ESSENTIAL
ESSAYS
ON JUDAISM

ESSENTIAL
ESSAYS
ON JUDAISM

ELIEZER BERKOVITS

Edited by DAVID HAZONY

SHALEM PRESS

JERUSALEM

Third Printing, 2007

Chapters 1 and 10 appeared in *God, Man, and History*,
copyright 1992 by The Berkovits Estate

Chapter 4 appeared in *Crisis and Faith*,
copyright 1976 by Hebrew Publishing Company

Chapters 5 and 12 appeared in *Man and God: Studies in Biblical
Theology*, copyright 1992 by The Berkovits Estate

Chapters 6 and 8 appeared in *Towards Historic Judaism*,
copyright 1943 by Phaidon Press

Chapter 11 was originally published in
Tradition, Fall 1962

Cover photo: Copyright Dave Bartuff/Corbis

Printed by: Top Print Ltd., Tel-Aviv
Printed in Israel

10 9 8 7 6 5 4 3 2 1

ISBN 965-7052-03-3

⊗ The paper used in this publication meets the minimum requirements of
the American National Standard for Information Sciences—Permanence of
Paper for Printed Library Materials, ANSI Z39.48-1992

CONTENTS

ACKNOWLEDGMENTS   vii

INTRODUCTION BY DAVID HAZONY   ix

I. JEWISH MORALITY AND LAW

   1. Law and Morality in Jewish Tradition   3

   2. The Nature and Function of Jewish Law   41

   3. Conversion and the Decline of the Oral Law 89

   4. A Jewish Sexual Ethics   103

   5. The Biblical Idea of Justice   129

II. Jewish Nationhood

    6. On the Return to Jewish National Life   155

    7. On Jewish Sovereignty   177

    8. Towards a Renewed Rabbinic Leadership   191

    9. The Spiritual Crisis in Israel   201

III. Jewish Theology

    10. The Encounter with the Divine   215

    11. Knowledge of the World and Knowledge of God   235

    12. The Concept of Holiness   247

    13. Faith After the Holocaust   315

Appendix: Writings of Eliezer Berkovits   333

Sources   339

Notes   341

Index   385

ACKNOWLEDGMENTS

THIS COLLECTION OF ESSAYS is the product of the efforts of a number of people to whom I would like to extend my thanks. For their frequently eye-opening comments on the introductory essay, I am indebted to Mor Altschuler, Marc Gafni, Aryeh Morgenstern, Aviezer Ravitzky, Joel Rebibo, and Einat Shichor. Joshua Weinstein and Assaf Sagiv suggested wise improvements in both the introduction and the selection of essays. Yosef Yitzhak Lifshitz, my teacher and colleague, has been an inspiration and a source of important criticism of the project as a whole. Daniel Polisar, my editor-in-chief at *Azure*, has offered crucial editorial and substantive comments—as well as a great deal of forbearance—at every stage. For his belief in the project and decisive criticism, I thank my publisher (and brother), Yoram Hazony.

The people at Shalem Press have offered a professional, dedicated environment for the production and promotion of the book. In particular, I would like to offer my thanks to Anat Altman, Dina Blank, Rachel Cavits, Atara Kligman, Judy Lee, and Marina Pilipodi for their tireless efforts. Naomi Arbel and Kinneret Lapidot provided crucial logistical support throughout; Ayelet Rabinowitz, Moshe Spinowitz, and Avi Helfand assisted in the research in preparation of the essays.

Throughout the editorial process, I have enjoyed the support and encouragement of the family of Eliezer Berkovits. In particular, I wish to express my heartfelt gratitude to Avraham Berkovits of the Technion and Dov Berkovits of the Beit Av Institute, who have been involved in the project from the beginning, offering their important opinions on everything from biographical issues to the format and selection of essays.

Above all, my wife Abby has been a source of unending encouragement, dedication, and love. To her I owe everything.

David Hazony
Jerusalem
September 2001

INTRODUCTION

FOR NEARLY TWO CENTURIES, the institution of Jewish law has sustained withering criticism from religious thinkers who have argued that in submitting to a legalistic outlook, Judaism has abandoned the moral truths that were at the core of the ancient biblical teaching. Following Spinoza, these writers have argued that while the law may once have been necessary for the establishment of the ancient Jewish people, it was already showing signs of wear by the time of the prophets such as Isaiah and Jeremiah, and is certainly not relevant as law today; rather, it is the moral spirit expressed by these prophets that is the eternal message of Judaism. Thus according to Martin Buber, a leading spokesman for this approach, the central problem with the traditional view is that it "transforms the law into a heap of petty formulas and allows man's decision for right and wrong action to degenerate into hairsplitting casuistry," with the result that "religion no longer shapes but enslaves religiosity."[1]

Views similar to Buber's can be said to have reached the height of their influence during the first half of the twentieth century, at a time when modernist beliefs had become so accepted among Jewish religious thinkers that many openly doubted whether Jewish law would even survive the coming generations.[2] In our day, however, a reaction against such extreme positions can be felt throughout the spectrum of Jewish religious belief, a striking example being the platform adopted by the Reform movement in 1999, which broke with its century-long opposition to the application of Jewish law when it called for the "ongoing study of the whole array of *mitzvot*," and the renewed observance of classical practices previously abjured by many of the movement's leaders.[3] As a result, the question of the importance of the Jewish law, or halacha, has again become relevant in circles well beyond its traditional constituency, necessitating the reconsideration of fundamental questions concerning the nature and function of this law: If an approach to Jewish life based on law is not inherently at odds with the moral demands of the prophets, as some have argued, then what, if anything, is its moral value? Is it possible that the law, properly understood, could itself play an important role in creating the moral personality, and even that most elusive of aims, the moral society?

With such questions in the air, it is well worth a renewed consideration of the writings of Eliezer Berkovits, perhaps the one modern thinker who addressed these questions most directly and systematically, and who for this reason may prove to be the most significant Jewish moral theorist of the last generation. Berkovits, who died in 1992, is known principally for his writings on the Holocaust, as well as his essays on modern trends of Jewish philosophy.[4] His most important work, however, may be his exploration of the nature of Jewish morality—an effort spanning half a dozen books and many essays, which offers a comprehensive approach to Jewish faith that includes both respect for the traditional law as a binding norm and a belief in the normative supremacy of the values and vision articulated by the prophets.

This he achieved through a careful examination of the rabbinic and biblical literature, which led him to reach three important conclusions about Jewish morality: (i) That the halacha as presented in the Bible and Talmud is primarily about moral values rather than rules, and that any attempt to reduce it to a fixed set of rules violates its essence; (ii) that Jewish morality, as expressed by the prophets and as impressed upon the halacha, is concerned fundamentally with the consequences of one's actions rather than the quality of one's reasoning or intention; and (iii) that Judaism understands morality not only as a discipline of man's intellect or spirit, but no less as an effort which must be incorporated into the habits of his physical being, through the vehicle of law, if it is to achieve its goal of advancing mankind in history.

Perhaps there is no need to say that if Berkovits' description of Jewish morality is correct, then much of the fire and brimstone poured upon the halacha over many years may have been misguided, and the road may in fact be open for a serious reconsideration of the justifications and desirability of a law-observing Judaism in our own time. But perhaps of equal interest is the light which Berkovits' arguments shed on the defense of the law mounted by many of its staunchest adherents in recent years, which the central claims of his philosophy do much to call into question as well. In what follows, therefore, I have devoted one section to each of what I take to be the three central tenets of Berkovits' worldview concerning the relationship between Jewish morality and the traditional law. In so doing, I hope to show that, when considered together, they constitute one of the most potentially fruitful philosophies of Jewish morality in recent times; and to suggest that this effort may offer a path towards a more coherent understanding of the Jewish normative tradition.

II

Eliezer Berkovits was born in Romania in 1908, and received his rabbinical and philosophical training in the 1930s at the Hildesheimer Rabbinical Seminary in Berlin and the University of Berlin. After escaping Germany in 1938, Berkovits served as a communal rabbi in Leeds, Sydney, and Boston before assuming the chair of the philosophy department at the Hebrew Theological College in Chicago in 1958, where he taught until 1975. At that time, at the age of 67, Berkovits relocated to Jerusalem, where he lived and worked until his death less than a decade ago. Over the course of his career, Berkovits wrote no fewer than nineteen books, as well as many articles, which, while demonstrating an unflagging devotion to Orthodox Judaism, nevertheless reflected a sharp discontent with the dramatic changes that Orthodoxy had undergone during his lifetime.

In the decades that followed the Second World War, much of Orthodox culture underwent a transformation that the sociologist Menachem Friedman has described as a shift from "life tradition" to "book tradition," or from a popular religion based on deeply rooted traditional values and norms, in which the scholar was generally limited in his ability to determine practice, to one centered on rules made explicit in the codes of law and in the interpretations of those codes by the rabbis of the yeshivot.[5] This shift had its roots in the rabbinical seminaries of Central and Eastern Europe in the early nineteenth century, but became a dominant social trend only after the Holocaust; at that time, the disruption of centuries of communal life prompted Orthodox leaders to encourage massive yeshiva enrollment, in the hope of rebuilding part of the vast world of Tora scholarship that had been lost. The result was that by the 1970s and 1980s, Orthodoxy had come to be characterized not only by a changed institutional structure, but also by a new normative ethos, based far more on the authority of the written halachic codes and their interpreters.

Although this shift was by no means uniform throughout Orthodoxy, a few general points have been observed in describing it. The first is that authority in determining Jewish practice, once given principally to family and communal traditions and only secondarily to the learned elites of the yeshivot, shifted decisively in favor of texts, particularly codes of law, and therefore to the yeshivot where they are studied. The second was a new tendency towards stringency in halachic ruling—what Judaic scholar Lawrence Kaplan has described as an "ethos of *humra*" (i.e., an ethos of stringency), predicated on the asceticism characteristic of yeshiva life, as well as a belief in strictness as a kind of moral training.[6] Third, Jewish practice to a great degree lost its internal hierarchy of values, which was displaced by a new tendency to view all halacha, down to the most minor of prohibitions, as possessing equal importance.[7] As a result of these changes, a new Orthodox norm has emerged that is quite different from what prevailed a century ago, in which value distinctions within the halacha have largely collapsed, and the rule of texts has, for the most part, prevailed.[8]

Berkovits' writings represent the first and most concerted attempt by an Orthodox writer to resist these trends. The thrust of his argument is that the halacha, although a legal system, is nonetheless a fluid one governed by a fixed set of moral values; accordingly, it has always evolved, allowing change whenever particular rules, including biblical prohibitions, were understood to be in conflict with Judaism's own larger goals. To demonstrate this, Berkovits wrote a number of works on the nature of Jewish law, the best known of which is *Not in Heaven: The Nature and Function of Halacha* (1983).[9] In the excerpt included below (pp. 41-87) he describes what he calls the "priority of the ethical" in halacha, by which he means a flexibility built into the law to allow for the fulfillment of higher moral principles. One such principle is that of human dignity (*kevod habriot*), the application of which ranges from preserving the physical modesty of men and women to protecting the honor of the disadvantaged. According to the Talmud, the preservation of human dignity overrides all rabbinical regulations, as well as some biblical commands.[10] Moreover, Berkovits cites a number of cases in which the principle of human dignity inspired legal innovation. The Talmud cites the ordinances concerning funeral rites, in which rabbinic leaders obligated wealthy families to adopt the standards of the poor, who could not afford fancy coffins and shrouds, in order to allay the latter's shame. (p. 64) Another such value is the "ways of peace" (*darkei shalom*), the desire to prevent needless conflict both within the Jewish community and between Jews and Gentiles. While the principle of the "ways of peace" is not given the same legal weight as human dignity, the rabbis nonetheless felt it to be a fundamental principle, as expressed by the late amoraic statement that "the Tora in its entirety exists for the sake of the ways of peace." (pp. 59, 66) Berkovits cites additional principles which drive and at times override provisions of the halacha, including economic efficiency, public safety, and common sense (*sevara*).

The concern for such overarching values afforded the rabbis a remarkable degree of exegetical freedom, which—at least at some stages during the development of the halacha—permitted them to alter or even abrogate the practice of certain laws specified in the Bible. Occasionally this was done through technical innovations to circumvent the law, such as the institution of *prozbul*, a rabbinic writ enabling the extension of monetary loans beyond the sabbatical year despite a biblical injunction to the contrary.[11] More frequently, however, we find the plain intention of the biblical institution ignored. Berkovits cites a number of laws which, while explicit in both letter and spirit in the Tora, were either restricted beyond applicability or simply excised from the practical halacha: The case of the "stubborn and rebellious son" who, because of his vile and uncontrolled ways, is seen as deserving of death; the "city led astray" which is to be destroyed utterly because it has fallen to the temptation of public idolatry; or the "forty lashes" which the Tora prescribes as punishment for certain crimes, but which under the rabbinical interpretation are never to be carried out in full. (pp. 61, 71-72) In these and similar cases, what Berkovits calls the "halachic conscience" has been called in to amend the law for the sake of a higher moral principle. In some instances the rabbis explicitly cite the general moral verses of the Bible, such as "And you shall do that which is right and good in the eyes of the Eternal your God."[12] In others, no source was considered necessary to justify such steps.

Why did the rabbis allow themselves such a degree of flexibility in interpreting the law, if it is divinely revealed? According to Berkovits, such flexibility is central to the nature of the oral tradition. As he writes in "Conversion and the Decline of the Oral Law" (1974):

> Every written law is somewhat "inhuman." As a code laid down for generations, it must express a general idea and an abstract principle of what is right, of what is desired by the lawgiver. But every human situation is specific and not general or abstract.... The uniqueness of the situation will often call for additional attention by some other principle, which has its validity within the system.

According to Berkovits, the written Tora cannot and does not advertise itself as an exhaustive handbook of Jewish living. Rather, it presents laws together with moral values, and then depends on an oral tradition to derive, express, and apply these principles to the realities of human life. The role of the scholar is to internalize these values and translate them into functional rabbinic precedent, through what Berkovits calls the "creative boldness of application of the comprehensive ethos of the Tora to the case." Through a living oral tradition, the scholar of Tora gives the written law its applicability, makes it relevant for the life of his generation, and thereby redeems it from irrelevance and inhumanness: "The written law longs for this, its redemption, by the oral Tora." (pp. 96-97)

For this reason, in ancient times it was strictly forbidden to put the oral teachings into fixed, written form—a prohibition breached only reluctantly in the second century with the redaction of the Mishna by R. Yehuda Hanasi, when conditions of exile endangered the continued transmission of the oral law. However, as the exile deepened over the centuries, the need for increasingly concrete written representations of the halacha was felt, and the precedent set by the Mishna was repeated and expanded until, during the medieval period, the oral law was for the first time translated into the systematized written codes which are now understood to form the core of practical halacha. Today, codes of Jewish law have become central to yeshiva study; most rabbinical programs focus not on study of the Bible or Talmud, which contain mostly literary material or non-decisive legal discussions, but on the perusal of codes of law such as R. Jacob ben Asher's *Arba'a Turim* and R. Joseph Karo's *Shulhan Aruch*, and commentaries on these codes such as Karo's *Beit Yosef* and R. Yisrael Meir Kagan's *Mishna Brura*—the assumption being that through these will the student learn how to render proper halachic decisions when called upon.[13] Thus the recent shift in Orthodoxy towards an emphasis on "book learning" can be seen, in a way, as the extension of a trend that has spanned many centuries.

Berkovits reviews this history with no small measure of discomfort. In his view, this gradual transformation of the oral tradition into a written one was a "calamity," representing a "violation of the essence of halacha." (p. 101) While he admits that owing to the Jews' historical predicament, there may not have been any alternative (as some of the codifiers maintained in their own defense), Berkovits nonetheless views the codification of the oral law as a blow to the traditional goals of Jewish law itself. Echoing the criticism leveled against the codes when they first appeared in medieval times, Berkovits sees them as violating the purpose of an oral tradition by reducing what is supposed to be a system of values, the application of which necessarily eludes precise and permanent delineation, to a set of rules. What was once "halacha"—literally, a *way* of living—became a complex code which circumscribes life but cannot capture its most essential contents. The kind of approach to Jewish life that emerged as a result, and became dominant in Orthodoxy in Berkovits' lifetime, was the shadow of what had once been a dynamic, creative approach to life.

Berkovits does not argue for the abolition of the *Shulhan Aruch*. He accepts the premise that the halacha is a binding system of law, and that, as with any legal system, one must for the sake of the integrity and stability of the law be willing to preserve time-worn precedents. In this regard, Berkovits is no revolutionary.[14] But by reviving the debate over the effect of the legal codes, he is nonetheless raising the banner for a reconsideration of the way halacha is understood. If the codification of the halacha was a necessary response to the trials of destruction and exile, then the lawbooks which have come to be identified so fully with Orthodoxy are in some important sense alien to the law. Even if they are helpful in assisting a student to review or to organize the halacha, they are of limited value in allowing him to understand, internalize, and ultimately live the values that are the law's essence. For this reason, Berkovits called, in "Towards a Renewed Rabbinic Leadership" (1943), for a revision of the way Orthodox rabbis are educated, in order to foster a rabbinic type that would more closely resemble the creative, erudite thinkers of the Talmud. This, he hoped, would lead to a regeneration of the vital and dynamic character of the law. (p. 198)

Berkovits is not the only scholar of halacha to insist on the flexibility of the law. Such efforts have become especially popular in recent years, particularly among scholars of the Conservative movement; indeed, some of their arguments resemble Berkovits' quite closely.[15] Yet there is a significant difference between Berkovits' effort and that of these other scholars, which concerns the nature of the values which justify change. Underlying much of the argument of non-Orthodox scholars is an effort to justify change as part of an ongoing evolutionary process resulting from the continuous encounter between tradition and the evolving needs of the individual or society. In the words of Louis Jacobs, a prominent Conservative thinker: "The ultimate authority for determining which observances are binding upon the faithful Jew is the historical experience of the people of Israel"—meaning that history brings new situations before the Jewish people, and halacha must evolve accordingly.[16] Robert Gordis, another leading scholar of the Conservative movement, expresses a similar belief when he writes that "tradition constitutes the thesis, contemporary life is the antithesis, and the resultant of these two factors becomes the new synthesis. The synthesis of one age then becomes the thesis of the next; the newly formulated content of tradition becomes the point of departure for the next stage."[17] In these and similar writings, the emphasis is upon change as a response to new challenges posed by the flow of history, with little attempt to spell out exactly what are the eternal values, if any, that the openness to change is ultimately intended to preserve. Change is a product of the fluid encounter between the Jewish people and history, and therefore it does not follow any clear pattern; it is as variegated as history itself. As a result, it often becomes difficult to tell from these writings whether the need for change is determined through reference to principles that are themselves found within the Jewish tradition, or whether it is derived from somewhere else.[18]

From Berkovits' standpoint, this view is hard to reconcile with the moral message of the prophetic texts. These were clearly meant to deliver a message whose importance rested not in its success as a "synthesis" between

the traditional and the contemporary, but precisely in its ability to transcend the changing attitudes of history. Indeed, according to the Talmud it
was the criterion of eternal validity that determined whether a given text
was included in the biblical canon in the first place.[19] Instead, Berkovits
understands change in halacha to reflect the careful, incremental adjustment of legal means to further moral ends that are themselves intrinsic to
Judaism and unchanging. These moral ends are not an external "antithesis"
with which the tradition must come to terms by changing its internal
content in keeping with them; they are themselves the moral core of the
same revealed message from which the law receives its authority. Commenting on the statement of the medieval Jewish thinker Judah Halevi that
"God forbid that there should be anything in the Tora that contradicts
reason," Berkovits writes:

> The rabbis in the Talmud were guided by the insight: God forbid that
> there should be anything in the application of the Tora to the actual life
> situation that is contrary to the principles of ethics. What are those
> principles? They are Tora principles, like: "And you shall do that which is
> right and good in the eyes of the Eternal"; or "Her ways are ways of
> pleasantness, and all her paths are peace"... or "That you may walk in the
> way of good people, and keep the paths of the righteous".... (p. 59)[20]

While the law may change, the values which underlie it do not; on the
contrary, the purpose of change is to permit the continued advancement of
the Bible's eternally valid moral teaching under new conditions.

This difference is felt in the way in which Berkovits levels his criticism
of prevailing halachic practice. Berkovits believed that the halacha had
ossified to the point of inflicting real damage on some of its own moral
ends—two significant examples being the status of women in Orthodox life
(particularly with respect to marriage and divorce law), to which he dedicated two full books; and the question of conversion standards, the increas-
ing stringency of which was, in his mind, contributing to the dissolution of
the unified Jewish people.[21] At the same time, however, the values Berkovits
invokes are consistently those found in the biblical and rabbinic literature.
When calling for a reconsideration of the status of women in Jewish law, for
example, Berkovits shies away from Enlightenment concepts such as liberty
and equality, and instead invokes classical Jewish concepts such as human
dignity, the protection of the innocent, and the covenantal symbolism

which the institution of marriage is supposed to entail, in order to conclude that "we have reached a juncture at which the comprehensive ethos of the Tora itself strains against its formulation in specific laws."[22] In his theological writings, as well, Berkovits assumes that the Jewish tradition is driven by a set of moral values inherent to and derived solely from within that tradition. His *Studies in Biblical Theology* (1969) is an extensive and meticulous work dedicated to teasing out the essential moral principles of the Bible by analyzing its use of terms such as "holiness," "justice," and "truth."

Berkovits' emphasis on values rather than rules, and the kinds of change which such an approach implies, earned him no small amount of criticism from an Orthodox establishment that was, and continues to be, in the midst of a dramatic shift in the opposite direction.[23] Yet his account of the oral tradition resolves a number of difficulties which the more conventional accounts are at pains to address. For example, a salient feature of the Talmud is its interweaving of legal discussions into a single text with the anecdotal and legendary materials known as *agada*. From the structure of the Talmud, it appears as though the halacha and agada were originally studied together, as a single subject. But if the halacha is essentially a set of rules rather than values, there is no obvious reason why the Talmud (or the Tora, for that matter) should ever have mixed together two essentially unrelated literary forms. Indeed, the logic of separating them is sufficiently compelling that Maimonides and the other codifiers found no difficulty in doing away almost entirely with the agada in composing their legal works; similarly, it is common practice in most yeshivot today to skip over the agadic passages of the Talmud, on the assumption that they have no important bearing upon the halachic discussion.

Yet if, as Berkovits insists, the rules of the halacha are merely one reflection of a set of higher moral principles, and the rules alone cannot suffice to provide the content of these values, then the interspersion of agadic material becomes reasonable, for it is in the tales and aphorisms of the rabbis that these moral principles are presented as part of an actual life full of unique situations; it is these stories that permit the student of halacha to study the application of values in complex, living circumstances, in a way that the study of a cut-and-dry legal code never can. If the institutions of Sabbath and prayer, to take two examples, are not merely about following a particular set of rules, but in fact aim at creating a certain type of devotional experience of which the rules are only a part, then the many agadot which appear in the talmudic tractates of Shabbat and Brachot, and which are rich in theological statements about the nature of these institutions, constitute a crucial alternative path for understanding how to live them.[24]

Another difficulty which Berkovits' model addresses is the relation between the prophetic and halachic texts. It is no secret that inasmuch as the halacha, narrowly understood, has become the focus of the yeshiva world, it has been at the expense of study of the Bible, particularly the books of the prophets. Like the agada, the biblical stories and prophetic teachings appear to add little to one's understanding of a rule-driven law; in several places the Talmud even prohibits the deduction of laws from prophetic texts.[25] Yet from the standpoint of the tradition itself, the reduction of the prophets' status is a difficult pill to swallow: The rabbis of the Talmud not only possessed an encyclopedic grasp of the prophetic writings, as is evidenced by their extensive citation of them; they also underscored the importance of the prophetic books through various halachot aimed at preserving their sanctity (such as the public reading of the *haftara* on the Sabbath, or the declaration that scrolls containing books of the Bible "defile the hands"),[26] as well as through detailed midrashic commentaries on many passages throughout the Prophets and Writings. The deepest secrets of the Tora are understood by the rabbis to be contained within the opening chapters of the book of Ezekiel, whereas the book of Esther is said to contain the key to understanding the Jews' covenant with God.[27] If the teachings of the prophets are so irrelevant to living a proper Jewish life, as may be inferred from their place in the yeshiva curriculum, why were the rabbis of the Talmud so concerned with them?

From the perspective suggested by Berkovits, there is no necessary separation between "prophetic" and "rabbinic" Judaism, for the thrust of both is moral. The rabbis were no less concerned with the cause of morality than were the prophets, and Berkovits is not exaggerating when he casts them as the prophets' moral heirs. (p. 192) If there is a great difference between prophetic and rabbinic texts, it is due not to a diminution of the status of morality, but to its incorporation into an oral law charged with fashioning a formal normative system for a people living in dispersion. This does not mean that there were no real differences between the way the prophets understood the normative content of the Jewish law and the way it was understood by the rabbis. What it does mean is that the popular view of the rabbis as dedicated principally to the preservation and process of ritual laws, and only secondarily to moral principles, is the reverse of the truth; and that there need be no contradiction between a commitment to the halacha as a binding law and a belief in the primacy of morality in determining the content of that law. The moral realm is not only a part of the halachic tradition. It is its driving spirit.

III

Nowhere in his writings did Eliezer Berkovits offer us a systematic treatise on the nature of Jewish morality, as considered separately from halacha. Yet his writings are infused with a distinctive set of assumptions that amount to a systematic rejection of the Kantian style in ethics, which, with its nearly exclusive focus on purity of intention, has characterized the thought of almost every major writer on Jewish morality of the last century. The Jewish perspective, according to Berkovits, is not concerned with the attempt to identify absolute principles which should inform our intentions, for it is not primarily concerned with intentions at all. From Berkovits' perspective, what is important is not intentions, or even "actions" as such, as much as the consequences of action. The moral values which stand behind the writings of the prophets and the rabbis are, in other words, an attempt to describe a desired state of human affairs within the world, the achievement of which is the aim of moral behavior.

This belief plays an especially prominent role in his halachic writings. One of Berkovits' goals in writing *Not in Heaven* is to demonstrate that the halacha not only accepts the priority of the moral, but also, as a consequence, constantly concerns itself with what he calls the "wisdom of the feasible"—the willingness to accept change in the legal order when this is necessary in order to avert undesirable social consequences such as shame, injustice, waste, physical danger, or communal strife. Citing the talmudic dictum "what is possible is possible, what is impossible is impossible," Berkovits brings a number of cases in which the Jewish norm is determined not according to a strict application of abstract principle, but according to the "possible": That which can be reasonably expected to bear successful application, as measured by its consequences.

One example is the talmudic principle of "the end was permitted on account of the beginning," according to which emergency personnel, who are permitted to travel on the Sabbath in order to save lives, are allowed to return home on the Sabbath as well, even after the risk to life has passed, when in principle they should be required to remain where they are. Because of the concern that doctors, midwives, or firefighters would hesitate to take the steps necessary to save lives because of the prospect of being stranded until nightfall, the rabbis allowed continued travel even after the mission had been completed, in order to achieve the desired result of saving lives.[28] Another example concerns the willingness of the rabbis to add an extra month to the Jewish calendar—with the consequence of delaying the observance of biblically prescribed holy days—for the purely practical reason of avoiding the difficulties of conducting Passover too soon after the winter rains.[29] Flexibility in halacha is displayed primarily in an effort to bring about desirable social results, or to prevent undesirable ones. (pp. 51-52)

Similarly, Berkovits' theological writings consistently emphasize the consequential side of prophetic morality. In the essays of *Studies in Biblical Theology*, not only are overtly moral terms such as righteousness (*tzedek*) and charity (*tzedaka*) understood to be addressing the actual achievement of good, as opposed to one's intentions with respect to others; even terms which relate principally to the divine realm, such as the "spirit" of God or the notion of "holiness" (*kedusha*), are shown, convincingly, to refer to God's actions or representation as they are reflected in their consequences within the historical world (see, for example, "The Concept of Holiness," pp. 247-314). Not surprisingly, this position is most vividly spelled out in Berkovits' explanation of the biblical idea of "justice" (*mishpat*), which appears in "The Biblical Idea of Justice" (pp. 129-152). Berkovits' reading of the biblical text presents justice as concerned primarily with the bringing about of a just state of affairs, rather than possessing "just" intentions or adhering to "just" maxims; conversely, when justice is not done, it reflects not a violation of an absolute rule, but a betrayal of the actual widow, orphan, or oppressed, whose relative powerlessness has made them incapable of defending their righteousness.[30] Through a careful analysis of the biblical applications of the term *mishpat* and its cognates, Berkovits develops a larger understanding of justice built not on absolute ideals but on a divinely sanctioned notion of "an orderliness, an appropriateness, and a balanced relatedness of all things in nature without which life is not possible." The prophetic demand for justice is thus understood as a call for the establishment of a just order within the world. Justice is, in Berkovits' words, "an appropriateness, determined not by abstract consideration, but by the reality of man's condition and subserving the meaningful preservation of human life.... Justice is done not that justice prevail, but that life prevail; it is done out of concern with a concrete situation, in which life is endangered and calls for its salvation." (pp. 146-147)

To understand the significance of Berkovits' approach, it is instructive to contrast it with the powerful existentialist movement that had come to dominate Jewish philosophy by Berkovits' time, and which continues to set the tone for much of Jewish philosophy today. Inspired by the iconoclastic thought of Soren Kierkegaard and Franz Rosenzweig, many Jewish thinkers in interwar Germany turned away from the abstract ideals which were the focus of earlier German thought and instead turned their attention to the examination of the individual consciousness, out of the belief that only through such an "empirical" approach could they achieve a reliable philosophical understanding. In discussing the religious experience, thinkers such as Martin Buber and Abraham Joshua Heschel employed the classical Jewish sources with the aim of studying the religious experience of the individual, such as prophecy or mystic ecstasy.[31] When dealing with ethics, they tended to translate the moral teachings of the Jewish texts into an emphasis on "deeds"—ethical actions which derive their obligatory nature from one's consciousness of God and of other people. However, while their appreciation for the concrete over the abstract brought them to an emphasis on actions, it is a natural result of their subjectivistic outlook that the "deed" was seen and judged primarily from the inside, as something which draws its importance and relevance principally from its place in the world of the acting subject: Either as a tool for the development of desirable qualities within the individual, or as part of a desirable pattern of individual living. The result is that while the existentialists paid greater attention to the importance of actions than did their German-idealist predecessors, they retained the latter's rejection of consequences as a valid consideration in determining whether an action is moral. On the contrary, the weighing of consequences was understood to be a violation of the purity of intentions, which continued to be viewed as the essence of morality.

An extreme example of this position is found in Buber's ethical writings. In a collection of his early essays entitled *On Judaism*, Buber argues that morality in Judaism, like ethics according to Kant, is predicated on the idea of "unconditionality": That moral actions must be taken with the perfect intention of doing what is right, without regard for external consequence:

> Not the matter of a deed determines its truth but the manner in which it is carried out: In human conditionality, or in divine unconditionality. Whether a deed will peter out in the outer courtyard, in the realm of things, or whether it will penetrate into the Holy of Holies is determined not by its content but by the power of decision which brought it about, and by the sanctity of intent that dwells in it…. Unconditionality is the specific religious content of Judaism.[32]

Deeds that are performed in "conditionality"—that is, with regard for their consequences—are in Buber's mind impure, sullied in the "lowlands of causality."[33] While actions certainly have consequences, these consequences are so intricately woven within the vast fabric of causality that man cannot hope to fathom them. However, when man purifies his intentions and ignores the conditions of the world, his actions "affect deeply the world's destiny."[34] It is the goal of the Jew, therefore, to work to purify his intentions, so that he may perform that which is right purely because it is so. A similar position is offered in Buber's 1952 essay "Religion and Ethics," where he defines ethics to mean

> the "yes" or "no" which man gives to the conduct and actions possible to him, the radical distinction between them which affirms or denies them not according to their usefulness or harmfulness for individuals and society, but according to their intrinsic value and disvalue. We find the ethical in its purity only there where the human person confronts himself with his own potentiality and distinguishes and decides in this confrontation without asking anything other than what is right and what is wrong in his own situation.[35]

Similar sentiments are found in the writings of Abraham Joshua Heschel, despite his many differences with Buber. Like Buber, Heschel emphasizes the importance of ethical action taken in purity of intention as the focus of religious life. Heschel's ethical vision is guided not by the careful weighing of consequences, but by an ideal of "piety" which focuses on intentions rather than results as the touchstone of moral validity. Piety is "the orientation of human inwardness toward the holy," an orientation which is ahistorical, recognizing that "life takes place under wide horizons, horizons that range beyond the span of an individual life or even the life of a nation, of a generation or even of an era."[36] Quoting the rabbinical dictum that "it matters not whether one does much or little, if only he directs his heart to heaven,"[37] Heschel describes what he believes to be the true end of good actions according to Judaism:

> We exalt the deed; we do not idolize external performance. The outward performance is but an aspect of the totality of a deed. Jewish literature dilates on the idea that every act of man hinges and rests on the intention and hidden sentiments of the heart.[38]

The significance of deeds, according to Heschel, is not in what they are capable of achieving in the outside world, but for the attainment of what he calls "spiritual ends"—that is, ends that relate to the spiritual state or level of the individual actor.[39] "The purpose of performance," he writes in *God in Search of Man*, "is to transform the performer; the purpose of observance is to train us in achieving spiritual ends.... Ultimately, then, the goal of religious life is quality rather than quantity, not only *what* is done, but *how* it is done."[40] Thus while Heschel does call for a "leap of action," a decision to act that is more important than a leap of faith because it has a greater impact on one's soul, the goal of such a leap is not the direct improvement of the state of things in the world, but to be "ushered into the presence of spiritual meaning. Through the ecstasy of deeds he [i.e., the Jew] learns to be certain of the hereness of God. Right living is a way to right thinking."[41]

Berkovits also places a premium on "deeds," yet it is clear that when he uses this term, he has something different in mind. While he agrees that actions have an invaluable impact upon character, for him the most important perspective from which to view deeds is from the "outside," from a perspective that is historical and public rather than subjective and personal—and which therefore necessarily views consequences as essential. As he writes in *God, Man, and History* (1959):

> The deed… is essentially social; and in order to be, it must find its place in the external world of man. It is social because it is always expressive of a relationship…. The deed, directed to the outside, is always in relationship to "an other." This "other" may be the world, a neighbor, or God. However, in order to be, the deed must be effective; and it must be so in the place where it belongs—in the external world, in history. In fact, the deed is the stuff of which history is made.[42]

To understand morality purely from within the framework of the individual psyche, Berkovits argues, is inadequate to the nature of the Jewish norm, which is focused primarily upon one's relationship to "the world, a neighbor, or God." This focus on the external means that deeds are not simply connected with the outside world, but entirely dependent on it "in order to be." A deed that is not "effective," that does not achieve desired consequences, is not morally significant.

Understood more broadly, morality must consider consequences in history, because it is for the sake of history—the improvement of the condition of man and his eventual redemption—that morality exists. Berkovits explicitly deduces the nature of morality from the belief in an eventual redemption of mankind in history. "Man in all his creaturely existence is to be redeemed. Redemption is an event in history. This world is to be established as the kingdom of God. The deed, man's daily life in space and time, must find its place in the kingdom; it builds the kingdom…. The deed, being the stuff out of which history is made, is never private; it is always public, as history itself."[43] Morality does not concern merely the individual's adherence to the divine command, but is the individual's way of contributing to the biblical vision of redemption. In the moral deed, man takes responsibility for history.

In this, Berkovits' understanding of morality resembles Max Weber's "ethic of responsibility" governing the conduct of politics. In Weber's view, the moral political figure acts in full consideration of consequences because he is acting for the furtherance of certain results, and is held to account principally for his success or failure to bring them about.[44] Under such a system, right and wrong take on a different kind of meaning than under an approach based on the purity of intention, and require a different sort of discipline. Confronted with a situation that is unjust or dangerous to the public, the individual asks not which rules he is obligated to follow based on a theoretical ethics, but begins by asking what a just situation, or one which eliminated the danger, would look like; only then does he ask what is necessary in order to bring about such a state of affairs. The political figure described by Weber is motivated by a general sense of responsibility for outcomes, and is guided by his own understanding of what results are desirable. Moreover, because he is interested primarily in achievement rather than the correspondence of his actions to a set of rules, the kind of knowledge necessary for proper moral decisionmaking is vastly different under an ethic of responsibility than under an intention-driven ethics. If one must account for results, then one's understanding must include a due appreciation of all those things upon which results depend, beyond one's own intentions: Historical and cultural factors, the proclivities of political actors, human nature, and so forth.

It is such an ethic of responsibility that Berkovits sees being demanded by the Jewish understanding of the deed, which is "always public, as history itself." He finds in Judaism a moral perspective according to which our actions are determined out of a sense of responsibility for the attainment of certain results, be they on an interpersonal or on a communal level. This is not to say that Berkovits advocates the abandonment of the weighty rules of behavior which we ordinarily associate with morality. On the contrary, precepts such as the avoidance of lying, killing, and violating the property of others are essential elements in the creation of a society of the sort envisioned in the Bible, and it is for this reason that in addition to its articulation of a larger vision, the Bible provides a collection of strong precepts which are intended to contribute to its realization. But there is a crucial difference between the rules appearing under an ethic of responsibility and the moral law as understood by Kant's Jewish followers: Because the rules are derivative of a larger vision of society, they are also subordinate to that vision—that is, they are not "absolute" laws at all, but general principles which ought to be followed under most conditions, but which should not be binding in cases where their application clearly does more harm to that vision than does their neglect. The result is that even such clear-cut biblical precepts as the avoidance of shedding blood and infringing on the property of others are found—in the killing and expropriation experienced in wartime, for example—to be limited in their applicability when the greater good is truly at stake; and many other, often less weighty, biblical laws are affected in much the same manner. Moreover, the purity of intentions, which Kant posed as a minimal condition for moral behavior,[45] takes on secondary importance under an ethic of responsibility, in which intentions are only important insofar as they affect outcomes. And finally, as far as intellectual faculties are concerned, an ethic of responsibility places a far greater emphasis on one's ability to judge the weight of rules against the consequences of behavior in a given case than on one's ability to formulate a pure intention. Soundness of judgment, rather than purity of thinking, becomes the decisive element in the composition of the just soul.[46]

By introducing morality as an ethic of responsibility, Berkovits' understanding of Judaism avoids two common pitfalls of modern moral discourse. On the one hand, because rules governing right and wrong are not absolute, but are instead subordinated to outcomes, moral valuations cannot ignore the specific situation in which the individual finds himself and upon which outcomes depend; in no case are we left concluding that he has done something that is on some level "wrong" even though it was the best of all available options—a conclusion which follows easily from a morality based on absolute rules, but which violates our basic understanding that right and wrong are intimately linked to free will. On the other hand, because the biblical vision is an eternally binding one, the source of moral understanding is objective and external, so that man is not left groping for moral guidance solely from within the confines of his own immediate reality—a belief in the primacy of the "situation" which flows naturally from the existentialist enterprise, but which ultimately produces a morality that is hopelessly subjective and relativistic.[47]

In Judaism as understood by Berkovits, the moral actor adheres to the heteronomous precepts which the Bible and the tradition provide, but always keeps before his eyes the redemptive state of affairs which they are meant to bring about, and therefore understands that he must ultimately exercise his own judgment in determining where the applicability of a given moral precept reaches its limit. Morality for Berkovits is, like politics, an "art of the possible," the aim of which is not mere adherence to a code, but the advancement of a vision of reality through the application of the consequence-driven values articulated by the prophets and their heirs in the rabbinic tradition.

IV

Berkovits' argument with Kantian moral thought and its Jewish adherents is, however, predicated on a deeper critique of much of Western moral thought since pre-Christian times. This tradition has consistently sought to portray morality as a set of ideas which, once grasped and accepted by man's non-physical side (that is, his intellect or spirit or soul), will bring about a commensurate change in the behavior of his physical element. Thus for Plato the good is identified with knowledge; for the Christian with faith; for Kant with reason. What unites this tradition is its fundamental dismissal of the body as a significant factor of the good, the assumption being that once man's non-physical element is properly directed, the physical side will surely follow.[48]

However, as Berkovits points out, the physical side does not surely follow—and therefore it cannot be left out of the moral equation. Morality is distinct from other areas of philosophy in that it is about performance, which means that it cannot exist without the cooperation of the body. As he writes in "Law and Morality in Jewish Tradition" (1959):

> The spirit itself is powerless; it may act only in union with the vital or "material" forces in the cosmos. No one has ever accomplished anything merely by contemplating an idea. All conscious action is the result of some form of cooperation between the mind and the body. Matter— whatever its ultimate secret—without the mind is inanity; mind without matter is, at best, noble impotence…. The material world can be saved from the idiocy of mere being by the direction it may receive from the spirit; the spirit can be redeemed from the prison of its impotence by the amount of cooperation that it may be able to derive from the material world. (p. 18)

Here Berkovits confronts the Platonic-Christian moral tradition, which sets itself against the body and the material world it inhabits, with what he understands to be the traditional Jewish account of man's nature as comprising spiritual and material elements, both of which must be engaged and tutored if he is to redeem himself and his world.[49] In learning to act morally, man faces a dual task befitting his dual nature: His conscious self must learn to identify and desire the good, and his material side must learn how to carry it out. Because the material is no less intrinsic to morality than the spiritual, any moral system which does not account for both will necessarily fail to maintain its applicability for actual, physical man—and without applicability, morality can have no meaning.

Man's physical side, however, is notoriously unresponsive to the edicts of reason. The body is a cauldron of material energies, complex and conflicting forces which are, in Berkovits' words, "unaware of the existence of any moral code." The behaviors of the human body are guided by its needs and appetites, which have no innate knowledge of or care for the demands of moral behavior. The matter of securing the body's "coopera-tion" therefore becomes a central problem. "Only now are we able to appreciate the seriousness of man's ethical predicament," Berkovits writes. "On the one hand, the mind of man, the custodian of all spiritual and ethical values, is by itself incapable of action; on the other, the life forces and all the sources of material energy, without whose instrumentality no ethical action is possible, are by their very essence completely indifferent to ethical or spiritual values.... The human body, the tool of individual moral conduct, is essentially amoral." Moral behavior therefore requires full coor-dination between man's understanding of the good and his behavior as a physical being—a coordination which is itself no small achievement, and therefore which no discussion of morality can afford to ignore. (p. 19)

The mistaken belief that man can be made good solely through prepa-ration of the mind is, in Berkovits' view, the salient tragedy of Western civilization. The Greeks understood, to varying degrees, the nature of the problem.[50] But beginning with Christianity, which decisively parted from its Hebrew biblical tradition when it wrote off the body as part of an incorrigibly sinful world, Western man as represented by European thought has associated the question of morality almost exclusively with the question of what a truncated, spiritualized actor, possessing only reason or faith, ought to do. The question of how, once right action has been determined, one is to overcome inner obstacles to taking the proper action is under-stood, when it is considered at all, to be a separate issue, relating to other realms such as psychology or education. "Since the days of antiquity," Berkovits writes, "Western civilization has mistakenly believed that it is possible to convince the body by reasoning with it…. And so it hoped in vain for effective ethical conduct through education. At its best, Western civilization was talking to the mind and never really reached the body." (p. 22)

The result was that despite centuries of moral teaching, Western man was never able to overcome the intrinsic amorality of his material element. The rise of murderous regimes in the heart of the most philosophically developed civilization stood for Berkovits as testimony to the West's failure to grasp the nature of morality. "In this respect, there seems to be little difference between ages of greater or lesser enlightenment; except that, in times of greater intellectual advancement, as knowledge increases man grows in power proportionately and becomes correspondingly more dangerous…. Notwithstanding enlightenment, man seems to remain an essentially unethical being." (p. 14) Thus by focusing exclusively on the training of his reason, and leaving aside the very practical and consequentialistic question of how the body may be trained to follow the commands of the intellect, Western man was never adequately prepared to act decisively in the face of evil.

As opposed to this tradition, Berkovits argues that Judaism has consistently maintained the centrality of the question of the physical. The rabbinic tradition is deeply occupied with man's composite nature as it pertains to his moral behavior. In the midrashic literature, man is consistently described as dual, combining both the "upper" and "lower" realms, resembling both the angels and the animals.[51] Commensurately, he possesses a "good inclination" which must be trained to outwit and overcome the "evil inclination," a naturally more powerful immoral urge associated with man's animal side. In later times, as well, much of Jewish moral literature focused not on the derivation of correct beliefs but on the discipline required to bring about moral behavior.[52]

According to Berkovits, Judaism addresses the problem of the human body by creating a comprehensive normative system that relates to the material on its own terms. Unlike the mind, the body cannot be taught through logical persuasion, for its "knowledge" does not take the form of words, arguments, or even primarily emotions. Rather, it "understands" through habits, and through what Berkovits refers to as the "bodily awareness"—that is, through acquired, reflexive reactions to circumstances within the world. To train the body to be moral, an appropriate method must be introduced:

> The body is not accessible to logical reasoning. One can only teach it by making it do things. One does not learn to swim by reading books on swimming technique, nor does one become a painter by merely contemplating the styles of different schools. One learns to swim by swimming, to paint by painting, to act by acting.... This applies nowhere more strictly than in the realm of ethical action. (p. 22)

Morality, like any other performative skill, requires actual physical training. If man is to live a moral life, rather than merely to think moral thoughts, it is not enough that he study the nature of the good or the right; he must also educate his physical element through its habituation to moral behavior, which requires a regime no less demanding than what is required for other areas of life in which performance is the measure of success.

To illustrate what such training might be like, and why it is essential for morality, Berkovits draws an analogy to military training: Just as it is potentially catastrophic for a soldier to learn to fight only in the context of an actual war, without advance preparation, so too is it perilous to ask a person to inhibit his powerful, amoral tendencies in the face of a moral challenge if he has not had advance preparation. Just as training for war means subjecting soldiers to a regimen of rehearsed fighting as if there were an actual enemy, so too does the Jewish tradition recognize the need for a method of moral rehearsal even in the absence of an actual moral challenge. This it achieves through the system of ritual laws, which discipline man's material side to disregard its own desires and act instead according to the prescriptions of the mind, as if there were an actual moral challenge being faced. (p. 23)

Thus for Berkovits, even the "ritual" aspects of Jewish law which are devoid of obvious moral worth are nonetheless crucial for the moral training they provide. The dietary laws, for example, can be understood as preparation for a situation in which proper moral conduct may come into conflict with a specific physical urge, in this case the appetite for food. Through the continual, controlled inhibition of this appetite for the sake of a higher law, man learns to limit the influence of this urge upon his actions. When combined with similar training with regard to other physical inclinations, man's physical side as a whole becomes conditioned to responding correctly and accurately whenever emotions or inclinations conflict with moral demands:

> The aim is to teach... a new "awareness," one which is foreign to the organic component of the human personality. It is the awareness... of an order of being as well as of meaning different from that of organic egocentricity. The purpose of the inhibitive rules is to practice saying "no" to self-centered demands; whereas the fulfillment of the positive commands is the exercise of saying "yes" in consideration of an order different from one's own. (p. 25)

This does not, of course, mean that the ritual laws have no meaning beyond their utility. Berkovits is careful to avoid casting Jewish ritual solely in an instrumental light, at the expense of the symbolic, devotional, or historical meaning the rituals entail. In the selection from *God, Man, and History* included below, he describes how these commandments direct our composite selves not only toward moral behavior, but also toward a proper relationship between the individual and God. (pp. 27-39) What it does mean, however, is that the lattice of Jewish practices could not have simply been a collection of independently derived, socially encouraged devotional rituals, but needed to be a comprehensive system of law, if it were to fulfill its educational mission. Law, in the sense that it is meant here, means acting out of obligation, even in contravention of momentary desires. It means forcing our material side to act according to principle rather than inclination. Considered independently, symbolic rituals do not need to be "laws"; they can be undertaken on an individual basis, out of one's appreciation for their esthetic virtues, and perpetuated through convention. By presenting rituals as law, Judaism demands of man that he impose a discipline on his own material self throughout his life. In this way, the tradition trains him as a moral being in a way that no amount of discourse can.

It is this appreciation of physical performance which leads Berkovits to argue that there is a value, albeit a diminished one, even in the performance of commandments by "rote," without proper intention. The obligation of prayer offers an important case in point. Prayer is fundamentally a matter of devotion; through it, man expresses his most intimate thoughts and feelings to his creator. The intentions behind one's prayer are, perhaps more so than in any other religious act, essential to its nature. Thus Joseph B.

Soloveitchik, a leading Orthodox thinker of the Kantian tradition, insisted that intention constitutes the entirety and essence of prayer, whereas the physical recitation of prayers is merely "the technique of implementation of prayer and not prayer itself."[53] Heschel, too, was stating what appeared obvious to him when he wrote that "to pray with *kavana* (inner devotion) may be difficult; to pray without it is ludicrous."[54]

Yet by including prayer within a system of legal obligation, the halacha requires the Jew to pray at fixed times and in accordance with a fixed liturgy, with the result that many Jews often find themselves praying in the absence of proper intention. Seen solely from the perspective of the individual's spiritual connection with God, such prayer may indeed be empty and meaningless. Yet from the standpoint of man's material element, as Berkovits points out, the action is defensible, and even praiseworthy, because it both signifies and reinforces the body's subjugation to the conscious decision to pray, even if the mind has not fully succeeded in following suit. As he writes:

> Such, of course, is not the ideal form of prayer; at the same time, it is no small achievement to have taught the lips to "pray" on their own, without the conscious participation of the heart and mind. It shows that the human organism, from whose own nature hardly anything could be further removed than the wish to pray, has actually submitted to direction by the will to prayer…. Automatically "praying" lips may count for little in comparison with *kavana*, the directedness of the praying soul toward God in ecstatic submission; yet they too represent a form of submission of the organic self to the will to pray. (p. 26)

Thus the halacha is, for Berkovits, not a set of seemingly arbitrary rules dictated by God and the rabbis, but rather a necessary response to man's fundamental dualism—an approach to morality which views the body as no less significant than the mind, and which forms a part of a larger, normative Judaism spanning both the moral and legal realms. This is something which other Jewish philosophers have in some ways attempted. Both Buber and Heschel, for example, insist that their philosophies of Judaism address, in Buber's words, "the whole man, body and spirit together."[55] For this reason we find them not infrequently making statements similar to those of Berkovits concerning the importance of the body's involvement in moral actions. Yet they fail to articulate any kind of method for preparing the body for moral action, under the assumption that where the mind deter-mines to lead, the body will simply follow. Their moral teaching, it often seems, tacitly assumes that the human body is what the mind that inhabits it wishes it to be, rather than what it actually is.

The failure of so much of Western ethics to address the body as a moral question has a great deal to do with its emphasis on moral intention at the expense of the actual outcome of human actions. For if results are unimpor-tant, then actions, however important, are so only insofar as they are a reflection of one's intentions. Moral failings are necessarily perceived as failures of the conscious mind, and therefore the only redress is a further purification of intent. The inevitable result of this approach, however, is a disjunction between the demands of morality and the hopes of redemption: By detaching morality from consequences, these thinkers must also detach it from any reasoned hope that moral behavior will, in any clear way, bring about the betterment of mankind in history. If there is to be any causal link, no matter how distant, between morality and redemption—a basic tenet of Judaism which no major Jewish thinker has yet attempted to do without—then an intention-based morality must relegate it to the realm of the incomprehensible and obscure, and make of it a matter for faith alone; which is precisely what many of these thinkers, adopting a mystical ap-proach to history, advocate.[56] If, however, as Berkovits argues, morality is in its essence meant to bring about an actual improvement in the affairs of mankind, then one must view outcomes as the principal target of moral behavior, and the body as a central challenge to morality, since it is the agent of all moral outcomes.

V

The Jewish moral tradition brings together three distinct elements: A system of law incorporating both moral and ritual obligations; a set of moral values emphasized in the teachings of the prophets and in the rabbinic tradition; and a vision of the improvement of man's lot in history, which adherence to the Jewish normative system is meant to assist in bringing about. Because of the difficulty of maintaining a balance among all three elements—law, values, and vision—contemporary Jewish thinkers are often found attempting to escape the central role bequeathed to one or another of them by Jewish tradition. For some, traditional values such as *kevod habriot*, human dignity, are downplayed in the effort to transform the more concrete precepts of Jewish law into the central imperative of religion; among others, it is the law that is undermined in the pursuit of distilled moral values which, while possessing great appeal in their simplest form, frequently fall short in their ability to give clear guidance for moral action when confronted with the complexity of real life; and in many cases as well, the improvement of man's condition within history is relegated to the status of a wishful, mystical outcome resulting from one's devotion to either laws or ethical principles that are themselves derived without reference to their consequences in history, and so no longer seem to have any discernible purpose that reaches beyond the bounds of the subjective mind.

Of Jewish thinkers in the last century, it was Eliezer Berkovits who most successfully combined these diverse elements of the tradition, preserving for each a proper place within a balanced system of Jewish morality: For Berkovits, it is the values of Judaism which constitute its eternal moral fabric, which underlie the law, and which dictate the extent of change in the law over time; it is the prophetic vision which establishes morality as a vehicle for the advancement of man, and thereby determines the consequentialist character of these values; and it is the law—as law, not merely as traditional practice—which is needed to address the fundamental problem of man's corporeality, a problem that must be overcome if moral beliefs are to be translated reliably into moral outcomes. Taken together, these elements form a comprehensive approach to morality which seems to offer the possibility of a Judaism that is capable of holding fast before the tides of revolution, while at the same time safeguarding our humanity and offering us the hope of genuine improvement of our condition within history.

By incorporating all three elements into a single moral system, Berkovits poses a significant challenge to those Jewish thinkers who read the tradition as making compliance with halachic codes the sole test of religious behavior. No less important, however, is the challenge he poses towards those of the opposite inclination, who have for so long assailed Jewish law as a stumbling-block for moral behavior. For as the events of the past century demonstrate, all the mind's moral principles may come to nought if the concrete society which they are supposed to benefit lacks the practical discipline necessary to put them into practice—and this is a discipline that only law can teach. The renewed interest in Jewish law in recent years seems to reflect a disillusionment with the dominant assumption of twentieth-century Jewish thought: The belief that the Jewish people can successfully offer a moral example to the world while denying its tradition of heteronomous law. Eliezer Berkovits offers all Jews a compelling theoretical basis for rejecting that assumption.

Thus Berkovits provides a coherent alternative to both of these reductionist approaches, by suggesting that morality is ultimately about neither adherence to law nor proper intent, and that neither may therefore be understood as absolute. While cogently arguing for the very real significance of each for the emergence of a moral society, Berkovits reminds us that this does not mean that one should, for the sake of conceptual simplicity, forget their contingent nature. Only a rediscovery of the idea that morality is inspired by, and ultimately subordinate to, a vision of the improvement of mankind—and a conscientious application of that vision to reality in the form of our moral understanding and practice—can permit morality to emerge as a factor in human history.

David Hazony
Jerusalem
September 2001

I

JEWISH MORALITY
AND LAW

1

LAW AND MORALITY
IN JEWISH TRADITION

(1959)

THE PROPHETIC ENCOUNTER WITH GOD is of such radical impact that, in principle at least, it fully determines the nature of man's encounter with the "other"—that is, with God's creation. All encounters in this world are meetings of needs set in a context of value. The needs have their origin in the essential imperfection of creation; the value, in the act of creation. As I have discussed elsewhere, value without need, giving us perfection, would extinguish both man and his world.[1] Yet it is also the case that need without value would render all endeavor and striving unworthy of man. Only in response to the need that is at the heart of all meaning and value does man fulfill his destiny.

The paradigm of all encounters is man's encounter with God. God meets the other with concern and care. The manner of God's involvement in the world is the eternal example for meeting the other. Nothing that man may meet within this world can be as strange to him as he himself is to God. Yet God elevates man to "fellowship" with himself. Meeting the other, in the image of the paradigm of all encounters, is an act of creative fellowship through caring involvement. It is the essence of the religious way of life. It is the concept of *imitatio dei*, which has been introduced into Western thought by Plato,[2] and which the rabbis expressed in the following fashion in the Talmud:

> In the Bible it is written: "You shall walk after the Eternal your God."[3] But is it possible for man to walk after the Presence? Is it not written: "For the Eternal your God is a devouring fire"?[4] Rather, the meaning is: Follow him by imitating his dispositions. As he clothes the naked... so should you clothe the naked. As he visits the sick... so should you visit the sick....[5]

The "dispositions" are, of course, the relational attributes. Their ultimate significance is that they provide the original pattern for all relationship on earth.

Long before the Talmud and Plato, the idea found its classical expression in the words of the prophet Jeremiah, when he proclaimed:

> Thus says the Eternal:
> Let not the wise man glory in his wisdom,
> Neither let the mighty man glory in his might,
> Let not the rich man glory in his riches;
> But let him that glories glory in this,
> That he understands, and knows me,
> That I am the Eternal, who exercises mercy,
> Justice, and righteousness on earth;
> For in these things I delight,
> Says the Eternal.[6]

The knowledge of God surpasses all other possessions. Significantly, the prophet does not imply by it metaphysical meditation on the divine essence. God may only be known by his relational attributes—by the nature of his involvement in creation, by the fact that he exercises "mercy, justice, and righteousness on earth."[7] Most important, however, is the concluding phrase: "For in these things I delight, says the Eternal." That God relates to the world because he delights "in these things" establishes the *imitatio dei* as the divine law for man. Because "these things" are desired by God, the relational attributes become the example to follow. The encounter reveals not only God's concern, but also what he desires of man. The relational attributes are God's law for man. God, whose essence is hidden and who reveals himself by involvement with his creation, making manifest "these things" in which he delights, is of necessity revealed as the Lawgiver. The delight of the Eternal is his law for man. Since all revelation is divine involvement with men, and since all involvement is affirmation of the things God desires, revelation and law are inseparable. The encounter at Sinai revealed God as well as his law to Israel.

We may also express the idea as follows: As religion is inconceivable without revelation, neither is it possible without the law of God. God's involvement in the world and his law for the world are one. The law is the bond that preserves the relationship of divine concern beyond the fundamental religious experience of the encounter itself. The encounter passes quickly, but the law of the Eternal remains forever. As the crystallization of what God desires of man, the law is the guarantee of God's continued interest in man. As long as God's law stands, he too remains involved in the destiny of man. When the mystery of the encounter has faded away, God is still related to man by means of his law. When the precious moment in which man is granted the certitude of the Presence has sunk into the darkness of the past, the "fellowship" with God may still be maintained by doing the will of God. The law is the avenue of contact beyond the point of encounter.

The essence of the law is the same as that of the encounter itself: It is an expression of God's continued concern with man. That God commands man is the proof that he considers man. The law represents the highest affirmation of man, as well as his crowning dignity. By giving man the law, his Maker declares: I do care how he lives and what he does with his life. Charging him with the law, God testifies, as it were, that man is man enough to live under the law. The law is the sign that God has a measure of confidence in man. The command of God implies the encouragement: I order you because I know you can do it.[8] For who should know the nature of man better than his Maker? The law, being willed by God, is an indication that man—by fulfilling it—will reach the purpose contemplated for him by the Creator.

Thus, the law itself is a manifestation of God's love.[9] And so the rabbis taught in the Talmud: "Beloved are Israel, for the Holy One surrounded them with commandments."[10] Being fully aware of the implication of the law as God's concern for man, Judaism—far from considering it a burden—recognized in it an "object of desire"[11] revealed to the children of Israel. And so the psalmist was able to sing:

The law of the Eternal is perfect, restoring the soul;
The testimony of the Eternal is sure, making wise the simple.
The precepts of the Eternal are right, rejoicing the heart;
The commandment of the Eternal is pure, enlightening the eyes.
The fear of the Eternal is clean, enduring forever;
The ordinances of the Eternal are true, they are righteous all together.
More to be desired are they than gold, than much fine gold;
Sweeter also than honey and the honeycomb.[12]

II

What is the purpose of the law? In asking the question, it is clear we are now walking on dangerous ground. Nor is it our ambition to try and fathom the intentions of the Lawgiver. It is enough for the believer to know he is to do the will of God. He rejoices in the thought that, by obeying the command of God, he may relate to his Maker and walk "with him" or "before him."[13] He is elated by the thought of the law as the lasting testimony of God's concern with his welfare. When asking about the purpose of the law, then, I wish to consider those aspects which seem significant in the context of our human condition and its problems.

The interpretation presented earlier emphasizes the ethical significance of the law of God. This was borne out by the quotation from Jeremiah. The relational attributes as a code for human behavior declare: When meeting the world outside, you do it by relating yourself to it, by establishing fellowship with it through caring involvement. This is the essence of the imitation of God, and it invests the law with an ethical purpose. This does not mean that the law is identical with ethics. The law has meaning on many levels of human existence, and only after analyzing them separately can we grasp its various implications for man. Undoubtedly, the law has meaning on the ethical level. It is the ethical relevance of the law that I shall address first.

Traditionally the laws of Judaism are divided into two main groups: One contains the laws ordering relationships between man and his fellow; the other, those of a purely ritual nature, as between man and God. At the same time, as is well known, the law of God in the system of Judaism is extremely ramified: It embraces the entire life of the Jew. Man in time and in space, man in society and man in the world, are the subjects of the law.

The rhythm of the day and of the week, of the year and of the years, is determined by numerous regulations concerning times of prayer and of rest, times set aside for holiday observances. The law also prescribes one's dealings with the world of things about us by the many rules about foods to eat and not to eat, clothing to wear and not to wear. The pursuit of agriculture, the building of a home, have their respective observances. And, needless to say, the same is true of man's intercourse with his fellow man in society or in the family, in the state and among the nations. All are circumscribed by the law. Every important event in the life of the Jew is brought under the dominance of the law. There seems to be no niche or nook into which the law has not penetrated. The law is present all the time and everywhere. The Jew is indeed surrounded by *mitzvot* on all sides.

Now, the ethical significance of the laws affecting human relationships can be readily acknowledged. The laws of the second group, however, the purely ritual part, present a serious problem of interpretation. One may accept the need for some basic ritual practices and yet be nonplused by the elaborate system of Jewish ritual laws. What is the purpose of the numerous rules and regulations that seem to suggest a purely mechanical practice, without any spiritual significance? In the *Shulhan Aruch* it is even pre-scribed in what order a person should get dressed in the morning.[14] Yet the picture is in fact far more complicated. On the one hand, as we shall see, nothing could be further from the truth than to claim that the "ritual" laws have no ethical function. On the other, the ethical code of the law regarding man and his fellow is not as free of problems as would seem at first glance. So the necessity for further inquiry is not eliminated even if one acknowl-edges only the ethical principles of the law as being spiritually meaningful.

The idea of a revealed law, even if limited to the rationally understand-able realm of ethics, presented quite a problem in the history of religious philosophy. At various times, religious thinkers inquired into the essence of a divine law. They wished to know in what its validity consisted. Was it valid because it conformed to reason or because it was willed by God? Already in early Islamic philosophy, two schools of thought grappled with the problem.[15] There were the "freethinkers" who maintained that the good must be inherently recognizable as such. Consequently, the intellect alone is the judge of its validity. The law is revealed by God because it has validity of its own, but it is not valid because it is revealed. The "fundamentalists," on the other hand, felt that if reason alone were to judge the validity of the law, this would make the event of its revelation superfluous. They, therefore, held that outside the will of God there was neither good nor evil. The good was good because it was commanded; and had God commanded its opposite, then what is now known as evil would have become good. This solution is, of course, far from convincing. It is difficult to accept the idea that God could have elevated what is now called evil to the dignity of the good in a divine code. Yet it is also true that if the validity of the law were to depend on the arbitration of the intellect, the paramount importance of the revelation of the law would be abolished.

These discussions left their mark on the development of Jewish philosophy. Saadia Gaon, influenced by the Islamic schools, divided the laws of the Tora into rational and revelational laws. Rational laws are those which may be recognized by reason; they were revealed so that mankind might enjoy their benefit before they could be discovered through the process of intellectual growth. The revelational laws are those on which reason passes no judgment. They were given by God in order to increase man's reward for obeying the divine will.[16] Saadia's solution is, of course, merely a compromise. Even regarding the "revelational" laws, it is hardly possible to say that they have no value of their own, and that their entire significance lies in that they, having been ordered by God, may render man worthy of reward or mark him for punishment, as the case may be.[17]

The same controversy flared up again several centuries later between Thomas Aquinas and John Duns Scotus. Aquinas, following in the footsteps of the Islamic "freethinkers," taught the rationality of the good, which might be known by the "natural light." Duns Scotus, on the other hand, in line with the Islamic "fundamentalists," affirmed the complete dependence of the determination of good and evil on the groundless will of God.

From the religious point of view, we seem to be left with an insoluble dilemma. The validity of the law must be rooted either in reason or in revelation. But if the law has intellectual validity, what need is there for revelation; and if the law is not acceptable to reason, what use revelation?

In the great centuries of the European Enlightenment, philosophy decided against revelation. In the name of natural religion, deism made itself independent of revelation, declaring the light of reason to be the only source of authority for the law. Immanuel Kant, for example, proudly proclaimed that "the true and only religion contained only such laws... of whose absolute logical validity we may become aware ourselves... [and] which we therefore acknowledge as revealed by pure reason."[18]

This bold cutting of the Gordian knot was, of course, no solution to the religious problem. The "true and only religion" whose laws are "revealed by pure reason" may be something noble; to call it religion, however, is justified only if we assume that everything true and noble is religion. This, however, is a compliment which religion, in loyalty to its essence, must refuse to accept.

It would seem, then, that not even the category of laws concerning man's relation to his fellow is free of problems. It is not easy to say which is the less perturbing difficulty: The question of what need there is for revelation, if the laws are to be accepted on the basis of their rationality; or our all-encompassing ritual code, which seems difficult to associate with any spiritual significance.

III

Before attempting to answer these difficulties confronting the idea of the law of God in Judaism, two basic problems of ethical theory, usually overlooked, must first be addressed. One is the question of the source of ethical obligation; the other is the examination of human behavior in the light of that obligation.

As to obligation, it is not enough to know the rational essence of the good and the right; one must also understand why it is imperative to adhere to the good and the right. The two are far from being identical.[19] And when we consider human behavior in the light of ethical obligation, the problem of all problems is, of course, how to induce man to act effectively in accordance with his obligation.

None of the extant theories of ethics are able to show that ethical obligation has its source in the essence of the good itself. Let us assume, for example, that hedonism is a logically valid theory. What law is there in reason to forbid a person to behave unreasonably and to act contrary to the pleasure principle? Reason may, of course, describe the consequences of such "foolish" action—but what if one does not care about the consequences? Or consider utilitarianism. Let it be granted that the greatest happiness of the greatest number is indeed the essence of goodness. How can it be proved that one ought to care about it, and that one should be morally condemned if one does not? It is not different with intuitive ethics either. Man may have some innate concepts of good and evil; he may even be able to entertain an intuitive appreciation that he ought to act in accordance with the standards of such an inborn ethical code. But since he is capable of disobeying his moral "instinct," what is there in the intellectual grasp of those intuitive ideas that will obligate him to obey?

Perhaps the most interesting illustration of this point is provided by Kant's categorical imperative. At best, Kant has shown that to act so that the maxims of our will may at all times serve as the principles of a general law is indeed an *a priori* requirement of "pure, practical reason." However, he overlooked the most important thing: To prove that man is *obligated* to act in accordance with this famous "factum" of reason. If Kant is right, one might say that an action which does not conform to his categorical imperative is not dutiful, as the term must be understood by practical reason. But he has certainly not established that it is man's duty to act dutifully in this sense. The categorical imperative might have been fully validated logically; it is unfortunate that it is neither categorical nor imperative.

Our second problem is even more fateful for human progress than the first. Assuming the obligatory character of an ethical code, whatever the source of obligation, how is mankind to be induced to act accordingly? Obviously, this is a question which ought to be of fundamental concern to all ethics. The finest rules of human conduct are of little worth unless people follow them. It is one of the recurring subjects of the dialogues of Plato: Is goodness teachable and how should it be taught? [20]

The Socratic-Platonic answer to the inquiry is well known. The highest form of goodness is a kind of intellectual grasp of the supreme idea of being, and its contemplation. Goodness is therefore knowledge itself and, like all knowledge, it is teachable. This leads to the theory of "involuntary evil." All evildoing is the result of some miscalculation. Moral evil is the cause of the greatest unhappiness. Therefore, says Plato, "let us remember that the unjust man is not unjust of his own free will. For no man of his own free will would choose to possess the greatest of evils." [21] Moral turpitude is always due to ignorance and is involuntary. The entire history of humanism to our own day breathes the same spirit of intellectualism in ethical conduct. Education is the panacea for all problems of ethics. What people need is enlightenment. Give them schools, teach the human race, and all will be well.

Within the realm of Western thought,[22] one may see in Christianity the extreme opposite of the Socratic teaching. From the Christian point of view, it is futile to expect to teach goodness effectively. As the result of the Fall, man is so constituted that he is incapable of goodness by his own exertion. Man would indeed be lost were it not for God, who, like a true *deus ex machina*, saves him by the miracle of grace. Christianity too seems to have a theory of "involuntary evil." Here evil is, of course, not due to ignorance; yet it ought to be known as involuntary, since it is due to a corruptness of human nature itself, which cannot be mastered by natural means. Man can only be saved; he cannot improve.

Between the Socratic and the Christian tradition we may place, in this context, Marxian and various forms of evolutionary ethics. Dialectical materialism appears to be in one respect even more optimistic in its outlook than Socratic Platonism. According to it, there is hardly any need to teach goodness. Nor would it be of much use; ideas in themselves are powerless. The only determining factors are the material conditions of human exist-ence. Organize them so that they serve the well-being of all men, and all will be well with mankind. Now, the optimism of Socrates at least has its logical justification in the light of the Socratic premise. There, the idea of the supreme good is ontological; it is the source of all reality as well as of all goodness. On this basis, the real and the good are of the same origin and essence. The good is also the cause of all order in the universe.[23] What *is* ought to be. Reality is on the side of the good. It may, of course, not be so at all; but, at least, this follows from the premises of the teaching. However, if one denies the reality of the realm of ideas altogether and considers every-thing dependent on a strict materialistic determinism, the expectation that any kind of a social order would solve the problems of men is a form of dogmatic optimism for which there is no justification at all, either in theory or in experience. The assumption that material satisfaction leads to noble deeds presupposes a blind confidence in the essential goodness of a human nature which only occasionally becomes perverted by hunger and cold. A dogmatic idealism is implied, ill-befitting a materialistic philosophy.

Nor is much gained by wedding materialism to what has been called evolutionary ethics. We need not here enter into a discussion of the many fallacies of such an ethics. Assuming that it does exist, its basic principle seems to be another categorical imperative, which might be formulated in this way: In all your actions follow the direction of evolution.[24] We take it that, on the basis of such a theory, "adaptive function" is also responsible for the "conscious purposes" of an ethical code. Acting in accordance with such a code, one would *eo ipso* follow the direction of evolution. One would exercise mercy, justice, and righteousness for evolutionary reasons.

Now, whether or not evolution explains the emergence of such terms, it is far from being an answer to our question: How does evolution induce man to follow its "direction"? By having brought about the emergence of "conscious purposes," it has also evolved consciousness. As a result of all this, man may follow the "direction" and be good or refuse to follow it and be bad. Assuming, again, that the evolutionary direction does lead to the ethically good, judging by experience it would seem that the human race, having evolved to the level of consciousness, refuses *en masse* to follow evolution. The vital question of ethical practice—how is goodness to be taught so that it becomes effective in human conduct—remains unanswered.

Of course, materialistic evolution cannot borrow the solution of its problems from Christianity. But it may perhaps adopt the Socratic-humanistic answer, that goodness depends on knowledge, by claiming that the key to ethical action is the contemplation of the direction of the evolutionary process. But if such enlightenment will indeed lead to ethical action, then it is proved that intervention by consciousness in the evolutionary process is possible because it falls in the line of evolutionary direction. And since whatever follows that direction is assumed to be good, all successful purposeful action would have to be called good. The test of evolutionary ethics would be success. Whatever survives is ethical. On such a basis, there is no need to pursue the discussion any further.

Henri Bergson, having distinguished between the rationality and the obligation of the good, also understood the gravity of the problem of human conduct. He differentiated between the lower, self-centered morality of the closed society, like the tribe, family, or nation, and the higher, universal morality of the open society of humanity. He rejected the Socratic-humanistic position that ethics may be acquired by any form of intellectual exercise and seemed to accept the Christian viewpoint in part, in that he too believed that human nature might not be relied upon for moral behavior. However, he let the *elan vital* perform the task which in

Christianity was the function of divine grace. Moral action, according to Bergson, is not left to conscious behavior. The human personality is much too fickle to be entrusted with so important a responsibility. Therefore, the *elan vital* assures effective ethical conduct by compulsion. In the closed society it takes the form of social pressure, which establishes moral action as a habitual reaction, corresponding to what is known as instinct in the animal kingdom. In the open society, morality—which is communicated by the individual genius of saints and prophets who appear "like the creation of a new species"—exercises a more or less irresistible attraction.[25] Social pressure and the rise of the "social ego" are facts resulting from creative evolution. All morality, therefore, "be it pressure or aspiration, is in essence biological."[26] In other words, according to Bergson, too, man cannot help himself. He is in need of salvation; but the savior is the *elan vital* that redeems biologically.

Bergson's was a bold attempt to solve our problem. The *elan vital*, which unlike materialistic evolution does comprise the spiritual and purposeful, entrusts the effectiveness of ethical principles to the safekeeping of powerful biological forces which may not be thwarted. Unfortunately, the French thinker did not seem to realize that he had impaled himself on the horns of a dilemma. He saw clearly that the conscious acceptance of an ethical code did not guarantee its realization. He therefore called in a form of biological compulsion to assure the effectiveness of moral principles. But the moment ethical obligation becomes a form of compulsion, however ingeniously implanted in the workings of evolution, it ceases being ethical. As Bergson himself points out, ethical obligation presupposes freedom of action.[27] Man acts ethically, when, choosing among alternatives, he decides to act in conformity with the ethical demand. Therefore, either there is morality in freedom, and where there is freedom there is also the threat of failure; or there is creative, evolutionary compulsion and no ethics. Thus the problem remains unsolved. In reality we find that—assuming that mercy, justice, and righteousness are indeed nature's own "end" for man, as Bergson would have it—man seems to command sufficient freedom to be able to reject these ends of nature, and makes ample use of his freedom to do so. The *elan vital* does not seem to have been very successful.

We are thus left with the Socratic and Christian answers to the question of how goodness may be acquired by man. Neither of them, however, is supported by experience. Man may have ample knowledge of the good, yet more often than not he will act against his better insight. Moreover, the conduct in history of nations and societies, of classes and castes, provides us with a record of inhumanity that reduces to irrelevance the most sadistic crimes of individuals. In this respect, there seems to be little difference between ages of greater or lesser enlightenment; except that, in times of greater intellectual advancement, as knowledge increases man grows in power proportionately and becomes correspondingly more dangerous. The evil done by the power that knowledge provides has always eclipsed the good done by the same power. Notwithstanding enlightenment, man seems to remain an essentially unethical being.

Historic experience inclines us toward the Christian view, of the corruptness of human nature. On the basis of our experience, it is much easier to make a case that man cannot learn goodness than one that supports the Socratic-humanist position. But while history provides ample material for a theory of the hopelessness of human nature, it shows no convincing signs of salvation through divine grace. Since the day when such an act of salvation is supposed to have taken place, the criminality of man has not receded, not even in the wide realms of Christendom. Jews especially do not have to wander far afield for proofs. For them it is enough to recall what has befallen them during almost two millennia of exile in the Christian countries. The fate of the Jews in Christian lands, which in our own day was brought to its logical climax in the extermination of six million Jews, is irrefutable evidence that to this day mankind has remained unredeemed. All claims to the contrary are swept away like chaff in a windstorm before the martyrdom that Israel suffered at Christian hands through the ages.

IV

The two problems of the revealed law of God, which we discussed earlier, are not unrelated to the two problems of ethics. In what follows, I hope to show that the divine law has its ethical significance in that it offers a solution to those ethical dilemmas from which ethics is unable to extricate itself by its own strength. What appeared to be the predicament of religion in its ethical context was mainly due to the fact that the two fundamental problems of ethics were not understood.

The misunderstanding of the function of reason has been the tragic mistake which the Western world inherited from the Greeks. According to Plato, the ideas have power as well as authority. The same may be said of the forms of Aristotle. With the Stoa, the laws of reason are identical with laws of nature. Reason institutes laws, and it is also the most effective principle of order. This idea was adopted almost unquestioningly by Western thought. Once it could be shown that an ethical principle was reasonable, the need to prove that it was also obligatory was hardly ever appreciated. It was taken for granted that the reasonable was also obligatory. Similarly, it was assumed that once the reasonableness of the good was understood, reason itself would cause man to act ethically. Reason was believed to have authority to command, as well as power to compel. Starting from such premises, it was of course not possible to appreciate the significance of a revealed law. Only against the backdrop of such an understanding of the function of reason could the problem of revelation arise. If reason were sufficient to command and to make a person obey, then indeed the question was justified: If the law is reasonable, what need for revelation; if it is not reasonable, what use revelation?

But reason as such may neither command nor induce action. Reason is the faculty of understanding, of recognition and interpretation, of analysis or synthesis. Reason may tell the difference between right and wrong; perhaps even the difference between good and evil. It cannot, however, provide the obligation for doing good and eschewing evil. The source of all obligation is a will, and the motivation of a will is a desire.[28] Reason knows no desire, though man may desire to be reasonable. What ought to be ought, perhaps, to be reasonable; however, it ought to be not *because* it is reasonable, but because someone wants the actualization of that which is reasonable. Reason may describe what is; it cannot prescribe what ought to be, except hypothetically. If we wish to reach a destination, reason may advise us how to get there; it cannot, however, tell us what destination to choose unless it is informed in advance what we desire to find at our destination. All authority of reason is hypothetical. The very laws of logical processes possess only such hypothetical authority. If one desires to think logically, one must observe them. But there is nothing in the laws of logic to obligate man to logical thinking, should he prefer foolishness to wisdom. Or to use a previous example, Kant's categorical imperative is essentially hypothetical: The entire *Critique of Practical Reason* proves only that if one wishes the approval of pure, practical reason, one should respect the categorical imperative. It is always a desire, and not objective reason, which by setting a goal moves the will, and it is the will that issues the command. Not everything that is desired and willed is good; but the good does not become an obligation until it is desired and willed. The nature of the obligation depends, of course, on the will from which it emanates. The source of the obligation may be individual desire. A man may recognize something to be good. If he desires it, determining his course of action by his desire-motivated will, he becomes his own lawgiver. Or society may be the source of the law; desiring certain common objectives, it may safeguard them by legislation. The essence of justice may be described in terms of reason; its obligation must forever be based on a will. This, however, is tantamount to saying that all law derives its authority from some form of "revelation." The lawgiver must make his will known to establish the law. Let a law be ever so rational, if it has not been instituted as such by the will of the legislative authority, made manifest in one way or another, it is not obligatory; in short, it is no law.

We may now appreciate how misguided has been the controversy concerning revelation and the rationality of the revealed law through the ages.[29] The arguments between "freethinkers" and "fundamentalists," between enlightened deists and traditionally inclined theists, were never resolved. Nor could they have been resolved along the lines on which the discussion was conducted. Both schools of thought were right as well as wrong. The "freethinkers" were right in maintaining that a law that could not be subjected to the test of reason was worthless; they were wrong in assuming that justification in reason makes revelation even partially superfluous. The "fundamentalists" were right in insisting that a law not revealed by God could not be considered of divine origin; they were wrong in asserting that the quest for intellectual affirmation was immaterial. Their dilemma was due to the confusion between logical validity and ethical obligation. They did not realize that the *summum bonum* might be rational and yet not obligatory, unless it were willed by someone in authority to command. The law of God may indeed be "perfect"; however, it becomes his law because it is willed by him. Were the intellect to grasp, through the faculty of its "natural light," a divine truth, this would mean entertaining a divine concept in the mind of man. If man desired and determined to act in accordance with that insight, he would make a divine truth his law of conduct. The intellectual validity of the law would then be divine; the ethical obligation, however, would have its origin in the will of man. An eternal truth becomes the law of God when action in accordance with it is explicitly desired by God. It is the *will* of God that makes the good obligatory as the law of God. Just as religion itself cannot be based on logical proofs for the existence of God, but only on the experience of God's concern for man,[30] so too the law of God cannot be established on the logical validity of any system of ethics, but only on the manifest will of God. We know of the law of God, as we know of any other law, because it has been revealed to us by the lawgiver.[31]

From what has been said, it follows that the concept of the law of God does not exclude the possibility of a secular ethics. In view of the difference between the logical validity of a code and its source of obligation, a valid code of ethics can be based on the exercise of mercy, justice, and righteousness and be made obligatory because man or society "delights in these things." Human behavior according to such a code would be ethical, yet it would be independent from a divine law. The same ethical code may be desired by society or by God; the difference will lie in the nature of the obligation. The binding force of a code instituted by society or the state is relative; the force of the one willed by God is absolute. It is not, however, in the difference in the rigor of its application that the distinction between relative and absolute obligation is reflected. A secular society need not be less exacting in its demand for obedience to its laws than a community governed by a divine law. Mercy as well as justice are the things in which God delights. But a law instituted by a will of relative authority admits of compromise for the sake of expediency; the law of absolute authority will not be overruled by such considerations. All secular ethics lack the quality of absolute obligation. They are as changeable as the desires and the wills that institute them; the law of God alone is as eternal as his will. Secular ethics, derived as it must be from a relative will, is subjective; God alone is the source of objectivity for all value and all law. Relativistic ethics, serving the goal of subjective desire, is essentially utilitarian; the desire of God alone makes the object of the desire an end in itself.

V

It is not enough, of course, to be able to point to the source of the obligation of ethical principles. As already indicated, the task is to induce man to implant the demands of morality in human conduct. We have observed that the dismal record of human performance in this area testifies to man's most tragic failure in history. This failure, I have suggested, is due mainly to the belief that reason implies both authority and power. The foregoing discussion addressed the matter of authority; what remains is the question of reason's power.

Assuming that the mind possesses power of its own, the Socratic theory of "involuntary evil" is correct. If ideas indeed possess a vital potency, then once they are grasped and contemplated, they will—most certainly—determine the actions of man. On the basis of this assumption, goodness becomes teachable via the intellect. All one needs in order to act in accordance with ethical principles is their conscious realization. Reason will then cause man to obey. The truth, however, is that the mind is incapable of action of any kind. The spirit by itself, within the realm of human experience, is impotent. It has rightly been observed that the higher forms of being, as well as the higher categories of value, are by themselves the weaker ones as measured in material potency.[32] The realm of existence which is blind to the ideal of truth as well as to any concept of morality—that is, inorganic nature—represents also the most powerful concentration of material energy in our experience. The spirit itself is powerless; it may act only in union with the vital or "material" forces in the cosmos. No one has ever accomplished anything by merely contemplating an idea. All conscious action is the result of some form of cooperation between the mind and the body. Matter—whatever its ultimate secret—without the mind is inanity; mind without matter is, at best, noble impotence. Power by itself is purposeless; purpose on its own is powerless.[33] The material world can be saved from the idiocy of mere being by the direction it may receive from the spirit; the spirit can be redeemed from the prison of its impotence by the amount of cooperation that it may be able to derive from the material world. Meaning is realized in this world by the interpenetration of mind and matter. Matter must be informed by mind, and mind must be rendered potent by matter.[34] Without interpenetration of the two realms, reality would simply be a jungle of blind forces, entangled with one another and, perhaps, contemplated by some mind that rationalizes the impotence of the spirit into stoic serenity.

Nowhere is this more true than in the realm of ethics. The ethical deed represents the unity of mind and matter; it results from an intimate cooperation between the ethical intention and the human organism which "agrees" to be guided by it. Without a living body, there is for man no possibility of doing good. (Without a normally functioning brain, one cannot even *think* of goodness.) All ethical principles depend for their materialization on the vital, organic element, which is inseparable in this world from the human personality. In the ethical deed, the mind guides toward a desired goal, and the organic element provides the practical means of reaching it. The spirit of man may recognize the end of ethical aspirations intellectually; his physiological and biological inheritance, constituting the human body, is alone the instrument of ethical realization. Without the cooperation of the body, the mind will achieve nothing.

Only now are we able to appreciate the seriousness of man's ethical predicament. On the one hand, the mind of man, the custodian of all spiritual and ethical values, is by itself incapable of action; on the other, the life forces and all the sources of material energy, without whose instrumentality no ethical action is possible, are by their very essence indifferent to ethical or spiritual values. All forms of energy are indifferent to considerations of righteousness or mercy; all biological needs or desires are unaware of the existence of any moral code. The human body, the tool of individual moral conduct, is essentially amoral. Indeed, since the prototype of all ethical action is God's encountering the world with care and concern, one might even say that the instruments of ethical realization are not only basically amoral but, indeed, anti-moral. As in the divine prototype, care and concern for the other require self-limitation and even self-denial.[35] But all the inorganic concentrations of energy in the universe meet their environment with the full impact of their self-concern. All the organic needs in nature seek their own satisfaction exclusively. Physiologically and biologically, the organic nature of man strives to preserve its vitality and effectiveness in an essentially selfish way.

At the core of human existence is the source of man's ethical dilemma. Man, taking his place in the realm of the spirit as well as of matter, is committed to ethical action. He is obligated to meet the other, the non-self, in a relationship of caring involvement. But he can do this only through the instrumentality of a physical organism which is in essence under the sway of laws of self-centeredness. Man appears to have nothing with which to overcome the dualism of his being, except this nature of his, within which the two principles are alive and at cross-purposes with each other.

From the ethical point of view, Plato was right when he defined man as a soul using a body. He was wrong, however, in going on to say that knowledge would ensure that man would make the right use of his body.[36] Knowledge by itself is never the cause of action. Already Aristotle subjected the Socratic-Platonic view of the teachability of goodness to pertinent criticism. He pointed out that the mind, being calculative and speculative, "is never found producing without appetite."[37] It is true that Aristotle also says that "appetite alone is incompetent to account fully for movement." Often one appetite has to contend with another and, at times, we may even resist temptation and follow the advice of the "practical mind"; but only because the "practical mind" itself subserves an object of appetite.[38] Ethical practice must be motivated by an emotional urge, and its effectiveness depends on the outcome of conflicting emotions and desires.

Aristotle, in his criticism, was anticipating Spinoza, who many centuries after him proclaimed that the intellect as such was powerless against emotions. He maintained that our knowledge of good and evil is unable to restrain emotions which are in conflict with such understanding, unless our knowledge itself becomes an emotion or a desire for the good, more powerful than the opposing desires.[39] While this insight is valid independent of his system, it is regrettable that Spinoza's solution to the problem of making intellectual concepts emotionally effective makes sense only on the basis of his own premises. What we observe in actual experience is the fearful impotence of the mind to curb, let alone rule, emotions. Only emotions seem to be potent enough to control or master emotions. All this seems to lead us to the Marxist position. It was Karl Marx who asserted that ideas become potent when they capture the *imagination* of the masses. This, of course, means that ideas, in order to be powerful, must serve goals that are emotionally desired by a great many people.

The Marxist rebellion against Socratic-humanistic intellectualism was fully justified. It was right in affirming the impotence of the spirit, as such, in the realm of events and actions. It was wrong, however, in concluding from such "material" impotence the nonexistence of an independent realm of valid ideas and values, which ought to inform events and guide actions.

VI

Bearing in mind the complex nature of the ethical dilemma, how then is effective ethical conduct possible?[40]

The law, itself an expression of God's care for and confidence in man, outlines the human share of responsibility in man's salvation. There is a great deal man can do and, therefore, ought to do in the cause of his own redemption. At the same time, the extent of the law, which leaves no part of life untouched, should be understood as an indication that Judaism does not accept the facile optimism of the Socratic-humanistic tradition that all man needs for the good life is the intellectual study of the essence of goodness. According to Judaism, man judged by his own nature is not as hopeless a creature as Christian theology would have; neither is he as easily led to goodness as humanism imagines. There is, indeed, a great deal man is able to do for his own redemption, but much more is needed than the contemplation of the good.

It is to the problem of ethical practice, of how to induce man to live in accordance with an ethical code which he acknowledges intellectually or by faith, that the seemingly irrelevant elements in the system of Jewish law provide the solution.

The motivation of all action being a desire, the ethical deed requires an "appetite for goodness." Judaism assumes that such an inclination is indeed implanted in human nature. It is the good inclination (*yetzer hatov*), which—like its adversary the evil inclination (*yetzer hara*)—has its seat "in the heart."[41] It is an emotional force, a desire for the good.[42] It is present in all men, but—unfortunately—it is helpless in the conflict with the other, self-centered and self-regarding urges and needs of physical man.[43] It is therefore necessary to foster the emotional force of the desire for the good, to increase its intensity and its hold over the emotional pattern of the human personality. In order to achieve effective ethical conduct, not the mind alone, but, foremost, needs and appetites have to be educated; the seat of desire in human nature must be so influenced that emotional forces are willing to submit to the discipline required for moral action. This, however, is not enough. Beyond the education of needs and desires, it is also necessary to make the physical organism of the human body, the "tool" of all action, receptive to the emotionally accepted purposes of the spirit.

This is a twofold task, the accomplishment of which is pursued along two lines, converging on a common goal. One may increase the intensity of the desire for the good by sublimating some of the egocentric inclinations of human nature. But the sublimation of desires is brought about by inhibition.[44] Preventing the satisfaction of natural wishes, we erect emotional dams, creating reservoirs of emotional energy. The resources of such reservoirs may then be so channeled as to increase the emotional "charge" of the desire for the good, thus enabling it to seek its own satisfaction more potently. Within the system of Judaism, the purpose of the method of inhibition is achieved by such "ritual" laws as belong to the category of the negative commandments (*mitzvot lo ta'aseh*). "You shall not do any kind of work on the Sabbath day" has obviously an inhibitory function as well. The same is true of the numerous dietary laws and of many other "purely religious" injunctions. There is within Judaism a code of commandments which achieves the inhibition of some natural needs and desires.

However, beyond inhibition—which as we shall see leads to sublimation—the law proceeds to the task of "educating" the human body, the indispensable instrument of all action, for the ethical deed. But how does one educate the body? Since the days of antiquity, Western civilization has mistakenly believed that it is possible to convince the body by reasoning with it, by telling it what it may and may not do. And so it hoped in vain for effective ethical conduct through education. At its best, Western civilization was talking to the mind and never really reached the body. The body is not accessible to logical reasoning. One can only teach it by making it do things. One does not learn to swim by reading books on swimming technique, nor does one become a painter by merely contemplating the styles of different schools. One learns to swim by swimming, to paint by painting, to act by acting. One learns how to do anything by doing it. This applies nowhere more strictly than in the realm of ethical action. The only way of educating the bio-physical instrument of action is by making it perform. This task is fulfilled by the other group of "ritual laws," which has its place in the category of commandments of positive injunction (*mitzvot aseh*), prescribing certain religious performances.

However, it may look as if we were running around in a circle. Was not our original problem how to make the bio-physical part of human nature submit to the commands of the spirit? Now we seem to be suggesting that the only way of doing it is by making it submit. We inhibit needs and desires, we make a reluctant body perform all kinds of "religious" duties. If, however, we can do that, why not come directly to the point and satisfy ourselves with prescribing the ethical deed alone?

The problem is not essentially different from the one we face when teaching any other distinctive form of behavior or action. One does not teach the act of warfare merely by lecturing to recruits. One learns how to wage war best by waging it. On the other hand, to wait until a martial conflict actually arises would be foolhardy; it may then be too late to learn. The solution to the problem is, of course, military training. In this way one teaches the art of war by warring, except that the process of learning takes place in a situation of unreality. The peacetime maneuvers of an army may be planned to be as close a replica of the conditions of real warfare as possible; yet such maneuvers do not take place in the situation of real war. This, of course, is right and proper. It is true that one can learn to act in a certain way only by performing the action which is required. However, while one is learning one ought to be able to make mistakes without serious consequences. Therefore, one teaches people to behave and to do by making them behave and do, but in a situation that is artificially created for the specific purposes of "training." To send an army of raw recruits into battle may be the most direct method of teaching the art of warfare. Those who survive will learn fast and thoroughly. But the direct method is obviously not the wisest; and the more powerful the enemy, the smaller the chances of victory. All training teaches behavior by making a person do what he is expected to do. It is always partly inhibitive and partly prescriptive. It can be successful because it adopts what we may call the "indirect" method of teaching conduct. One is taught to act in an artificial situation, as if one were acting in a real one. One may succeed in acquiring a skill or an art because there is always a "second chance." In the "as if" situation of training, mistakes are hardly ever fatal and, therefore, one may try and try again.

Similarly, the ethical significance of the two categories of "ritual" laws, which we have been discussing, consists in that they ready the bio-physical organism, the only means of ethical conduct, for effective ethical action by setting up the classical training situation. Any one commandment of the Decalogue—"you shall not commit adultery" or "you shall not kill" or "you shall not covet"—is an ethical injunction directed to a real situation of conflict or temptation. In order to obey it, one must inhibit powerfully aroused passions. But one does not learn the art of self-control merely by reading the Bible. One learns it by actually controlling oneself in the face of a challenge. However, when the challenge actually arises in all seriousness, it may be too late to inhibit and to act ethically and effectively. To delay one's preparations for meeting the challenge until it actually presents itself would be the direct method, which usually leads to failure. The direct attack on the amoral and, perhaps, even anti-moral egocentricity of the physical organism is as unwise an undertaking as the sending of untrained recruits into the firing line. Emotions will be mastered only by stronger emotions. The dynamic charge of vital urges will be held in check by the more potent charge of opposing and no less vital desires. But, originally, the desire for the good, as one of the vital urges within human nature, is outnumbered by opposing forces.

The educational significance of the inhibitive as well as positively enjoining "ritual laws" is that they represent the *indirect* attack of Jewish intention on the essential self-centeredness of the bio-physical element, the unwilling yet indispensable partner in the ethical life. Both the inhibitive and the prescriptive regulations of this code, from the point of view of ethical training, follow the indirect method. By referring to them as "ritual" laws, we express the idea that there is no logical reason for their being laws at all. There is, for instance, nothing in the real situation of man to suggest that it is harmful to partake of food that is forbidden by the dietary laws. It is the law itself that creates an artificial situation, as it were. It orders people to behave "as if" it mattered what type of food they consumed. Or let us take another example, one which is not inhibitive but prescribes some form of action: The commandment of the daily wearing of phylacteries. Again, there seems to be nothing in the real situation of man to require such an exercise. It is the law itself which creates a situation in which the perform-ance of this religious duty is treated as seriously as if something important depended on it. It is the typical "as if" training situation. Judged by the reality of the immediate situation, the soldier engaged in camouflage exercises, his helmet adorned with branches and leaves, not daring to move lest an enemy take a shot at him, when obviously there is no enemy, does a silly thing. Seemingly, he is engaged in an equally absurd task when he aims his rifle, loaded with make-believe bullets, at a make-believe target. Yet on such make-believe may indeed depend his very life, should the "as if" situation ever turn into a real conflict.

The training method of the "ritual laws" approaches the citadel of biophysical egocentricity indirectly: It never demands complete self-denial from it, as is exacted in the real situation of conflict and temptation. At no time, for example, does the observance of the dietary laws require complete denial of one's need for food, meaning the absolute suppression of "appetite." The inhibition is always partial and temporary.[45] Similarly, in those regulations that prescribe certain duties to be performed, what is demanded is of course not what the human organism, following the promptings of its own nature, would normally be inclined to do. Yet the submission exacted by the law is again only temporary and partial. To put on the phylacteries, to observe the three times of daily prayer, to pronounce a blessing before the enjoyment of the fruits of the earth—these require some submission, some discipline, some sacrifice. However, the self-regarding interests of vital needs and inclinations are not radically challenged. In submitting to the discipline of the "ritual laws," the egocentricity of man's organic nature is not directly assaulted. Because of the limited objective of the law in this context, it is possible to achieve some success by making appetites and desires obey, by curbing some of their exclusive self-seeking, and by causing the body of man to perform at the bidding of a will whose desire does not have its place among bodily desires and needs. The indirect method deals cunningly with the "evil inclination."[46]

We may now say more exactly what is being accomplished in the interest of ethical conduct by the observance of the "ritual laws." The aim is to teach purely subjective emotions, needs, and desires a new "awareness," one which is foreign to the organic component of the human personality. It is the *awareness of the other*, of an order of being as well as of meaning different from that of organic egocentricity. The purpose of the inhibitive rules is to practice saying "no" to self-centered demands; whereas the fulfillment of the positive commands is the exercise of saying "yes" in consideration of an order different from one's own. By such training, one breaks down the exclusiveness of man's organic selfishness. The obedience to the rules and commands is itself an exercise in behavior that is not purely self-regarding and orients a person toward an other. Submission to the law becomes submission to an other; awareness of the other means acknowledging and considering it.

We are dealing with the reactions of the human body. The awareness of which we are speaking cannot, therefore, be conscious. Physical awareness is instinctive or habitual. The acknowledgment of an other must be made habitual in order to be effective. This may be accomplished by a method of training that is comprehensive and continuous. The religious system of Judaism, which disciplines the Jew in every situation all through life, establishes habitual patterns of physical reaction and conduct, which testify to an acute physical "awareness" of an order of reality that is not of the body. When, for instance, a religious Jew feels nauseous when forbidden food is placed before him, such a reaction is not natural; it is not in keeping with the laws of his original physiology. The reaction shows the awareness of an outside will and law that the physiological element has somehow acquired.[47] In a sense, the nausea reflects the partial transformation of the natural desire for food, which has become retrained by the desire of the lawgiver. People who pray regularly and on all the occasions prescribed by religious law at times find that their minds have wandered far from the meaning of the prayer. Yet their lips—apparently guided unconsciously— continue to form the words automatically. Such, of course, is not the ideal form of prayer; at the same time, it is no small achievement to have taught the lips to "pray" on their own, without the conscious participation of the heart and mind. It shows that the human organism, from whose own nature hardly anything could be further removed than the wish to pray, has actually submitted to direction by the will to prayer. The physical element has become "aware" of that will in the same way in which it is "aware" of anything else, i.e., habitually; it has absorbed guidance from the intention to pray, and it respects its existence. Automatically "praying" lips may count for little in comparison with *kavana*, the directedness of the praying soul toward God in ecstatic submission; yet they too represent a form of submission of the organic self to the will to pray. In the Talmud is found the remark that we owe a debt of gratitude to the head because it bows, as prescribed when we reach the paragraph of *modim* in our prayer, without waiting for the explicit order from our consciousness to do so. It bows mechanically, as it were, even when the mind has digressed from the contents of the prayer.[48] No doubt, such behavior is not the most ideal approach to God. However, we believe the value of a culture is not expressed in what people think consciously, but rather in what they do habitually. The civilization of the highest order is that which succeeds in teaching man's physical self to show, in its own "automatic" way, respectful submission to an order that is determined by the desires of the spirit and the longings of the soul.

Through the all-encompassing discipline of religious observances, the awareness of the other affects the habits of the entire physical element of the human being. The inhibitive regulations establish a pattern of behavior which disciplines the self-regarding impulses and, therefore, directs the "attention" of the unspent emotional energies toward an outlet by means of sublimation. At the same time, the prescriptive laws develop physical dispositions and skills to act at the behest of a will outside the physical realm. All this is pursued by the discipline practiced in the "as if" situation, by means of the "ritual laws."[49] But when the real situation of temptation, or the conflict of impulses and intention, arises in all seriousness, one has already practiced inhibition for the sake of an "other"; in innumerable previous situations, one has actually considered the other by making the body act as commanded by a will from outside the realm of organic self-centeredness. In the situation of serious challenge, one may therefore count on a measure of preparedness to obey instructions issuing from a higher order of values.

VII

At this point the question may be asked: Assuming that the "indirect method" does indeed condition the vital drives and train the body for behavior that is not exclusively egocentric, what need is there for associating such an education with laws that emanate from God? Could such discipline not have been devised equally well by some human agency? Man has created many such systems of disciplinary training. The impressive history of military art in all ages is a case in point; the English public school system may be considered another; the art of yoga may also serve as a particularly convincing example. In all these cases, without any specific reference to

God, success has been achieved in educating a new form of "awareness" and in establishing habitual patterns of behavior previously unknown.

Our question might be answered as follows: Since God desires of man that he practice mercy, justice, and righteousness, and since he desires this because he is concerned about his creation, it need not be contrary to good sense that he also prescribe a method that would help man in reaching the goal set for him by his Creator. Such an answer is problematic, however, because it limits the significance of the "ritual laws" to the function they perform in resolving the dilemma of effective ethical conduct. But the "ritual laws" are not merely the handmaid of ethics. Their meaning is far from exhausted by the "indirect method" with which they address the problems of successful moral action. Rather, their immediate significance is to be described in purely religious terms.

The "indirect method" helps in deciding the conflict within man in favor of the good; it serves as a bridge between the image of God imprinted on man and the material component of human existence. All this belongs in the realm of ethics. There is, however, another dualism—perhaps even more critical—that must be resolved, in the realm of religion. We have seen that the basic religious experience is one of relationship between God and man.[50] God cares for man and makes himself accessible to man. But the relationship, when it is established—either in the acute phase of the encounter or in the latent one of faith[51]—may occur only between the spiritual personality of man and the manifestation of the divine Presence. It would seem that the bio-physical component of human nature is incapable of any relationship with the divine. The "organism" is not only amoral but fundamentally profane. This is the origin of the "religious" rejection of the body. Most higher religions are unable to make sense of the body. They see in it the throne of evil and suggest that man would be better off without it.

What the idealism of numerous religions and philosophies overlooks is that man without a body is as little to be considered human as man without a soul. Whatever the plight of the soul after death may be, in this world man is a composite being, consisting of mind and matter, of soul and body. That God made him that way means that he has to make sense of his life in the form in which he was granted life. Any rejection of the body is a rejection of man himself, of man as God created him for the tasks of this world.

If religion is relatedness to God, then the whole human being must be so related and not man as soul only, for as such he does not exist in this world. Man, soul and body, must enter into the relationship. This may actually happen in the prophetic encounter itself. There man is not at all in his own power; he is completely overwhelmed, as well as completely sustained. At the manifestation of the divine Presence, body and soul become one in their nothingness and, as one, are sustained in the elevating love of God. In the encounter itself, the dualism of human nature is overcome by the power as well as by the love of God. But in the post-encounter phase of religion, when the relationship is maintained by historic memories and the art of faith[52]—and this phase comprises all the life of most men and most of the life of all men—how is man's physical being to participate in the relationship? Is only the conscious element of the human personality to be related to the religious experience? Is only the soul to live in the divine Presence? If so, then man as man would be incapable of religion.

The task of relating the physical component of the human being to God can be accomplished only by a divine law. The body cannot meditate divine truth; it can only do or not do, behave one way or another. It may enter into the religious relationship only by means of its own nature—through action and behavior, undertaken in fulfillment of a divine command. It is true that the purely ethical function of the "ritual laws" might be achieved without their being divine commands; but their religious function cannot. On the religious plane, the indirect method of ethical concern becomes direct religious commitment. The training by the indirect method conditions the human organism for non-egocentric action; the origin of the law in the divine will, however, turns the non-egocentric conditioning into theocentric behavior. The "awareness" established is not directed merely toward some outside order, but toward a divine one. It is not just "an other" which the organic component of the human being senses, but the "Wholly Other" that is God. From the ethical standpoint, inhibiting some of the radically self-regarding impulses is a negative act; but in the religious context, by inhibiting one fulfills a divine command. Not only does one learn to submit to an outside will; one obeys the will of God.

By obeying the command of God, the human organism itself becomes related to God; by *doing* the will of God, it is enabled to enter into relationship with the divine. The dietary laws, for instance, not only have the disciplinary significance of "educating" man's appetite; by obeying divine injunctions in one's eating habits, a basic human need enters into the religious situation. Or consider the traditional way of observing the Passover festival. Spiritually, one could commemorate the miracles that God wrought in Egypt by some form of intellectual exercise, such as thinking of the Exodus, remembering the events that led up to the liberation of our people, or contemplating the debt of gratitude we owe God for his intervention on behalf of Israel. All this is, of course, included in the traditional observance. But the physical element cannot participate in any form of spiritual celebration. The body may be induced to "remember" and to observe Passover only by our making it do things that have a bearing on the meaning of the festival; by refraining from all leavened bread, by partaking of the *matza*, by reclining at the Seder table. To cleave to God is, undoubtedly, a deeply religious concept, and one may have a pretty good idea how the soul may attempt to do it. But such cleaving will be of a spiritual nature. However, the body of man may learn how to cling to him only by performing some physical action symbolic of the spiritual meaning. The daily wearing of the phylacteries, for instance, may be considered such an action of "binding" the body, too, to God.

The religious significance of the "ritual laws" is that they create a material "awareness" of the divine Presence. Again, this kind of awareness is not the same as that of the mind. It is not a conscious awareness; it is more akin to instinct. It must become a habit, to some extent subconscious, in order to assert itself in practice. Therefore, as seen earlier from the standpoint of ethical conduct, and now from the religious point of view as well, the system of the ritual laws must be all-embracing in order to develop the awareness of God as a secondary instinct, as it were, for man's physical being. The so-called ritual laws are the only way for the physical component in man to become oriented toward the divine; through them, the body too may cleave to God. By fulfilling the commandments of God, the body too may enter into the relationship that is the essence of religion.

The spiritual quality of both the worship and the service of God has been exalted too often. But such service applies only to one part of the human being; and as such, it underscores the religious impotence of the other. If the relationship to God is to be complete, it must engage man in his entirety. We can know nothing of the religion of a pure soul. Our task is to establish the religious reality of man. In the history of religious thought, a great deal of unjustified criticism has been heaped on the mechanical, ritual performances of religion. What is more important, the conscious worship of the mind or the quasi-automatic performances of the body? The question is meaningless. The body cannot worship consciously, and the mind is incapable of serving by way of "ritual" practice. Since man is neither only soul nor only body, but both joined to each other, both these constituent elements must be related to God, each in a manner adequate to its own nature. On the level of the soul, the relationship is spiritual and conscious, but it cannot be expressed in action; on the level of the body, the relationship has to become "materialized" in action.

These two expressions of the religious life are not meant to exist parallel to each other as the religion of the soul and as that of the body. The *mitzva* is the union of the two. It is never only thought, nor is it a mere reflex movement of the body. In its ideal form, the *mitzva* is a deed; and, like all true deeds, it is of the spirit and of the body at the same time. In fulfilling a *mitzva*, the Jew consciously orients himself toward God; by doing the will of God, he knowingly places himself in rapport with the divine Being. But all this is the internal and invisible content of the *mitzva*; its external reality is constituted by the action of the body.[53] In fact, only because of the conscious element in the *mitzva* are the ritual laws able to establish the new bodily "awareness" as habitual orientation toward God. The conditioning of the body toward the will of God is the result of continuous conscious suggestion. Through the *mitzva*, man overcomes the dualism of his nature in the God-oriented deed. In the *mitzva* man is one; as a whole he relates himself to the one God.

The most revealing example in this connection is, perhaps, the case of prayer. No doubt, it is possible to pray "in one's heart," without words and without any movement of the body. One may pray in silent meditation. However, while such prayer may be appropriate for a being that is pure mind or soul, it is certainly not the adequate prayer for a being like man. The perfect prayer on earth is the one prayed not only by the soul of man but by the whole of the human being, body and soul. As the psalmist exclaims: "All my bones shall say: Eternal, who is like unto thee?"[54] Man's situation requires that his very bones should be capable of "prayer." But this is only possible if prayer too becomes a *mitzva*, unifying body and soul. Prayer, therefore, cannot be only silent meditation; it has to be a spoken word.[55] It has to be physical action, informed by intention. Physical prostration before God is no less essential for prayer than is spiritual concentration. The prayer of man should be human and not angelic.

The idea is magnificently formulated in the *nishmat* hymn of the Sabbath morning service:

> Therefore, the limbs which you have apportioned in us,
> the spirit and the soul which you have breathed into our nostrils,
> and the tongue which you have placed in our mouths,
> shall all thank and bless, praise and glorify, extol and revere,
> hallow and do homage to your name, our King.[56]

What is here said about prayer applies to religion in general. It is comparatively easy to serve God as a spirit; the challenge is to serve him in the wholeness of man's earth-bound, and yet soul-indwelt, humanity. Immanuel Kant once wrote: "The true [moral] service of God is… invisible, i.e., it is the service of the heart, in spirit and in truth, and it may consist… only of intention."[57] This, indeed, is the noble formula for the historic bankruptcy of all "natural," as well as "spiritual," religions. The invisible service of God is the prerogative of invisible creatures. When man adopts such service for himself, he makes the dualism of his nature itself a religion. He will expect *Gesinnung* (sentiment) and noble intentions of the soul, and will readily forgive the profanity of the body; he will have God "in his heart" and some devil directing his actions. He will serve God on the Sabbath and himself the rest of the week. He will worship like some angelic being in the specified places of worship and follow his self-regarding impulses everywhere else. And he will find such an arrangement in order. For should not the true service of God be invisible? And is not the physical organism—and together with it, all the material manifestations of life—therefore incapable of religion?

Contrary to Kant, Judaism teaches that man's "true service of God" must be human. It should be invisible, as man's soul is invisible; and it should be visible, too, because man is visible. It must be "service of the heart, in spirit and in truth" as well as of the body. It must be service through the *mitzva*, the deed in which man's spiritual and material nature have unified. It is a much higher service than that of the spirit alone. It is the religion of the whole man.[58]

The essence of such service has been beautifully expressed by a latter-day rabbi, who said that of all those commandments that are "between God and man," he loved most that of dwelling in the succah. In entering the succah, one steps into the *mitzva* with one's very boots on. This is, indeed, basic Judaism. It is comparatively easy to relate the spiritual to God; it is as easy as it is ineffective in history. The real task is to orient the whole world of man, matter and spirit, toward God.

VIII

Thus far, only continuous sacrifice has been demanded of man's material nature. The indirect method, as training for ethical conduct, inhibits natural impulses and undermines the self-centeredness of man's physical being. On the religious level, too, the creation of what we have called a physical "awareness" of the divine Presence is achieved at the cost of considerable physical self-denial. However, once the idea is accepted that man as a whole being is to relate himself to God, the self-denial of his material nature reaps its own reward. In the *mitzva*, which is realized by the union of the spiritual and material, the vital needs and functions of the physical component of man receive their affirmation. If they too are to participate in the relationship that is the religious life, then they too are wanted by their Maker; they too are acknowledged by God. The insistence that the oneness of man be achieved by overcoming the dualism of his nature implies that the material and organic have their own positive value. Far from being rejected, they are actually desired. In the attention given them, they are vindicated.

This vindication finds its expression, first of all, in the general acceptance of life as a basic value. The preservation of life is a fundamental religious commandment, which—with three exceptions—takes precedence over all other religious laws.[59] To preserve one's health and not expose oneself foolishly to danger is itself a divine command. Unlike Plato, Judaism does not look upon the body as "a prison of the soul."[60] It is, rather, essential and prerequisite to human existence. In view of the long history of idealistic misconceptions, it cannot be repeated often enough that the soul as such is not human. Man needs life, in the purely biological sense of the word, if he is to fulfill his divinely ordained destiny on earth. Life itself is God-given; it possesses meaning and worth in its material, organic manifestation.[61]

However, apart from the vindication of life as such, in the attempt to relate the whole of man to God, the particular needs, urges, and appetites of man's bio-physical aspect find their affirmation as well. Again we may look to the example of the dietary laws. In fostering certain eating habits, these laws implicitly acknowledge the claims of a purely biological need and desire. The Jew who, in submission to God, satisfies his hunger by curbing the self-centeredness of an organic impulse has succeeded in serving God, even by the purely material activity of keeping his body alive. Even when eating, he lives in the presence of God.[62] "Blessed are you, Eternal our God, who brings forth bread from the earth," the blessing a Jew says before eating bread, is not only a form of divine service, but also encourages man's enjoyment of bread as God's creation.[63] The enjoyment itself, essentially biological, becomes oriented to God, because the blessing prepares for it spiritually. "He who sees handsome people and beautiful trees," the rabbis taught, "should say: Blessed be he who creates beautiful things."[64] By reciting the blessing, which at first intervenes between man and his enjoyment, man turns his sensual delight into an act of thanksgiving to God for his creation. In this way, earthly delight becomes justified through its relatedness to God.

Such affirmation of earthly needs and impulses is characteristic of the whole system of the law of Judaism. Sabbath and holidays are not observed "spiritually," nor should they be. Man is not a spirit. On the Sabbath, therefore, not only the soul should find peace, but the body too should rest. One celebrates the day not only by meditation and prayer, but also by wearing Sabbath clothes and by enjoying the Sabbath meals. The Sabbath meal itself is a *mitzva*; it is divine service. Properly performed, it is service of a far higher quality than that of prayer and meditation alone; it is the service of the whole man. Body and spirit celebrate the Sabbath in communion. The Jew who keeps the Sabbath may say that the material enjoyments of the day enhance his spiritual elation, and that his spiritual elation renders the material enjoyments more gratifying. In the unifying act of the *mitzva*, the Sabbath acts as a "spice" to the palate, elevating the spirit of man.[65]

The biological functions, under the discipline of the law, fulfill the purpose desired by the law. The prohibitions of the law themselves imply a proper direction for these functions. Sexual morality, for instance, through its many inhibitive rules, prescribes the positive function of sexuality. As a result, we find that within Judaism it would be inconceivable to regard marriage as a "lesser evil," which, as a compromise in a hopeless situation, may be allowed to the lesser breed of men. Nor is marriage merely permitted, but rather an important religious obligation. According to the Bible, after the creation of man, God blessed him with the words "Be fruitful, and multiply, and replenish the earth."[66] The words of Isaiah that God created the earth "not a waste; he formed it to be inhabited"[67] were understood by the teachers of the Talmud to mean that man's duty is to ensure that the earth not become a waste, and that it remain inhabited by people.[68] Of the bond between husband and wife, the rabbis had the boldness to say: "If husband and wife merit it, the divine Presence dwells in their union."[69]

One should serve God with one's entire being. But one can do this only if the self-centeredness of man's vitality is curbed and his organic reality conditioned for the awareness of the divine. Through the education of man's physical component in the will of God by means of an all-embracing system of religious observance, the biological functions themselves become dedicated; man's nature becomes purposefully directed and may now fulfill itself and yet serve God. Only here do we reach the most intimate interpenetration between mind and matter, the closest union between spirit and body, between the needs of the creature and the purpose of the Creator. It is possible for man to satisfy all his needs in doing the will of God.[70] It is here that man's dual nature is brought to harmony. It is the vindication of matter through its union with the spirit and its association with a divine purpose.

This vindication of matter is itself an essentially religious task; it is part of the basic religious obligation which we have described as *imitatio dei*. The original religious experience is man's encounter with the divine. In this encounter we discern God's care and concern for man. From this follows the religious duty to meet the "other" as God meets man, with care and concern. Now, one of the most elementary meetings with an "other" is the confrontation between man's conscious self and his material condition. The body does not meet the spirit, but the spirit does meet the body. Whatever the distance between the two, it is as nothing when compared to the abyss that originally separates man from God. Notwithstanding God's nature as "Wholly Other," the love and pity of God for man allows the encounter to take place. How much more should the spirit of man, in imitation of God, meet the body with pity and care.[71] The rejection of man's physical nature is an act of irreligion; it is conceit of the spirit and irreverence toward God's creation. While such rejection may occasionally be acclaimed as the unnatural triumph of rare individuals, in the history of man it always leads to the undoing of the spirit by the vengeance of the neglected drives of human nature.[72]

For the soul of man to meet the body of man, it should become the helpmate of the body, directing its impulses toward an acknowledged goal that is acceptable to those needs as well; it should work for their dedication in such a way that they may find fulfillment and at the same time perform the bidding of God. When matter becomes vindicated in this way, and the harmonization of human nature is thus accomplished, the soul of man has made its insights available for the guidance of the body, and the body of man has lent its vital effectiveness to the aspirations of the soul. Through their union in the *mitzva*, the great transformation takes place: The spirit becomes "materialized" and, therefore, effective; the body is "spiritualized" and, thus, oriented towards the divine. This is holiness.[73]

The spirit is never holy by itself; there are no holy ideals or holy intentions. Holiness is only possible where the danger of profanity is close at hand. Only in the realm of defilement may the act of sanctification be performed. The encounter between the spirit and the "other" is the origin of holiness. Holiness may evolve only where the spirit is in contact with its opposite. When the "ideal" begins to penetrate the kingdom of the "material," there is the beginning of sanctification. Where natural needs and urges become directed toward goals which may be acknowledged in the presence of God, and where spiritual aspirations become effective through their "communion" with the material sources of vitality, there alone may holiness be found. Only life is capable of holiness. Any ascetic rejection of the world of the senses excludes the possibility of sanctification. It is not the will that is holy, but the deed, because in it the spiritual and the material unite.[74] And it is through the holy deed alone that body as well as soul may be sanctified.

IX

Our discussion of the meaning of the law within Judaism ought to be summed up at this point. We may say now that the division of the laws of Judaism into rational or ethical laws and religious or ritual observances is not quite justified and, taken at face value, may be misleading. We have seen that even the so-called rational laws, concerning human conduct toward one's fellow, cannot derive their obligatory quality from reason. It is always a desire and a will that make a law obligatory; and the meaning of the revealed law in Judaism is that the law's obligatory nature derives from the expressed will of God.[75] This, of course, means that all the "rational" laws are also "religious" at the same time. Their justification may be reasonable; their reasonableness, however, is law for the Jew because of the divine command. Thus all the laws traditionally described as "between man and his fellow" (*bein adam l'havero*) have their place also in the category often referred to as "between man and God" (*bein adam lamakom*). One's conduct toward his neighbor is at the same time conduct toward God, and every hurt caused to another is also a sin against God.[76]

On the other hand, what appears to be purely religious observance has its ethical relevance through its indirect education of the material element in man. Through its creation of a physical awareness of an "other" and its demands, the system of religious observances educates the body for behavior that is not exclusively egocentric. The "purely religious," therefore, always has indirect influence on moral practice. In obeying the "ritual laws," which regulate the relationship between man and God, one indirectly brings greater order into one's relationships with other people. In a sense, by establishing habitual awareness of an "other," the indirect method achieves a measure of man's liberation. The claims on man which attempt to enslave him are innumerable—claims of his own nature, of economic forces, of social convention. But a system of law that teaches man to say a limited "no" to the promptings of his own nature and to the urgings of economic need, as well as to the dictatorship of social custom, and that at the same time develops within him an inclination to say "yes" to the commands of an authority that is not of this world, helps man to establish his independence in facing the world. Man is not required to refuse the claims of the world on him, but he may now withdraw himself from their pressure, and put some distance between himself and their importunings; he may now pause before committing himself. The discipline of living, which is one of the aims of religious observance, makes man free by enabling him to act in the world rather than react to it.[77]

However, the most important function of the "ritual laws" is the orientation to the divine which they achieve for the physical being of man. The commands of action (*mitzvot ma'asiyot*)[78] make it possible for the material element to enter into the relationship. From awareness of an "other," which is ethics, we proceed to the awareness of the "Wholly Other," which is religion.

It is on the level of religion that one may hope to overcome the dualism of human nature. Within ethics, the sensuous, impulsive nature of man has to surrender to the ethical command, which is foreign to it. On the religious level too, at first, the awareness of "the other," who is God, requires submission to the will of God, which is no less foreign to man's material nature than is the ethical command. However, on the religious level, the surrender to the will of God is the first phase of reconciliation and harmonization. As we saw, the religious insistence on relating the physical to God in submission to his command implied the vindication of physicality in its own right. The physical is, thus, accepted as meaningful and capable of guidance: It may seek its own fulfillment and yet serve the purpose that God has given man in the world. Only here, where the spirit need not deny the body and the body need not feel shame in the presence of the spirit, in the deed of unification between the two, may we find the culmination of all religious aspiration—the sanctification of life.

One may also put it this way. In the realm of ethics, the body of man is the servant or tool of the spirit. In the religious sphere, a measure of self-denial and submission is still demanded of the body; however, not as a mere tool of the spirit but for its own sake, so that—together with the spirit—the body too may participate in the religious experience of relatedness to God. This is the opening move in the overcoming of dualism. Both body and soul live in the presence of God. On the level of holiness, however, where the material in an act of self-realization can also do the will of God, one is almost inclined to say that the spirit becomes the servant of the body. Now, the spirit submits its own insights to be made use of in setting the direction for material self-affirmation.

It is important to appreciate that these various realms for which the law is significant do not exist independently of each other, nor can they be traversed by man one after the other. They represent the whole of man's responsibility. Man lives in all of them at the same time. They continually influence and sustain each other. The ethical, finding the source of its obligation in the will of God, depends on the religious. And since the human organism is the instrument of ethical action, its religious conditioning for submission to the will of God is itself important for the effectiveness of ethical conduct. On the other hand, the religious awareness of the "Wholly Other" is reached via the ethical awareness of an "other." Therefore, the more successful the ethical training by way of the "indirect method," the more promising the prospects of a physical awareness of the divine become. Every defeat in one realm is a defeat in all realms, and every achievement in one realm has its effect in all realms.

I do not mean to suggest that these various functions of the law are ever fully realized in the life of man; but they do reflect the direction which the Jewish way of life pursues, the goal at which it aims. According to rabbinical teaching, the Tora has been given in order to purify mankind.[79] When the task of purification is completed, the law will be fulfilled. In that state, to exercise "mercy, justice, and righteousness on earth" will have become the natural desire of the whole man. When, as the result of the sanctifying deed, mankind as a whole will "delight in these things," the law will no longer be needed. But there are no shortcuts in history. Only through the law will the law be overcome. When that phase is reached, mankind will have fulfilled its destiny, and history will be at an end.

2

THE NATURE AND FUNCTION OF JEWISH LAW

(1983)

THE TORA IS ALL-INCLUSIVE. It embraces the entire life of the Jewish people. Halacha, therefore, has to interpret the intention of the Tora for all areas of Jewish existence: The spiritual, the ethical, the economic, the social. It also has to define the functions and powers of the teaching and implementing authority envisaged by the Tora. In what follows, I will examine three important ways in which the halacha translates the intention of the Tora into application in the real-life situation: (i) As guided by common sense, or *sevara*; (ii) as the wisdom of the feasible, according to which the law must maintain its applicability in practice; and (iii) as the priority of the ethical, according to which it is understood as furthering the larger moral principles embodied in the Tora. In the concluding section, I will explore in detail the ways in which these principles are put into practice, as shown in the example of marriage and divorce laws.

I. COMMON SENSE

All interpretation is first of all an activity of the intellect. It is important to note the degree of authority that the Talmud ascribed to logical thinking, to the insights of common sense, which the rabbis refer to as *sevara*. In a number of talmudic passages it is taken for granted that the *sevara* is no less authoritative than the biblical text itself. Often, when one of the rabbis attempts to justify an opinion by basing it on a verse in the Tora, the question follows: "What need is there for a verse? It is a *sevara*"—that is, the opinion may be based on reasoning alone.[1] The meaning of the question is: Since the opinion under discussion may be established by common sense, the text used for its validation seems superfluous. But since there can be nothing superfluous in the Tora, the text quoted must be teaching something else.

The principle of the *sevara* is effective in every area of talmudic law. We shall consider several examples. Two rabbis of the Talmud discuss the legal form of acquiring movable property. According to Resh Lakish, one has actually to take possession of the object by pulling it, lifting it from the ground, or causing it to move. He bases his opinion on a verse in the Bible. R. Yohanan, on the other hand, maintains that possession is taken when the purchase money is handed over to the seller. However, he cites no biblical proof for his view. Writing in the fourteenth century, the commentator R. Yosef bar Habiba explained: "R. Yohanan does not derive his opinion from a biblical text. He bases it on *sevara*. For most property is actually acquired by means of money."[2] It is significant, however, that while R. Yohanan has no biblical proof for his view, he considers it sufficient to state that "it is the word of the Tora"—that is, it is by the authority of the Tora that money is the legal means of acquiring movable property.

In another context we learn that if a woman, of whose marital status nothing is known, appears before a court and asserts that she had been married but is now divorced, she is believed; she may remarry without providing any further proof that she is divorced. The ruling is based on the principle that "the mouth that bound her [as a married woman] is also the mouth that releases her [by also stating that she is now divorced]." One of the rabbis in the Talmud, R. Asi, attempts to justify the principle by pointing to a verse in the Bible that supports it. This justification, however, is rejected, for "what need is there for a biblical proof? It is a *sevara*—the same mouth that bound her also releases her."[3] If you trust her statement that she was married, you also have to trust her statement that she was divorced. The principle is applied in numerous other areas.

The authority of the *sevara* emerges clearly from two other examples. Since the commandments of the Tora were given to us that we may live by them, the rule is that if a Jew is forced to violate any commandment under threat to his life, he should transgress rather than die. However, there are three exceptions to the rule. They are idolatry, sexual prohibitions such as adultery and incest, and murder. One must accept death rather than commit any of these three sins. Whereas the rule in the first two cases is derived from the Tora, in the case of murder one relies on a *sevara*. It is told that once a person came to Rabba and told him that the ruler of the city had ordered him to kill someone; if he disobeyed, he himself would be killed. What was he supposed to do? Rabba answered him succinctly: "What makes you think your blood is redder than that of your fellow man?" Maimonides offers the following interpretation: Reason tells us that one may not destroy a life in order to save another. It is remarkable, therefore, that this rule in the case of sexual prohibitions is derived from the rule concerning murder; according to talmudic understanding, the Bible compares the seriousness of a sexual attack on a married woman to that of an attack upon the life of a person. Just as one should die rather than commit murder, so should one refuse to violate the sexual laws, even under threat to one's life.[4] The Talmud bases the ruling in one case on a comparison to the ruling in another—but to one that is nowhere mentioned in any biblical text and whose authority is assumed to be known on the strength of its reasonableness.

In another case, the power of the *sevara* is affirmed even more boldly. According to the biblical law, if a woman remarries after a divorce, and the second husband then divorces her or dies, she may not return to her first husband. The Talmud discusses the question of whether this law applies only when the marriage to the second husband had been consummated or even when the woman was only formally betrothed to him.[5] The majority view holds that even if only the legal betrothal had taken place, the woman, once divorced from her second husband, may not remarry the first.

This view, however, presents us with a hermeneutical problem. The biblical text tells us the reason for the prohibition of remarriage to her first husband: "Since she had been defiled."[6] How does this apply to a woman who was only engaged to another man but did not live with him? The rabbis explain that this reason applies only to the case of an adulteress, whose husband is barred from remarrying her. This, of course, contradicts the plain meaning of the text. The Bible speaks in general terms that apply to every case in which a divorced woman remarries and after a second marriage wishes to return to her first husband. To limit the ruling to the case of an adulteress renders the text unintelligible. Moreover, we have a rule that in no interpretation may the plain meaning of the text be disregarded. One of the most authoritative commentaries on the Talmud, that of the Tosafot, explains that in this case, the plain meaning of the verse was suppressed because it did not seem to be right to say that a woman who married another man was "defiled" by that marriage. Her second marriage was legal and completely moral.[7] Only an adulteress may be described in such language. In this case, on the strength of a *sevara*, a new meaning was forced upon the biblical text, violating its simple meaning.

Occasionally, even a new law that departs from a prevailing rule may be created by a *sevara*. According to a well-established principle, the Tora frees a person from responsibility for the results of external compulsion, any "act of God," any normally unexpected event or unforeseen circumstance (*ones rahmana patrei*). Nevertheless, Rava, one of the great talmudic authorities, declared that this rule does not apply to cases of divorce: If, for instance, a man hands his wife a writ of divorce on condition that the divorce will take effect only if a certain event takes place, he cannot later deny the divorce by arguing that the event took place unexpectedly, against his will, outside the normal course of possibility. In other words, a woman who would have remained married according to the generally recognized biblical rule, since the conditions of her divorce would have not been considered fulfilled, is judged to be a divorced woman, free to marry again, according to the new ruling of Rava.

How may this exception to the rule be justified? Rava ruled on the basis of his own *sevara*. He was saying: Let us consider the likely consequences of the general rule. Assume that a man gave his wife a writ of divorce with the explicit condition that the divorce would take effect only if he did not return from an upcoming trip to a foreign country within twelve months. If he then does not return, there are two possibilities: Either he does not wish to return, in which case the divorce is effective; or he does wish to return but because of some "act of God" is prevented from returning, in which case, in accordance with the general rule, the writ is not valid and his wife is not divorced. Assuming that there is no possibility of communication between the husband and wife, what might be the consequences in such a situation? The more conscientious woman will in most cases assume that if her husband has not returned at the end of the given period, he is probably unable to return due to circumstances beyond his control. She will consider herself still married and possibly remain an *aguna* for the rest of her life.[8] Another woman, less conscientious in matters of marital fidelity, will readily be inclined to believe that her husband has not returned because he does not wish to; therefore, the condition of the divorce has been met, and she is a divorced woman, free to look for another mate. Both, of course, may be wrong. In actual practice such a situation would be intolerable. Therefore, the general rule governing external compulsion cannot function in the area of divorce. If a divorce is given conditionally, the husband and wife are to be informed that once the condition is fulfilled, no matter for what reason, the divorce becomes valid.[9]

We have seen, then, that:

(i) Principles from a *sevara*, sound common sense or logical reasoning, have the validity of a biblical statement;

(ii) The Tora itself makes reference to a ruling by a *sevara*, assumes it to be known, and by comparison to it establishes its own ruling in a case in which the *sevara* on its own would not have been able to give the biblically required decision;

(iii) A *sevara* may be so convincing that it may compel one's conscience to suppress the plain meaning of a biblical injunction and force upon a verse in the Bible a meaning that it can hardly bear textually;

(iv) A *sevara* may show that in certain areas the consequences of a generally prevailing law would be unacceptable and, therefore, that those cases must be exempted from the authority of that law.

The importance of the *sevara* also throws light on another aspect of halachic legislation. In case of disagreement between rabbinical opinions in the Talmud, the rule is, in accordance with the biblical verse, to follow the majority opinion. Yet on numerous occasions this principle was not followed; the opinion of an individual was accepted against that of the rest of his colleagues.[10] In most of these cases, no reason is given for the deviation from this biblically based rule, but occasionally one may derive from the talmudic discussion what it was that guided the teachers of halacha in this matter. R. Yose maintains that one may not grant power of attorney to another person by sending him word via a messenger. The majority of the rabbis disagreed with him. Yet Shmuel taught that the halacha was according to R. Yose. When the son of R. Yehuda Hanasi remonstrated with him about this, Shmuel answered him: "Be quiet, my son, be quiet. Had you known R. Yose personally, you would realize that he always had his reason for his opinion."[11] In another case, R. Elazar, the son of R. Shimon, disagreed with the view of his colleagues. One of the rabbis ruled that the halacha was not according to R. Elazar. The Talmud asks: "That is obvious! [There is no need for saying so, since the rule is that] when an individual goes against the many, the halacha is according to the majority." The Talmud answers that in this case, it was necessary to state explicitly that the rule was not according to the minority, because otherwise one might determine that the minority opinion was correctly reasoned, and, therefore, one would have to decide against the majority; it was stated in order to prevent that mistake.[12] In the case of R. Yose, we accept the minority opinion because it is more convincing than that of the majority; in that of R. Elazar, one has to warn against the minority opinion because the reasoning behind it might be seen as convincing. Other examples of this nature appear in the Talmud. On one occasion an opinion of Shmuel is contradicted by an authoritative earlier source. The verdict presented on Shmuel's view is *tyuvta*, which normally means defeat in talmudic discussions. But despite this, the halacha follows the teaching of Shmuel, because his reasoning is sound.[13] Sound reasoning overrules an authoritative text.

Thus we have gained an insight into the functioning of the majority rule. That an opinion is held by the majority of scholars is no proof that it is true. A majority may be no less mistaken than a minority. Therefore, follow the opinion that is based on logically valid reasoning. If the *sevara* of the minority, even if it be a minority comprising a single person, is convincing, accept it. When there is no reason to prefer the minority view to that of the majority, when logically the two are equally compelling, only then follow the majority. The majority rule is not a logical principle but a pragmatic one. Thus, the rabbis were able to say that the minority opinions have been preserved in the talmudic sources, and not just those of the majority, so that if a rabbinical court at a later time should for some reason of its own agree with the minority, it would have the right to invalidate a previous ruling according to the majority. And it could do so even if the first ruling was handed down by a rabbinical court greater in learning as well as in number than was the second.[14]

II. THE WISDOM OF THE FEASIBLE

Especially since the time of Immanuel Kant, a distinction has been made between two kinds of reason. One is theoretical, dealing with the categories of logical reasoning; the other is "practical," and its subject matter is the laws of ethical reasoning. Correspondingly, in halacha, theoretical reason found its application in the "Thirteen Rules" in midrashic and talmudic literature that the rabbis used in interpreting the biblical text. A comprehensive study of the Thirteen Rules would give us a treatise on talmudic logic. Our concern, however, is chiefly with the "practical" reason of halacha. We use the term in a twofold sense: Halacha facing the practical needs of human existence, and halacha teaching the application of ethical principles in the midst of the daily life of the Jewish people.

That the Tora was not given to the ministering angels of the Almighty is self-evident. A number of halachic rulings were based on this insight. But if so, the Tora must pay attention to human nature, to the human condition, to human needs. That this is indeed so, the rabbis found confirmed in an important biblical injunction.

In order to humanize the conduct of soldiers engaged in a war, the Jews were commanded:

> When you go forth to battle against your enemies, and the Eternal your God delivers them into your hands, and you carry them away captive, and see among the captives a woman of goodly form, and you have a desire for her, and would take her to you for a wife, then you shall bring her home to your house; and she shall shave her head, and pare her nails, and she shall put the raiment of her captivity from off her, and shall remain in your house, and mourn her father and her mother a full month; and after that you may go unto her, and be her husband, and she shall be your wife.[15]

Considering the barbarous behavior toward women in conquered territories in time of war prevailing even in our own day, this law of the Bible was revolutionary. According to rabbinic interpretation, one could take a captive woman only for a wife, and one had to treat her as a wife.

Notwithstanding its ethically innovative nature, the rabbis of the Talmud thought that the law needed further justification. The Bible obviously condemned the lawlessness and cruelty with which conquered people, and especially women, were treated by victorious armies. Why did it not forbid the taking of captured women against their will altogether? The explanation given is that this law was given with a view to the "evil inclination" (*yetzer hara*), which is part of human nature.[16] In light of the force of the sexual instinct in man, in the prevailing conditions it would have been useless to command its complete suppression. By ordering the soldier who desired her to take her for a wife, the Tora was educating people toward humane behavior, toward an understanding of the injustice done to the captive woman.

This interpretation reflects the talmudic understanding that the Tora does not command anything that man, because of his intrinsic nature or the prevailing conditions, would not be able to do. This realization is the basis of a ramified series of halachot. According to the Tora, one must not marry the divorced wife or the widow of a brother. But if a man dies without leaving any offspring, it is a biblical commandment for his brother to marry the widow, so that through the building of a new family may the name of the deceased brother be preserved. This is known as *yibum*, or levirate marriage. If, however, the brother refuses to marry the widow, the ceremony of *halitza* is necessary, by which the woman is freed to marry whomever she pleases. According to this rule, the levirate marriage takes precedence over the *halitza* separation.

Nevertheless, during the mishnaic period, the rabbis reversed the order, arguing that *halitza* is preferred.[17] What was the reason for this? The explanation given is as follows: As a rule, a man must not marry the former wife of his brother; an exception, however, was made in the case of a brother who died without leaving children. In such a case, one fulfills a divine commandment by marrying the widow, in order to raise a family that will be considered as if it were the family of the deceased brother. However, it was found that most people who would marry the widow would not do so for the sake of the *mitzva*, in order to preserve the name of a brother. People usually marry for personal reasons, because of attraction or other personal interests. Given human nature as the rabbis knew it, the biblical commandment was not realizable. Therefore, according to some commentaries, the levirate marriage was forbidden; according to others, it was only discouraged. According to the one, a biblical law was abolished; according to the other, it was greatly reduced in meaning and importance.

To understand this, it is important to recall a talmudic principle: "Where it is possible, it is possible; where it is not possible, it is not possible."[18] Let us look at some of the examples given. Assume an elderly or sick man lives away from his wife in a "land across the sea," a faraway country without the possibility of communication. He might be a man without children. If he should die, his wife will not be free to remarry whomever she wants, for the man has a brother, who may want to fulfill the commandment of the levirate marriage, or else will have to release her through the *halitza* ceremony. The husband wishes to relieve his wife from such dependence on a brother; therefore he sends her a writ of divorce. It takes some time before the messenger arrives. In the meantime the husband dies because of illness or old age. In such a case, the divorce ought to be invalid, for a divorce cannot take place after the husband's death. Nevertheless, the Mishna states that the messenger should hand the woman the writ under the assumption that the husband is still alive. This accords with the halachic principle of *hazaka*, or presumption, according to which a condition, once established, is legally assumed to continue unchanged until the opposite has become known.

In another authoritative source, however, it is taught that if a *kohen*, a member of the priestly caste, gives a writ of divorce to his wife under the condition that it will take effect just before his death, his wife must immediately refrain from eating food that is *teruma* (the share that was given to a priest from the yield of the land). In this case, the wife is of Israelite parentage; as long as she is married to a priest, she may benefit from *teruma* on account of her husband. But once she is divorced, she returns to her Israelite status; like any other Israelite, she is barred from deriving any benefit from the priests' share. In this case, as soon as she receives the writ of divorce, even though it becomes valid only immediately prior to her husband's death, she is already considered an Israelite woman. This is due to the possibility that her husband may die at any moment, in which case she would already be divorced now.

The two sources seem to contradict one another. In the case of the divorce document sent from a faraway country, the husband is presumed alive as long as we do not receive information to the contrary; in the case of a woman married to a *kohen*, we do not make that assumption, and instead take into consideration the possibility of his death. In attempting to resolve the contradiction, the Talmud offers: "You are comparing *teruma* to divorce? *Teruma* is possible; divorce is impossible."[19] The meaning is: For the woman married to a priest, it is relatively easy to make arrangements to live on food that does not have the sanctity of *teruma*. But the consequences of assuming the death of the husband in the first case would be much more serious. The faraway husband, knowing that a writ of divorce sent by a messenger would have no validity, would refrain from sending one. As a result, his wife would become an *aguna*, neither married in fact nor able to remarry, since her husband might still be alive.

The "principle of the possible" is expressed in another, even more striking case, again concerning the levirate marriage and the *halitza* ceremony. According to biblical law, if the wife had given birth to a child before her husband died, the levirate marriage does not apply. This is true even if the child died immediately after birth. The rabbis, however, held that if the child was born prematurely, the birth is considered sufficient to disqualify the levirate marriage only if the newborn was fit for life. As to the question of what constitutes fitness for life, the Talmud offers two differing opinions. According to R. Shimon ben Gamliel, if the child lived for at least thirty days, we are certain that it was fully developed. But if it died within that period, there is a possibility that it was not quite fully developed. The rest of the rabbis, on the other hand, maintain that there is no need for a thirty-day period.

Assuming now that the widow remarried even though her child did not live thirty days, R. Shimon ben Gamliel would rule that because of the doubt regarding the child, she would still have to go through the *halitza* ceremony in order to be free from the ties to the brother of her former husband. This may lead to unpleasant consequences, for there is a rule that a priest may not marry a woman "rejected" by means of *halitza*. Therefore it was decided that in case of a remarriage to an Israelite, we assume that the child was not viable, and therefore the woman must go through the ceremony. If she married a *kohen*, we assume that the child was completely developed; the mother is free to marry whomever she wants. In one instance we follow the opinion of R. Shimon ben Gamliel, in the other that of the other rabbis. How so? If she is married to an Israelite, the Talmud argues, "it is possible"; if she is married to a *kohen*, "it is not possible." An Israelite may marry a woman who performed *halitza*; therefore, *halitza* is "possible."

A priest is forbidden from marrying such a woman; therefore, to require *halitza* is not "possible." [20]

In these examples the principle of the possible is explicitly used. In other cases it is not mentioned, but it is clearly the guiding consideration. On the Sabbath, for example, one is prohibited from leaving one's city or community and walking in an undeveloped area beyond a distance of two thousand cubits. However, there are a number of exceptions to the rule. For instance, a midwife who is called to a delivery, a person needed to help fight a dangerous fire or to save people in a flood or in an attack by pirates, and so on—such are not only permitted but required to go wherever they are needed. However, a problem arises after they have completed the task to which they were called. According to the law, one who journeyed beyond the two-thousand-cubit limit must remain where he is until the end of the Sabbath. It is true that in our case the person was permitted to go beyond the Sabbath limit, but that was because of the emergency. Now that the emergency is over, is one tied down to the spot where he finds himself after the event? R. Gamliel the Elder, the head of the Sanhedrin, ruled that people who are allowed to travel for the sake of an emergency are to be considered as inhabitants of the city to which they have gone in order to help; like the latter, they too may move a distance of two thousand cubits in all directions. His reason was that if they were to be immobilized until the end of the Sabbath at the spot where they rendered help, they would not leave their homes to help in the first place. Thus, "the end was permitted on account of the beginning" is the talmudic formulation in this case. [21]

Similar considerations of the possible were obviously decisive in the formulation of two other principles. The halachic authorities have the power to issue restrictions on certain practices, out of a concern that they may lead to the violation of biblical commandments. However, it was also determined that no edicts of this kind may be issued if their nature is such that the majority of the people may not be able to obey them. Such edicts, if issued, lose their validity automatically. [22] Similarly, it was taught that if the people engage in certain practices contrary to the obligations between man and God (the "ritual" commandments), and if there is reason to assume that reproving them will influence them to change their ways, one should do so. But if it cannot be assumed that they will change their ways if told that what they are doing is in violation of the law, then, says the Talmud, "Leave Israel alone; it is better that they should transgress out of ignorance than that they should do it intentionally." In one talmudic passage, it is said that this principle applies only to violations of rabbinic interdicts, but not in matters that the Bible itself forbids. A second passage, however, shows that it is valid even for biblical commandments.[23]

A careful examination of the examples discussed will show that in the application of the principle of the possible, the impossible is not the objectively impossible, but that which is not reasonably feasible. The category of the possible (*efshar*) represents that which, in view of human nature and with proper attention to human needs, is practically or morally feasible. Illustrations of pragmatic and moral feasibility are found in certain rules observed in the calculation of the annual calendar. Because of the difference between the solar and lunar years, it is necessary, at certain points within a multi-year cycle, to add an additional month, a second Adar, to the Jewish year. Apart from this, occasionally the second Adar was inserted for purely practical reasons that had nothing to do with the planetary order. And so it was taught:

> One introduces the additional month because of the roads, because of the bridges, because of the ovens for roasting the paschal lamb, and because of Jews who left their homes in exile [with the intention of going to Jerusalem to celebrate Passover there] but have not arrived yet.[24]

Because of the winter rains, the roads to Jerusalem were washed out, bridges were carried away by floods, the ovens were damaged. It was, of course, a practical necessity to postpone the celebration of Passover by one month, so that the necessary repairs might be made. Most significant, however, is that it was even postponed in order not to disappoint travelers from Babylon who were on their way to celebrate the festival in Jerusalem but had been delayed, for whatever reason. The second Adar was added to the annual cycle of that year in order to enable them to arrive in time. The entire sequence of the year's holy days was thus moved by one month out of consideration for their feelings. To do anything else would have been "impossible," because it would not have been morally feasible.

The principle of moral feasibility is recognizable in other halachic decisions as well. Two examples are among the boldest. Guards of gardens and orchards are not obligated to fulfill the commandment of building a succah for the holiday of Succot. The discussion in the Talmud seems at first to assume that the reason for this was that since the orchards are usually outside the built-up areas, there are no festival booths available for the guards. Thus, the objection is raised: "Well, let them build their succah in the place where they keep watch." Upon which the answer is given: "The Bible says, 'you shall dwell in Succot': 'To dwell' means to live in them as one lives in one's home." But what does this mean? Explains Rashi: To dwell as one lives in one's home would require that the guards move into their festival booth in the orchard a great deal of their normal household— including beds, bedding, and other implements. It would put them to too much trouble. For this reason, they are freed from the obligation of dwelling in a succah.[25] The other ruling that attracts our attention deals with a specific aspect of the Yom Kippur observance. One of the five forms of abstinence that a Jew undergoes on the Day of Atonement pertains to washing. Apart from a minimum of cleaning the hands and eyes, among other pleasures one also forgoes on that day that of washing and bathing. According to some of the halachic authorities, this is a biblical command. However, one of the exceptions to the rule is a bride during the thirty days after her marriage. She may wash herself on Yom Kippur so that she should be beloved to her husband.[26] In both these cases, the morally feasible was the deciding factor.

Pragmatic feasibility is clearly the main consideration in talmudic regulations in the economic field. A number of problems arose from the implementation of the biblical commandments regarding the sabbatical year. Every seventh year, no agricultural work was to be done in the fields and the gardens, and all debts were canceled. The cancellation of debts had serious economic consequences. As the seventh year approached, people would refuse to lend money to their fellows. Thus, the situation developed against which the Tora had warned:

> Beware that there be not a base thought in your heart, saying: "The seventh year, the year of release, is at hand"; and your eye be evil against your needy brother, and you give him nothing; and he cry unto the Eternal against you, and it be counted as a sin against you.[27]

Hillel saw that the entire purpose of the biblical injunction regarding the release of all debtors from their debts had been foiled. He therefore introduced the regulation of *prozbul*, according to which, as the seventh year approached, a creditor could hand over the promissory notes in his possession to a rabbinical court, declaring that he himself would not demand payment on them.[28] In this way, private debts in a sense became public ones. Unlike the private creditor, the court did have the right to demand payment, and then could transfer the funds at a later date to the lender. As the Talmud explains, this regulation had a twofold purpose, serving both the rich and the poor: The rich did not lose their money; the poor, in need of a loan, were able to find people who were willing to lend it to them.

The sabbatical year also caused other problems for the poor. In other years, there was usually something for them from the crops. They could go gleaning in the fields; any sheaf forgotten was theirs by law. In addition, every farmer was obliged to leave the corners of his field unharvested as the share of the poor. All this was lost for them every seventh year. More serious was the problem of unemployment. In a normal year they could hire themselves out for work with the farmers. In the sabbatical year, there was no work for them in an agricultural society. This was a serious problem already at the time of the return of the Jews from Babylon. As a solution, the returning community intentionally did not include numerous areas that had previously been Jewish land into the "sanctity" of the land of Israel. Thus, in the sabbatical year, the poor would find work, as well as the other benefits due them from the yield of the fields, in those districts.[29]

The problems caused by the sabbatical year pertained not only to the poor, but to society in general. Thus, the month that occasionally had to be added to the calendar cycle was never introduced in a sabbatical year, but usually in the year immediately preceding it. On these occasions, astronomical calculations were disregarded. The reason was economic: Had the seventh year been thirteen months long, the period during which the land had to lie fallow would have been lengthened. This was to be avoided. But it was useful to lengthen the preceding year by one month, thereby allowing the farmers additional time to complete all their work in the fields.[30]

The Talmud relates that R. Yanai said to the people: "Go and sow in the seventh year because of the *arnona*," that is, the land tax that had to be paid to the non-Jewish authorities.[31] Had they not worked their land, they would not have been able to pay the tax. The commentaries endeavor to explain how R. Yanai could tell the people to violate a biblical commandment. Rashi maintains that R. Yanai must have believed that since the dispersion of the Jewish people, the sabbatical year had lost its status as a biblical commandment and was now only a rabbinical institution—a matter about which there is disagreement among the mishnaic teachers. Because of that, in times of need, it could be disregarded. The Tosafot, on the other hand, maintain that even if one is of the opinion that the sabbatical year still has biblical authority behind it, R. Yanai's message to the people may nevertheless be justified, for if they had not been able to pay the required tax, they would have been imprisoned and might have been killed. It is, however, rather difficult to accept this explanation. The problem was not that of an individual but of an entire community, and it is unlikely that they would all have been thrown into prison. More likely they would have been fined; perhaps part of their land would have been taken from them. All this might have created serious economic problems for the people. There is no proof at all of what R. Yanai's view was regarding the nature of the seventh-year observance. It need not surprise us that because of the serious economic consequences, he allowed the people to work their land in the sabbatical year, even if the commandment had retained its biblical authority over the course of time.

A number of other halachic arrangements were, in fact, corrections upon biblical laws under the pressure of economic needs. According to biblical rule, in all cases of litigation, the imposition of an oath on one of the parties can only free him from payment. On the strength of an oath one can never gain payment for a claim. However, a modification of the rule was introduced in the case of a wage dispute. If a laborer claims that he did not receive his wages, and his claim is denied by the employer, in the absence of proof on either side, the laborer swears and receives his wages. The decision is based on two reasons. First, the wages are essential for the laborer's livelihood. Second, the laborer's claim is less likely to be mistaken than that of his employer. The laborer has only one employer, one wage to look forward to, whereas the employer often has many workers and is more occupied with his affairs than with each of his workers.[32]

Another modification of a rule concerning an oath is the following. If a person against whom a claim is made for payment of a loan admits to a part of the claim, he has to take an oath that he does not owe the part that he denies, even when there is no evidence against him. But once again, an exception was allowed. What if someone finds a lost object and returns it to his owner, and the owner then claims that only a part of it was returned, and demands full return? The finder does not have to take an oath to affirm his statement, even if he does admit to part of the claim against him. The reason is based on the consideration that if an oath were placed on the finder, people would not return lost objects.[33]

Let two more examples show how halachic innovations were introduced because of the concern for the effective functioning of the "market." One example is actually called a "market regulation" (*takanat hashuk*).

> If one recognizes his implements or books in the possession of another, and it is known that they have been stolen from him, the one who bought the objects declares by oath how much he paid for them, and against payment the original owner receives his property back.[34]

It is, of course, assumed that the buyer was unaware that he had bought stolen goods. The goods were always the legal property of their original owner. Nevertheless, he has to buy them back. This was a regulation in order to protect the normal functioning of business transactions. As the commentary of R. Shlomo Yitzhaki (Rashi) put it: "Since the buyer bought in the open market [without knowing that the goods were stolen], if the original owner would not return the price he paid, no one would dare buy anything for fear that it was stolen. Thus, all business would come to a standstill."[35]

A regulation regarding collateral for loans was also formulated with a similar view to safeguarding the normal functioning of credit arrangements. It states that any loan given on the basis of a promissory note automatically becomes a mortgage on the landed property of the borrower. In case of nonpayment, the creditor can collect the debt from the mortgaged property. This is true even if the property was sold to someone else in the interim; the buyer then has a claim against the original owner. However, if the loan was arranged orally, it does not become a mortgage on the borrower's property. In case of nonpayment, the creditor may not collect from any landed property that the borrower might have sold in the meantime.

This, however, is not the biblical law. There are two opinions recorded in the Talmud as to what was the original biblical rule in these matters. Ula is of the opinion that according to the Tora, all loans, whether in writing or by oral agreement, became mortgages on immobilia. Such a regulation, however, was commercially not feasible, for in the circumstances prevailing in talmudic times, only loans against an IOU, signed by two witnesses, would become public knowledge. Therefore, anyone who bought any of the borrower's property would know of the existence of the loan and would be able to protect himself against the risk he was taking. But loans by oral agreement are completely private affairs, publicly unknown. However, since they, too, would mortgage property, a potential buyer would never know what chances he was taking. The result would destroy the realty market. For this reason, the halacha determined that only loans that became public knowledge, in the circumstances of the times, became mortgages, but not the private ones granted by oral agreement only. Rabba, on the other hand, maintains that biblical law does not recognize that any kind of loan becomes a mortgage. But in that case, a creditor would have no security for the money he lent. It would mean that people in need of credit would not be able to get it. This would greatly disorganize the economy. It was, therefore, decided that the creditor could receive a guarantee of repayment by insisting that he be given a duly executed promissory note, by which all landed property of the borrower becomes mortgaged to the creditor up to the amount of the loan.[36]

To these halachic rulings to safeguard the efficient functioning of the economy corresponds a principle, derived from a biblical text, that "the Tora treats protectively the money of Israel." The talmudic rabbi Rava often made use of this principle in order to reach halachic decisions. In at least two cases he applied it as one of the arguments to rule in a question of food forbidden or permitted to be eaten.[37] In a similar discussion, R. Akiva called to his interlocutor: "How long will you waste the money of Israel?"[38] In a number of rulings, the course of leniency was chosen out of consideration of the financial damage that might accrue from an opposing view.[39]

It is important to realize that all these rulings of pragmatic feasibility are not to be separated from moral considerations. The idea found its classical expression in a comment by R. Shimon concerning the festivals. As he explained it, the festivals of Passover and Succot last seven and eight days, respectively, but the festival of Shavuot lasts only one day. Why so? In the spring, when Passover falls, as well as around Succot, after the harvest, there is little work in the fields; therefore, let them celebrate for eight days. But Shavuot falls in the busiest work season of the year. One day of festival will suffice. According to R. Shimon, in a spirit similar to that of the Tora's concern for the property of the people, this too teaches us that the Tora is protective toward Israel.[40] Concern about the material welfare of society is not materialism, but an expression of moral responsibility for the life of the people.

To illustrate the point further, it is worth concluding with an example from the Mishna. According to the Bible, a woman who gave birth brought a sacrifice to the Temple after the period of purification. If she could afford it, the sacrifice was a lamb "as a burnt offering" and a turtle-dove or pigeon "as a sin offering"; if she was poor, she brought another dove or pigeon in place of the lamb.[41] Now, if the woman failed to do this and went through a number of other births, she had to make offerings for each birth. For instance, after five births, she had to bring five such sacrifices. However, she did not have to do it all at once. After the first sacrifice, she would be considered ritually pure again (meaning that she may now partake of the meat of animals offered in the Temple). Now, it apparently happened quite often that women neglected to offer the prescribed sacrifice after every birth, so that the number of sacrificial obligations was accumulating. Women owed three, four, five, or more such sacrifices. In accordance with the law of demand and supply, the price of pigeons usually went up. As the Mishna tells it:

> It happened once that the price for two such pigeons went up to a golden dinar. R. Shimon ben Gamliel, the head of the Sanhedrin, then took an oath and said: "I shall not go to bed tonight until the price goes down to a silver dinar." He went into the study house and taught: "A woman, even if she gives birth five times, brings only one sacrifice; the rest are no obligation upon her." Soon after, the price for the pigeons came down to half a silver dinar.[42]

Some of the commentaries are aghast. How could R. Shimon rule against the law? Rashi explains that even though R. Shimon was treating a biblical commandment lightly, it was an occasion "to act for the sake of God."[43] For if the prices did not go down, women would not bring even one sacrifice but would, nevertheless, eat of sacrificial meals in their ritual impurity. This was, indeed, one of these cases when one rules against the law for the sake of the law. But even Rashi, the great classical commentator on the plain meaning of all biblical and talmudic texts, was hesitant to accept the ruling of R. Shimon, as one may see from the fact that he had to give it a ritual justification—a reason for which there is not the slightest suggestion in the text. We are inclined to follow the view of Maimonides, who cites R. Shimon's declaration without any further comment.[44] In this case, we have before us a perfect combination of economic and moral feasibility. Not to allow the exploitation of the poor was indeed acting for the sake of God.

III. THE PRIORITY OF THE ETHICAL

We have seen how interrelated pragmatic and moral considerations are in the halacha. In this section we will address the power of the ethical in the halacha. In his *Kuzari*, Judah Halevi writes: "God forbid that there should be anything in the Tora that contradicts reason." The rabbis in the Talmud were guided by the insight: God forbid that there should be anything in the application of the Tora to the actual life situation that is contrary to the principles of ethics. What are those principles? They are Tora principles, like: "And you shall do that which is right and good in the sight of the Eternal"[45]; or, "Her ways are ways of pleasantness, and all her paths are peace" (according to talmudic teaching, this refers to the ways and the paths of the Tora)[46]; or, "That you may walk in the way of good people, and keep the paths of the righteous."[47]

In summation of such principles, the Talmud would say: "The Tora in its entirety exists for the sake of the ways of peace."[48] Quite clearly, these principles, and such an understanding of the meaning of the Tora, give priority to the ethical demand. In what follows I hope to show how this influences biblical interpretation, how it reaches out beyond strict legality, and how it even renders explicit biblical commandments inapplicable.

The festival of Succot is celebrated with the combination of the "Four Species." Two among them are the palm branch (*lulav*), and the myrtle boughs (*hadas*). The Talmud, however, wishes to know why only the palm, and why only the myrtle? There are two other plants that would meet the exact meaning of the original Hebrew text of the Bible. In place of the palm, one could use the plant called *kufra*, and in place of the myrtle, another called *hirduf*. Answers Abaye: Neither of these plants could be meant, for it is written: "Her ways are ways of pleasantness." Explains Rashi: "*Kufra* is a thorny plant. With its many thorns it would hurt the hands." The same applies to the *hirduf.* The ends of its leaves are sharp as needles; it would be difficult to handle it without being stuck by them. The Tora could not have meant those two plants, for it would not be in keeping with "ways of pleasantness." For the exclusion of *hirduf,* Rava has another explanation: "The Bible could not have meant that plant, for it is written: 'You shall love truth and peace.'" Explains Rashi: "*Hirduf* is a plant from whose sap a lethal poison is distilled. The use to which this plant is put contradicts the idea of 'truth and peace.'"[49]

On the Sabbath one must not carry any kind of burden in a public domain. Thus the Mishna teaches: "A man should not walk out with a sword, bow and arrow, shield, spear, or lance." R. Eliezer disagreed. He was of the opinion that those weapons were an ornament for a man, and one may carry ornaments attached to the body on the Sabbath. The halacha was decided according to the other rabbis, who retorted to R. Eliezer: "Those weapons are nothing but a shame to man, for did not Isaiah prophesy that a time would come that 'the nations shall beat their swords into plowshares and their spears into pruning hooks; nation shall not lift up sword against nation, neither shall they learn war any more'?"[50] If that is the ultimate ideal of universal history, the rabbis ask, how may weapons have any ornamental significance?

However, much more significant is the dominating influence of these principles in interpersonal relationships. Once again we refer to the laws governing the levirate marriage. It was the rule that a widow who had given birth to a child would marry outside the family of her former husband. If the child should die after her remarriage, even though there are no other offspring of her late husband, she need not go through the *halitza* ceremony in order to be released from her levirate bonds. From the point of view of talmudic reasoning, this was not at all obvious. A rule of talmudic deduction[51] is employed to argue that really the woman ought to perform *halitza*. But all logical reasoning is pushed aside by the statement that such could not be a law of the Tora, for it is said of the Tora: "Her ways are ways of pleasantness." In other words, it is inconceivable that the Tora would in this case require *halitza*. The woman is already married. To subject her to such a ceremony would be humiliating for her vis-a-vis her present husband.[52]

The reference to the overruling ethical principle is not always explicit in halachic decisions. It is, however, obvious that it plays a decisive role in the final conclusion. People ignorant of Judaism quote "an eye for an eye, a tooth for a tooth" as a principle of Judaic justice. Apart from the fact that the translation itself is questionable, the halachic interpretation as early as the mishnaic period (ending around 200 C.E.) concluded that the Bible was referring to monetary compensation. The effort made to justify this interpretation is most impressive. Almost all the arguments are of an ethical nature. For instance: If you take "an eye for an eye" literally, then the law itself becomes inapplicable: Surely, "an eye for an eye," but not an eye for an eye and a life. But occasionally, by taking a man's eye one may be taking much more than that, depending on the success of the operation or on the state of health of the person involved; it may even cost him his life. Therefore, the Bible can only mean monetary compensation for an eye or a tooth. Whatever the logical validity of the arguments, the halachic decision was not literally an eye for an eye, but payment of damages for the eye lost.[53]

A similar reinterpretation of the plain, literal meaning of the biblical text is given in another connection. The Bible says that if an ox was "wont to gore in the past, and warning has been given to its owner, and he has not kept it in, but it has killed a man or a woman; the ox shall be stoned and its owner also shall be put to death."[54] Once again the halachic teachers, with the help of other relevant biblical passages, ruled that monetary damages to be paid to the family were meant, for "one puts a person to death if he himself kills, but not for killing by his ox.[55] It is quite obvious that independently of all adduced "collaborating" biblical material, the halachic conscience could not accept the idea that a man, though not guiltless (he had after all been warned about the wildness of his animal), should be put to death for the goring of his ox.

The halachic humanization of the textual regulations governing the punishment of flogging, prescribed for certain transgressions, is illuminating. First of all, it was decided that flogging was to be carried out with a strap made from the skin of a calf, which is much softer than one made from the skin of a full-grown animal. Secondly, it was shown that the forty stripes that the Bible prescribes were really only thirty-nine. This is important, because it was further shown that the flogging was not to be administered to one part of the body, but had to be divided into three parts, one part to the front of the body, and two parts to be divided between each of the shoulders.

The consequences of this tripartite division could be rather significant. Prior to the punishment the condemned person would be examined in order to decide how many lashes his body could endure without harming his health. If the opinion of the experts was that he could endure not more than twenty, he would be given only eighteen, because twenty is not divisible into three parts, equally to be distributed on three sections of the body. The officers who administered the punishment had to be physically weak but of keen intelligence. They needed the understanding to be able to discern, as they were proceeding, whether the ordered number of lashes was too much for the health of the transgressor.

Finally, there was also a law that if the original judgment was for thirty-nine stripes, but in the course of flogging it was noticed that the person could not tolerate more than twenty, the flogging had to stop. On the other hand, if he was condemned to twenty lashes, and as the punishment was given it became evident that he could very well endure the full measure of thirty-nine, the punishment had to stop nonetheless in accordance with the original estimate. Rashi explains: "Once a person has received a flogging, even though not the prescribed number of lashes, he has been humiliated for his transgression. That is enough." The idea has its basis in a strange biblical formulation that states, at the end of the description of the punishment, "and your brother shall be dishonored before your eyes."[56] The word "dishonored" in Hebrew (*nikleh*) strongly suggests another word that has the same letters and with a slight change in the order of the letters means "be beaten" (*nilkeh*). The rabbis took the hint and interpreted: "Once he has been humiliated [for his transgression], he becomes again your brother."[57]

All the above rulings are somehow based on textual interpretation. But quite clearly, it is the halachic conscience that creates the interpretation.

The halacha was not very comfortable with the idea of corporal punishment. There was an element of insult in it to the dignity of man. And the concern for respect for the individual (*kevod habriot*) is an authentic halachic principle. Its corrective implication in matters of biblical law is derived from the Bible itself. The Tora orders that if an animal, even one belonging to one's enemy, collapses under the weight of its burden, one is obligated to help the owner lift the goods from its back. By the midrashic method of interpretation, it is concluded that an old man or a scholar for whom it is not befitting to engage in such menial efforts is exempted from this obligation. The exemption is then formulated as a halachic principle: "Great is the importance of a person's honor, that it overrides a biblical commandment."[58]

The same principle is applied in an entirely different case. According to biblical law, a member of the priestly caste, for reasons of ritual purity, must not have any contact with a dead body (except that of a close relative). However, when a corpse is found and there is no one to attend to its burial other than a priest, he is obligated to bury the dead. The reason is the same: "For great is the importance of a person's honor, that it overrides a biblical commandment." Only this time, the honor is the respect due to the dead. Nonetheless, the dignity of man is being protected. In the Babylonian Talmud, the general validity of the overriding power of this principle is limited to monetary regulations. (The case of the *met mitzva*, the person who dies and has no one to take care of his burial, is considered an exception.) In all other matters, only rabbinical laws may be superseded by consideration for respect for the individual. The Jerusalem Talmud makes much greater use of this principle. Occasionally, it overrides there even biblical commandments in non-monetary matters.[59]

In cases where there was no question that the written word might impinge on the human dignity of a person, the halacha was mindful not to allow practices that would put to shame the ignorant and, especially, the poor. The Bible prescribes the reading of an appropriate text at the annual offering of the first fruits at the Temple in Jerusalem. Originally, those who could read would read the verses themselves. Someone else would read on behalf of those who could not. However, this practice shamed the illiterate, and they refused to come. Thus, a new regulation was introduced: An official of the Temple had to read the prescribed text on behalf of everyone without distinction.[60]

A more significant example: During the Temple period, a great many laws about ritual purity were in effect. At the same time, it was known that an *am ha'aretz*, the Jew ignorant of the Tora (a rather incomplete description of the type, but sufficient for our purpose), was not too careful in observing the laws of purity. Therefore, a scholarly observant Jew would not eat food or drink wine touched by an *am ha'aretz*. However, an exception was made during the three annual pilgrimage festivals. During the festival period, all Jews were treated as if they were scholars. This meant that the foods and wines in the stores, which were, of course, handled by the many pilgrims, including numerous ignorant ones, were all deemed to be "pure," permissible to be used by a scholar. Were the reasons for the exemption economic? Rashi explains it by saying that discrimination against the ignorant on those occasions would have been a public insult to them—meaning that one would have had to declare publicly to beware of all food touched by an *am ha'aretz*, or, perhaps, special stores for them would have had to be established.[61]

A number of regulations regarding customs of mourning and burial were guided by considerations of respect for the feelings of the poor. The rabbis taught:

> Originally, the food [traditionally brought to the house of the mourner after the funeral] was brought to the rich in silver and gold baskets, and to the poor in baskets made of stripped willow twigs. The poor felt ashamed. Because of the honor of the poor, it was ordered that to all homes one would have to come with twig baskets.
>
> Originally, in the houses of the rich the drinks would be offered to the mourners in costly white glass; for the poor, they would use cheap colored glass. The poor were ashamed. Because of the honor of the poor, it was ordered that in all homes only the colored glass was to be used.
>
> Originally, the faces of the dead of the rich would be uncovered [for the funeral]. The faces of the poor, however, would be covered because often they would show the signs of starvation. The poor were ashamed. Because of the honor of the poor, it was ordered that at all funerals the face of the dead was to be covered.
>
> Originally, the dead of the rich would be carried to their burial on couches; but of the poor in cheap wooden boxes. The poor were ashamed. Because of the honor of the poor, it was ordered that all dead were to be carried in boxes.
>
> Originally, the apparel in which the dead were clothed for the funeral was so expensive that the poor could not afford it, so that [it was said] it was harder for them to raise the money than even to bear their sorrow for the dead. They would leave the body and run away. Until R. Gamliel, the head of the Sanhedrin, ordered "irreverent" treatment of himself, that he be carried out in a cheap cotton shroud. After that, the people followed his example, and they too used cheap shrouds made from cotton.[62]

However, on happy occasions, too, social behavior was guided by sensitivity towards the poor. It is told that there were no holidays in Israel like the fifteenth of Av and Yom Kippur. It seems that on those two days, a popular festival took place that enabled the daughters of Israel to go out and look for suitable husbands in all modesty. The happy mood of the festival was due to the fact that girls did not go out in fashionable clothes according to the financial status of the family. They all had to dress in borrowed, white garments, including the daughters of the king. Everyone had to borrow from someone lower on the social and financial scale than oneself. This was the rule, in order "not to embarrass those who did not have any" nice clothing.[63]

Often, in the area of interpersonal relationships, corrective innovation had to be employed with respect to the law. This was necessary because the law is always general. Its very generality, however, is at times unable to do justice to the particular or specific. There are certain laws that determine the formal requirements for the legal transfer of property. One form of acquisition is by way of a yard that a person owns: Any object placed in a yard with the intention of transferring it into the possession of the yard's owner is legally acquired. This form of acquisition was extended to include the case of any ownerless object or valuable that lies in (certain) areas within a radius of four cubits from where one is standing. The regulation was introduced that whatever is found within that space becomes the property of the person standing there. This was done in order to eliminate quarrels between people; if a more technical form of taking possession were required in such cases, it would very often lead to quarrels; for instance, if one person was in the process of bending down to take hold of an object lying in front of him, and someone else anticipated him by a quick movement. In order to reduce such cases to a minimum, the rabbinical regulation (*takana*) was introduced.[64]

Other innovations were instituted in order to prevent hatred between people. We shall here cite only one example from among many. According to R. Yehuda Hanasi, the editor of the authoritative version of the Mishna, a person could legally betrothe a married woman with the condition that she become his wife after the death of her husband. Similarly, since according to biblical law (even in times of polygamy) one was not permitted to marry a sister of one's wife, one could conclude a marriage contract with a woman with the condition that she become one's wife after the death of her sister, the present wife. In general, agreements of such a nature had, according to R. Yehuda Hanasi, full legal force. According to the law, therefore, in case of the death of the parties concerned, the marriage thus concluded would take effect automatically. Yet the rabbis ruled that in these cases the general law did not apply. Marriage arrangements of this nature would lead to enmity between husband and wife, between sister and sister, between one man and another. This consideration invalidated a marriage contract that was legally binding according to the biblical law.[65]

A great many regulations were introduced because of the "ways of peace." Some of them deal with relationships to non-Jews. "The rabbis taught: Because of the ways of peace, one is obligated to support the poor of the Gentile together with the Jewish poor; to visit their sick as one visits the Jewish sick; to bury the non-Jewish dead as one buries the dead among Jews." In another passage it was added that one should comfort Gentile mourners, as demanded by the "ways of peace."

Another group of regulations instituted because of the "ways of peace" are actual deviations from the generality of the law. Animals, birds, and fish that are caught in traps and nets do not become legally acquired property as long as they remain in the traps or nets. One can acquire property by placing it in any container; but neither a trap nor a net is considered a receptacle that holds objects as a container. Nevertheless, it was ruled that for a stranger to remove the catch from them would be equal to robbery. A similar case: Children and the mentally ill are not considered legal personalities in the sense of being able to acquire property. If they found a lost object, it would not pass into their possession, and anyone could come and take it away from them. However, it was ruled that to do so would be robbery. In these examples, the rabbis went against the law or beyond it because of the importance of the "ways of peace." In fact, it was in the context of all such regulations that the statement was made that the entire Tora is "for the sake of the ways of peace."[66]

In cases that are not directly related to social peace, the halacha urges the Jew to forgo certain advantages that he might gain from a strict adherence to the law. In interpersonal relationships, this is known as "the deed that they should do." Leniency and generosity toward fellow human beings are urged upon the Jew by the rabbinical interpretation of certain passages in the Tora.

Earlier in this essay, we saw that because of respect for their honored status, old men and scholars are not obligated to help raise an animal that has collapsed under the burden on its back. Yet at the same time, these respected people are urged not to make use of the exception and to act in accordance with the law that is generally binding for all; but to remain "within the line of the law" (*lifnim mishurat hadin*), even though legally they could go farther. This is a regulation that applies to all situations in which, because of special circumstances, one is freed from obligations toward another person that normally would be binding. Thus, the same Tora that grants the exemption also urges the Jew not to take advantage of it.[67]

In other cases, the halacha not only urges a person not to insist on rights which are his by law, but obligates him to forgo them. According to the law, a person may sell his property to whomever he wishes; and so anyone has the right to buy any property that is for sale. Yet this right was limited by the "law of bordering property" (*dina debar metzra*). When someone wishes to sell a tract of land, the owner of the property bordering on that land has the prerogative of buying it. If it was not offered to him first but was sold to someone else, the buyer has to return the land to the neighbor, who reimburses the buyer according to the price he had paid for it. The reason given is that the Tora says: "And you shall do that which is right and good in the sight of the Eternal."[68] To appreciate the significance of what we have called creative interpretation, it is worth recalling the context in which these words occur:

> You shall diligently keep the commandments of the Eternal your God, and the testimonies and statutes which he has commanded you. And you shall do that which is right and good in the sight of the Eternal....[69]

The teachers of the halacha did not read these verses as having only one meaning: Do the right and the good by keeping my commandments. The words "you shall do that which is right and good" were understood as an additional commandment. In addition to observing the laws of the Tora, also do that which is right and good. This could mean that it is sometimes necessary to go beyond the law, which in itself is right and good, in order to do what is right and good.

A case that caused some confusion among the talmudic commentators in these matters is the following. Some workers hired by Rabba bar Bar Hana dropped a barrel of wine and caused him considerable damage. According to the laws of damages, the workers were responsible and obligated to pay. Rabba bar Bar Hana took away some of their clothing, either to ensure payment or in lieu of it. They turned to Rav for help. He ordered that their clothes be returned to them. Rabba bar Bar Hana asked: "Is this the law?" Rav answered: "Yes, for it is written: 'That you may walk in the way of good people.'" He returned their clothes but did not pay their wages. Once again they turned to Rav, saying: "We are poor people. We have toiled all day. We are hungry and have nothing"—upon which Rav ordered Rabba bar Bar Hana to pay their wages. Once again he asked: "Is this the law?" and was answered: "Yes, for it is written [in the second part of the same verse]: 'And keep the paths of the righteous.'"[70]

The commentators struggle with the question of whether this was indeed the law or only a form of moral admonishment addressed by Rav to Rabba bar Bar Hana. Rashi and others accept the latter opinion; but there are also halachic authorities who maintain that Rav gave a legally enforceable ruling. A comparison with a similar story in the Jerusalem Talmud may help us to appreciate better the significance of the story as told in the Babylonian one. There we read that R. Nehemia the potter handed some of his pots to a worker, who then broke them; R. Nehemia took the man's clothing as a deposit against payment. The man took the case to R. Yose bar Hanina. He advised him to go back to R. Nehemia and tell him: "That you may walk in the way of good people." When R. Nehemia heard this, he gave back the clothes. But he did not pay the man's wages. So R. Yose told him: "Go back and quote him the second half of the verse: 'And keep the paths of the righteous.'" When R. Nehemia heard this, he paid the man his wages.[71]

This is clearly not the same case history told differently in the Babylonian Talmud. Such occurrences obviously happened quite often. The differences in style between the two narratives are considerable. R. Yose does not give instruction directly to R. Nehemia but advises the laborer how to appeal to him. R. Nehemia could have refused to be moved by the plea. Not so in the story in the Babylonian Talmud: Rav does not give advice; he pronounces law. There is a direct encounter between himself and the employer, upon whose challenge Rav insists: Yes, this is the law. Quite clearly, there is a difference here between the Jerusalem view and the Babylonian view. According to the former, to "walk in the way of good people and keep the paths of the righteous" is a moral injunction that contradicts the law of damages and is not enforceable. The Babylonian view, however, is that with all due respect to the law of damages, there are cases when it is overruled by a superior ethical principle which, in those cases, becomes itself the overriding law.

In the foregoing example, the law in its generality was sustained, and only its application in exceptional cases was limited. Occasionally, however, the ethical conscience of halacha weakened the very purpose of the law and even declared it to be inoperative. One of these laws concerns the status of the "bastard" (*mamzer*). According to the Bible, "a bastard shall not enter into the congregation of the Eternal."[72] This means that a bastard can only marry another bastard. He is not permitted into the family community of the Jewish people. It is important to understand that the bastard referred to in the Bible is not the illegitimate child of Western civilization. A child born to an unmarried woman is, according to the halacha, fully legitimate. Rather, a bastard (*mamzer*) is the offspring of a biblically forbidden union, such as adultery or incest.

The law intended to discourage such unions, to cause the parties to think of the very severe consequences for the child born of them. But those very consequences for the innocent child caused the rabbis a great deal of ethical discomfort. They expressed their moral reservations in the form of a midrashic interpretation of a verse in Ecclesiastes. This is the biblical text:

> So I returned and considered all the oppressions that are done under the sun. And behold the tears of the oppressed, and they had no comforter. And on the side of their oppressors there was power, but they had no comforter.[73]

The midrash asks who is meant by "the oppressed." All kinds of answers are given. In the end we hear the interpretation of Daniel the tailor. He maintains that the author has the bastards in mind.

> "Behold the tears of the oppressed." Their fathers sinned, but what has it to do with these insulted ones? The father of this one went to a woman forbidden to him, but how did the child sin, and how does it concern him? They "had no comforter," but "on the side of their oppressors there was power." Those are the hands of the Great Sanhedrin, which move against them with the authority of the Tora and remove them from the community because it is written: "A bastard shall not enter into the

congregation of the Eternal." "And they had no comforter." Therefore, says the Holy One: "It is upon me to comfort them." In this world there are those among them who are unworthy; but regarding the messianic era, Zechariah prophesied: "Behold I see them all like pure gold"; for this is symbolized by his vision: "I saw, and behold, it was an oil lamp of pure gold."[74]

With greater simplicity, it is said in the Talmud in the name of R. Yose, whose opinion is accepted, that "in the days of the Messiah, bastards... will be pure."[75]

One follows with astonishment the boldness of these rabbis, who certainly believed that the law of the Tora was divine and yet criticized it in the name of God, as it were. In their words, God himself realizes that this law has to be changed. The "bastards" too will be declared pure. God himself will comfort them. We ought to see, however, that the criticism is also based on the Bible, for the Bible deplores the injustice done to the oppressed, whose tears are disregarded, and who are surrendered into the hands of the established authorities. On the other hand, what is the Great Sanhedrin to do? They function by the power entrusted to them by the Tora.

This is one of those situations in which the halacha is called in to function. There is a law whose purpose is a positive one; namely, to protect the moral health of the family. But there is also a biblical view about the seriousness of the injustice done to innocent people in general. And in this specific case innocent people suffer because of the valid concern and care for the ethical foundations of the community. It is as if the happiness of the bastard were sacrificed to a greater good. It was unquestionably an injustice done to an innocent human being.

The halachic way out of the dilemma was a very circumspect application of the law of the illegitimate child. First, there is the ruling of R. Yitzhak that in the case of a family in which a bastard has "submerged" (that is, his status as such is not publicly known), we let him be submerged—one does not make investigations to discover who is a bastard and who is not (as Rashi mentions, in any case in the end all families will be declared pure). On the basis of this ruling, R. Yohanan, one of the leading sages of the Jerusalem Talmud (often quoted also in the Babylonian one), took an oath that he could easily prove the presence of bastards in some families in the land of Israel. "But," said he, "what can I do? Some of the great men of this generation are among them." Again, the same situation emerges: The application of the law concerning bastards could not be the only consideration. The law was not applied because of weightier considerations. Finally, while the law giving expression to an idea that was in itself meaningful was acknowledged, it was also decided that it was forbidden for anyone to reveal that someone is an illegitimate child.[76]

Much more far-reaching were the results of the halachic conscience in some other conflicts with the written law. One example was the case of the "stubborn and rebellious son" who was "a glutton and a drunkard" and did not listen to the voice of his parents. If his father and mother together agreed that there was no other recourse for them but to hand him over to the "elders of the city," then, says the Bible, he should be put to death. "So shall you put away the evil from your midst; and all Israel shall hear, and fear."[77]

One may judge such a law rather cruel. From the beginning it required justification. It was said that the "stubborn and rebellious son" was put to death because of his threatening end. The Tora understood where his ways were leading him. He would consume the property of his father. Finally, not finding the means to satisfy his addictions, he would become a highway robber. Said the Tora: Let him die while he is still innocent, rather than later, when he is guilty.

The regulations attached to the law by the teachers of the halacha were so numerous and so meticulous that even if one had followed the biblical injunction, in practice the law would have been implemented only very seldom. In fact, R. Shimon, one of the halachic authorities of the mishnaic period, declared that a case of the "stubborn and rebellious son" never happened and would never happen. The reason he gave had nothing to do with halacha. For, "because this son ate meat to the value of a *tartemor* [an ancient Greek coin] and drank half a *log* [a large liquid measure] of good Italian wine, his parents would hand him over to be stoned to death?" Such things do not happen. The law may say what it pleases; it has no application in human experience.

Another mishnaic teacher, R. Yehuda, went even further. He "interpreted" the biblical text in such a manner as to show that if you followed its literal meaning, it would hardly be possible to make any use of this law. According to the text, the parents have to appear before the elders and declare: "This our son is stubborn and rebellious; he does not hearken to our voice; he is a glutton and a drunkard." Commented R. Yehuda:

> "Does not hearken to our voice," says the Bible. "Voice" is in the singular. Now, a father and a mother may agree in this matter and speak as if with one voice, but in actual fact they each have a voice of their own. But the Bible says, "our voice"; it can only mean that their voices are alike also in the physical sense. But if their voices must be indistinguishable, then it means that the parents also have to be alike physically in appearance and height. All these conditions, of course, can never be met. Therefore, it never happened, nor will it ever happen.

And now follows the most surprising conclusion of this entire discussion. "If so," R. Yehuda asks, "why was it written?" The answer is: "To interpret it [showing that it was not meant to be implemented] and to receive divine reward for its study."[78] As if it were a test for the intelligence and the conscience of the student and the teacher.

A similar "interpretation" was also placed on another law of the Tora. The Bible decreed that if an entire city is led astray to idol worship by some of its inhabitants, it should be destroyed, including its inhabitants and all their property. The law was an expression of Judaism's desperate struggle against polytheism. Faith in the one God was the *raison d'etre* of Jewish existence. Without monotheism there could be no Jewish people. Yet to destroy an entire city was not an easy matter. Thus we hear that this law was never enacted. "The case of the 'city led astray'—it never was, nor will it ever be." How so? The answer given is that the Bible commands: "And you shall gather all its spoil into its broad place, and shall burn the city with fire...."[79] Now it is impossible that at least one of the doorposts in the condemned city should not have a *mezuza* (a parchment scroll containing verses of the Bible) attached to it. But since it contains the name of God, a *mezuza* must not be burned. The commandment says: "And you shall gather *all* its spoil" and burn it. This law cannot be fulfilled. Part of the "spoil" would be *mezuzot*, and they cannot be burned. Therefore, this commandment was given "in order to be 'interpreted' and to be rewarded" for an interpretation that shows that the law was never meant to be applied.[80]

One might say that all these cases—the law about the "bastard," the one regarding the "stubborn and rebellious son," and the "city led astray"—intend mainly to impress the importance of an idea upon the consciousness of the Jewish people. There are, however, many other examples of rulings that are meant either to limit or even to frustrate completely the implementation of the law in actual life situations.

The halachic authorities were extremely hesitant about imposing the death penalty, even though it is provided for in biblical law. Thus, the Mishna rules: "A Sanhedrin that condemned even only one person to death in seven years was called a killer court." This tradition was corrected by a mishnaic teacher to read "once in seventy years." Finally we hear the words of R. Yishmael and R. Akiva, who said: "Had we been there [i.e., had we been members of the Sanhedrin], no one would ever have been put to death."[81] (They lived after the legislative authority of the Sanhedrin had already lapsed.) The Talmud explains that they would have found reasons to show why the death penalty could not be imposed. Once again we find a tension between the written law and the living conscience. The law is not to be abolished. It is the law of the Tora. And, indeed, there are crimes and sins for which one may well deserve the death penalty. But whether to put a human being to death by human hands is another matter. When R. Yishmael and R. Akiva declared that they would not have done it, their decision was also based on the teachings of the Tora. For halachic reasons, based on the Tora, this biblical law, valid in itself, would not be put into practice.

IV. THE EXAMPLE OF MARRIAGE AND DIVORCE LAW

It is doubtful whether the halachic conscience is anywhere more strongly in evidence than in the area of the marriage and divorce laws. In these matters we find a full understanding of the legal weakness of the status of the woman. As is the way of the halacha, great efforts are made to retain the meaning of the legal principle and yet to find solutions to the daily problems arising from the confrontation between the written word and the moral demands of the concrete situation.

Some of the halachic rulings deal with the laws of marriage (*kidushin*); most of them deal with those of divorce (*gitin*). According to the law, a man may enter into marriage by authorizing another person to betrothe a woman on his behalf, by the prescribed ceremony. But Rav, the most respected halachic authority in Babylon, forbade marrying a woman by proxy. His reason was that when the man meets his wife, he might find her disagreeable. But the Tora commanded: "You shall love your neighbor as yourself."[82] One who marries by proxy exposes himself to a situation in which he will not be able to fulfill the commandment of loving his wife as himself.[83] A similar ruling of Rav (or, according to another opinion, of R. Elazar) concerned the marriage of minors. For social reasons, in conditions that no longer prevail, the Bible authorized a father to marry off a daughter who is a minor to whomever he pleased. According to the later ruling, the practice of this law was forbidden. The halachic authorities ruled that a father may marry off a minor only if she explicitly declares that she is willing to marry the person her father chooses for her.[84]

Neither were the rabbis satisfied with the legal situation of the married woman. Biblical law mentions a threefold obligation of the husband toward his wife. He must provide her with food and clothing and must respect her conjugal rights. In the rabbis' view, this was inadequate. Thus, they introduced the formal marriage contract, or *ketuba*, in which the mutual obligations of the marriage partners are set out, among them a sum of money that the husband has to pay his wife should he divorce her. With the introduction of the marriage contract, all kinds of conditions were, as a norm, included in writing: For instance, the husband's obligation to pay for medical treatment in case of the wife's illness, to pay ransom should she be kidnapped, to pay for all burial expenses, and to arrange for her to be maintained from his estate as long as she remained a widow.[85] All these were revolutionary innovations introduced no later than the mishnaic period.

The most significant aspect of the introduction of the marriage contract was that it established the halachic possibility of including all kinds of other conditions in the marriage agreed upon by the parties. The payment to the wife in case of divorce, provided for in the set formula of the contract, could be increased as a condition of the marriage. In times and places of polygamous practices, the bride could demand that the contract contain the condition that the groom obligate himself not to take another wife. It could also be clearly stated what the consequences would be if the husband broke the agreement. The marriage contract was meant to strengthen the status of the woman and to see to it that it should not be easy for the husband to divorce her. R. Meir declared that it was forbidden to marry without a contract. The conditions introduced by the halachic authorities as the minimal norm for every marriage were assumed to be automatically implied in every marriage contract and were binding upon both partners even if they were not explicitly set out in the *ketuba*.[86]

There is at least one case in which the halacha denies a husband his right to divorce his wife: When the woman is insane. This was a complete departure from biblical law. Legally a husband may divorce his insane wife as long as she understands the meaning of the divorce. This was interpreted to mean that after she is handed the writ of divorce, she does not return to the house of her husband. Now, it may occur that such a woman is capable of understanding what a divorce is, yet is completely incompetent to look after herself. In talmudic language, she can keep her writ but cannot keep herself. The rabbis ruled that such a woman must not be divorced, that she may not become treated as one abandoned. She remains a married woman, and her husband must take care of her.[87]

One area in which the woman was most severely disabled was that of divorce. There she was completely in the power of her husband. Whereas the husband could divorce his wife at any time at will, she could not divorce him. The matter was further complicated by the fact that a writ of divorce, or *get*, given by the husband under duress was invalid. Often this law is morally intolerable. The Mishna suggests a way out: "These are the husbands whom we compel to divorce their wives: A person with severe boils, one suffering from a bad odor from the nose, the worker whose task it is to collect the excrement of dogs, a copper miner, and a tanner."

Apart from the first, in all these cases the reason is that a bad odor is attached to the people who suffer from those illnesses or earn their livelihood in such a manner. It was assumed that one may not compel the wife to stay with her husband in those circumstances. R. Meir is of the opinion that the wife may insist upon a divorce even if she knew prior to the marriage of the condition of her husband or his work and agreed explicitly to enter into the marriage with him in spite of it. She may plead: "I thought I could endure it; now I see that I cannot." While the majority opinion did not take R. Meir's view, there is general agreement among the talmudic teachers that one compels the husband to divorce his wife if the circumstances of his bodily state were not known to her prior to the marriage. The commentators understood that "to compel" here means even by physical punishment.[88] (In our day it would probably mean imprisonment.)

But does not biblical law state that the *get* has to be handed to the wife of the husband's free will? A way out of this dilemma was found by the surprisingly original idea that since it is right and proper that a husband divorce his wife in such a case, if he refuses to do so, "we compel him until he declares: Yes, I do wish to divorce her." This, of course, requires explanation. In his code, Maimonides cites the ruling as follows:

> Whenever the law requires that a husband be ordered to divorce his wife, and he refuses to do so, the Jewish court in any place and at all times imposes corporal punishment on him until he says, "I am willing"; he writes the *get*, and it is valid. Similarly, if he is thus compelled by a non-Jewish court that orders him to act as demanded by the rabbinical court, and the Jews are pressuring him through Gentile hands until he divorces his wife, the divorce is valid. And why does such a divorce not become invalid? After all, he is forced to act against his will, regardless of whether it is by the rabbinical or the non-Jewish court. [The answer is] that we consider compulsion only if one is forced to do something that the Tora does not obligate him to do…. But one who is driven by his evil inclination to nullify a positive commandment or to commit a sin and is then compelled until he agrees to do what he is obligated to do… is not considered to have been forced. It is he who forced himself by his evil intent.[89]

The first impression one may gain from this "explanation" is that Maimonides is of the opinion that the punishment frees the husband from the clutches of his evil inclination, so that he may be free to act as he really wants. The idea becomes somewhat more sympathetic in its concluding elaboration. This is how Maimonides sums it up:

> Therefore this man who does want to divorce his wife, since he does want to be a Jew and does want to fulfill all the commandments and avoid all sins, and since it is his evil urge that overwhelmed him at the moment, if as the result of his punishment his urge has been weakened, and he is therefore able to say, "I am willing," he then divorces his wife out of his own will.[90]

Assuming that we are dealing with a person who lives according to Tora law, and therefore approves in principle of the halacha that orders husbands to divorce their wives in certain situations, it does make sense to say that this husband who refuses to obey the rules of the Tora because it affects him personally is indeed his own prisoner.

In somewhat more general terms, one might say that as long as a person is a member of a society and does not leave it, *eo ipso* he obligates himself to adhere to its laws. He freely surrenders his freedom in all matters in which the law imposes its discipline. Occasionally, coercion is needed to remind him of the terms of his membership. In less legalistic language and closer to contemporary ideas about the truth that "man is to freedom condemned," one might also say that a human being is always confronted with choices. He may rebel against the laws of his society, in which case he chooses to face the consequences of his rebellion. If the society then punishes him as the law provides, that was his choice. If, on the other hand, he decides to give up his rebellion and because of the pressure of the punishment obeys the law provides, that too was his choice. He acts as he does now because he has chosen obedience over rebellion. Be that as it may, the important thing here is that there were situations in which one could not expect a woman to continue in marriage. A way was found to dissolve that marriage, a way not originally provided for in the law.

There are a number of other cases in which the husband is to be urged, or even compelled, to divorce his wife freely. We shall here discuss only two more examples, that of the "rebellious husband" and that of the "rebellious wife." On the basis of the corresponding talmudic sources, the *Shulhan Aruch* rules as follows:

> If a husband rebels against his wife and says, "I will provide for her sustenance, but I refuse conjugal relationship with her because I hate her," then [at first] one adds weekly… to her *ketuba* [i.e., to the sum the husband has to pay her in case of divorce], and she may continue living with him so long as she desires. But although the value of her *ketuba* increases continually, the husband is still violating a biblical commandment [by denying her conjugal rights]…. Thus, if she wishes, one compels him immediately to divorce her and pay her *ketuba*.[91]

Even more significant is the halachic ruling in the case of the "rebellious wife." Here it is the woman who refuses to have conjugal relations with her husband. The talmudic statement on the subject is ambiguous; it allows two interpretations. Among the classical commentators, some are of the opinion that in such a case one compels the husband to grant his wife a divorce. The most sympathetic view in this matter seems to be that of Maimonides. He cites the law as he understands the relevant statement in the Talmud and adds to it his own personal reason for the law, one not mentioned explicitly in the talmudic sources:

> A woman who refuses conjugal contact with her husband is called "rebellious." One has to ask her why she rebels. If she says: "I dislike him and cannot have intercourse with him," one compels her husband to divorce her. She is not like a captive woman [the reference is to the law regarding the enemy woman captured in a war, discussed earlier], that she should submit to one she dislikes.[92]

Some of the leading halachic authorities agree with the decision of Maimonides. Others who interpret the relevant talmudic text differently disagree with him. The discussion shows that the vehement disagreement with Maimonides is based not so much on the talmudic source material as on personal apprehension of the conditions to which the view of Maimonides may lead. If a husband can be coerced to divorce a "rebellious wife," then any woman who "set her eyes on another man" could claim that she could not endure her husband and would thus get a divorce.[93] Obviously this is no solution to the problem. The argument against Maimonides perceives an easy way out for the *prutza*, the dissolute woman, if his opinion were adopted. Of course, the real problem exists not for the *prutza* but, on the contrary, for the honest woman. The more honest she is, the less is she able to continue living with a husband with whom she is incompatible.

Much greater understanding for the plight of the "rebellious wife" is shown by a halachic authority whom one of the medieval commentators calls "the rabbi," without mentioning his name. The rabbi does not fully share the view of Maimonides, but neither does he accept the opinion of his opponents. Whereas it is generally assumed that the rebellious wife, if she is divorced, loses the monetary compensation set out in the marriage contract, the rabbi writes as follows:

> If she says she dislikes him, one does not compel her to stay with him by warning her about the loss of the value of her *ketuba*. One leaves her to her attitude [toward her husband]. Since her husband is displeasing to her, she is like one coerced in the matter. She cannot help herself. Even a good and pious woman cannot submit to a husband whom she rejects… even if no

faults are visible in him. Such things happen quite often. This is not unlike the case of a person who is unable to eat a certain kind of food that is detestable to him. There is no way here to coerce her. One should rather intercede with her, to influence her to accept him. Furthermore, if we were sure that what she says was true, that he is indeed repulsive to her and she did not just "set her eyes on another man," we would compel the husband to divorce her as in the other cases in the Mishna regarding the "husbands whom we compel to divorce their wives," for similar reasons.... In this case, we happen to doubt the honesty of her statement, because we do not find in her husband those faults that she claims.... Therefore, we cannot compel the husband to divorce her; but neither dare we punish her with the loss of the monetary value of her *ketuba*. Maybe she does speak the truth, for [it is written]: "The heart knows its own bitterness."[94]

There seems to be little doubt that in cases where the rabbinical court would find a basis for the pleading of the wife, the anonymous rabbi would agree with the decision of Maimonides, and those others who think as he does, that one compels the husband to divorce his wife, because she is not his captive.

To what extent the opposition of some authorities was due to personal attitudes rather than solid halachic foundations one may judge by the following. Among those whose interpretations of the talmudic source differ from that of Maimonides is R. Isaac Alfasi. After having stated his view that according to the Talmud, in the case of the "rebellious wife" one does not compel the husband to divorce her, he continues: "This is the talmudic law. However, nowadays in the rabbinical courts of the yeshivot, this is how we rule in these cases: When a woman comes and says, 'I do not want this man; I want him to give me a *get*,' she should be given the writ of divorce immediately...." This is also reported by Rabbenu Gershon, one of the great halachic authorities of the medieval period. In the name of R. Hai Gaon, it is cited that such was the practice for over three hundred years in the Babylonian schools of the gaonic period. And yet, the great Spanish medieval commentator R. Solomon Aderet (Rashba), opposes it sharply, dismissing the gaonic practice by saying that "maybe" they meant it only as an emergency measure, a temporary arrangement that no longer has any authority behind it.

Most surprising about the attitude of Aderet is the fact that his suggestion to dismiss the gaonic practice had already been rebutted a generation earlier by Nahmanides, who is considered his teacher. Nahmanides went to the defense of Alfasi against the criticism of R. Zerahiah Halevi (known as Ba'al Hama'or), who long before Aderet also asserted that there was no gaonic practice in the matter, for the deviant ruling from the Talmud was only a temporary measure meant for a specific time and situation. This is how Nahmanides rejected the suggestion:

> He [Alfasi] was more familiar with the rulings of the Geonim than anyone else. Undoubtedly, he means to say that they ruled for the future too. The words of the Ba'al Hama'or are another way of saying that he disagrees with the Geonim and maintains that in this matter we have to follow the talmudic law, but he says it in polite language. The truth, however, is that they introduced their ruling for generations to come. In the days of our master [i.e., Alfasi] this had been the firmly established practice for five hundred years. This is known from their [the Geonim's] responsa.... It is also found in the works of the early as well as the later authorities. And they knew well how it was intended.

This is clear and convincing enough. Yet in conclusion Nahmanides wrote: "However, if someone wishes to be strict and not compel a husband to divorce [a 'rebellious wife'], as is the law in the Talmud, he has lost nothing; and may he be blessed."[95] One remains astounded at such words. To be "strict" in matters of divorce and overlook the happiness of the woman may often be extreme leniency in the implementation of the not insignificant biblical commandment "And you shall love your neighbor as yourself."

In a later period other problems arose. There was the case of the husband who mistreated his wife by quarrels, anger, or beatings. The husband who repeatedly forced his wife out of the house was compelled to give her a divorce. But in the case of wife-beating, one opinion is that it is a sin, and that this fact should be impressed upon the husband. One might be in greater sympathy with the other opinion, also quoted in the *Shulhan Aruch*, that if the man does not listen to "one or two warnings" by the rabbinical court, he should be compelled to divorce.[96]

We shall consider a case that is discussed in the thirteenth-century responsa of R. Samson ben Tzadok. He was asked what the law was to be for a woman whose husband caused her such continuous suffering that she despised him. "It is well known that he is a very hard man. She cannot endure him because of the continual quarrels. He also lets her starve. She has come to hate life itself." In his response, R. Samson discusses the problem from a number of angles, quoting also the talmudic saying that one cannot expect anyone "to live with a snake in the same basket." Finally, he quotes the Mishna which lists the cases in which one compels a husband to divorce his wife, among them that of a man who has chronic bad breath, and concludes: "If one forces him for the odor of the mouth, how much more so for unceasing suffering that is worse than death." Most significant is the concluding comment in his responsum, which employs several talmudic sayings to make his point: "Even though I know that one finds in the works of great latter-day authorities that in such a case one does not compel the husband at all, but neither are we 'mere reed-cutters along a pond,' and in matters that depend on common sense, 'the judge has to rule by what his own eyes see.'"[97]

Problems similar to that of the "rebellious wife" take on a more serious dimension with respect to the biblical laws regarding the levirate marriage, which demanded that if a man died without leaving any children, one of his brothers had to marry his widow. Once again, we shall look at the Mishna that is introduced with the words: "And these are the husbands whom we compel to divorce their wives." We saw above that R. Meir was of the opinion that even if the woman explicitly agreed to marry the man in spite of his physical condition or profession, she might refuse to live with him after the marriage by explaining: "I thought I could endure it; now I see that I cannot." The other sages disagreed with him in this case. At the same time, the Mishna continues: "It happened that one man, a tanner, died leaving no children. He had a brother who was also a tanner. Declared the sages: In this case, the woman has the right to say: 'I was willing to accept your brother; I cannot accept you.'"

In such a case even the rabbis who disagreed with R. Meir accepted his opinion that one compels the brother-in-law to perform the *halitza* ceremony, by which the widow is freed to marry whomever she pleases.[98] But what happens when the refusal of the widow is not connected with the bodily odor of the brother-in-law inseparable from his occupation, but is of a purely personal nature; for instance, when the widow and her brother-in-law are not suited for each other? Such possibilities are discussed in the Talmud. Assuming the age difference is too great to favor a successful marriage: "If he is a mere youth and she is an old woman, or he is an old man and she a child, they say to him: 'Why would you want to marry someone so much younger than you, someone so much older than you? Go, seek someone like yourself and do not bring quarrel into your home.'" This advice that must be given to him is based on the biblical verse: "And the elders of his city should call him and talk to him." In the case of an "unsuitable" brother-in-law, one must urge *halitza* rather than levirate marriage. In the Talmud itself there is no definition of suitability, but the following story is provided to illustrate the point: The brother-in-law wanted to marry his sister-in-law, but it was obvious that his only intention was to acquire her money. The man was tricked into freeing the widow by *halitza*. He was promised a sum of money if he performed the ceremony, and after the ceremony the wife reneged; still, the *halitza* was considered valid. Thus, in order to deal with the problem of the "unfitting" brother-in-law, the principle was laid down that a *halitza* ceremony executed under a false assumption on the part of the brother-in-law is nevertheless valid.[99]

This was, however, only a partial solution of the problem. What was to be done if the unfitting brother-in-law did not allow himself to be misled? The question was attacked more fundamentally with the case of the widow who refused to marry her brother-in-law, not because of any shortcoming of his, but simply because she had no desire to marry him. This is not the place to present the entire halachic discussion of the subject by the halachic authorities. Needless to say, all those authorities who ruled that the woman who refused to continue a marriage must be given the desired divorce would also rule that the brother-in-law must submit to *halitza*. But even the halachic authorities who would not allow an enforced divorce in the case of a marriage are inclined toward leniency in order to free a widow from her levirate bonds.

Among the authorities who disagreed with Maimonides' ruling in the case of the "rebellious wife" was R. Asher ben Yehiel (Rosh), who lived in Germany and Spain in the late thirteenth and early fourteenth centuries. Yet in the case of a brother-in-law whom the widow refused to marry because he was young and ignorant, he ruled that one compels the brother-in-law to agree to *halitza*.[100] Once again it was R. Samson ben Tzadok who asserted that if the widow, for reasons of her own, refuses to marry her brother-in-law, he has to be forced to free her through the *halitza* ceremony. He fortified his decision with the statement that even those who disagree with Maimonides' opinion in the case of the "rebellious wife" respect the plea of the widow to be freed by compelling the brother-in-law in this case. His argument was that "the teachers in the Talmud were stricter in matters of divorce than in those of *halitza*." Actually there is a clear talmudic statement that one "must not suppress the pleas of the widow'" (i.e., who refuses to marry a brother-in-law).[101] While this may be understood in various ways, the interpretation that the widow has the right to refuse to enter into the levirate marriage is accepted by the classical commentator of the Talmud, Rashi, and is expressed in one of the earliest and most authoritative halachic codes, the ninth-century *Halachot Gedolot*.

A number of other innovative regulations were introduced by the talmudic teachers in order to remedy the legally weak status of the married woman. One of their major concerns in this regard was to protect the wife against becoming an *aguna*, a woman whose husband for whatever reason cannot be reached for purposes of a divorce. She is legally married, but she has no husband and yet cannot remarry. (The Hebrew word *ogen* means "anchor"; the woman is "anchored," tied to a situation from which there seems to be no release.)

Various laws that generally apply were declared inoperative in divorce proceedings in order to reduce the likelihood of a woman becoming an *aguna*. For instance, a messenger who brought a writ of divorce, or *get*, sent by a husband to his wife, from Babylon to the land of Israel, had to testify that the divorce document was written as required by the Tora, "in his name and in her name and for the purpose of divorce." (According to the law, if a *get* is written on behalf of one man to divorce his wife, and after its completion it is handed to another man whose name and whose wife's name are identical with those that appear in the document, it is invalid; so is a *get* written for the sake of writing practice.) Normally, two witnesses are required to testify. In this case, however, it was ruled that the testimony of the messenger alone was sufficient. The reason for this had to do with the conditions of the time. There were not many travelers between Babylon and the land of Israel. Had one insisted on two witnesses, considerable delays might have occurred in the sending of a writ of divorce; in numerous cases, the writ would never have been sent, and the woman would have become an *aguna*. In order to prevent this from happening, "the rabbis were lenient."[102]

Another example: A *get* required the signatures of two witnesses. Assuming now that the witnesses who were available could not sign their names, what was to be done? The decision was that the signatures were prefigured in the document in such a manner that the witnesses had only to fill in the ink. This was the only document where such a practice was permissible. Said R. Elazar: "This was done so that the daughters of Israel not become *agunot.*"[103]

In this case the deviation from the norm was not from biblical but only from rabbinical laws: Since the majority of the Babylonian scribes were familiar with the rules of writing *gitin*, the demand for testimony was only a rabbinical requirement. Similarly, the filling in of a prefigured signature by a witness was not against a biblical law. However, we find that even when the problem presented concerned a biblical injunction, the rabbis found a way, outside the generally valid norm, to save a woman from the status of *aguna*. This was the case of the wife whose husband went to "a land beyond the sea," a faraway country with which there was no possibility of normal communication. One witness arrived from that land and testified that the man had died. According to the Bible, facts are to be established in court on the strength of the testimony of two witnesses. Nevertheless, the rabbis of the Talmud allowed the woman to remarry. They went even further. According to the biblical law, one may testify only from direct personal knowledge, but not on the basis of knowledge learned from another person's testimony. Neither is the testimony of a woman or a slave admitted. But in this case, it was ruled not only that the testimony of one witness was sufficient, but that the witness may testify on the basis of hearsay, and that the witness may be a woman or even a slave.

Why was all this permitted? The Talmud explains it as follows: Should the husband still be alive and eventually return after his wife's remarriage, the consequences for her would be extremely serious; for even though she was still married, she had entered into another, illegal marriage. According to the law, she would have to leave her second "husband," but she could not return to her original husband. She would be adjudged an adulteress. Her children by her second, legally invalid marriage would be considered illegitimate. She would also have forfeited any compensation due her from the first marriage contract in case of divorce. Because of the very serious consequences of mistaken testimony, it was assumed that the woman would be most careful. Before entering into another marriage, she would consider the entire situation, investigate herself, and make sure that the testimony was reliable. "Because of the dire consequences [in case of error] at the end, one was lenient at the beginning." The final words in the discussion of the subject are: "Because of the danger of her becoming an *aguna*, one made it easier for her."[104]

One of the boldest halachic innovations was the annulment of marriage in certain situations. Since a divorce could be effected only by the husband handing a *get* to his wife, the husband also had the power to cancel the writ of divorce before it reached her. He could send the document by a messenger, and before the messenger had time to deliver it, the husband could appear before a rabbinical court and declare that he had invalidated the writ, in which case the divorce did not take place. Without a writ there could be no divorce, and this *get*, having been canceled, became a mere piece of paper. Legally, the husband could cancel the validity of the divorce document even without notifying his wife or his messenger. This could lead to the unfortunate situation of a woman receiving such a document and believing that she was now divorced. If she then entered into a new marriage, she had technically committed adultery, with all the disastrous consequences involved. In order to remedy the situation, R. Gamliel the Elder, who lived in the first century C.E. and was one of the most respected heads of the Sanhedrin, instituted an ordinance "that one should not cancel a *get* in the absence of his messenger or his wife," that is, without their knowledge. One should not do it "for the sake of the correction of the world" (*tikun olam*).

But what happened if a person disregarded the edict of R. Gamliel the Elder? A later generation of mishnaic teachers, R. Yehuda Hanasi and his son R. Gamliel, debated the issue. Both were descendants of R. Gamliel the Elder. R. Yehuda Hanasi was of the opinion that if a husband, defying the ordinance of R. Gamliel the Elder, did cancel a writ of divorce, the document became invalid. For indeed, according to biblical law the husband does have that right. His son R. Gamliel, however, ruled that after the edict of R. Gamliel the Elder any cancellation of a *get* without the knowledge of the wife or the messenger is ineffective. The writ remains valid, and the divorce does take place. "Otherwise," he argued, "of what worth is the authority of the court of law?" A powerful attack was mounted in the Talmud against his view: "Is there such a thing as a divorce that is invalid according to biblical law, and merely because 'of what worth is the authority of the court of law?' we free a married woman to marry whomever she pleases?" The Talmud's answer: "Indeed so: He who marries a woman does so with the understanding that the legal basis of the marriage is the law as perceived by the rabbis [Rashi's explanation: In the formula the groom says to the bride, 'You are sanctified to me in accordance with the law of Moses and Israel']. They retroactively annulled this marriage."[105]

The principle of the annulment of marriage is applied in the Talmud in a number of different situations. Earlier we discussed the ruling of Rava that in matters of divorce, the generally valid principle of *ones rahmana patrei*—that a person is not responsible for an action that takes place due to unexpected circumstances beyond his control—was inoperative. Accordingly he ruled that a divorce given with the condition that it should take effect only if the husband did not return after a specified absence is valid, and the woman is considered duly divorced, even if the husband desired to return but was prevented from doing so by the unforeseen intervention of some superior force or circumstance. His reasons were twofold. First, the loyal wives would become *agunot*, for even when a husband refused to return, they would assume that he was prevented from doing so against his will and would thus consider themselves still married. Second, the less loyal wives, on the contrary, would only too easily conclude that the husband intentionally did not return and would consider themselves divorced, even though the husband was prevented from returning because of unexpected circumstances and, therefore, they were really not divorced. Here, too, the question was raised: According to the biblically valid principle of *ones*, that writ was not valid and, therefore, there was no divorce. Rava, because of his personal consideration of the possible consequences of a biblical law, nonetheless declared women who are married according to biblical law to be divorced. Again, the act was justified by reasoning that since all marriages are concluded on the basis of the halacha as understood by the rabbis, they also have the authority to annul them retroactively.[106]

An even more striking example of the function of this principle may be understood from the following example: According to biblical law, a father can arrange a marriage for a daughter who is a minor. (We saw earlier that already in the second century the rabbis in the Talmud attempted to curb this in practice.) The death of the father could cause serious social problems. In such a case, often there was no one to look after the minor. The rabbis of the Talmud decreed that the mother or the brothers of the minor could also conclude a marriage on her behalf. However, such a marriage was a rabbinical one; it had no biblical basis. According to biblical law, the young girl was not married to the husband to whom she had been given in marriage by her family. According to one opinion, when such a child-wife came of age, another marriage ceremony had to be performed. In the discussion of this theme the story is told: Once, when such a child came of age, the "husband" led her to the marriage canopy in order to marry her again in accordance with biblical law. As they were preparing for the ceremony, another man came, grabbed the bride, escaped with her, and formally married her. In this case, according to biblical law she was married to the second man. Yet the talmudic teachers invalidated this marriage. To the question of how they could annul a marriage concluded in accordance with biblical law, the answer is given: "He acted improperly, so they dealt with him 'improperly' and annulled his marriage." Once again explains Rashi: Since marriages are concluded in accordance with the rules of the rabbis, they have the authority to invalidate a marriage concluded by improper means.[107]

It is quite obvious that the rabbis were fully aware of the legally disadvantaged status of the woman. They were disturbed by it and endeavored to correct the situation through innovative rulings and rabbinical regulations. The process continued for centuries after the conclusion of the Talmud in the fifth century. Among the best-known post-talmudic regulations are the tenth-century bans of Rabbenu Gershon against polygamy (a ruling foreshadowed already in the Talmud) and against the husband who divorces his wife against her will. The ban of Rabbenu Gershon implied the exclusion of the violator from the community. R. Asher ben Yehiel, father of the author of the *Arba'a Turim*, the code upon which the structure of R. Joseph Karo's *Shulhan Aruch* was based, in one of his responsa remarked that the purpose of Rabbenu Gershon in requiring the wife's consent to a divorce was "to equalize the power of the woman to that of the man: As he divorces only by his free will, so can she not be divorced either except if she freely agrees to a divorce."[108]

3

CONVERSION AND THE DECLINE OF THE ORAL LAW

(1974)

OUR CONCERN HERE is not with the political struggles usually associated with the subject of conversion. Strictly speaking, our chief interest is not with the question of conversion at all. What I would like to discuss is the meaning of the common phrase *al pi halacha* ("according to halacha"); I shall use the problem of conversion in the State of Israel, which has embroiled us so long and generated so much bitterness among Jews, as an example to illustrate the fundamental problem of halacha in our days.

The laws regarding conversion are really very simple. For a conversion in accordance with the rules of halacha, there has to be the acceptance of the commandments of the Tora; in the case of a male convert there has to be circumcision; and finally there has to be immersion in the ritual bath. The requirements of the law in this matter are clear. There is no problem there. The problem, of course, is that while there is the law as stated in the Talmud and crystallized in the codes, there are also a great many Jews who either do not accept the Talmud as the ultimate authority for their own religious conscience, or give to the law regarding conversion an interpretation which differs widely from the one given to it by Orthodox Judaism. The real question, therefore, is not what the *Shulhan Aruch* says about conversion. That is well known. The question is what to do about all the Jews who do not accept the Orthodox view in this matter. It makes little sense to argue that since the unity of the Jewish people is at stake, all Jews must accept the Orthodox viewpoint. It makes no sense at all; not because the question of conversion is not important. It is of vital importance: We are dealing with the very essence of the nature and meaning of Jewishness. Rather, it makes no sense because in this way we shall not safeguard the unity of the Jewish people. On the contrary, in this way the gap widens, and the essential nature of being a Jew becomes more and more diluted for more and more Jews. One might, perhaps, retort: We are not concerned with the practical consequences. Here is the law; we insist that it be adhered to. But would this still be a halachic position? Is it indeed so that authentic halacha is free of meaningful practical considerations? We shall come back to this question later in our discussion.

Apart from the practical considerations, there is also a moral question to be raised. By insisting that in matters of conversion the Orthodox view must prevail exclusively, we have, of course, stated that our numerous non-Orthodox brothers and sisters have to be excluded from having any say in such a vital issue as what it means to be a Jew. Do we have the moral right to make such demands? It is true that we maintain that Tora is revealed to the Jewish people by God and, therefore, the law regarding conversion has divine authority. I, too, believe that, together with all Orthodox Jews. Nevertheless, I cannot overlook the fact that, no matter how strongly I believe it, it is still only my personal belief. And if there are tens of thousands of us who so believe, the faith in Tora "from heaven" will still remain *our* belief. No matter how convincing our reasons and our proofs for the faith may be for us, they will still be no more than reasons and proofs *for us*; enough for me, clear and convincing, like the brilliance of a clear and cool morning, yet inseparable from my subjectivity. It is true that our opinion in this matter of conversion is identical with that of the great Tora scholars of our generation. But again, this too is our recognition of their greatness. If we should be mistaken, if the great Tora scholars themselves should be mistaken, then their own greatness would be of little consequence. But, of course, we are right, our faith is true, and the greatness of the "great ones" is unquestionable. Indeed—so we believe. That Tora is "from heaven," *min hashamayim*, so I believe; but I cannot help recognizing that the fact that I so believe does not make my belief a faith that is itself from heaven. The Tora is from heaven, but my faith that it is so is not; neither is my interpretation of the meaning and consequences of that faith from heaven. If so, how can we deny Conservative and Reform rabbis and scholars the right to their interpretation? Of course, we Orthodox are the only Jews faithful to the demands of Tora. But no matter how much we insist on this, it will, nevertheless, remain our own subjective insistence. Could not, then, our non-Orthodox brothers and sisters turn to us and say with equal right, since our interpretation of Tora and Judaism is mistaken, that we do not represent "Tora-true" Judaism and that only theirs is the true way?

Of course, an Orthodox Jew might say: I don't care what they maintain. I have my own convictions, and I shall not depart from the letter in the *Shulhan Aruch* regarding conversion, even by a hair's-breadth. Indeed, one does have the right to such a decision. But, for the sake of intellectual honesty, one should have a proper understanding of the meaning of such a decision. In a sense, in its consequences, this would be a decision of seceding from community with non-Orthodox Jews or excluding them from community with us. Or, to say the least, it would be a decision regarding the rights and status of our non-Orthodox brothers and sisters within the community of Israel. However, if this is fully understood, we will have to concede that this is no longer a question purely of conversion, but of the importance of the unity of the Jewish people, the idea of the community of Israel, *klal yisrael*, in relationship to the laws of conversion.

How to convert to Judaism is not a halachic problem. It is all stated clearly in the *Shulhan Aruch*. The problem is that in this case the prescribed laws on conversion are in conflict with another important principle of Judaism, that of preserving the unity of Israel, the idea of *kneset yisrael*, through the obligation of *ahavat yisrael*, the love for the people of Israel. Only when we understand this have we raised the halachic question. For, indeed, such is the classical halachic "problem": That the strict adherence to one law is in conflict with the strict adherence to another obligatory principle of Judaism. In the case at hand, any Orthodox Jew has the right to say that for him, the importance of the laws of conversion are so vital that for their sake he will push aside all the important obligations regarding the ideal of unity of Israel and love of Israel. But where does he find the authoritative basis for his decision? In the *Shulhan Aruch* in the section on conversion? Certainly not. There he will find all the rules on how to convert a non-Jew. What he will not find there is the answer to our problem of halacha, i.e., in view of the importance of the idea of the unity of Israel and all that it involves. For Judaism according to the Tora, what should be our attitude to a vast number of fellow Jews who do not observe the laws of conversion as we do? Where, then, will he find the answer to his question— in which book, in which code? In no book, in no code. He must make this decision by himself, in his own Jewish conscience. But how so? He will accept the authoritative validity of the law on conversion, and at the same time he will acknowledge the importance of the unity and love of Israel; he will then seek resolution of the conflict from within the comprehensive ethos of Judaism, from what Judaism is about in its totality, according to his understanding and commitment. Moreover, this is an understanding and commitment which has grown into a measure of maturity as the result of the dedicated study of the classical sources of Judaism and of adherence to a way of life inseparable from it. This is not a purely subjective decision; but just because of the subjective element involved in it, it will be a truly halachic solution to a genuinely halachic problem.

It has now become necessary to give thought to the essence of halacha, the nature of the halachic problem and the characteristic quality of the halachic solution. Only by dealing with this aspect of our theme do we approach the core of our problem; indeed, not only the specific problem of conversion but the problem of halacha in the widest sense in the contemporary situation of the Jewish people. What is halacha? Halacha is the "Oral Tora," as distinct from the Bible itself, which is the "Written Tora." In other words, the Bible alone is not enough; the written law cannot fulfill the function or the purpose intended by the Tora. Why not? Let us see how halacha functions, what is the work that halacha does. Let us look at some well-known examples, as well as others less well-known.

A famous case of a halachic problem and its solution is the case of Hillel's *prozbul*. To put it concisely and perhaps not quite accurately, it was the transformation of private debts, which otherwise would be forfeited in the sabbatical year in accordance with the written law of the Bible, into public debts. This was a bold innovation, which Shmuel, of a later generation, would have liked to abolish. How and why was it instituted by the great Hillel? He was committed to the law of the sabbatical year. But, in his time, this law came into conflict with other valid concerns of Judaism. On the one hand, there was an obligation dictated by the Tora to protect the interest of the poor who, as the seventh year was approaching, could not receive any loans for fear that in the sabbatical year the money would be lost. On the other hand, there was also the important practical consideration for the effective functioning of the economy—also a valid concern of Judaism. R. Hisda expressed the meaning of the term *prozbul* in the etymologically monstrous yet essentially correct interpretation: *Pros buli ubuti*, an ordinance in the interest of the poor and the rich.[1]

Where did Hillel find the authority for his innovation? Where was it written in the Tora? It was, of course, not found in any text or code. He found it within himself. There was a clash between equally valid laws, principles, and concerns of the Tora. He had to find a resolution to the conflict. There was no text, no Written Tora to tell him which course to follow. He could find the solution to the problem within his own understanding of the comprehensive ethos of Judaism, as he was able to gather it in his own heart and in his own conscience from the totality of the teaching and way of life of Tora.

Let us consider another example. According to the written law of the Bible, two witnesses are required in order to establish a fact in court. Yet in the case of a husband who has disappeared, the rabbis of the Talmud accepted the testimony of one witness alone in order to prove the death of the husband, so that the wife may remarry. How could they rule in this manner against an explicit law of the Tora? Many interpretations were offered to explain this bold innovation.[2] However the technicality of the ruling may be explained, the decisive motivation behind it was clearly stated in the Talmud: "The rabbis were lenient because of the *aguna*," meaning that in order to save the wife from the status of an *aguna*, a woman bound to the end of her days to a man who has disappeared, they applied the law leniently to her case.[3] Once again, it is the authentic halachic problem. There is the written law of the Bible, but it has come into conflict with another obligation of the Tora-committed Jew, the care and concern for a woman whose husband has disappeared. Once again, there was no written code to consult. On the basis of the rabbis' understanding of the overriding intentions of the Tora, formulated nowhere explicitly but absorbed into their own consciousness as the result of a life of dedication to Tora and its living realization, they gave the answer, a halachic solution to a halachic problem.

The examples are innumerable. For instance, the case of Rabba bar Bar Hana, who had hired workers to carry barrels of wine. Somehow, the workers broke one of the barrels, and the wine was lost; whereupon Rabba bar Bar Hana confiscated their cloaks, as a guarantee for, or in lieu of, damages to which he thought he was entitled. They brought the case for adjudication before Rav, who ruled that the clothes were to be returned to the workers. Asked Rabba: "Is this the law?" And the answer was: "Yes, for it is written: 'That you may walk in the way of good people.'" The clothes were returned. The workers, however, were not satisfied. "We have worked all day, and we are hungry," they said, claiming their wages. Ruled Rav: "Go and pay them their wages." Once again Rabba asked: "Is this the law?" and the answer was given: "Yes, for it is written: 'And keep the paths of the righteous.'"[4] Legalistically speaking, Rabba was, of course, right. Such was not the law. But the case before Rav presented one of those characteristically halachic problems. There was the law of damages. But there was also the obligation to care for the disadvantaged. Once again, the decision was made on the basis of a rabbi's appreciation of the more comprehensive concern of the Tora. Rav's decision was in accordance not with the specific law of damages, but with the overall purpose of the law of the Tora. It was halacha.

The cases which illustrate the point are numerous in talmudic literature. Two more are worth consideration. In recent times, due to a *cause celebre* in Israel, the problem of the *mamzer*, of the bastard according to biblical law, became, for a while, the preoccupation of many of us. Without commenting on the case itself, it is worth noting how certain aspects of the problem were dealt with in the Talmud. There is, for instance, a statement by R. Yohanan, the leading teacher of his time in the land of Israel, who swore that he could prove that *mamzerim* were present in a family. According to the law, that would disqualify the family from intermarriage with the "pure" families. Yet he refrained from revealing the facts. As he said: "What can I do? Some of the great men of this generation are among them."[5] The question might well be asked: Who gave R. Yohanan the authority to disregard a biblical commandment and allow marriage with members of a family who were, by the law of the Tora, to be excluded from the community? But once again, we have before us the typical halachic problem. There is the law on illegitimacy in conflict with another law and concern of Judaism, the respect due to great rabbis in Israel, who are bearers and teachers of the Tora, whose function is vital for the preservation of Judaism and the Jewish people. There was no code to tell R. Yohanan how to act. On the basis of his understanding of what Judaism demands of the Jew, he decided not to reveal the facts. In the Talmud, his decision is related to a principle formulated by R. Yitzhak: "Once a *mamzer* has 'sunk' into a family, leave him there," meaning that even if one could determine which part of the family is "pure" and which is not, do not investigate, do not ferret out the *mamzer*. The principle is further broadened into the rule that if one knows with certainty of a bastard in a family who could be simply singled out, but the case is not generally known, one is not permitted to reveal the truth. One might wonder how such leniency could be justified in the face of a clear biblical ruling on the exclusion of the bastard and his descendants in all generations from intermingling with the community. Undoubtedly, here, too, biblical teachings in conflict with each other in a given situation had to be considered: On the one hand, the law of the *mamzer*; on the other, considerations of justice and pity for the innocent bastard and his offspring. (The rabbis in various places had the courage to question the justness of the law regarding the *mamzer*.) Thus, with true halachic boldness, out of their comprehensive interpretation of Judaism's meaning, they limited the application of the law.

We conclude with one of the most striking examples of halachic boldness and independence found in the Talmud: The great debate about the oven of Achnai. The subject matter of the debate itself is irrelevant to our discussion. The dispute over the law in this case raged between R. Eliezer ben Horkenos and the other masters. Since his colleagues did not accept his arguments, the great R. Eliezer wrought a number of miracles to prove he was right. The miracles were disregarded. Finally, a voice from heaven came to the support of R. Eliezer, declaring: "What do you want from R. Eliezer? The halacha is always as he teaches it." What was there for the rabbis to do? The Talmud continues the story: R. Yehoshua then stood up and said (quoting from the Bible somewhat out of context): "It is not in heaven!"[6] And this explanation is given: Said R. Yermia: "What does it mean, 'It is not in heaven'? The Tora has already been given to us on the mountain. The answer is that we pay no attention, not even to a heavenly voice, because God has already written in the Tora at the mountain: 'Decide according to the majority.'"[7] (This, of course, is itself a "halachic" reinterpretation of the literary meaning of the verse.)

Needless to say, the second part of the story is no longer about the oven of Achnai. It is about the confrontation between the divine voice, which the rabbis clearly received, and their own conscience as to what was the right decision in the case of the oven. How did they resolve the confrontation? They beat the divine voice with God's own words, as they understood those words. However, their own personal share in the decision is obvious. For one could have easily argued with R. Yehoshua: It is true that one should rule in accordance with the majority opinion, but only when the discussion is among men. However, in a debate with God himself, how dare you rule against God? How, indeed, dare you enter into a debate with him? Yet the rabbis did rule against a voice from heaven. Once again, there was a conflict between two demands of the Tora: To obey the heavenly voice, or to administer the law in a given case as they were able to understand it. Once again, the conflict was resolved on the basis of a more comprehensive principle which, in the rabbis' own estimation, deserved priority. The story itself finds its charming conclusion as follows: R. Natan met the prophet Elijah (who, in Jewish lore, occasionally walks among the people and reveals himself to them) and asked him, "What did the Holy One do in that hour [of the great debate]?" Said Elijah: "He laughed and exclaimed, 'My children have defeated me! My children have defeated me!'"[8] The postscript to the story is decisive. To his own joy, God is overruled. A specific word of God is controlled by a more comprehensive divine command. Therein lies the secret of the creative vitality of the halacha. We might now formulate it more generally. When, in a given situation, a specific law is in conflict with another law, principle or concern of the Tora, the specific law may be limited in its application, reinterpreted, adapted, suspended, or changed in this one situation but not abolished, by the overruling concern of the comprehensive Tora.

We may now be in a better position to understand why the Written Tora is not enough, why it needed to be completed by an Oral Tora, and why the halacha could not be anything else but oral teaching. Every written law is somewhat "inhuman." As a code laid down for generations, it must express a general idea and an abstract principle of what is right, of what is desired by the lawgiver. But every human situation is specific and not general or abstract; in a sense, every human situation is unique. No general law speaks to the specific situation. The uniqueness of the situation will often call for additional attention by some other principle, which has its validity within the system. Two witnesses are necessary to establish a fact. That rule has general validity. But the woman whose husband has disappeared is in a specific situation. The law of the Tora itself calls for responsible care for her specific plight. Resolution can be found only in the totality of the ethos of the law. But no written code can provide the resolution. The code can deal only with the general, not with the specific. Once you write it down as a code, you have generalized it. Only the Oral Tora, alive in the conscience of the contemporary teachers and masters, who can fully evaluate the significance of the confrontation between one word of God and another in a given situation, can resolve the conflict with the creative boldness of application of the comprehensive ethos of the Tora to the case. Thus, the Oral Tora as halacha redeems the Written Tora from the prison of its generality and "humanizes" it. The written law longs for this, its redemption, by the Oral Tora. That is why God rejoices when he is defeated by his children. Such defeat is his victory.

According to an opinion in the Talmud, God concluded his covenant with Israel only on account of the oral tradition.[9] A covenant is a relationship of mutuality. The covenantal relationship could find no expression in the revelation and acceptance of the Tora at Sinai. It was a case, as the Talmud puts it, in which "he hung a mountain over them like a barrel"—a law given, imposed. Only in halacha is the covenant, as mutuality of relationship, fully present. Halacha is not subjective adjustment at all (though a specific law may be adjusted, but not for the sake of adjusting to the situation). The essence of covenantal mutuality cannot be subjectivity; but neither can it be without subjective involvement on both sides. Halacha is not subjective, but it has a subjectively creative element to it. The halachist recognizes the will of God as expressed in the Tora; he is wholly committed to the law and the teaching of the Tora. But in the mutuality of the covenant, the responsibility has fallen to him to take upon himself the risk of determining, in the light of the totality of the Tora as teaching and living, the manner in which the will of the other party to the covenant is to be realized in a specific situation. Ultimately, he has to do that in the independence of his own conscience, which is imbued with Tora.

This is our share in the covenant, the existential component of our participation in it. Loyalty to the Tora, to the divine partner to the covenant, demands that we accept the responsibility, notwithstanding the risk involved in the subjective aspect of our participation. Only in this way may the generality and abstractness of the Written Tora be transformed into *torat hayim,* a Tora of life, its realization in whatever situations Jews find themselves in the course of history.

We may now return to the question of conversion "according to halacha." As pointed out earlier, this is not just a matter of conversion but, rather, the problem of how to decide in the case of a conflict between the laws of conversion and one's obligation according to the Tora of preserving the unity of Israel, and of having love for all of Israel. Only because of the confrontation between two equally binding principles of the Tora do we have an authentic halachic problem on hand. Is there now any further principle in the totality of the system of Judaism that might be used as the basis for a halachic solution?

One could perhaps make the following suggestion. It is true that the laws of conversion do prescribe that a non-Jew be accepted into Judaism only if he is willing to accept all the commandments of the Tora in all sincerity, and if he is circumcised and immersed in a properly prepared ritual bath. However, it is also established that if this were not the case, but a person converted without the religious responsibilities having been explained to him, even if he or she undertook this step for the sake of marrying a Jew or for any other ulterior reason, even if the conversion had taken place in the presence of three laymen, ignorant of the laws and teachings of Judaism, the conversion is still valid. Of course, this is allowed only *bedi'avad,* after the event of conversion has taken place. But as a rule, from the start of the conversion process, it is not permissible. On the other hand, there exists a general principle of halacha that all cases of severe need or urgency are to be treated as if they were *bedi'avad,* after the fact. In other words, what normally would be admissible only post factum, under the pressure of circumstances, is allowed from the start. Now, I do not hesitate to say that the preservation of the unity of Israel and the practice of love of Israel are matters of utmost urgency. With this understanding of the problem, I might well think that a compromise with our non-Orthodox brethren was possible. I imagine that I would have every right to approach them somewhat as follows:

We have our own views on what constitutes genuine conversion, and you have yours. We disagree on this point. We shall not force our view on you, as you will not force yours on us. But insofar as we are both part of the people of Israel and desire to have our place of responsibility in it, we do have in common our concern for the preservation of the unity of Israel, and are equally motivated by the love of Israel. Therefore, in this matter of conversion, your problem is very similar to ours. It is not really a question of how to admit a non-Jew into Judaism. It is a "halachic" problem for you no less than for us, namely, how to resolve the conflict between your requirements for conversions and your commitment to the unity of Israel. We know well what your *a priori* position on conversion is. But since this is a case of severe need, what would be your post factum position in view of the need for Jewish unity and for the sake of your love for your fellow Jews? In view of the urgency dictated by our understanding of Judaism's call for love of Israel and for the safeguarding of unity of Israel in our relationship to you, we are, *bedi'avad*, willing to forgo the demand for full adherence to the requirements for conversion as we accept it for our own conduct. How far can you go in allowing your obligation to unity and commitment to a common destiny to control and modify your requirements for conversion?

I disagree with Reform Jews as to what these requirements ought to be. As to Conservative Judaism, I understand from some of its leading spokesmen that the majority of the Conservative rabbis do adhere to the laws of conversion as stated in the *Shulhan Aruch*, though I assume that the Orthodox interpretation as to what constitutes "acceptance of the yoke of the commandments" may differ from theirs. But notwithstanding the disagreements, I do have sufficient respect for the leading rabbinical and scholarly personalities in both the Conservative and Reform groups to know that, in moral responsibility, they could not, and would not, refuse to respond positively to such an approach on the part of those who came to them in the name of halacha. At least, instead of shouting at each other, we might start talking to each other.

Is this the solution? Perhaps. Is there no other way? Perhaps there is. What concerns us here, however, more than the actual solution to this specific problem, is the fact that in all this controversy it has occurred to no one to define the problem "halachically" in the manner suggested above. Instead, what should have been resolved in the spiritual dimension has been degraded to a political struggle, one which, to our humiliation, has been silenced for the time being only by the booming of Syrian guns. Is this Tora? Is this halacha?

We have discussed this problem of conversion "according to halacha" because it illustrates the problem of halacha in our time in the widest sense. In the course of the ages a calamity has overtaken the Oral Tora. In the course of time, what was to be oral teaching became more and more committed to writing. The first "text" of the Oral Tora was the Mishna. In the Gemara, which is usually understood to be the explanation of the mishnaic text, one notices the struggle of the Oral Tora, still very much alive, with the mishnaic phase of its solidification. There is a continuous tension between the oral teaching and the written word of what, too, was in its origin Oral Tora. The text is "corrected"; a law often formulated in the Mishna as a general principle is interpreted to mean only a single rule in a specific case. The plain meaning of the text is often changed into its very opposite by an insertion. Interpretation is often "creative," in that it often disregards syntax and literal meaning. The whole of the Gemara testifies to the unavoidable struggle of the spoken word of the halacha with its solidification in a text. But, then, the Gemara too was "concluded." And now the Oral Tora has been committed to two texts. However, the second text has much less a solidified form of the oral teaching than the first. There is an essential difference between the spoken and the written word. Whereas the Mishna was indeed a transformation of the spoken word into the written one, the Gemara was the writing down of the spoken word in a manner that preserved its essential spoken quality. The Mishna is a text; the Gemara is more like notes for a text.

Then came the third phase, that of the codifiers. Maimonides, for instance, in his monumental halachic work, *Mishneh Tora*, imitating the mishnaic style, transformed the "notes" of the Gemara into a text and, thus, he transformed the entire extent of Oral Tora into a new kind of Written Tora. The ultimate outcome of this process was, of course, the *Shulhan Aruch.*

Thus, what was not meant to be did come about: The Oral Tora became a written one. In fact, this whole development took place in actual violation of a principle of the Tora, according to which it was forbidden to commit to writing the Oral Tora.[10] Why, then, was it done? One might apply to this entire development what was said in the Talmud of R. Yohanan and R. Shimon ben Lakish, who allowed themselves to study the written version of certain parts of the oral tradition. It is said that they did it following a verse in Psalms which, in a famous talmudic interpretation, reads: "When it is time to act for God, one may violate his command-ment."[11] They meant to say that since it was impossible to preserve the entire body of the oral teaching in memory alone, some parts of it had to be put to writing, especially in the light of the vicissitudes, uncertainties, distinction of communities and talmudic academies, and exiles in the history of the Jewish people in many lands. This conclusion is supported by Maimonides' introduction to his *Mishneh Tora.*

This means that the transformation of the Oral Tora into a text was due to political history. It was an unavoidable violation of the essence of halacha when the spoken word was forced into the straitjacket of a written mold. It was no one's fault; nevertheless, it was a spiritual calamity of the first magnitude. Orthodoxy is, in a sense, halacha in a straitjacket. Having had to transform the Oral Tora into a new written one, we have become Karaites of this new Written Tora, forced upon us by external circum-stances. It was part of the spiritual tragedy of the exile that exactly what halacha in its original vitality and wisdom intended to protect us from has happened. In a sense, we have become Karaites. God can no longer rejoice over his "defeat" by his children. It is a condition we have had to accept. It is the price we have paid for the preservation of our identity and Jewish survival.

Today, however, we are faced with unprecedented new challenges, problems of a true halachic nature, which require solutions in the true halachic spirit. This is true in the free societies in which Jews live, but it is compellingly manifest in the State of Israel. When some leading rabbinical authorities there maintain that halacha can solve all of the problems that may be raised for Judaism in a modern state, they are right and they are wrong. They are right, for halacha in its original strength could solve all such problems. Yet they are wrong. Halacha in its present state cannot fulfill that function.

This is certainly no plea for reform. Many of our inherited molds are leaking and cannot meaningfully contain the life that has fallen to the lot of our generation. What is needed is to retrace our steps. To return to the original halacha, to rediscover it, and, having rediscovered it, to restore it to its original function. If the problem were thoroughly understood, it would liberate us from the burden of this type of halacha. We would then see that in this generation we have been called upon, as it were, by another "divine voice" to accept the responsibility to make use of whatever is still left of the

Oral Tora in its textual solidification. It would be the beginning that would lead us back to the original source and strength of halacha. It would be the beginning of its restoration to its original vitality and dignity, for the sake of which God concluded this covenant with Israel. What is needed is not less study of Tora, but better study of Tora; not less dedication to halacha, but more faith in halacha. Where there is greater faith, greater boldness is justified.

As in the past, because it was a time to act for God, shackles had to be placed on the Oral Tora in violation of God's command, so now the hour has come when the need to act for God places upon us the responsibility to free the Oral Tora from its shackles, in obedience to God's original command. There are risks involved in such an undertaking. Because of it we need not less but more fear of heaven. But possibly most of all, we need more love of all Israel, to illuminate our love of Tora. And to pray to God for his guidance.

4

A JEWISH SEXUAL ETHICS

(1976)

IN THE CONTEXT of contemporary secular civilization, the sexual revolution had to come. It derives its energy, as well as its plausibility, from a variety of sources. Above all, however, it is the open manifestation of the rebellion against Christian sex ethics that had been occurring under the surface for several generations. It is a revolt against the Christian denigration of the human body and against the Christian approach to sexuality which for many centuries determined the official moral climate in the West. In spite of all the developments in Christian thought since its early days, Christian theology could not fully emancipate itself from the apostle Paul's teaching on sex, according to which "it is good for man not to touch a woman," and "if they cannot contain, let them marry: For it is better to marry than to burn."[1] Thus sex could never completely free itself from the tarnish which was attached to it, as well as to everything else that was of the body, in early Christian thought.

In fact, only because of this begrudging submission to sex on the part of the Western religious conscience could the ideas of repression and guilt gain such overwhelming importance as they were given in modern psychology. Yet the fact that the rebellion broke into the open with such self-assurance is chiefly due to man's only more recently acquired self-understanding, which is inseparable from his view of the cosmos and his own place in the scheme of things. On the basis of modern scientific progress contemporary man has formulated his view of life and existence, views which, however, have not been—and cannot be—scientifically validated, and which are often no less dogmatic than the dogmas of the most religiously orthodox. One should not call this a philosophy, but rather a meta-science. According to this meta-science, the cosmos in its entirety is a chance event and man himself, of course, an absurdly insignificant chance event in the unlimited ocean of a basically meaningless universe. The shattering of the Tablets of the Law, also the direct result of this meta-science, and the subsequent relativization of all values, led in fact to a destruction of all standards, with man walled in on all sides by absurdity. As if this were not enough, modern psychology completed the reduction of man to the level of an animal, a rather complex one but still only an animal. Norman O. Brown, who in a brilliant volume attempts to give us a psychoanalytical explanation of the meaning of history in the Freudian tradition, has the following to say about the present age:

> For two thousand years or more man has been subjected to a systematic effort to transform him into an ascetic animal. He remains a pleasure-seeking animal. Parental discipline, religious denunciation of bodily pleasure, and philosophic exaltation of the life of reason have all left man overly docile, but secretly in his unconscious unconvinced, and therefore neurotic.[2]

The affirmation that try as he might, man can never be anything but an animal presents him with only one choice: He can either strive to become an ascetic animal, and since he will never fully succeed, he will be a neurotic; or he can recognize himself for what he is, a pleasure-seeking animal, and live accordingly. That is what the contemporary sexual revolution is all about: Man, accepting himself as an "animal," wishes to get rid of his neurosis. Now, not all psychologists are Freudians who would accept Freud's meta-psychology, according to which man is fully comprehended by the pleasure principle. Yet all of them that dominate the climate of the age, following a meta-psychology of their own, reduce what used to be considered the essence of man's humanity to an accidental derivative of his specific animality.

Given this kind of a meta-science and meta-psychology, which are uncritically accepted by a generation that they begat, the sexual revolution against all repression and inhibition is fully justified. On the basis of its premises, the resulting principle of a liberated sex ethics—that every kind of sexual activity and relationship between consenting adults is permissible—cannot be gainsaid.

II

As with every other aspect of Judaism, a Jewish sexual ethics cannot be maintained meaningfully without an understanding of the presuppositions on which it is based. The statement that the world is creation implies that all the vital forces in which human nature shares, that are present within man and carried into life through man, have their place within the scheme of all things. Thus, human sexuality has its Creator-intended function within the plan of creation; it is world-related, handed to man with a goal directed beyond the individual.

That God created man in his own image, that he breathed into man's form the breath of life, is of course an uncompromising rejection of all meta-science and all meta-psychology, which reduce man to a mere member of the animal kingdom. But that man is not an animal is a Jewish affirmation that cannot be given up without surrendering Judaism itself. Man's humanity is not something derived, an epiphenomenon of his animality; it is as originally given as his instinctual equipment and biological frame. Because of that man's "animality" too is human. Whereas the secularist of today animalizes the human, Judaism humanizes the so-called animal. Our great teacher Hillel considered caring for the body a *mitzva*, a religious responsibility, because it meant looking after the "divine image" in which man was created. Notwithstanding all the theological problems of anthropomorphism presented by the concept, it is the whole man, body and mind, instinct and spirit, that was created in God's image and as such, in his complex entirety, represents that image on this earth. Nor is this just teaching, unrelated to man's experience. It is more than doubtful that the reduction of man does justice to his existential reality. The reductionist theories are contradicted by the daily behavior of the human being. Man not only desires instinctively, he wills, plans, chooses, accepts responsibility, and creates.[3] In a public debate with a "radical" Jewish theologian, I induced him to clarify his goal for man. He wanted man to be a healthy animal. What he was unable to grasp was that it is impossible for man to be a healthy animal, for the simple reason that in order to be that, man has to make a choice, a decision. But no healthy animal, because it is healthy, could ever *want* to be a healthy animal. Only a sick man could want to be a healthy animal.

The point of view presented here has been succinctly expressed by Ignace Lepp, who wrote:

> Only a false reductive method, which takes the most rudimentary for the most natural, would permit us to speak of human instincts as if they were essentially identical with animal instincts. All human instincts are intimately penetrated by psyche. This is why purely psychic traumas can provoke respiratory and digestive troubles. And the more evolved man becomes, the more his biological instincts become bio-psychic. If we try to deny this state of things we will end not with "pure" animal nature but with a mutilation of human nature.[4]

Because of what man is, human sexuality cannot find its fulfillment in the simplicity of primitive satisfaction. As a rebellion against the repression and inhibitions of a society that has no spiritual, religious, or even mere philosophical basis for its sexual taboos, a "return" to primitive sexuality may have its validity. But because man is human and not animal, primitive, purely biological sexuality is bound to leave him empty and wretched. Ultimately a return to the purely biological is not open to him. The natural for man is never purely biological, it is always psychosomatic, or, to use Ignace Lepp's terminology, bio-psychic. Back to nature can only mean back to human nature. Any other kind of "return" is unnatural.

III

What are the consequences of these presuppositions? Firstly, just because even the biological and instinctual in man is not purely biological, but in its bio-psychic nature is altogether human, it is not to be rejected, but on the contrary, it is to be accepted. Judaism does not allow for any denigration of the body. The body is not bad; it is not the source of all evil. Saadia Gaon, the outstanding talmudic scholar and Jewish philosopher of the tenth century, had occasion to state unequivocally:

> As to the objection that is raised against the defilement and the contamination of the soul consequent upon its union with the body, we say, in reply thereto, that the body of man contains no impurity in and by itself. It is, on the contrary, entirely pure, for defilement is neither a thing subject to sense perception nor a requirement of logic. It is purely a decree of the Tora. This law has declared unclean certain secretions of human beings after their discharge from the body, although they do not defile while they are within the body. The aforementioned allegation can be maintained only if he that makes it will impose upon us rules that he has invented out of his own mind and make it obligatory upon us to consider as reprehensible what he so regards. That, however, we shall not permit him to do.[5]

In other words, while there are indeed in the Bible some ritual laws regarding certain bodily secretions, the body as such is "entirely pure" and as such, according to Saadia's understanding of Jewish teaching, is not only a worthy abode, but even an appropriate companion for the soul on this earth. Integrating Saadia's view with the idea of man as a bio-psychic unity, we would say that the body is body only in man's death, just as the soul is soul only after his death. In life, however, they are linked to each other in such a manner that they interpenetrate. Because of this psychosomatic unity, a denial of either one of them is a betrayal of both. Within Judaism, man is acknowledged in his bio-psychic reality. This is the basis of a Jewish sexual ethics. It excludes primitive biological sexuality as well as sophisticated asceticism.

This does not mean that there is no adequate appreciation of the power of internal drives, of the libido, especially in its sexual manifestation. On the contrary, there is a great deal of understanding for the struggle in which a person may be involved in trying to control his sexual desire. There is recognition for the fact that human beings may at times, in certain situations, not be able to control their sexuality. For example, a married woman who is forced to submit to sexual intercourse and, as the act proceeds, becomes cooperative is not considered an adulteress, because once she was forced into that situation she was acting against her will—"clothed with desire"—and became powerless against her instinct.[6]

The rabbis in the Talmud are not a bit prudish when they discuss sex. According to their opinion, no one is secure in the face of sexual temptation. The most remarkable stories are told about some of the greatest teachers and their weakness of the flesh. Such a story is told of R. Amram the Hasid ("the pious"). One day they brought to Nehardea some women who had been kidnapped and ransomed. They put them up in the attic of R. Amram, taking care to remove the ladder to the attic. It happened that the flames of the fire illuminated the face of one of the women and R. Amram noticed her. He took the ladder that—according to a bit of exaggeration, we assume—could normally be moved only by the combined strength of "ten men," and set it in the opening in the attic. As he was climbing up, feeling that by himself he could not control his desire, he started shouting, "There is a fire in the house! There is a fire in the house of R. Amram!" thus arousing his neighbors and exposing himself to disgrace.[7]

While R. Amram was still able to save himself in the last minute by his own exertion, the matter was not so simple in the case of R. Akiva and R. Meir, two of the most distinguished teachers of the Talmud. It is told that each of them in his time had derided sinners who could not resist temptation. For their proud self-assurance they were tested by the Tempter. To R. Akiva he appeared in the shape of a woman in the top of a palm tree. R. Akiva went and started climbing the tree after her. To R. Meir, the Tempter appeared as a woman on the opposite bank of a river. There was no bridge, so the rabbi got hold of a rope that was tied to both sides of the river and started pulling himself across. According to the story, both rabbis were saved from sinning because the Tempter was ordered to desist. Because of their merits as great teachers of the Tora, they were protected by a special act of divine grace.[8] Yet, not always did temptation find such favorable resolution in the life of talmudic teachers. Occasionally there is failure which leads to spiritual tragedy.[9]

The rabbis in the Talmud had nothing to learn from Freud regarding the tremendous power of the libido. Nevertheless, they had a very positive evaluation of its function. R. Shmuel bar Nahman, for instance, comments on the words of the Bible that at the end of creation God saw everything that he had made and behold it was *tov me'od*, very good: *Tov*, good, that is the *yetzer hatov*, the good inclination in man; *tov me'od*, very good, that is the *yetzer hara*, the evil urge in him. The question is, of course, asked: How is this to be understood, how is it possible to call man's innate inclination for evil "very good"? The midrash responds: "This is to teach you that were it not for the evil inclination, man would not care to build a house for himself, he would neither marry nor beget children, nor would he attend to the affairs of human existence."[10] What R. Shmuel calls the *yetzer hara* seems to be rather close to the Freudian libido, or id. It is the vital energy that sustains the life of man and is the source of the sexual drive. Its function is necessary; without it human life would not be possible.

The same idea is expressed in a rather moving story from the life of Abaye, one of the outstanding teachers in the post-mishnaic talmudic period. He once overheard a man and a woman making arrangements to set out together early in the morning on a journey on foot. Said Abaye to himself: I shall follow after them in order to keep them from sinning. He followed behind for three parasangs across meadows. It turned out that as far as the two travelers were concerned, it was a very innocent trip. As they reached their destination, Abaye heard them take leave of each other with harmless civilities: "It was a long way. Our company was pleasant. So long." Abaye was rather ashamed, recognizing that he himself could not have traveled with the woman so innocently. "Leaning against a door, he was visibly upset and pained until an old sage came by [to whom Abaye must have told the reason for his mental anguish] and taught him: The greater a man, the stronger his *yetzer*, his instinctual drive"—or perhaps we should render it, "the stronger his libido."[11] Sexuality is vitality; but human greatness is also a manifestation of vital energy. Normally, only non-vital people will enjoy comparative freedom from sexuality, but neither will they be burdened with creative potential for human greatness.

The positive value of universal sexuality is maintained with a sense of humor in the following tale. On a propitious occasion, the Jews asked for merciful support against the *yetzer hara* of sexual excess (or as we might also say in modern parlance, against the sexual libido). Their prayer was granted, and the *yetzer hara* was handed over into their power. However, a prophet warned them: "Look out now! If you kill this one, the world will be destroyed." They tied it up for three days. At the end of the three days, when a fresh egg was needed for a sick person, they searched for one in all the land of Israel but could not find a single one. What to do now, they wondered. Should they kill it? They would destroy the world. "Let us then ask that it be reduced to half size [meaning that the sexual drive should be limited to marriage alone]. But no half things are granted by heaven." So they decided to blind its eyes, which helped somewhat to reduce its strength.[12] There is in this tale an understanding of sexuality as a universal principle that serves life, as well as of the interrelatedness and unity of all life forces. One has to accept the *yetzer hara* in its universal reality, for without it man could not maintain himself. He depends on nature's "libido" for his sustenance. But one cannot desire it for the life of nature and limit it only to certain forms of personal life. No half things are granted by heaven. One has to acknowledge the *yetzer hara* in the wholeness of its universal function.

IV

However, just because sexuality is a universal life force, it surfaces in man originally as an impersonal drive. It is not what man does, but what is happening to man. One could very well leave it at that, if man were nothing but nature—that is, an animal. There is reason to assume that in the animal kingdom sex is indeed utterly impersonal. It is not what an animal does, but something cosmic that enacts itself through the animal (although the talmudic teachers were able to discern signs of the personal in the sex act in certain cases even in the animal world).[13] However, since the sexual instinct finds its normal satisfaction in union with a member of the other sex, this fundamentally impersonal drive points powerfully to another person. In the animal realm it is essentially a pointing from genital to genital; in the human experience it is a call from one bio-psychic being to another—in other words, a call from person to person.

True enough, just because man is not merely instinct but also will, not only pleasure-seeking but also meaning-pursuing, he may, if he so chooses, consciously attempt to reduce himself to the genital level of sexuality, and thus instead of becoming a healthy animal become a sick human being. But if he accepts himself in the fullness of his bio-psychic reality, he will find that this most impersonal drive of his nature directs him to the realm of the personal in the most fundamental of all human encounters. The contact between two human beings is never so close, never so intimate or so total as with bio-psychic union between a man and a woman. Unless one sees clearly how in the sexual union the crudely impersonal calls for its accommodation within the most fundamentally personal, one fails to understand the nature of human sexuality. Joseph Fletcher, possibly the most influential protagonist of situation ethics, writes for instance, with true "pharisaic" self-assurance:

> The ethical "pharisees"… fail to see that the most evil and destructive traits are not those of the sexual appetite, which is biologically given and morally neutral in itself, but the irrational emotional passions such as hate, fear, greed, ulcerous struggles for discreet status—all of our self-regarding ("sinful") and antisocial impulses.[14]

What Fletcher apparently does not understand is that while what he says about the sexual appetite is indeed true on the animal level, it is not true at all on the level of man. Because in the human experience this most impersonal of all instincts demands its satisfaction in the most personal of inter-human relationships, what is biologically given loses its natural innocence and moral neutrality. In the context of the most intimately personal, the impersonality of the sexual impulse becomes, due to its incomparable energy and driving power, the most self-regarding and the most antisocial of impulses which man has to personalize. Because the sexual union is the most elementary of all inter-human encounters, in which the most impersonal instinct seeks its satisfaction in the most intimately interpersonal realm of human existence, the manner of its satisfaction cannot but fatefully determine the resolution of the conflicts as they arise when the other "self-regarding and antisocial impulses" break into the interpersonal domain. It may therefore very well be that how man deals with personalizing the impersonal in his sex life is the core of all human morality.

It should be obvious by now that the fundamental principle of the sexual ethics that we have in mind is to personalize the impersonal. It is Jewish because it derives from the two presuppositions of the Jewish worldview that we indicated earlier, namely that the world is creation, and that man is a bio-psychic being. We shall now attempt to develop in more detail the consequences that follow from the basic principle in the light of the two presuppositions. What is the significance of the idea that the cosmos is creation in this context? We saw that the rabbis in the Talmud saw sexuality as a universal force that sustains the life of the world. Its function in nature is quite obviously procreation in its universality. However, what in nature is a given function, in creation is a purpose intended by the Creator. In support of the idea, the Talmud quotes the verse from Isaiah:

> For thus says the Eternal that created the heavens,
> He is God;
> That formed the earth and made it,
> He established it,
> He created it not a waste;
> He formed it to be inhabited...[15]

To that last line of this verse the Talmud attaches the comment that the purpose of creation, as far as man is concerned, is to understand that the earth must be sustained not as a wasteland but as a place to be inhabited. But since the earth as an inhabited place can be maintained only by procreation, the rabbis were able to formulate their insight by saying: The world was created for procreation. Obviously they do not mean the absurdity that the purpose of the creation was human procreation. The phrase on which they base their interpretation is set in the cosmic context of the creation of heaven and earth. They have in mind "procreation" as a universal purpose. Nevertheless, from these words of Isaiah they derive man's responsibility "to multiply and to increase."[16] The universality of the sexual instinct places man by way of his sexuality in the universal context; only this time the universe is creation. The impersonal drive that takes hold of man seeks the realization of divine purpose through him. But the purposeful, the goal-oriented, is found only in the realm of the personal. In man the impersonal, universal sex impulse seeks its satisfaction in a personal world. Once again the impersonal points to the other, only this time the other is God. Once again the impersonal is to be personalized, this time in an encounter with God by accepting responsibility for the function of the sexual instinct that was allocated to man by the Creator, by consciously making oneself available for God's purpose in life.

To personalize the impersonal sexual instinct is thus a twofold responsibility, towards God and towards one's partner in the bio-psychic encounter of the sexual union. However, on the level of the interpersonal encounter, responsibility stems from the biblical commandment: "And you shall love your neighbor as yourself,"[17] which in the area of the God-man encounter receives the formulation "You shall love the Eternal your God with all your heart, with all your soul, and with all your might."[18] Rather significantly, the rabbis in the Talmud interpreted the phrase "with all your heart" to mean with both your inclinations, with the *yetzer hatov*, the good inclination, and with the *yetzer hara*, the evil inclination. But we have seen earlier that they also identified the evil inclination with the libido.[19] Indeed, through the personalization of the libido in its sexual manifestation by using it consciously in the service of a God-intended purpose, one loves God with one's whole heart, even with one's *yetzer hara*. (Of course, the sexual instinct is not only the manifestation of the *yetzer hara*.) It is doubtful whether in the entire course of man's history anyone has degraded the reality of love in the world more than Freud, who saw in it nothing but libido energy displacement resulting from frustrated sexuality. We owe him the delightful idea that, for instance, tenderness between mother and child is nothing but the energy residue from aim-thwarted sexuality. It is the unavoidable deduction from the reduction of man to the animality of the pleasure principle. The truth that we affirm is the recognition of love as an originally given force in the wholeness of the bio-psychic reality of man. It is the most truly personal, as the libido is the most truly impersonal. It is through love in the interpersonal encounter that the libido in its broadest meaning is redeemed from the prison of its impersonality.

V

The fully personalized sexual union is the fully humanized one. It relates one at the same time to the Creator as well as to a fellow being in the wholeness of each other's humanity. What in nature is assumed to be purely biological is integrated in its humanized form into the bio-psychic structure of man. However, since humanization implies also the acknowledgment of the divine purpose of the sexual function, the personalized and thus humanized sex act becomes a *mitzva*, legalistically formulated, a divine commandment; in its existential quality, it is an ethical deed within the structure of a deocentric personal life. In fact, talmudic texts occasionally call the sex act a *devar mitzva*, a matter of *mitzva*, not only in its God-relatedness, but also as what takes place on the interpersonal level between a man and a woman.[20] Similarly, one might call any act of kindness and care for another human being a *devar mitzva*. It is rather different a phrase from the four-letter word which designates the sex act in its biologically impersonal and, we might now say, dehumanized form. As a *devar mitzva*, the biologically impersonal is transformed into the human and personal. Jewish sexual ethics can perceive the sexual act in its most humanized and personalized transformation as an act of sanctification. To sanctify oneself at the moment of intercourse is the ideal of sexual fulfillment.[21]

One may even say that the humanized transformation of the impersonal quality of the sexual instinct is the climax in man's striving for sexual liberation. We indicated earlier in our discussion that the contemporary sexual rebellion that wishes to do away with the taboos of this civilization has its justification. A civilization which has brought upon itself the collapse of all value standards, which has exiled meaning from the cosmos, whose summation is correctly expressed in the idea of the absurdity of existence, has indeed no grounds on which to base those restrictions on sexual activity which were accepted in the past. However, liberation from sexual codes that can no longer be supported by the basic affirmations of contemporary society throws man back once again into the domain of the biologically impersonal. Because of the tremendous power of the sexual instinct, man falls into the thralldom of mighty impersonal forces when he liberates himself from social taboos. The sex act is not so much an act as a letting go. It is not man who acts; rather it is something that happens (the impersonal does not act) through man. This, of course, may be enjoyable for a while, but as man allows free entrance to the impersonal into his life, and as the impersonal gets hold of him with its powerfully driving energy, in the long run it cannot but depersonalize man as a whole, "dehumanizing" him far beyond the sexual aspect of his life. Freedom, like love, is of the very essence of personal existence. He who submits to the biologically impersonal is held captive by necessity, the essence of the impersonal. It is not enough to free oneself from meaningless taboos. If one wishes to be human, one has to commit one's freedom to personalizing the impersonal within man's bio-psychic reality.

The humanizing of the impersonal does not in any way take away from enjoyment of the sexual act. It does not attempt to "spiritualize" the act. It wants what it says, to humanize it, including also its full enjoyment within the bio-psychic human reality. In fact, the enjoyment itself is part of the living realization of Judaism. In talmudic times, a *talmid hacham*, a Jew who leads a life of piety informed by Jewish learning, would engage in the sexual act once a week. But it was customary to do so on the night of the Sabbath. R. Shlomo Yitzhaki (Rashi), the classical commentator on the Talmud who lived in the eleventh century, explains the reason for the custom thus: "It is the night of joy, of rest, and of bodily pleasure."[22] The context into which humanized sensuality is integrated brings about its joyous sanctification.

Such affirmation of earthly needs and vital impulses is characteristic of the whole system of Jewish law. The Sabbath and holy days are not observed "spiritually," nor should they be so observed. Man is not a spirit. On the Sabbath, therefore, not only the soul should find peace, but the body too should rest. One celebrates the day not only by meditation and prayer, but also by wearing Sabbath clothes and by partaking of the Sabbath meals. The Sabbath meal itself is a *mitzva*; it is divine service. And if properly performed, it is a service of a far higher quality than that of prayer and meditation alone; it is the service of the whole man. The enjoyment of the Sabbath is neither spiritual nor material; it is *wholly* human. Body and spirit celebrate the Sabbath in communion. The Jew who keeps the Sabbath may say that the material enjoyments of the day enhance his spiritual elation, and his spiritual elation renders the material enjoyments more gratifying. In the unifying act of the *mitzva*, the Sabbath acts as a "spice" to the palate and as an uplifting joy for the spirit of man.[23]

All this may well be said also of the sensual joy of the body. The spiritual in man is never purely spiritual, as the biological is never purely biological. Thus, we may say that it is not only the pleasure of the body that enhances the *oneg shabbat*, the joy of the Sabbath; it is also the joy of the Sabbath that dignifies the pleasure of the body. However, what is said here in the special case of the Sabbath may only be so stated because of its applicability to the widest range of Jewish living. Sensual enjoyment is fully accepted within the purposefully directed experience, which is the essence of its personalization. The biblical commandment "and you shall rejoice before the Eternal your God"[24] is addressed not to the spirit of man or to his soul, but to his entire bio-psychic reality. To rejoice before God in the wholeness of human nature is the *mitzva*.

The Talmud tells the story of a man who was extremely careful in the observance of the commandment of *tzitzit*, of wearing ritual fringes on the four corners of one's garb. Once he heard that there was a prostitute in a city by the sea whose fee was four hundred gold pieces. He sent her the four hundred gold pieces, and a time was arranged for him. When the day arrived, he went to the door of her house. Her maid went in and told her: "That man who sent you the four hundred pieces of gold has come and sits at the door." Said she: "Let him enter." He entered.

She had prepared for him seven beds, six of silver and one of gold. They were arranged one above the other, and between each there was a ladder made of silver. The highest bed was the one of gold. She climbed up to the top and lay down naked in the golden bed. Then he too climbed up to sit beside her in the nude. At this moment the *tzitziot*, the four fringes of his garb, came and slapped him across the face. At this, he broke away and sat down on the ground. She too came down and sat on the ground. Said she to him: "By the Capitol of Rome! I shall not let you off until you tell me what blemish you saw in me."

Said he to her: "I swear I have never seen a woman as beautiful as you, but there is a commandment that God commanded us, and its name is *tzitzit*. The words in which it is written contain the phrase 'I am the Eternal your God' twice, meaning: I am the one who calls to account; I am the one who will reward. Now, the *tzitziot* appeared to me as if they were four witnesses."

Said she to him: "I shall not let you off until you tell me your name, the name of your city, the name of your rabbi, and the name of the school where you study Tora." He wrote it all down and placed it into her hand.

Then she got up and divided all her property into three parts: A third for the government, a third for the poor, and a third she took with her, apart from "that bed linen" (which was included in the division). She proceeded to the study house of R. Hiya and said to him: "Rabbi! Command that I be made a convert." Said he to her: "My daughter, is it perhaps that one of the students appealed to your eyes?" She took the note that the man had given her from her hand and gave it to R. Hiya. After reading it, he said to her: "Go and take possession of what you have acquired." The story concludes with this moral: "And so the same bed linen that she once spread out for the man to serve his lust, she now spread out for him in consecrated union. This was the reward for the *mitzva* of *tzitzit* in this world. How much in the world to come, who can tell?" [25]

Apart from a very few stylistic alterations, I have intentionally told the story with the same simplicity as it is found in the Talmud, because every part of it and almost every phrase is important for understanding the teaching that is being communicated.

The story begins with a full recognition of the almost irresistible force of the sexual instinct. The young man is a talmudic scholar, a pious man. As used to be customary, in addition to observing the commandments of the Tora as befits a student of the Tora, he dedicates himself to the strictest observance of one specific commandment. His sexual desire in this case is not a momentary temptation. The prostitute is extremely expensive, and he has to sacrifice a small fortune in order to get to her. He has to wait for the appointed day, and he has to go on a long journey, for she lives in a city "by the sea." When he arrives, he has to undergo the indignity of having to sit at her door until he is admitted. None of this deters him. He is like one possessed. It is not accidental to the story that the young man had chosen the commandment of the fringes for especially conscientious observance. For of this commandment the Bible says:

> And it shall be unto you for a fringe, that you may look upon it and remember all the commandments of the Eternal, and do them; and that you go not about after your own heart and after your own eyes, after which you used to go astray.[26]

Now, quite clearly, sexuality is that instinct in man which is most likely to lead him astray after "his own heart and his own eyes." If our young Tora student dedicated himself to the strictest observance of the *tzitzit* commandment, it was due to the fact that he realized his own weakness in the face of temptation and was struggling to overcome it.

As he enters the prostitute's boudoir there is no meeting between them. It is nudity that meets nudity; his sexual desire meets her greed. It is an accommodation between a man who has been reduced to the pleasure principle, and a woman who has been reduced to cupidity. It is sex in its classically impersonal manifestation. What could be more impersonal than an appointment between lust and greed?

The fringes that take on a life of their own and slap his face are the symbolic expression of his own resistance. The merit of the *mitzva* saves him from complete failure. As he is about to sink into the ecstasy of impersonality, a kind of an ego death, he is called back to the personal level of his being, and tears himself away and sits on the ground. The sight of him on the ground calls her from the impersonality of prostitution. She sits down with him on the ground. They sit there, still naked, but no longer in the nudity of lust and desire, but in the nakedness of their frail humanity, amidst the ruins of their human dignity. And now, *mima'amakim*—from the depths—to use a phrase of the psalmist, they call to each other. "She said to him" and "he said to her," and so again and again. When he first heard about her, she was the celebrated prostitute whose fame was spread across the lands. He had not even set eyes on her; she was the anonymous symbol of sex to him. But now, sitting opposite each other on the ground, he recognizes her as the most beautiful woman he ever saw. He acknowledges her in her full feminine dignity and is able to appreciate her beauty without the eyes of lust. When he first appeared at her door, he was nameless. He was "that man who sent her the four hundred pieces of gold." That was enough, nothing else mattered. But now she asks him about names: His name, the name of his city, the name of his rabbi, the name of the house of study where he learns Tora—so many names! Having emerged from the wilderness of impersonality, she is longing for personalization: Who are you, where do you come from, who made you what you are, and how was it achieved? As she meets him as a person, she finds herself as one. It is one of those revelational I-Thou encounters about which Martin Buber has taught us and which have within themselves the mystery of sudden transformation. It is redemption from impersonality. She comes out of it a changed human being. And so, we assume, does he. Finally, his struggles with the heart and the eyes that lead one astray are over. He has gained himself a new heart and he sees with new eyes. Now, the *mitzva* of *tzitzit* is fulfilled, not only in ritual observance, but also in recovered personal dignity.

The understanding between the man and the woman is subtly hinted at in the story. She says to him: Tell me your name and all the other names. But he does not tell. He writes it all down for her on a piece of paper, and "placed it into her hand." The text does not simply say that "he gave her the note," for that would have meant the mere technicality of conveying an object from one person to another, the purely physical act of handing over a piece of information. "He placed it into her hand" is the entrusting of something precious into safekeeping. It is not just handing over, it is communication. He did not answer her questions by word of mouth. He wrote it all down. "Please, do not forget—this is who I am. That is where I come from. This is how I became what I am. All this I place into your hand. Keep it." The importance of the note is revealed at the end of the story. The rabbi asks her: is it perhaps that one of the students appeals to your eyes? Once again the eyes appear in the story as doors of temptation, against which the young man sought protection by means of the *mitzva* of the fringes. Now, this is actually what she wants, one of the rabbi's students. But she does not answer, she does not explain, she does not defend herself. She is silent. And as he, without answering her questions, entrusted the note into her keeping, so now she, in silence, hands over the note to the rabbi. And once again the phrase is used which corresponds exactly to the phrase used for his entrusting the note into her hands. The text does not say, "she gave the note to him," but instead, that she brought the note out from her hand and gave it to him. The rabbi sees it and accepts her.

What did R. Hiya see? How was his question answered? There was a beautiful woman in front of him who could have had the great ones of Rome at her feet. Yet she was coming to his door to be converted. It is a matter of ultimate importance to her, yet she does not plead her cause. Is there a man involved? She is silent, but with one of those silences that tell more than any words could tell. A silence of truth and trust. Yes, indeed, there is a man. She hands him his paper. The rabbi notices that she had been treasuring it as a trust, which she now surrenders from her hand into his safekeeping as it was entrusted to her. The rabbi reads: There is a man who desired to be known by this woman for what he was, a Jew, who has a master, a student of the Tora. And who wanted her not to forget him. She kept his trust and now placed their joint destiny into the rabbi's hands. Not a word is said. The rabbi understands. Strangely, as he gives his blessing to their union, the rabbi uses what one might think is most inappropriate language in the situation: "Go and take possession of what you have acquired." It would seem to us that these words are chosen intentionally to make the point of her transformation. Originally, in her state of impersonality, she wanted possession in its impersonal form. She did not want him, but his gold pieces. But now that the impersonality of their relationship has been redeemed, it is person who takes the place of possession.

There is one more aspect to this story. Though redeemed from his lust, the man is fully open to the woman's beauty. She, on the other hand, does not hide the fact that she desires the man, but the whole man, in his bio-psychic completeness. The story ends with a statement of the sensual enjoyment of their union, that is seen as the this-worldly reward for the careful observance of the *mitzva* that protects a man against going astray after his "heart" and his "eyes."

This story contains all the basic principles of a Jewish sex ethics. It recognizes the force of the sexual instinct while illustrating how this instinct in its impersonal givenness depersonalizes a human being. It need not be repressed. Indeed, it can be raised to the personal level of human existence as the natural outcome of the personalization of the relationship between a man and a woman who encounter each other in the completeness of their bio-psychic being. Finally, as in our earlier systematic presentation, so in the story too, personalization is twofold. It is accomplished between the Jew and his God, and between the man and the woman. Thus they are rejoicing together in the presence of God. Once redeemed from the bondage of the impersonal, neither the eye nor the heart has to be denied. They lead, but do not lead astray.

One might ask: Is this kind of a transformation of the sexual instinct possible? In answer, one might point to the sex life of the Jewish people through the many centuries during which they remained within the struc-ture of their own religious culture and civilization. This kind of personal-ized sensuality has indeed been generally practiced by Jews through many generations, and has been one of the main sources of the effectiveness of the sexual morality of the Jewish people. Whereas, for instance, according to Freud's theory of instincts, as civilization progresses, the guilt feeling continues to be intensified and increased, there is nothing of this found in the moral history of the Jewish people.[27] This is no argument against the Freudian psychoanalytical technique of treating neurosis, but it is indeed a refutation of the fantastic meta-psychological myth created by the genius of Freudian imagination. We have to remember that Freud, though himself a Jew by birth, was creating the meta-psychological superstructure to his psychoanalytical technique against the background and within the confines of a non-Jewish civilization. As we indicated at the beginning of our discussion, it was a civilization that in its religious manifestation equated sex with sin and in its secular expression reduced man to the level of an animal. Within such a worldview, guilt, repression, and inhibition have, of course, an entirely different quality and force than within the Jewish worldview we have outlined. Where sex as such is accepted as the positive, life-sustaining principle of divine creation, the thought of it does not automatically generate a feeling of guilt. The woman in our story divided all her property, but "that bed linen" she carried with her along the long road of her own transformation, which in the end led her to her man.

The idea of repression as it is used by Freud may have its place within a culture that sees the body as bad and fallen; it has, however, no place at all beside the recognition of the validity and dignity of physical human existence. Within a Jewish sexual ethics one might speak of inhibition, but not of repression. However, in Judaism even inhibition has significantly less negative a connotation than within the Freudian construction. With Freud, inhibition is altogether imposed from without. When the pleasure principle clashes with the reality principle, civilization is born as a result of the inhibition of the id. Inhibition is not a choice, but a necessity, and since man is an animal, completely comprehended by his libido, the necessity is alien, external to his nature. No wonder, then, that with the progress of civilization, inhibition becomes more and more oppressive, the sense of guilt deepens, and finally, one day, the individual may no longer be able to bear the burden, and civilization itself will collapse in a universal neurotic conflagration. However, where inhibition is not altogether alien to human nature, when it is not altogether externally imposed, when it is not only a necessity but a choice of man, then inhibition is not merely repressive but also positively formative. It has a positive, intrinsically goal-inspired direction.

The fifteenth-century Jewish philosopher R. Joseph Albo has an interesting comment on human nature, which has some bearing on our discussion. In the story of the creation the Bible says at the end of each day: And God saw what he had made, and behold it was good. However, after the creation of man, this statement is missing. Albo explains: There are two kinds of perfection, of nature and of man. Nature's consists in its being, man's in his becoming. Nature is always in the present; therefore judgment could be passed upon it. As it was created, so it was completed. Man, however, is goal-directed; he was, therefore, incomplete at his creation. The evaluation had to be left in abeyance.[28] For the purposes of our discussion we might say an animal is a creature of an enduring present. It lives completely in the "now." A human being, on the other hand, is open to the future, goal-oriented. Inhibition is a denial of the "now." If one sees man as an animal, inhibition is denial. An animal, because the future is closed to it, cannot tolerate delay in the satisfaction of its instincts, but within the Freudian meta-psychology the progress of civilization is a progressive delaying of satisfaction, a progressive violence done to a creature that is completely enrapt in its "now." On the other hand, within a religious culture like Judaism, man as a bio-psychic entity is seen as essentially future-oriented. Inhibition in such a context is not delay, but postponement. But whereas delay is frustration, postponement is growth; whereas delay is violence against the "now," postponement is care of tomorrow; whereas delay is denial, postponement is promise. Within the Jewish sexual ethics one should replace the term inhibition with that of discipline. Inhibition imposed upon a creature of "now" is oppression, while discipline chosen by the future-oriented man is liberation.

Herbert Marcuse explains that Freud found his theoretical analysis corroborated by the great diseases and discontents of contemporary civilization: "An enlarged cycle of wars, ubiquitous persecution, anti-Semitism, genocide, bigotry, and the enforcement of illusions, toil, sickness, and misery in the midst of growing wealth and knowledge."[29] Could it not be that, rather than the "diseases and discontents" corroborating the theory, it is the theory that is responsible for them; not just Freud's theory of the instincts alone, but it, too, within the scientism of the modern age, which for several generations now has been disabusing man of his "illusions" regarding his human status and teaching him with such pervasive intellectual lucidity that man is really "nothing but"? Small wonder that he is acting more and more like one who is "nothing but."

VI

Two consenting adults engaging in intercourse have little to do with any kind of ethics. It is an arrangement, admittedly more civilized than rape. Jewish sexual ethics is not about sex, but about the union between a man and a woman that includes sexual fulfillment. But why marriage? Could the personalized relationship between them not be realized in the presence of God and yet within the privacy of their consciences? What need is there for its official legalization? In all honesty, one would have to say that the ethical character of the union, as we have defined it, may not automatically require such public recognition. And indeed, some of the leading rabbinical authorities, like R. Abraham of Posquieres (died 1198) and Nahmanides (died 1263), were of the opinion that such a union was in theory permissible.[30] Nevertheless, it was frowned upon and generally forbidden in actual practice. Nahmanides was of the opinion that if allowed, it would lead to promiscuity. By this he meant that while the ethical character of the union may not in itself require public sanction, given human nature, and leaving the conclusion and termination of the union completely to the individual conscience, it would in most cases lead to unchastity, to the pursuit of sexual activity on the impersonal level. It may not be true in every case, but the ethical rules and laws of a culture and society have to be formulated with a view to the anticipated behavior of the generality of mankind.

However, there is something more profound involved. The highest form of the personalization of the relationship between a man and a woman finds its expression in their complete dedication to each other. It includes unquestioning trust in each other, the full acceptance of one's partner in his or her comprehensive humanity. A love that does not have the courage to commit itself "forever" is lacking in trust, in acceptance, in faith. Love fully personalized desires to be final, ultimate. But how can one commit oneself forever? Only by accepting the bondage of the responsibility of the commitment. In the ups and downs, in the struggle of daily existence, the trust and the faith are tested, often as if by fire. The highest form of personalization of the union is the ultimate of love; but it does not come easy. It is a continuous challenge, it is a task at which man and woman have to work unremittingly. It is not simply a matter of working at sexual compatibility, but at the realization of the potential of their mutual humanity. To persevere often in difficult situations, when it might seem that one's original hopes have faded, is the highest expression of trust in the human potential of oneself as well as one's partner.

To persevere with the task of personalization is an expression of one's faith in the possibility of renewal and regeneration. It is faith in man's capacity for interpersonal care, trust, and love. It is trust that this capacity can be awakened through faith in its existence. It is love in its universal significance. It is confidence that notwithstanding frustrations and disappointments, there is a basic quality of preciousness present in the human being to whom we originally committed ourselves "forever," on which one may continue to work for the realization of the meaning of the original commitment. And this is decisive. This is the secret of personalization of the bio-psychic relationship. It is not an event that is achieved in one moment of grace, but a process that may take a lifetime, requiring a lifelong commitment. Bearing in mind the power of the sexual instinct, and in recognition of the demanding task of its personalization which is insepara-ble from the continued maturing and deepening of the interpersonal rela-tionship between a man and a woman in the widest sense, the official character of the marriage bonds is an ethical requirement for the surrender-ing of one's freedom to dissolve the union at a whim, because of a momen-tary disaffection or disillusionment. It is indeed a serious business. The binding formality of the marriage is the mutual acceptance of the responsi-bility to persevere in the task of the full actualization of each other's potential for the interpersonal life; it is a commitment to the trust in that potential and as such an affirmation by innumerable daily deeds of one's faith in the human being on the universal plane. The formal marriage is not to be based on the present love that at this moment unites two human beings, but on the trust in the self-transcending power of that love, in its as yet unfathomed potential which, through care, devotion, and the practice of basic humanity and decency, will carry two human beings to the richest fulfillment of which they are capable. However, just because personaliz-ation is the goal, the Jewish marriage does not include the commitment "till death do us part." Failure is always possible, mistakes are often made, and the relationship may degenerate into such an abysmal failure of impersonal-ity that divorce may become a moral necessity.

Thus far, we have discussed marriage only from the angle of the purely personal and, in a sense, self-centered relationship between a man and a woman. However, as we saw, personalization has to be pursued also on the cosmic level, by relating the interpersonal union to the divine purpose of creation that seeks its realization through it. It includes the conscious identification of a man and a woman with that purpose, of merging by choice with the cosmic stream of continued propagation of new life, thus becoming partners of God in the work of creation. This new life, the life of a new generation, is no longer a purely personal matter. Because of its manifold implications and consequences, it is a matter of communal rel-evance and concern. This aspect of the task of personalization asks for the integration of the Jewish marriage within the religious ethics of the totality of Jewish living. This is the public share in every marriage. In the interest of the new life, it has to ensure, as far as humanly possible, the durability of the union. However, there is a specifically Jewish concern with every Jewish marriage. One might say that at the start of the way of the Jews through history stand the words which God said of their father Abraham:

> For I have known him, to the end that he may command his children and his household after him, that they may keep the way of the Eternal, to do righteousness and justice; to the end that the Eternal may bring upon Abraham that which he has spoken of him.[31]

The conscious identification with the divine purpose of the life-propagating cosmic principle is not simply a commitment to the biological transmission of life from generation to generation. This would still be an act of impersonality. As far as the Jew is concerned, the cosmic principle is personalized when it is made to serve the transmission of the life of Judaism from generation to generation. What God had "spoken of Abraham" was never meant to be "brought upon him" in his own lifetime. It was to find its fulfillment in the course of the fullness of the bio-psychic history of all his children. Judaism is a process through history, beginning with Abraham, the father, moving towards its culmination in Abraham's child, the Messiah, when all history will be fully redeemed from the bondage of the impersonal. Because, in history, Judaism is forever striving for its realization, it is always lived with a sense of the "not-yet." It is forever lived in the future and with responsibility toward that future. It is what it will yet be. A Jew, who desires to be one, is always a link in the generations, a child who receives and a parent who transmits with the intention and the freely accepted responsibility of furthering through time the bringing about at the end of time of what God had "spoken of Abraham." Personalization of the union between a man and a woman is to be sought on the interpersonal level, in the presence of God, with the acceptance of responsibility for the historic destiny of all Israel. That is what Jewish ethics means by marriage and family. That is what we mean by the marriage formula: "You are sanctified to me in accordance with the law of Moses and Israel."

VII

We have analyzed what we consider to be the basic principles of a Jewish sexual ethics that may be crystallized from Jewish tradition. We shall now deal with some of the consequences for actual behavior that follow from these principles.

Originally, it was customary for marriages to be arranged by a match-maker or even through a *shaliah* (an agent with the power of attorney), without the groom and bride seeing each other first. However, Rav, one of the most authoritative teachers of the Talmud in the second century, taught: "It is forbidden for a man to espouse a woman without having seen her first, for he might find some blemish in her that might alienate him from her." Significantly, the reasoning why such a situation should be prevented from arising is based on the biblical verse: "You shall love your neighbor as yourself."[32] In other words, not simply because of possible disappointment, but because the personal relationship of love between one human being and another may be prevented from becoming a reality.

Another teaching of Rav should be read in a similar light. Child marriages were once an acceptable practice, but Rav declared: A father is forbidden to give his minor daughter in marriage until she has sufficiently grown to be able to say: "This is the man I want to marry."[33] Rav also warned people against marrying for the sake of money.[34] The words of the Bible, that you should not go astray "after your own heart and after your own eyes," were interpreted a generation earlier by Rav's teacher, R. Yehuda Hanasi, editor of the Mishna, as including the warning: "A man shall not drink from one cup while setting an eye on another." Several generations later, another teacher in the Talmud applied this not only to a case when a man is intimate with his wife while thinking of a strange woman, but even to a case of polygamy where a man is thinking of another one of his wives.[35] Another talmudic teacher, R. Asi, taught that a man is forbidden to compel his wife to have intercourse. Others before him had already enjoined that a man should be extremely considerate in intimacy with his wife. He should be aware of her needs, he should please her before the intercourse, he should communicate with her before the act and even during it, bringing joy to her.[36] In a striking passage, R. Levi, also of the second century, gave a rather surprising interpretation to the following words of God through the prophet Ezekiel: "And I will purge out from among you the rebels and them that transgress against me...."[37] Says R. Levi: "These are the people who compel their wives into intercourse, who are intimate with their wives even though they hate them... who quarrel with them when they are together, who have sexual relationships while drunk, who engage in the sex act even though they have already divorced their wives in their hearts...."[38] The medieval commentators explain this passage with particular reference to the drunk. One says: His sex act is not true union but an act of prostitution, for he is bent only on the act itself. Another says: Because of his drunkenness, he does not consider his wife at all.

Because of the nature of the relationship between man and woman, all these rules of sexual behavior are enjoined on the husband. But there are also some statements which speak of the conduct of the wife in the sex act. For example: "Our masters said: 'When a woman lies with her husband and thinks of a man whom she saw in the road, there is no greater lewdness than that.'"[39] The very strong phrasing is an indication that from the point of view of the most intimate interpersonal relationship, this was considered a worse degradation of its moral character than even the act of outright sexual unfaithfulness. All these rules and principles of behavior have one thing in common: They all aim at the elimination of the impersonal from the sexual union and its consecration through personalization. They are equally binding on both sexes. They are directed against using another person as a sex object. In accordance with talmudic methodology, the rules are usually derived from, or homiletically related to, some verse in the Bible. Most impressive, however, is the statement of R. Levi, who, as we saw, applied the terms "rebels and transgressors against God" to people who degrade the satisfaction of their sensual desires to the level of the wholly impersonal. It is considered rebellion and transgression against God. This is in keeping with our main thesis. Personalization includes relatedness to the divine purpose. Sex indulged on the impersonal level is not only a degradation of one's sexual partner, but also a rejection of what God intended sex to be.

A few more words have yet to be said on the question of birth control. Does our presentation not exclude it completely? This is not the place to give a comprehensive or even somewhat adequate discussion of the subject.[40] It should be stated, however, that Jewish sexual ethics does not insist that the sex act always be directed towards procreation. If that were so, marriage could not continue beyond the wife's childbearing age. Marriage to a woman who was not fertile would then be against Jewish law. While at one time such a marriage was to be dissolved after ten years, the custom is—as explicitly stated in the *Shulhan Aruch*—no longer to be observed.[41] Cases of actual birth control, permitted or even required, are discussed in the Talmud and ruled upon in the codes.[42] Special cases of rape, of threat to the health of the mother, and numerous others have been discussed in the rich responsum literature through the ages. It is not the intention of our presentation to give rulings in specific cases. What we should bear in mind is that whenever birth control is permissible or even mandatory, or when a certain union, even though childless, is yet to be maintained, what then follows in practice is, just because it is done in the light of the teaching of the Tora, still an act of personal relatedness to God, the creator of life. Because it is undertaken in conscious accordance with Judaism, one acts then in full awareness of one's responsibility towards the divine purpose that seeks its realization through us.

Jews today disagree as to what extent Judaism requires of them that they adhere to the interpretation of halacha as promulgated by one or the other trend within Judaism. It seems to us, however, indisputable that anyone who desires to live his life as a Jew will have to adopt a sexual ethics whose goal it must be to personalize his sexual relationship on the threefold level that we have indicated: The interpersonal, as between man and woman; the cosmic, as between God and man; and the historic, as between the individual Jew and the destiny of the Jewish people through the ages. Of a union established on such foundations, R. Akiva would say: If a man and a woman are worthy, the divine Presence dwells in their union.[43] Through their achievement in the personalization of their relationship, their life together makes room for God within the bio-psychic fulfillment of human existence—for a God not of asceticism or of life-denying spirituality, but of life-affirming and life-desiring sanctification.

5

THE BIBLICAL IDEA
OF JUSTICE

(1969)

TO UNDERSTAND what is meant in the Bible by justice, it is necessary to examine the various uses to which the noun *mishpat* ("justice") and the verb *shafat* ("to judge") are put. *Mishpatim* are rules, laws, or ordinances, which are often mentioned together with *hukim*, statutes, which God gave to the children of Israel that they perform them and live by them. They cover a wide area of civil, criminal, and ritual law.

Often *mishpat* is the case before the court, the entire process of administering the law. When the Bible says, "You shall not respect persons in *mishpat*; you shall hear the small and the great alike; you shall not be afraid of the face of any man,"[1] the term is not used in the narrower sense of judgment. The injunction refers to the entire conduct of the case in court. *Mishpat* is the suit before the judge. When the daughters of Zelophehad made their claim to the possession which was due their father, the Bible says: "And Moses brought their *mishpat* before the Eternal."[2] Moses brought their case before God, as well as the question of whether their claim was justified or not. We do not think that King Solomon asked God for an understanding heart to discern judgment or justice in the abstract.[3] He asked for understanding *lishmoa mishpat*, to hear wisely, with the proper insight, the suits brought before his court.

Mishpat may also mean the specific verdict delivered in a certain case, the judgment delivered by a judge. *Mishpat* is, for instance, used in this sense in the case of King Solomon, who judged the case of the two women before him.[4] In one place, at least, *mishpat* stands for the place where justice is administered: "Therefore the wicked shall not stand in the *house of justice* (*bamishpat*), nor the sinners in the congregation of the righteous."[5] This translation is suggested by the parallelism, which the verse seems to demand.

Mishpat may also mean the law in the abstract sense. This is how it is used, for instance, in the verse: "You shall have one manner of *mishpat*, as well for the stranger as for the home-born."[6] This injunction employs the concept of *mishpat* as the general idea of a law equally binding on all people. However, *mishpat* may also mean, simply, justice. When Abraham exclaims before God, "Shall the Judge of all the earth not do *mishpat*?"[7] what he means is: Shall not God himself act justly, shall he not enact justice?

Obviously, all these various meanings derive from the basic idea of what is meant by *mishpat* or *shafat*. It is normally understood that basically these words mean law and justice or judging in accordance with the law and administering justice. What is the meaning that the Bible itself expresses by these terms?

Often, the meaning seems indeed to be: Justice, judgment in accordance with strict principles of justice, the full application of the law in all its consequence; so that the psalmist has reason to say: "My flesh shudders for fear of you; and I am afraid of your judgments."[8] There is reason to fear the *mishpat* of God, even though in the same context the psalmist has occasion to affirm that "Righteous are you, O Eternal, and upright are your judgments."[9] To judge may even mean to execute judgment, so that *mishpat*, or its verb form, becomes the equivalent of punishment. The psalmist speaks of this kind of *mishpat* when he prays: "I know, O Eternal, that your judgments are righteous, and that in faithfulness you have afflicted me."[10] God's *mishpatim* in this case were judgments actually executed which were the psalmist's affliction. Quite often this is the significance of *mishpat*. It is the punishment following the judgment and in accordance with it. We shall quote a few important examples of this usage.

Isaiah once expresses God's indignation over the nations in the words: "For my sword has drunk its full in heaven; behold, it shall come down upon Edom, and upon the people of my ban, for *mishpat*."[11] Needless to say, the sword does not come down in order to judge Edom, but in order to execute the judgment already passed over Edom—in other words, to punish. In the same sense Ezekiel speaks of the doing of *mishpat* by God.[12] When Jeremiah announces the downfall of Moab, he introduces the terrible description of its collapse with the words, "And *mishpat* is come upon the country of the plain." He repeats the same phrase at the close of his prophecy of doom, saying: "Thus far is the *mishpat* of Moab."[13]

Of the fallen Babylon it is said:

> We would have healed Babylon, but she is not healed;
> Forsake her, and let us go everyone into his own country;
> For her *mishpat* reaches unto heaven,
> And is lifted up even to the skies.[14]

If Babylon cannot be healed, she must already be afflicted. The *mishpat* that reaches unto heaven is the measure of her punishment. Because of the vastness of the punishment, Babylon cannot be healed. In the prophecy concerning the future of the house of Eli, which was intimated to the young Samuel, God did not say—as the translations would have it—that he would judge Eli's house forever. A judgment is pronounced once; there is no such thing as a continuous judging for a crime once committed. What God said was that the punishment would not depart from Eli's house. As it is also stated explicitly "that the iniquity of Eli's house shall not be expiated... forever."[15] The prophet Zephaniah calls upon the daughter of Zion to sing and to be glad and rejoice for

> The Eternal has taken away your *mishpatim*,
> He has cast out your enemy;
> The King of Israel, even the Eternal, is in the midst of you;
> You shall not fear evil any more.[16]

Again, quite clearly, *mishpatim* are not only judgments, but judgments already executed which afflict the daughter of Zion. This comes to expression more dramatically in the Hebrew original, which should better be rendered: "The Eternal has *removed* your *mishpatim*." Something to which they have already been subject is taken from them. The enemy has already entered Zion. But now that this punishment, the *mishpat*, has been removed from them and God, instead of the enemy, dwells in their midst, there is nothing to be feared.

In all the cases which we have quoted, and in numerous others, *mishpat* stands for the strictness of the law and its implementation. And God is the judge who executes such justice and law. It is in view of this aspect of divine activity that it is said of God in Deuteronomy that "the Eternal your God, he is God of gods, and Lord of lords, the great God, the mighty and the awful, who regards no persons, nor takes reward."[17] It is the description of the mighty and powerful judge who is impartial and who cannot be deterred from his course of executing judgment. It is, however, important to note that immediately after these words the text continues: "He does execute justice for the fatherless and widow, and loves the stranger, in giving him food and raiment."[18] This very stern judge, who "regards no persons," does regard the fatherless and widow. He exacts justice for their sake. His insistence on justice is motivated by his concern for the weak and the oppressed. He executes justice just as he loves the stranger. Because of his love for the oppressed, he judges the oppressor. He may be "awful" as he judges, but he judges because he is "a father of the fatherless and a judge of the widows."[19] As terrifying as he may appear to those whom he judges, as comforting is he to those for whose sake he executes judgment. God's insistence on justice is dictated by his concern for those to whom justice is denied.

It is for this reason that the biblical command to do justice is so often connected with the injunction to protect the rights of the weak and helpless. Typical of this attitude is the commandment in Exodus: "You shall not wrest the judgment of your poor in his cause. Keep far from a false matter; and the innocent and the righteous slay not; for I will not justify the wicked."[20] Any justification of the wicked is not only an offense against an abstract ideal of justice, but the actual betrayal of the poor and the innocent. Every perversion of justice is also the imposition of suffering on someone who is unable to defend himself against it. It is with the one who is so imposed upon that the biblical demand for justice is concerned. As it is also written: "You shall not pervert the justice due to the stranger, or to the fatherless; nor take the widow's raiment to pledge. But you shall remember that you were a bondman in Egypt, and the Eternal your God redeemed you thence; therefore I command you to do this thing."[21]

It is the continually recurring accusation of the prophets that the people do not espouse the cause of the poor and the oppressed, that their denial of justice to the fatherless and needy is what brings on the anger of God. Jeremiah, for instance, expressed it in indelible words:

> They are waxen fat, they are become sleek;
> Yea, they undertake deeds of wickedness;
> They plead not the cause, the cause of the fatherless,
> That they might make it to prosper;
> And the right of the needy they do not judge.
> Shall I not punish for these things?
> Says the Eternal;
> Shall not my soul be avenged
> On such a nation as this?[22]

It is the denial of justice that causes God to exact justice. His anger has its source in the compassion for those who, by the denial of the justice due to them, are made to carry the yoke of human wickedness. When God calls upon the people to repent and to purify themselves, he says to them through the mouth of his prophet Isaiah:

> Wash you, make you clean,
> Put away the evil of your doings
> From before my eyes,
> Cease to do evil;
> Learn to do well,
> Seek justice, relieve the oppressed,
> Judge the fatherless, plead for the widow.[23]

To seek justice is to relieve the oppressed. But how else is the oppressed to be relieved if not by judging the oppressor and crushing his ability to oppress? History is not a Sunday school where the question is whether to forgive or not to forgive. The toleration of injustice is the toleration of human suffering. Since the proud and the mighty, who inflict the suffering, do not as a rule yield to moral persuasion, responsibility for the sufferer demands that justice be done so that oppression be ended. When the psalmist calls on God, "to whom vengeance belongs,"[24] to render to the proud their recompense, his concern is not with the principle of justice that has been violated, nor with the letter of the law that must be fulfilled. What does concern him he states clearly when he follows up his call to "the Judge of the earth"[25] with the words:

> O Eternal, how long shall the wicked,
> How long shall the wicked exult?
> They gush out, they speak arrogance;
> All the workers of iniquity bear themselves loftily.
> They crush your people, O Eternal,
> And afflict your heritage.
> They slay the widow and the stranger,
> And murder the fatherless.
> And they say: The Eternal will not see,
> Neither will the God of Jacob give heed.[26]

The psalmist's concern is with the reality of an intolerable human situation. God's people are being afflicted and crushed. Who are the people of God? They are represented by the widow, the stranger, and the fatherless. They are the weak, the helpless, the oppressed, and the persecuted. Compassion for them, love for them, demands that an end be put to the arrogance and power of the proud and the wicked. God must see and give heed. Love for man is at the root of the demand for justice. All injustice is human suffering. Once more we quote the words of the psalmist to illustrate the intrinsic connection which exists between the two in the biblical interpretation of the reality of human existence. Of God, who made heaven and earth and "who keeps the truth forever,"[27] the psalmist also says:

> Who executes justice for the oppressed,
> Who gives bread to the hungry.
> The Eternal looses the prisoners;
> The Eternal opens the eyes of the blind;
> The Eternal raises up them that are bowed down;
> The Eternal loves the righteous;
> The Eternal preserves the strangers;
> He upholds the fatherless and the widow;
> But the way of the wicked he makes crooked.[28]

Justice alone will not feed the hungry or raise up those who are bowed down, but without justice neither of these acts of kindness and compassion can be performed. The love for the righteous and the concern for the stranger will be mere sentimentalism if injustice is permitted to be rampant. One cannot uphold the fatherless and the widow without at the same time protecting them against the arrogance of the mighty. One must make the way of the wicked "crooked." One must not let it lead to its goal, if the way of the innocent is to be straight before them. There is no other alternative in history.

II

The purpose of judgment is to save the innocent from injustice. The idea is so deeply anchored in biblical thought that "to judge" becomes the equivalent of "to save." Of the terrible anger of God the psalmist says: "You caused sentence to be heard from heaven; the earth feared, and was still. When God arose *to judgment, to save* all the humble of the earth."[29] God judges in order to save. Ezekiel expressed the same idea in the following manner: "Because you thrust with side and with shoulder, and push all the weak with your horns, till you have scattered them abroad; therefore will I *save* my flock, and they shall be no more a prey; and I will *judge* between cattle and cattle."[30] He who wants to save the flock must judge between cattle and cattle. Isaiah says it in his own majestic style:

> My favor is near,
> My salvation is gone forth,
> And my arms shall judge the peoples;
> The isles shall wait for me,
> And in my arm shall they trust.[31]

If salvation is to go forth, judgment is to be instituted. And indeed from numerous passages in the Bible emerges the idea that the function of the judge is to save. In the case of unintentional homicide, the Bible decrees:

> Then the congregation shall *judge* between the smiter and the avenger of blood according to these ordinances; and the congregation shall *deliver* the manslayer out of the hand of the avenger of blood, and the congregation shall restore him to his city of refuge.[32]

The commandment to judge is the responsibility to deliver. According to Jeremiah God speaks to the house of David, saying:

Execute justice in the morning,
And *deliver* the spoiled out of the hand of the oppressor,
Lest my fury go forth like fire,
And burn that none can quench it,
Because of the evil of your doings.[33]

The association between judgment and deliverance is so intimate that they are, at times, interchangeable. Isaiah, for instance, could say: "We look for *mishpat,* but there is none; for salvation (*y'shu'a*), but it is far off from us."[34] The justice or judgment they were looking for would have been their salvation.

In two places in Samuel, the verb *shafat* actually means to save. David, fleeing and hiding from Saul, on one occasion confronts his enemy with the words: "The Eternal therefore be judge, and give sentence between me and you, and see and plead my cause, and deliver me out of your hand."[35] The English translation, as so often, hides what is the most characteristic feature of the Hebrew original. In our case it is the phrase which is here rendered as "and deliver me out of your hand." The Hebrew says: *Veyishpeteni miyadecha,* which, translated literally, yields, "and judge me out of your hand." Of course, one cannot say it this way in English, because in English to judge does not mean to deliver. But it is essential for the understanding of the biblical concept of justice to know that the Bible does say it so. Needless to say, judge one out of the hand of someone else does mean to deliver him. The Hebrew phraseology underlines the connection between judging and saving; the English translation hides it.

How dangerous is such inattention to the implied meaning of the Hebrew idiom, one may realize by examining carefully two passages in the book of Samuel. The tragic story of Absalom's rebellion against his father ended with Absalom's death. The question arose of who should bring the news to the king. At first Ahima'atz volunteered. He said: "Let me now run, and bear the king tidings, how the Eternal has avenged him of his enemies."[36] Joab, however, did not allow Ahima'atz to go. Instead, the Cushite was sent. When the Cushite stood before the king, he communicated the news of the death of Absalom in terms very similar to those proposed by Ahima'atz. He said to David: "Tidings for my lord the king; for the Eternal has avenged you this day of all those who rose up against you."[37]

Nothing could be more misleading than such a translation.[38] There is nothing in the Bible about God's having avenged David of his enemies.

The Hebrew idiom in both these passages is identical with the one used by David himself, when he confronted Saul and asked that God be judge between them. It is *shafat... miyad.* For some reason both the Revised Version and the Jewish Publication Society edition translate the phrase when spoken by David as "to deliver from the hand of," but when spoken to David as "to avenge someone of." In writing English there may be justification for such literary freedom. But in translating, the disregard for the Hebrew idiom is a form of rewriting the biblical text in a manner that actually misrepresents biblical thought. As in the case of David, so also in that of Ahima'atz and the Cushite, *shafat... miyad* means the same thing: To deliver one from the hand of someone else. Only in Hebrew, because to judge in Hebrew is also to save, we say: To judge someone out of the hand of someone else. What Ahima'atz and the Cushite actually said was rather different from what the translations maintain that they said. They did not speak of vengeance, but of deliverance. Ahima'atz's words were: "Let me now run, and bear the king tidings, how the Eternal has delivered [judged] him out of the hand of his enemies." The Cushite, too, expressed himself similarly, using the same idiomatic phrase and saying: "Tidings for my lord the king; for the Eternal has delivered [judged] you this day out of the hand of all those who rose up against you."

We are now in a position to understand a rather unusual title that the leaders of the Jewish people had at a certain time in history. After Joshua, and up to the election of Saul to kingship, the leaders of Israel were called Judges. But why Judges? They were of course judges, too, but that was not their chief function. They were the heads of the people, fulfilling the function that later on was that of the kings. It is strange that they should have been called Judges. However, it is strange for us only if the meaning of the word is its meaning in the English language. The title, however, is quite proper if we attempt to think in biblical terms. What does the Bible say about the Judges?

> And the Eternal raised up *judges*, who *saved* them out of the hand of those who spoiled them.... And when the Eternal raised them up *judges*, then the Eternal was with the judge, and *saved* them out of the hand of their enemies all the days of the judge.[39]

This makes, of course, very poor sense in English. Since when is it the task of judges to save their people out of the hand of their enemies? This sounds altogether different in Hebrew, especially as one recalls that instead of "who saved them out of the hand of those who spoiled them," one could almost say "who judged them out of their hands"; or as one remembers that, as we saw, Isaiah uses *mishpat* (judgment) and *y'shu'a* (salvation, deliverance) as parallels. Since to judge in Hebrew may well mean to save, the judge may well be the savior or the one through whom God sends deliverance to his people. How inseparable is the function of the judge from that of the savior comes to magnificent expression in the words of Isaiah:

> For the Eternal is our Judge,
> The Eternal is our Lawgiver,
> The Eternal is our King;
> He will save us.[40]

III

However, the positive meaning of the biblical concept of justice is not yet adequately understood. We have learned that to judge means the passionate rejection and combating of injustice, protection of the innocent and the poor and weak. In this way, the term seems to achieve its significance as an act of deliverance. But as yet, we have not discovered the contents of the idea of *mishpat* itself. What is the biblical concept of justice? Of what does biblical justice consist?

It is probably the most surprising aspect of the idea of *mishpat* that it is able to keep comfortable company in the Bible with such other biblical ideas as *hesed* (love or loving-kindness), *rahamim* (compassion or mercy), and *tzedaka* (any good deed not obligatory upon the doer—or, simply, charity).[41] In Jeremiah, for instance, God is called "the Eternal, who exercises loving-kindness (*hesed*), justice (*mishpat*), and charity (*tzedaka*)."[42] Even a single passage like this one ought to suffice to show that the biblical *mishpat* is not to be confused with the idea of justice as it is understood in the context of Western civilization. It is doubtful that in Western thought a single text might be found to parallel this one in Jeremiah, in which justice is placed between loving-kindness and charity. Within the sphere of Western culture and religion, the three concepts cannot be coordinated. Justice there is opposed to loving-kindness as well as to charity. For the Western mind, he who exercises loving-kindness and practices charity forgoes the implementation of justice. *Hesed* and *mishpat*, *tzedaka* and *mishpat* are opposites within the frame of reference of practically all cultures and their religions. A judge is either just or merciful. One exercises either *hesed* or *mishpat*. But no judge may exercise loving-kindness, justice, and charity, and certainly not in that order. One either loves or judges. And God, too, is either a God of love or a God of justice. Not so in the Bible. The meaning of *mishpat* must be different in its essence from that of justice, as the word is understood in most languages, if it is possible to say of God that he exercises loving-kindness, justice, and charity on earth, for "in these things he delights." Most surprising of all is the placing of *mishpat* between *hesed* and *tzedaka*, as if it were the required order, whereas in all Western literature the sequence would be illogical. The logic of the Western mind may be able to move on from justice to love and charity or to charity and love, but never from love to justice and then from justice to charity.

That we are confronted here with a uniquely biblical—and, because of the inevitably misleading translations, hardly ever understood—concept is proven by the fact that the close association between *mishpat*, on the one hand, and *hesed*, *rahamim*, and *tzedaka*, on the other, is a continually recurring theme of the Bible. What is it that God requires of man, according to Jeremiah? To do what God himself does: To do *mishpat* and to love *hesed*, to exercise justice and to love practicing loving-kindness. The European does not know how one may be called upon both to do justice and to exercise loving-kindness. Like Jeremiah, Hosea, too, associates *mishpat* and *hesed*, when he says: "Therefore turn to your God; keep *hesed* and *mishpat*, and wait for your God continually."[43] Even more impressive are the words in Zechariah: "Execute true *mishpat*, and exercise *hesed* (loving-kindness) and *rahamim* (compassion) every man to his brother."[44] Whereas Hosea called upon Israel to keep *hesed* and *mishpat*, Isaiah's admonition is to keep *mishpat* and to do *tzedaka*.[45] *Mishpat*, justice, seems to be a member of the same group of values to which loving-kindness, compassion, and charity, too, belong.

The association between *mishpat* and the other members of the group seems to be even closer than the passages quoted thus far suggest. Isaiah speaks mysteriously about God when he says of him:

And therefore will the Eternal wait, that he may be gracious unto you,

> And therefore will he be exalted, that he may have compassion upon you:
> For the Eternal is a God of justice (*mishpat*),
> Happy are all they that wait for him.[46]

The difficulty of interpretation cannot be overlooked. It is a moving thought that God himself waits impatiently for the right moment to be gracious to Israel and to exercise compassion (*rahamim*) toward them. And as God waits for that moment, so let Israel, too, wait for God. However, the reason given for God's anxious desire to show grace and compassion for Israel requires explanation. How can one say that God is waiting to be gracious and compassionate because he is a God of justice? Is God merciful and gracious because he is just?

The usual translation of *mishpat* as justice, law, or judgment breaks down completely when we hear the psalmist pray:

> Hear my voice according unto your loving-kindness (*hesed*);
> Quicken me, O Eternal, according to your *mishpat*....
> Great are your compassions (*rahamim*), O Eternal;
> Quicken me according to your *mishpatim*.[47]

The words of the psalmist belong to the same world of discourse as those of Isaiah. There is some intrinsic, almost causal connection between *hesed* and *rahamim*, on the one hand, and *mishpat*, on the other. All this compels us to conclude that the biblical concept of *mishpat* has little in common with what the idea of justice connotes in Western thought. What, then, is meant by *mishpat*? What is justice in the Bible?

It would seem that the original meaning of *mishpat* is to be sought on a more primary level of human interest than that of justice or law.

When Joseph interpreted the dream of Pharaoh's butler and told him that the latter would be restored to his office, he said to the butler: "And you shall give Pharaoh's cup into his hand, after the former manner when you were his butler."[48] Now, the Hebrew version of "after the former manner" is: According to the former *mishpat*. Obviously, *mishpat* here is neither justice nor law. It is more habit, the way a thing was customarily done.

There are many examples in the Bible which show this or a related usage of the word *mishpat*. For six days the children of Israel went around the walls of Jericho in a certain order. On the seventh day, says the Bible, they rose early at dawn "and compassed the city after the same manner seven times."[49] On the seventh day they surrounded the city following the same order which they had adopted on the previous days. Again, the Hebrew for "after the same manner" reads: According to the same *mishpat*. On the seventh day they were really following a routine which they had devised on the previous six days. *Mishpat* might well be rendered here as "routine." Of the spies from the tribe of Dan the Bible tells us that they came to the city of Laish "and saw the people that were therein, how they dwelled in security, after the manner of the Zidonians, quiet and secure."[50] For "after the manner of the Zidonians" we have in the Hebrew: "According to the *mishpat* of the Zidonians." *Mishpat* here would be a certain manner of living, a certain style of conduct.

Mishpat may even mean the character, appearance, or nature of someone or something. Ahaziah, king of Israel, sent messengers to Ekron to inquire of its god whether he would recover from his sickness. The prophet Elijah met the messengers on the way and sent them back to the king with the message that he would die. When they came before the king, he asked them: "What manner of man was he that came up to meet you, and told you these words?" Their answer was: "He was a hairy man, and girt with a girdle of leather about his loins."[51] For "what manner of man" we have in the original: "What was the *mishpat* of the man?" meaning: What were his characteristic marks? What was typical of him? Of the heathen population which was transplanted from Babylon to Samaria, the Bible tells: "They feared the Eternal, and served their own gods, after the manner of the nations from among whom they had been carried away."[52] Here, too, "after the manner" corresponds to "according to the *mishpat*," that is, according to the customs.

The word *mishpat* is used in a most interesting context in the book of Samuel. The people ask for a king. God tells Samuel to listen to their request and says: "But you shall earnestly forewarn them and shall declare unto them the manner of the king who shall reign over them."[53] "The manner of the king" is *mishpat hamelech*, which is described as the way he would rule over them, making the people his servants, exacting tribute for his personal aggrandizement, taking from them the fruit of their labor. *Mishpat* is here the custom of the king, the manner in which he usually exercises his authority, the way he acts toward his people. One can, of course, easily see how customs of a king, and of a people as well, may one day be regarded as laws, yet we have to bear in mind that the original meaning of *mishpat hamelech* is the manner in which the king customarily exercises his authority. It is the characteristic mark or nature of kingship, the way in which kings behave.

What can be said of kings may also be said of God. When the king of Assyria first settled people from the provinces of his empire in Samaria, they were plagued by wild animals as a punishment from God, whom they refused to acknowledge. The explanation given to the king was that this visitation came over the new settlers because they "know not the manner of the God of the land."[54] Here, too, the manner is the *mishpat* of God. According to the understanding of the Assyrians, the God of the land, like the gods of other lands, had his customary way of behavior; he ruled over the land in a certain manner and was wont to make certain demands on the inhabitants of the land. To know his ways was to know his *mishpat*. And he who wished to live securely in the land had to adjust himself to the *mishpat* of God. Such was the Assyrians' understanding of the matter. Yet it was not too far from the truth. None other than the prophet Jeremiah spoke in similar language of the *mishpat* of God. Desperate over the stubbornness of his people who refused to return to God, the prophet said:

> And I said, "Surely these are poor,
> They are foolish, for they know not the way of the Eternal,
> The *mishpat* of their God.
> I will get me unto the great men,
> And will speak to them;
> For they know the way of the Eternal,
> The *mishpat* of their God";
> But these had altogether broken the yoke,
> And burst the bands....
> Their transgressions are many,
> Their backslidings are increased.[55]

Careful attention to the Hebrew syntax shows that *mishpat* in our text is synonymous with *derech*, way.[56] The *mishpat* of their God is not another object of their ignorance, but an explanatory parallelism to "the way of the Eternal." This causes no difficulty of interpretation if we recall that *mishpat* means manner of action or customary behavior. As the Assyrians spoke of "the *mishpat* of the God of the land," so did Jeremiah, too, use the phrase "the *mishpat* of their God." Taken in this sense, the *mishpat* of God is indeed synonymous with the way of the Eternal.

It is in this sense that the psalmist uses the term *mishpat* in the surprising passage that we quoted above:

> Hear my voice according unto your loving-kindness (*hesed*);
> Quicken me, O Eternal, according to your *mishpat*....
> Great are your compassions (*rahamim*), O Eternal;
> Quicken me according to your *mishpatim*.[57]

It is God's *mishpat*, his way, his manner of acting toward his creation, to grant life and strength to those whose strength is failing. He does this according to his loving-kindness (*hesed*) and his compassion (*rahamim*). In this sense, both *hesed* and *rahamim* might be considered God's *mishpat*, God's customary way of exercising providence.[58]

Needless to say that Jeremiah's understanding of "the manner of their God" was rather different from what the Assyrians meant by "the manner of the God of the land." For them the *mishpat* of God was probably quite similar to the *mishpat* of the king, as it was presented to the people by Samuel. All lands had their gods, and all gods had their own ways. For Jeremiah the *mishpat* of God, the way he acted, the manner in which he ruled the universe, the way he treated man and was concerned about his creation, was the right way; the way one ought to act. God's way with his creation is God's law for his creation. God's law for man emanates from God's way with man. All law is God's way, appropriately reflected onto the realm of human existence. All biblical law, in a sense, is *imitatio dei*. To practice *hesed* and *rahamim*, which is the way of God, thus itself is God's law for man. This is in keeping with the numerous passages in the Bible to which we have referred earlier in our presentation and which require of man that he act in loving-kindness, compassion, and charity. But of course, *mishpat* is also used in a specific sense, in which—as we saw—it is coordinated with *hesed*, *rahamim*, and *tzedaka*. It must be one specific aspect of God's way with the world which may become, in its application to human conduct, *mishpat* in the specific sense of justice and right. What is the material content of such *mishpat*? Can we define it?

There are a few passages in the Bible which may help us in our effort to define it. A well-known passage in Isaiah provides a useful starting point:

Who has measured the waters in the hollow of his hand,
And meted out heaven with the span,
And comprehended the dust of the earth in a measure,
And weighed the mountains in scales,
And the hills in a balance?
Who has meted out the spirit of the Eternal?
Or who was his counselor that he might instruct him,
With whom took he counsel, and who instructed him,
And taught him in the path of *mishpat*,
And taught him knowledge,
And made him know the way of discernment? [59]

What could be the meaning of *mishpat* in this context? It does not seem to be an ethical or legal concept. The text emphasizes God's omnipotent mastery over the universe and not his dealings with men and nations. In our text *mishpat* is coordinated with counsel, knowledge, and discernment. It must be something upon which understanding and wisdom have some bearing. Now, we may well see how counsel, knowledge, and discernment related to the first verse in our quotation. The measuring of the waters and of the dust of the earth, the meting out of the boundaries of the heavens, the weighing of the mountains and the hills is not just a poetic description of the Almighty's play with his toy, the universe. This measuring and weighing is the establishment of the principle of balance among the various parts of the universe; it is the introduction of the right proportion among the contending forces without which God's creation could not last, but would instead tumble back into the primordial void of *tohu vavohu*.

To have meted out to each its share, and to have placed them in a balanced proportion to each other, that they may stand together, was to have established God's creation as a universe. Such a deed, among men, normally requires counsel, knowledge, understanding. But the prophet exclaims, who was there to be God's counselor and teacher, and who taught him in the path of *mishpat*? There is only one thing left in the text with which we may identify *mishpat*: It is the measuring and the weighing, the establishing of the balance by which alone the universe is able to stand, the bringing together of the various universal forces in harmony so that in mutuality they may constitute the cosmos. This is the way God made the universe, and his way of doing it is the law of the universe. We would then say that *mishpat* here is the cosmic principle of balance and harmony required for the preservation of God's creation.

This *mishpat*, because it is the sustaining law of the universe, embraces the whole of existence, all created reality. Whatever exists is due to its functioning, and man encounters it continually. If man desires to live, he must take cognizance of the ramifications of cosmic *mishpat* in his own sphere of existence and cooperate with them. In a rather surprising passage, the prophet Isaiah describes the implications of *mishpat* in the labors of the plowman:

> Give ear, and hear my voice;
> Attend, and hear my speech.
> Is the plowman never done with plowing to sow,
> With the opening and harrowing of his ground?
> When he has made plain the face thereof,
> Does he not cast abroad the black cumin, and scatter the cumin,
> And put the wheat in rows and the barley in the appointed place
> And the spelt in the border thereof?
> For he does instruct him to *mishpat*;
> His God does teach him.
> For the black cumin is not threshed with a threshing-sledge,
> Neither is a cart-wheel turned about upon the cumin;
> But the black cumin is beaten out with a staff,
> And the cumin with a rod.
> Is bread corn crushed?
> Nay, he will not ever be threshing it;
> And though the roller of his wagon and its sharp edges move noisily,
> He does not crush it.
> This also comes forth from the Lord of Hosts:
> Wonderful is his counsel, and great his wisdom.[60]

The *mishpat* which God teaches the plowman is not essentially different from the one by which, measuring and weighing the various parts of his creation, he establishes their relationship to each other and makes the universe an enduring and functioning entity. It is the same *mishpat* of relatedness and balance, applied to the corner of the world in which the plowman performs his task. How the earth is to be plowed, how the various seeds are to be sown in relationship to each other, how each of the seeds is to be treated after having yielded the hoped-for harvest, all has to be done according to a *mishpat* which is from God and which, like the original comprehensive, universal *mishpat*, reveals God's wonderful counsel and wisdom. But why was it so important for the prophet to draw the attention of the people to the *mishpat* that the plowman has to obey? Surely he was not lecturing to them on the art of agriculture. The point he was making was that *mishpat* is a universal principle. It prevails everywhere, in the realm of the spirit no less than in the realm of nature. As there is an orderliness, an appropriateness, and a balanced relatedness of all things in nature without which life is not possible, so is there also the same kind of *mishpat* in all matters of the spirit. Not to take cognizance of them leads to disaster.

The idea is expressed with somewhat greater clarity by Jeremiah. Complaining about the backsliding of Israel, God, speaking through the mouth of the prophet, says:

> Yea, the stork in the heaven
> Knows her appointed times;
> And the turtle and the swallow and the crane
> Observe the time of their coming;
> But my people know not
> The *mishpat* of the Eternal.[61]

If we understand *mishpat* to mean ordinance, law, or commandment, the comparison between Israel and the seasonal birds who follow their instincts is difficult to interpret. If, however, the *mishpat* of the Eternal is a cosmic principle of measured, balanced relatedness which applies to the whole of life, to the realm of the spirit no less than to the realm of nature, then the meaning of these words of Jeremiah becomes clear. These seasonal birds know their appointed times, they sense the orderliness and interrelatedness in nature, thus they know when to come and when to go; but Israel does not acknowledge the same *mishpat* as it prevails in the spiritual life of the world.

How shall we formulate this cosmic principle of *mishpat* when it is projected onto the scene in which human beings find themselves in contact with each other? Is it not also a weighing and a measuring of claims, drives, and desires, a balancing and harmonizing of the whole with a view to its preservation and its God-intended functioning? Justice and law are like God's *mishpat* in the act of creation: An appropriateness, determined not by abstract consideration, but by the reality of man's condition and subserving the meaningful preservation of human life. Because it is not mere adherence to an abstract principle or ideal, but a principle of order that has its place within the cosmic balance of the coordinated interrelation of all life, it is a justice that is exacting. Its implementation may be frightening, especially when it is done by God himself, who intervenes in the course of history in order to restore the disturbed balance that threatens life itself. Justice is done not that justice prevail, but that life prevail; it is done out of concern with a concrete situation, in which life is endangered and calls for its salvation. Thus, while *mishpat* may be grim, it is always also an act of saving and deliverance. *Hesed*, loving concern for life itself, may well be the source of such *mishpat*.

That *mishpat* means such a principle of measure and appropriateness, whose very purpose is to sustain life, comes to beautiful expression in two passages in Jeremiah. In one place the prophet has Israel pray: "O Eternal, correct me, but in *mishpat*; not in your anger, lest you diminish me."[62] The meaning of *mishpat* here, far from being an exception, reveals its true meaning. It is a principle of preservation; the restoration of a disturbed balance which is needed because life has become unbalanced. As if in answer to this prayer of Israel, Jeremiah also has God speak to Israel and say:

> For I am with you, says the Eternal, to save you;
> For I will make a full end of all the nations whither I have scattered you,
> But I will not make a full end of you;
> For I will correct you in *mishpat*,
> And will not utterly destroy you.[63]

God is with Israel to save it, yet God is also judging Israel to correct it. To save and to judge are not exclusive of each other. The *mishpat* that is imposed may itself have its origin in God's nearness and concern. It is difficult to state exactly where in such *mishpat* loving-kindness ends and objective justice begins. A justice that never loses sight of the actual human situation with which it is benevolently concerned is never wholly objective. Its main concern is not with what is due to a person, but with what may hurt a person. It is not a formal legal concept, but a material, moral one. Of his servant, upon whom he put his spirit, God says in the words of Isaiah that he shall make *mishpat* go forth to the nations. And of his *mishpat* it is said: "A bruised reed shall he not break, and the dimly burning wick shall he not quench; he shall make *mishpat* go forth according to the truth."[64]

Mishpat according to the truth is the non-abstract, the non-objective justice. A justice that does not respect persons in judgment, but does consider their need. It is a justice that does not break, but delivers; and if it breaks, it is in order to deliver. Such justice may easily be coordinated with loving-kindness and compassion, and it may unashamedly call for the practice of charity, as we saw was the case in numerous passages in the Bible. At times, it even merges with *hesed*. Because he is a God of *mishpat*, we heard Isaiah say, he waits for the moment when judgment has passed and he may again be gracious and compassionate toward Israel. When Moses said of God: "The Rock, his work is perfect; for all his ways are *mishpat*,"[65] he could not have meant that all God's ways were justice. That would not be true. According to the entire testimony of the Bible, God is not only just, he is also merciful and long-suffering, compassionate and loving. But he could well have meant the *mishpat* which we have found to be the cosmic principle of the measured balance and harmonized coordination, the divinely implanted appropriateness of the universal order. It is because of that *mishpat* that his work is perfect. Therefore all his ways, along which his work grows, are ways of *mishpat*. But since this *mishpat* is the order of all life and its preservation, one might also say that what God does as *mishpat* is itself *hesed* from the viewpoint of his creation. As indeed the psalmist put it:

All the paths of the Eternal are loving-kindness and faithfulness[66]
Unto such as keep his covenant and his testimonies.[67]

IV

The problem that often occupies man's mind is, however, not that God is a judge who is too exacting, executing justice without mercy and charity, but rather that he so often seems to be indifferent toward the evil perpetrated by man and the suffering of the innocent. It is not the task of this study to discuss the age-old theological problem of theodicy. However, one classical version of theodicy has a direct bearing on our immediate subject. It is the version found in the book of Job.

The story is well known. Job queries the justice of God. One ought to appreciate the seriousness of Job's inner struggle. Not his undeserved suffering is his chief preoccupation, nor the self-righteous affirmation of his innocence. His concern is with the nature of God. How can God be unjust? It is the most serious problem that may perturb a believing soul. It is for this reason that he must reject all the arguments of his friends. The issue is a fundamental concern of religious faith. It must not be blurred over with pious words. How can God be unjust? And we, who read the book and know from the introduction what was hidden from the eyes of Job, also know that what was done to Job was not justice. Demanding justice of God, Job is the great hero of faith who struggles for the honor of his God. He will not rest until he is given an answer, until he understands. For it cannot be, it must not be, that God should not act justly; and yet, he has experienced injustice at the hand of God. The issue must be faced for the sake of God.

The more one senses the believing fervor with which Job struggles to understand the God in whom he puts his trust, the more is one puzzled by God's answer:

> Then the Eternal answered Job out of the whirlwind, and said:
> Gird up your loins now like a man;
> I will demand of you, and declare you unto me.
> Will you even make void my judgment (*mishpat*)?
> Will you condemn me, that you may be justified?
> Or have you an arm like God?
> And can you thunder with a voice like him?
> Deck yourself now with majesty and excellency,
> And array yourself with glory and beauty.
> Cast abroad the rage of your wrath;
> And look upon everyone that is proud, and abase him.
> Look upon everyone that is proud, and bring him low;
> And tread down the wicked in their place.
> Hide them in the dust together;
> Bind their faces in the hidden place.
> Then will I also confess unto you
> That your own right hand can save you.[68]

Upon this reference of God to his own overwhelming power follows the great poetic description of the majestic might of some of his creatures, like the behemoth and leviathan. Can Job compete with that? And God continues:

Who then is able to stand before me?
Who has given me anything beforehand, that I should repay him?
Whatsoever is under the whole heaven is mine.[69]

The more we read on, the more we are surprised at God's answer. The answer seems to sidestep the issue. God owes no one anything—except justice. No one doubted God's omnipotence, but to take a stand on it does not seem to meet Job's quest for divine justice. If one is puzzled by God's answer, one is mystified by Job's reaction to it.

Then Job answered the Eternal, and said:
I know that you can do everything,
And that no purpose can be withheld from you.
Who is this that hides counsel without knowledge?
Therefore have I uttered that which I understood not,
Things too wonderful for me, which I knew not...
I had heard of you by the hearing of the ear;
But now my eye sees you;
Wherefore I abhor my words, and repent,
Seeing I am dust and ashes.[70]

Job is duly impressed by God's omnipotence and omniscience. But what has become of the heroic struggle with the problem of divine justice? Has he been answered or only silenced? One may well understand that God's self-revelation would overwhelm a mere man who would then be willing to abhor and repent the words which he had uttered; but then, after having posed the question mightily, we are left without an answer. Yet Job's conduct after God has revealed himself to him suggests that somewhere along the line Job was given an answer which brought peace to his anguished soul.

A great deal has been written on the mystery of the conclusion of the book. It would seem, however, that a great deal depends on the proper understanding of the word *mishpat* in the key line in God's answer: "Will you even make void my *mishpat*?" If we translate the word in this context as justice, or as judgment, then indeed what follows becomes rather questionable. It would seem to us that such an interpretation is excluded by the very words spoken by God to Eliphaz after the denouement. When all was said, God turned to him with the words:

My wrath is kindled against you, and against your two friends; for you have not spoken of me the thing that is right, as my servant Job has.[71]

One may wonder: If the answer to Job was that one should not dare question the justice of an omnipotent God, in which way did Job speak rightly about God, whereas his friends did not? Were not the arguments of his friends rather similar to the ultimate answer which he was given, namely, that one must not question God's justice? Having done just that, having demanded justice even of God, in which way did Job speak of God "the thing that is right"?

Therefore it may be reasonable to conclude that "Will you even make void my *mishpat*?" does not mean, Dare you question my justice (or judgment, in the sense of executing justice)? Job did say the right thing about God. What was done to him was not justice. He did ask the right question: How can God be unjust? Job spoke correctly about God, unlike his friends who tried to defend what was not justice as God's just judgment. They were distorting justice in order to defend God. That was speaking wrongly about God. God does not stand for the bending of justice for the greater glory of his name. He is a just God. But he is God and not man. Apart from justice, he also has other considerations in the management of his universe, like—for instance—the terrifying testing of the faith of the righteous, as was the case with Job. Such a thing cannot be justified on the basis of justice. But it may have its place within God's *mishpat*, if we understand the term in the sense of the cosmic principle of universal appropriateness, as we found it used in Isaiah: "Will you even make void my *mishpat*?" means: "Will you invalidate the way in which I run the universe?" So understood, the mocking challenge to Job, whether he had an arm like God, whether he could thunder like God, was justified. God was not reproaching Job for having doubted the justness of what befell him. But God taught him that in the plan of a universal Creator there are other considerations, too, apart from that of justice alone, whose validity may be understood only from the viewpoint of the Creator alone. In order to understand God's *mishpat*, the principle of cosmic appropriateness by which he sustains his creation, one would have to be God himself.

If we said earlier that the ways of God with men become the laws of God for men, it applies only to the extent to which those ways may be projected onto the human scene. Insofar, however, as God's way is God's *mishpat* as the cosmic order of divinely envisaged appropriateness, no *imitatio dei* is possible. Thus, in history, a chasm may open between the way of God that is just and the one that, though not justice, is nonetheless *mishpat*. And the heart of faith, which alone may bridge the chasm, plays with the thought that in the end, when all is known, even God's inscrutable *mishpat* may turn out to be one of those paths of God, of which it has been said that they all are loving-kindness and faithfulness.

II

JEWISH NATIONHOOD

6

ON THE RETURN
TO JEWISH NATIONAL LIFE

(1943)

TODAY WE ARE just as far from solving the religious and cultural problems of modern Jewry as we were when these problems first appeared in the last century. The position of the Jews, however, is much worse now than it was then. We no longer have the strength and vitality of the ghetto behind us. Instead we see a succession of gradually declining Jewish generations. This is not very encouraging. Much of our former strength has been wasted. We are very much weaker than, say, 150 years ago. Besides, today we are living in a restless world, a world of gigantic transformations in which the fundamentals of human life are being critically reviewed. The whole world is being recast. Amid these transformations—which, as usual, are especially felt and suffered by Jews—we carry the additional load of our own problems. In such circumstances, to prepare the Jewish future, after an unfortunate period of misapplied Jewish emancipation, is a task more formidable than probably any other that a Jewish generation has had to face since the exile. It will not do for us to unload our difficulties onto others. For in this respect the nations are very honest; they always return the load to us whenever we try to discard it. Besides, however keen Jewish youth may be on building a happier world, we shall never find our place in it unless we have already managed to solve the problems of Judaism. But before this can happen, we have to face unflinchingly and sincerely the real problem of our existence.

Elsewhere I have tried to show how both Liberal and Orthodox Judaism have failed in their attempts.[1] In fact, as theologies or philosophies both already belong to the past (in practice they may persist through inertia for quite a long time). What we have to consider is why they have failed. From the very beginning, it seems both attempts were doomed to failure. In order to understand this, we must consider one important aspect of our exile: The rigidity of the structure of Judaism as it has been handed down to us.

Our Judaism, as we know it today, is based on the Talmud. Now, the Talmud is a very great work. It is tragic that, under the influence of ignorant and mischievous non-Jewish misrepresentation, there are so many Jews who look upon it as a work of hair-splitting Pharisaism. On the contrary, it is a wonderfully vivid record of the religious, cultural, and social life of the entire Jewish nation, covering a period of at least seven centuries (this without taking into account the old and usually anonymous parts of the Mishna which go back almost to biblical times). There is every reason for a Jew to take pride in this great creation of his nation.

The antecedents of talmudic Judaism were far different from those of contemporary Christian civilization. Its memories went back to Ezra and Nehemiah, to Isaiah and Jeremiah, to Hosea and Amos; its actual everyday life was imbued with the Bible. The Talmud came into existence because a whole nation, and not just a few saints, took the Bible seriously, and tried to make it the foundation of their everyday life. The teachers of the Talmud wore the mantle of the prophets. It is, therefore, misleading to say that the Talmud closed about 500 C.E. It would be more correct to say that it was concluded 1,300 years after Isaiah. When the last word was inserted in the Talmud, Judaism was looking back over thirteen centuries of prophetic teaching. This was not the world of 500 C.E. Thirteen hundred years of prophetic tradition, lived and taught, produced a world much nearer to us than to its contemporary Christian world. The great teachers of the Talmud are even today "modern personalities" in a much deeper sense than many of the great Europeans ever have been. Their message is still to be taken to heart, although it is the message of a life that was actually lived many centuries ago.

Since its conclusion, all religious and spiritual authority in Judaism has been centered within the Talmud. Every decision in Jewish life, great or small, has been taken in accordance with talmudic authority. This was a historic necessity in the life of a nation that had no state of its own, that was dispersed all over the world, its branches continually in danger of extermination. Such a nation had to vest its unifying authority somewhere where it did not depend on either geography or material well-being, the two factors over which the Jewish people had no control. The Talmud became the spiritual authority—voluntarily accepted by the whole nation. Jews were persecuted, murdered, hunted throughout the world, catastrophe following upon catastrophe; but the unifying authority remained firm all the while, for it was rooted in the voluntary acceptance of spiritual values. The Talmud was the most successful experiment in the history of national constitutions, in that it functioned without executive power and without compulsion. It preserved a whole nation against the continuously stupid and wicked enmity of the entire world. That, notwithstanding its physical weakness, there still exists a Jewish nation which has witnessed the breakdown of mighty empires and vast tyrannies, that it is still there, young in spite of the heavy disappointments—all this we owe to the Talmud.

Nevertheless, we made a very serious sacrifice in constituting that great work as it stood at 500 C.E., as the only authority in Judaism, an authority that could be commented upon but never overruled. Until the end of the fifth century C.E., authority rested in living institutions—in the land of Israel in the office of the *nasi*, the prince of the Jews, and his court; in Babylon in the person of the exilarch, and the heads of the great Babylonian academies. Though these institutions had been losing influence over time (as we shall see later), they were nonetheless *living* authority. Living authority is always elastic, for it has in itself the possibility of development, it is able to make its decisions in accordance with the necessities of life. It can guide and direct life, not in the shape of compromise, but by applying to it the living spirit of tradition, thus not only preserving traditional values but developing them in faithfulness to their intrinsic sense. Living authority is always built upon tradition, but as it is alive it can exist only when there is a possibility of an organic evolution in the application of tradition. When, owing to the hard facts of Jewish history, owing to the insecurity of Jewish life, living authority was no longer practicable, and authority had to be transferred to the book, the Talmud, the records of a once-living authority, Judaism had to sacrifice the possibility of organic development; it renounced the great principle of the evolution of traditional teachings. The structure of Judaism became rigid, for it had lost its evolutionary strength. For many centuries this was not felt to be hampering Jewish existence. The Jewish people was living for the most part amid semi-barbaric surroundings, however high-sounding their names might be, which were at a stage of cultural development far behind the world of the Talmud.

But when, through Jewish emancipation, European Jews entered the circle of modern civilization and experienced the conflict between that new world and their own Jewish world of old, the rigidity which they had taken upon themselves resulted in an inability to adapt, rendering all the important problems arising out of that conflict insoluble. Jews began to share more and more in a life that was rapidly changing, while at the same time they remained in a spiritual and religious world that had lost its capacity to develop. In such a situation, all attempts at reconciliation were doomed to failure. Nothing was possible but the Liberal method of breaking the rigidity and thus breaking Judaism (for there was no other Judaism apart from that which was bound to tradition), or the unsatisfactory compromise of Neo-Orthodoxy, a compromise which had to be renewed with every changing day.

II

In order to understand how serious is the predicament of Judaism, we must not forget that Judaism originally was not lacking in the potential for development. The prophets and their successors, the teachers of the Mishna and Talmud, were not Orthodox Jews in the sense in which we understand the word today; and to try and compare them with anything liberal would be quite devoid of meaning. The Talmud tells us, for instance, that R. Eliezer, in a controversy with R. Yehoshua, called for miracles to testify to the truth of his opinion, and in the end a voice from heaven declared that everywhere the opinion of R. Eliezer was decisive halacha. And yet, R. Yehoshua was able to say, "The Tora is no longer in heaven; we are not obliged to obey the miraculous voice from heaven."[2] Such a Judaism, claiming an independence that could not be influenced either by miracles or even by a direct "message from heaven," was surely not lacking in intellectual courage. In another rabbinic legend, the story is told that when God introduced Moses into the study house of R. Akiva, Moses was unable to follow the lectures of that great master, and regained his peace of mind only when he heard R. Akiva replying to a pupil that what he was teaching was nothing new but in fact a tradition directly "received by Moses from Sinai."[3] A legend like this expresses in a striking manner the evolutionary unfolding of Judaism in the course of Jewish history. Not even Moses himself is able to recognize the Judaism of R. Akiva at first glance, for it is somehow different, something new. Nevertheless, it is still *torat moshe*, the Tora of Moses, for it is indeed his teaching, organically unfolding itself in the life of the nation. Everywhere in the Talmud and midrash we meet this courage to apply the spirit of the ancient word to new situations and in so doing to give the word a new shape. The Tora is not eternal in the sense that it retains for all time that shape in which it was first understood by men. It is eternal because it has the miraculous power to reveal to each generation new meanings which are yet the old ones, which have waited just for this generation to be lifted into the sun of the passing day.

The inflexibility of Judaism, as it has been handed down since the conclusion of the Talmud, is not of the essence of Judaism. The static quality is certainly no religious dogma or article of faith. Had it been so, the exigencies of our life would have jettisoned such a belief long ago, without endangering the essential contents of Judaism. As it is, the rigidity is something far more serious, for it is a concrete fact. Judaism has indeed lost its flexibility, its strength of development. You may override principles; you cannot overlook historic facts. For that reason, any attempt to reform or reshape Judaism must fail. Reform is only possible where there is flexibility. It is folly to treat Judaism today as if it were flexible. Whoever tries to break its rigidity is not building anything new; he is only destroying the old mold that was useful for so many centuries, and that even today is more useful than the shortsighted innovations by which reformist bodies are bringing about the dissolution of Judaism.

Before we can begin to address the predicament of modern Jewry with any hope of success, Judaism must regain its original capacity for development. Nothing will ever be achieved, and we shall ultimately face disaster, if we fail to understand this. Before anything can be done to overcome the dualism of our modern existence, we shall have to bring about those conditions in which alone may Judaism unfold itself naturally, in the line of previous Jewish history.

III

Is it possible to bring about such conditions? On the answer to this question depends the future of Judaism.

It must be said that this great change in the structure of Judaism is at least a theoretical possibility. Whether it will be actually achieved depends on whether Jewry understands the gravity of the present situation, and whether it will concentrate all its spiritual energies on this task.

But before addressing the question of how to effect such a change, we have to examine the causes of rigidity in Judaism. It is not enough to say that with the closing of the Talmud, Judaism lost its evolutionary capacity. For the closing of the Talmud itself was a product of the time: It was in itself the effect of certain historical causes. To understand the underlying causes, we must restate some fundamental facts concerning the nature of Judaism.

The teachings of the Tora were not suspended in mid-air. They were closely related to living human institutions. Judaism looks upon life as the raw material which has to be shaped in conformity with the spiritual values contained in the Bible. Judaism is a great human endeavor to fashion the whole of life, every part and every moment of it, in accordance with standards that have their origin in unchallengeable authority. Its aim is not merely to cultivate the spirit, but to infuse prosaic, everyday existence with the spirit. Its great interest is not the human soul, but the living human body controlled by the forces of the soul. It is in and of this world. It will never yield to the obstinacy of that gigantic mass of raw material which we call life, and which so reluctantly allows itself to be molded by the spirit. It will never reconcile itself to a divided existence of which part is Caesar's and part God's. The whole of life is of one piece; the whole of life is the testing place for man. Judaism is in love with life, for it knows that life is God's great question to mankind; and the way a man lives, what he does with his life, the meaning he is able to implant in it—is man's reply. Actual life is the partner to the spirit; without the one the other is meaningless.

The teachings of the Tora can therefore reveal their real sense only when there is a concrete reality to which they are applied. On the one hand we have Tora, trying to give shape to the raw material of life which is so reluctant and evasive; on the other, each bit of Tora-shaped life: In social institutions, in economic arrangements, in the relations between man and his neighbors, in the street and in the market as well as in the places of worship—living Tora, acting on the very intentions of Sinai. For just as Tora shapes life, so does Tora-shaped life, in its turn, direct and thus unfold Tora. It is as if the Tora were using its own experiences to set the course of its development. And in each new phase, it strives again to fashion our lives, which, once refashioned, will again inform the meaning of the teaching as it has been previously revealed. And so on to eternity: Tora leading life, and Tora-led life unfolding Tora. This is the inner meaning of the partnership between Tora and prosaic, everyday life; and out of this partnership emerges a Judaism capable of unlimited development. It is the spirit developing life, and that life with its new necessities challenging the spirit to unfold new meanings. The eternity of the Tora lies in being able to accept the challenge and to reveal new meanings from among those latent in the original Sinaitic tradition.

But this is possible only as long as the partnership exists, as long as there is a corporate Jewish existence controlled by a group of people who are prepared to realize the Tora in everyday life. The Tora could unfold itself as long as there existed such a corporate Jewish reality, which, guided by the Tora, was able to affect the Tora in return. (The great record of such mutual guidance is the Talmud.) The degree to which the corporate life exists is the measure of the evolutionary strength of Judaism. As that life is lost, Judaism commensurately loses its elasticity. Naturally, Jewish corporate life does not mean only the synagogue or Hebrew classes or the intimacy of the famous "Jewish home." It implies the total life of the Jewish people, under the control of the Jewish people. This kind of Jewish reality we lost centuries ago; we lost it with the destruction of the ancient Jewish state, with the exile. Large chunks of it remained for a time in Palestine, for even under Roman domination the country remained for a time Jewish; there were also corporate arrangements in Babylon and other countries where Jews lived in close and large settlements. But even these gradually crumbled into smaller and smaller pieces, so that by the time the Talmud was closed, Judaism had in fact reached a point where development was no longer possible, for the great partner of Tora, Jewish reality, was lost. From then on, the Jewish nation has more and more been subjected to conditions which the Jews, as Jews, had no say in shaping. The examples of Jewish communal autonomy in the centuries that followed were of great cultural and religious importance in their days, but they could not remedy the basic anomaly of Jewish existence. For Jews from now on had to suffer an existence imposed upon them by others. The great spiritual tragedy of the exile consists in the breach between Tora and life, for exile means the loss of a Jewish-controlled environment. This, as far as we Jews are concerned, is the crux of the whole problem.

It is incorrect to speak, as it is so often done among Jews, of the conflict between Judaism and modern life. For as yet there is no modern Jewish life. We are only sharing in modern non-Jewish conditions of life. Many of the baffling problems of modern Jewry would look entirely different against the backdrop of an environment which, however small, we Jews would control. For instance, the problem of observing the Sabbath in modern times is a very difficult one. For we are part of an economic system that works on Saturdays. Hebrew prayers represent another difficult problem, but only because life around us is not Hebrew. But consider how different the position would be if we had an economic system resting on the Sabbath. What a great day the Sabbath could be to us! And if the mother tongue of our children were Hebrew, consider what a different meaning could be given to the services in the synagogue. What we could do with our Hebrew Bible!

The conflict between Judaism and non-Jewish surroundings is always present, and does not present any theological or philosophical problem. For Judaism was never so ambitious as to try to dominate a non-Jewish environment. Being a Jew does not mean that one has to prove the compatibility of Judaism with a life built on non-Jewish foundations. It is, therefore, not right to call for the reform of Judaism under the pressure of the hard facts of modern life. It is certainly very uncomfortable to be a Jew in the midst of a Christian world, but a reform of Judaism on those grounds alone means sacrificing Judaism on the altar of Christian civilization for the sake of individual comfort. The only justification for a call to reform would be the exigencies of a Jewish-controlled environment: For instance, a modern Jewish life in an autonomous land of Israel. The necessities of Jewish life are necessities of Judaism. The demands of a Jewish-owned environment are justified demands on Judaism and must be satisfied by Judaism. But exigencies arising out of the anomaly of the "Christian existence" of Jews in

Western civilization, demands resulting from the difference between the rhythm of Judaism and some other culture, these are not problems of theology or philosophy; they are part of the great Jewish tragedy. They all go back to the political problem of the exile. Naturally enough, they are influencing the religious and cultural atmosphere of Judaism. As to them we say: Rather should we perish in defending Judaism than subject it to a reform that can mean only dissolution and destruction. Our "Christian existence" in exile is no reason whatever to reform Judaism. As long as Jews live in exile, the conflict between Judaism and non-Jewish surroundings will remain; we shall have to endure the strain, that cannot be helped. (Perhaps we can alleviate the strain considerably, but of that later on.)

Any further development of Judaism is possible only by the creation, somewhere on this earth, of a complete Jewish environment, one wide enough to embrace the whole existence of a Jewish national entity. Only by the creation of such a Jewish environment can we give back to Tora the great partnership of life which alone is capable of freeing Judaism from its present exilic rigidity, and create the circumstances in which evolution will again be possible.

True enough, in a modern and autonomous Jewish society there will be many conflicts arising out of the modern organization of life, and there will always be the discussion between religion and science; but a Judaism again rendered elastic by life that is fully under our own control will be able to face these conflicts, unfolding itself in the effort to do so.

Let us consider in this connection the often heard argument for the renewal of the Sanhedrin, the ancient rabbinic legislative and judicial council, with the aim of creating an authoritative body to decide religious questions in accordance with the necessities of the day. This idea is nothing more than thoughtless play with a word which, in spite of its historic associations, would be devoid of any meaning today. The Sanhedrin is not the academic gathering of seventy-one illustrious Jewish scholars. It is an organ of a truly corporate Jewry. It is an institution of a Jewish nation that is master in its own house, and its function is to keep order in that house. It is no academy for the furtherance of the knowledge of Judaism. The Sanhedrin can only be a constitutional body in the Jewish state, in an autonomous Jewish society, or, at least, in a self-contained society in which the great factors of life are Jewish. Its authority is not that of knowledge or that of election; its authority has its roots in Jewish corporate existence. For that reason, it could never be established outside the land of Israel, and even there it ceased to be when Jewish life there had entirely lost its autonomy.

IV

The creation of an autonomous Jewish body corporate is the *sine qua non* for the regeneration of Jewish religion and culture. Without it, further development of Judaism is impossible; without it Judaism can hardly be saved in the present circumstances. On the other hand, such autonomy does not of itself mean religious and cultural regeneration, nor does it automatically bring about the healing of the breach between Tora and life. On the contrary, its reappearance may emphasize the breach by revealing the contrast between the new form of life and the world of an ancient tradition.

For two generations now, we have been witnessing the heroic efforts of an enthusiastic Jewish youth to create for itself a new Jewish life in the land of Israel. In many respects we can see clearly the regeneration of the Jew. A new Jewish type has arisen that is far different from the crippled and often degenerate Jew of the exile, a new youth in which any nation might take pride: Courageous, heroic, and beautiful—but, unfortunately, hardly recognizable as Jewish. Is this modern Hebrew in modern Palestine still a Jew? Of course he is according to the Nuremburg Laws, for racially he certainly is of Jewish stock. But can he be looked upon as continuing the spiritual life of Judaism? Is he handing on the great heritage of the past to coming generations? Is he giving back the newly created Jewish life of Palestine to Tora? In general, he is not; and many of his representatives will declare that they have never intended to do so. What was intended, and to a considerable degree achieved, was the regeneration of our people through the Jewish national idea and through the work to be done in its realization. What, as yet, we have failed to achieve is the regeneration of Judaism. The new Jewish reality in Palestine is, for the time being, of a nature that cannot be reconciled with the aims and intentions of historic Judaism.

It is important to face these facts calmly, not in the querulous frame of mind of those self-righteous people who are always prepared to pry into the "sinful hearts" of others, repeating phrases that hold no meaning for those to whom they are addressed. This sort of "criticism" will lead us nowhere. Rather than criticize, let us try to understand.

The Jewish pioneers who followed the call for national revival in the land of Israel had literally to take their lives in their hands. After two millennia of exile, the task of rebuilding the land and rejuvenating the nation was a living dream unparalleled in history. A nation for many centuries deprived of the possibility of ordinary manual labor, without agricultural experience, estranged from a natural life on the land, was returning to its ancient country that had been deserted for so many generations, a barren people back to a barren land. Over and above the recalcitrance of the neglected land itself, there were other difficulties. There was a whole nation in ruins, there was poverty and misery, there was lack of sympathetic understanding even among Jews. But in spite of this, there were the faithful, too, who possessed an unquenchable desire to build.

To achieve what has been achieved in such circumstances was made possible only by a fanatical will, fanatically concentrated on that one aim, to build. The least success could be achieved only by great efforts. There was only one way open: To concentrate all available energy, physical as well as spiritual, on the task at hand. Everything had to be subordinated to the one aim of returning to the land. This new generation consisted of fanatics and builders. For this reason it was one-sided; and so it had to be. No other Jewish type would ever have succeeded at the beginning. The "fanatics" had neither time nor energy to spend on the very intricate problem of fitting traditional Judaism into the new framework they were creating. For them to succeed, there was only one way open, to find the shortest way from the *bitza*, the swamp, to the sound foundations of a new *meshek*.[4] It is futile to blame anybody for such a development; it was dictated inexorably by the circumstances. To be blamed are those who sat back in their easy-chairs and wrote verbose protestations, instead of joining in the work and showing practically how Tora was to be realized while creating the new *eretz yisrael*. It will ever remain a stigma on a great part of Orthodox Jewry that they protested instead of encouraging, that they hampered instead of helping, that they stood behind instead of taking the lead, that they separated and did not join.

There is another point that should be considered in this connection. The land of Israel is Jewish *land*. Its requirements are of a different order from those of the single Jewish house, for instance, and of a far wider scope.

The observance of the Sabbath in the Jewish house, for example, is comparatively easy. The only thing one needs is a reliable "Sabbath goy." But what of a Jewish colony? Should it be handed over to the Sabbath goy on every Saturday and on holidays? Should the whole economic system of the country be given over to the Sabbath goy for fifty-two Saturdays and the several holidays of the year? We have only to picture such a thing to realize its impossibility. Are there indeed shortsighted people among us who ask for such arrangements? Unfortunately, there are many champions of the Tora who are so far from understanding it as to believe that such arrangements are compatible with the Tora's intentions. There are innumerable difficulties arising from the Jewish life in the land of Israel, and hampering that life. As yet, nobody has ventured to make the bold arrangements which could be looked upon as the answer of historic Judaism to the questions of a new day. What wonder, then, that the breach between Judaism and life not only continues to exist, but has been emphasized by the juxtaposition of the two, as has happened in the land of Israel? Whatever the situation there may be, no one of us has the right to shift the responsibility to other shoulders. Not all have a share in the successes in Palestine, but we are all responsible for the failures in the country. The failures in the land of Israel are failures of the whole nation and of Judaism as such. What we have achieved has been in spite of our faults; wherever we have failed it is because of them.

V

The most sympathetic understanding of the Zionist movement cannot deceive us into overlooking the fact that, as yet, we have been completely unsuccessful in regenerating historic Judaism. And it is from this perspective that the Jewish national renaissance should be examined.

Two thousand years of exile have undoubtedly crippled us. We have to overcome the anomaly of our existence in exile; we want to normalize the social, economic, and political structure of the nation. All this can be achieved only by returning to the land of Israel. For us the return is a necessity; we cannot survive without it. But do we intend to live exclusively by it? Is mere survival an ideal worth living for? What are we to do with our national regeneration? Is it to be an end in itself? Are we to emulate the "great Western civilization" in this respect too: Are we to become adepts in some form of European nationalism? Is all our endeavor to be directed towards becoming a "respected" member of the family of nations, towards the restoration of "Jewish prestige"? Do we intend to become, maybe, even a "great nation"? If so, may God guard us against such greatness. Is it really such a worthy ideal for us to show the nations that we too are capable of "great deeds," or deeds which they themselves must admire? Like the liberal assimilationist who was so eager to prove to his non-Jewish neighbor that an "Israelite" could also be a good citizen, are we going to Palestine now in order to live there too in the public gaze, to demonstrate to the world that a Hebrew can be just as gallant as any other of the "gallant nations" of Europe?

If so, this Jewish renaissance is just assimilation on a national scale. During the emancipation, Jewish religious and political assimilation emulated European liberalism; now, in a Europe gone mad with nationalism, we imitate this newest fashion. The assimilation of emancipation and this kind of national renaissance would have the same result: The destruction of Judaism; the one through individual, the other through collective assimilation. It may be granted that national renaissance is a better policy than assimilation, it may secure more personal happiness for its followers—at least for the time being. The controversy between the two policies, however, would become entirely opportunistic. Maybe it is better policy to be a Zionist than an assimilationist; but what of that? What if people still prefer to be English or French or American for the obvious reason that they have been living in those countries for generations and not in Palestine, that they speak the language of their native countries and not Hebrew, that they are imbued with the spirit and culture of modern European states and not with that of the Bible or the Talmud? What if they do not appreciate the new Hebrew literature which, however wonderful in itself, is still a poor thing compared with any of the literatures of the European countries? If Hebrew nationalism is to be a mere copy of European nationalism, its controversy with assimilation becomes a struggle between temperaments rather than ideals.

What is more, Hebrew nationalism provides a kind of justification of assimilation. For assimilation may not necessarily mean the imitation of the evil elements of Western civilization, whereas Hebrew nationalism is emulating its most dangerous idol, European nationalism. We Jews should understand this, for again and again we have had the unhappy experience of seeing the true nature of nationalism, without the mask. We ought to know by now that it is capable of being the worst murderer of history; its patriotic guise, lending it the mantle of the noble and the good, makes it all the more efficient. Have we forgotten all this so soon, we who have had the unique but unenviable opportunities of seeing it at work? Have we lived and suffered for so long only to fall victim to this infantile disease of half-grown Europeans? Are we now to become a "great nation" and live for our "honor" only? Should it not rather be our duty to exterminate this scourge of mankind, at any rate among Jews? In accordance with our historical experience and the highest teaching of Judaism, we are cosmopolitans, we are internationalists and pacifists.

The biblical conception of the Jewish state is the kingdom of God on earth. The basic demands of Judaism compel this outlook, the logical consequence of which for the modern man is opposition to the idol of the independent nationalistic state that is its own end and purpose. This will forever remain the great historic tradition of Judaism; whoever breaks with it breaks with Judaism. True enough, as long as there was a Jewish state in history, it was more often heathen than Jewish, which means, in fact, that it was mostly "European" in its essence, although on the Asiatic level of development. It is true that the history of the ideal of God's state is mainly a history of failures. But Judaism was always conscious of the failure, for it remained always conscious of the ideal. The histories of the heathen Hebrew states in ancient Judah and Israel concern us only inasmuch as they show the relentless struggle of Judaism against the obstinacy of human hearts clinging to their religious, social, and political ideals. The heroes of that period were not Saul or Ahab but Samuel and Elijah, not the great kings but the great prophets, not the warriors but the teachers. And they, our prophets and teachers, were fighting uncompromisingly against much which in modern terms we should call nationalism. The great traditions of the prophets were carried on by the scribes, the Pharisees, who were persecuted by the great kings because they would not compromise with Caesar and his heathen creations. They did not choose to give him what he claimed as his; for nothing was his in the eyes of those for whom there was only one truth and one God, and everything on earth was to serve God's kingship in one great unity of purpose.

We must not forget for a single moment that throughout all the failures to realize it, the ideal came nearer and nearer to fulfillment, until it had—at least in part—triumphed at the tragic moment of Jewish history when the Roman legions successfully stormed the walls of Jerusalem. R. Yohanan ben Zakai, smuggled out of the beleaguered city in a coffin, was the embodiment of the ideal triumphant over the obstinacy of human hearts. The establishment of the academy at Yavneh was not a sudden changeover from one form of Jewish existence to another; it was not a new invention of R. Yohanan ben Zakai aimed at allowing the nation to go on living; it was no clever trick frustrating the natural course of events, as it seems so often to be misread by modern Hebrew nationalists. It was, rather, an organic link in the continuity of the history of Judaism. The Jewish state lay prostrate, but in the midst of its destruction, Judaism was conquering the Jewish nation. In accordance with the teaching of its prophets and their rabbinical successors, the Jewish nation had overcome the seductions of such molochs of nationalism as national pride and national prestige.

From this aspect, the disaster of the destruction of the Jewish state in 70 C.E., and the endless exile that followed it, are seen to be necessary links in the long chain of the history of Judaism. At last, the ideal of the state of God on earth had partly triumphed. Partly, because it had won over the heart and will of the remnant of the people but could not maintain the concrete Jewish state as well. Judaism was winning the nation, but it lost certain elements which are indispensable to the existence of a nation. Now that, for the first time in its history, the nation as such was prepared to build the state of God on earth, it had no place on earth to build it. The concrete bases of its life were increasingly delivered up to and determined by factors outside its control.

This, however, was no accident; it was historic necessity. For no devotion and singleness of purpose on the part of one nation can ever succeed in establishing, let alone maintaining, the state of God in a world that is organized on lines constituting the very denial of such a state. We cannot say how far the ideals of the prophets with regard to national existence were already established within the Jewish state before its destruction; certainly the world would not accept them, and therein lay the weakness of the kingdom. It has been said in modern times that the world cannot exist half-free and half-slave; far less is it possible to create a state of God in one corner of the earth amidst a world of imperial Caesars and power politics. The Jewish state had to go under because its heathen basis of power and might for the sake of power and might became meaningless to the nation; the state of God, however, could not be established because the rest of the world lived for nothing but power and might.

Thus we went into exile to bide our time there, to wait, however long it might be, until the time when the establishment of the state of God on earth might be attempted once more.

Exile, therefore, is no break in the history of Judaism. It is an inevitable step on the way to its final realization.

We have always seen in the exile the "wrath of God poured out over us," and so it always has been, when measured by the appalling suffering it has entailed. It has maimed us, physically and mentally. But this unnatural existence has brought with it at least one great blessing: It enabled us to live and to wait without being responsible for the course followed by the world. At the moment when the Jewish nation was prepared seriously to attempt the upbuilding of a state of God, it could not proceed because other nations were not yet ripe for such a venture; their exclusive devotion to might and pomp was not only a tragedy for the Jews; it was a world tragedy. Might and pomp, national honor and "greatness," imperial majesty and power politics, are conceived in guilt and maintained in guilt. From the beginning of recorded history, collective or national existence has always been bound up with crime. Consequently, taking part in national life meant living in sin. Political transactions became synonymous with iniquity and corruption. There has been no place for us as Jews in international life. Our national history in exile has always been passive. We have had to accept the crumbs which "great civilizations" have graciously thrown out to us.

All this has been unpleasant, but thank God for it. Let us thank God that it was not we who were throwing out these soiled crumbs to others. Let us thank God that we were not the masters but only the pariahs of these great civilizations; that we had no share in their criminal inhumanities. We have often been trampled on, but let us thank God that it was not we who trampled upon justice, decency, freedom, and human dignity whenever it suited our selfish purposes. Let us be grateful to the exile; it has freed us from the guilt of national existence in a world in which national existence meant guilt. We have been oppressed, but we were not oppressors. We have been killed and slaughtered, but we were not among the killers and slaughterers. We have been hunted from country to country, but there were no fugitives fleeing from their homes because of fear of us.

For this reason we see in the exile no break in our history, but a very important phase in the realization of Judaism. It is not passive resignation to an inevitable fate. It was not purposeless suffering, but suffering for the sake of an ideal to which we remained faithful at all costs. Exile was more a blessing than a disaster. In the circumstances, they alone served "who only stood and waited."

Let us also be just towards the exile. Let us never forget that for centuries in the wretched, overcrowded, sordid ghettos—one of the crowning inhumanities of Western civilization—there was more humanity, justice, and kindness than in the rest of Europe. Let us not forget the endless galaxy of truly great men and women who lived and worked in the exile, children of the exile, humbly righteous Jews. Let us not forget for a single moment that much of what we detest in the exile, its squalid ugliness, its lack of harmony and beauty, is not Jewish but European: It is the stain of Europe on our life. The exilic Jew, his bent back, his distorted features, his often undignified outer bearing, what else are these but the seal of his "masters" on his body? The outer wretched appearance of the exilic Jew was the fitting counterpart of the moral wretchedness of the surroundings in which he had to live. It was not Jewish. It was the mark of Europe on the Jew.

Let us be just towards the exile. It has been a greater, worthier period of our history than the time of our independence in the past. We were incomparably more faithful to the ideals of the Bible in exile than we ever were in biblical times. Unfortunately, in the endless anomaly of Jewish suffering, the greatness of exile degenerated into assimilation. But woe unto us if the degeneration of the exile should lead us to a Hebrew nationalism along the European pattern. The Jewish nation two thousand years ago grew out of this kind of wickedness and shortsightedness. Are we to relapse into it today? Is it for such "glorious times" we have been waiting? Are we to erase two thousand years of Jewish history and render sterile all the sacrifice of numberless Jewish generations? Such a relapse would imply that the whole of exile was a meaningless tragedy. Let us think again before we seek to make the changeover from exile to *eretz yisrael*. Not every form of *eretz yisrael* is worth the trouble, and many a form could be unworthy of Judaism.

VI

Reason tells us that we cannot cancel the past; we cannot start Jewish history anew. If we sought survival on such terms, we should certainly go under. There is essentially no difference whether the dissolution of Judaism, and with it the disappearance of the Jew, is disguised as assimilation or as a perverted nationalism. True, national survival is possible only through return to Palestine, but survival is not an end in itself. Survival must serve continuity. Survival must aim at creating those circumstances in which the next phase of the organic development of Judaism is possible. Organic development is not synonymous with reform. Reform is consciously undertaken in opposition to the past; organic development takes place in conformity with principles that have prevailed in the past. Organic development cannot be "made"; what we can and must aim for is the creation of circumstances which make it possible. This is the only way of regenerating Judaism. Regeneration is not a "task" to be "tackled." It must grow.

There are two sources from which it can emerge: The one historic Judaism, the other a new Jewish life constructed and run by Jews; and it must come from both these sources simultaneously. Both are present in the land of Israel. There we already have Jewish life with its demands and its needs which cannot be overlooked. The authority of the living Jewish present will have to work miracles in freeing Judaism from its present exilic rigidity and in stimulating new phases of development. But before this can come about, the authority of the living present must recognize the spiritual authority inherent in the long past of our nation. It would be fatal if, because of the special form that Judaism had to take in the exile, we should now deny its claim to determine the meaning and aims of this new life for which Judaism has been yearning for thousands of years. It would mean not only introducing the great spiritual tragedy of the exile—the break between Tora and life—into the land of Israel, but perpetuating it there. If it came to that, then this return to our ancient homeland would prove to be another tragic aberration of the exile, and in the land of Israel itself we should be farther away from "home" than we have ever been in exile. Continuity alone will lead us home; and continuity, as we understand it, does not mean a mere repetition of the past. It is the road along which we are to move into the future, in faithfulness to the past. It is the only way of building "Altneuland."[5] That there should be some such continuity is widely felt in modern Palestine. The attempt to revive the Jewish festivals, for instance, is one of the many evidences of this tendency. The untiring endeavors of the poet Haim Nahman Bialik in the last years of his life aimed at fostering historic continuity.

Return to the land of Israel is a stirring ideal with great moral appeal so long as Jews live in exile. But once the return has been achieved, and the homecomers have settled down, when the struggle to conquer the neglected soil is over—what then? If there be nothing more than the ideal of return for the sake of return, disappointment is at hand, and emptiness lies ahead. Zionism is good for the exile, it is bad for Zion. Those who see the menace clearly and feel the responsibility for averting it will naturally enough turn to historic Judaism for help. But, with the exception of Bialik, all we have witnessed so far in this direction is more like fumbling in the dark; incoherent attempts without a clear-cut program, without knowledge of what we should be aiming at, without investigation of the conditions under which alone the appeal to historic Judaism can give us what we are in need of.

To what extent such fumbling in the dark goes on is shown by the case of the Bahad, the Movement of Religious Pioneers for Palestine. Here we have an intelligent and active group of pioneers that has already achieved remarkable successes in the colonization of the country and established itself as a separate group within the Zionist movement, dedicating all its work in Palestine to the ideal of the historic continuity of Judaism. Its basic formula, *tora va'avoda*, "Tora and Labor," under which alone this youth can envisage the realization of Judaism, is indeed a great and moving call. But is it yet a working program? Is it yet a reply to the many pressing questions that beset the modern Jew in Palestine? Unfortunately, no. The movement is laboring heavily under the burden of its religious idealism. Its members are well aware that its formula means a new order of social justice; the implications of *avoda* are well understood by them. Yet it cannot be said that there is a clear realization among them of the part that Tora is to play in the upbuilding of the country beyond the fulfillment of the daily commandments of religion by the members of the group. There is no conception of how Tora can be made the basic principle of social and political life in a modern Jewish state. Take, for instance, the great problem of the halacha. Halacha as we have known it in exile is bound to fetter the development of the country. The settlements of the *tora va'avoda* movement are, of course, already experiencing this difficulty, and yet no step whatever has been made towards the solution of the problem. If the left wing within Zionism is too impatient with the past, the right wing is too tender with it. What *tora va'avoda* actually does is to import exile-conditioned Judaism into Palestine, just as the parties of the Left and the Center are importing the exile-born and exile-produced negation of Judaism into the country.

Neither of them will prevail. Continuity, as the organic unfolding of historic Judaism, must be the aim. But we must create the circumstances in which new growth will be possible. We have already pointed out that in the new Jewish life of *eretz yisrael* the main conditions are present, for through it the vivifying partnership of Tora and life can be restored. We must realize, however, that man is the place of this restoration; it is in us that Tora and life must meet. It is in us that the old life must hand its principles and strength to the new life that is to be created and given direction. We are the link between the past and the future. It is through us that the past must pour itself into new channels. It is in us alone that Tora can be given back to life, and life may find its way back to Tora. The past must live in us before it can grow into the future.

The decisive proof of this is the experience of *eretz yisrael* itself. Whatever new culture has been created there that can rightly be called Jewish is the work of the former yeshiva student. On the other hand, all the cultural activities in the country with no relation to the past, undertaken without reference to continuity, have proved to be the empty projects of Hebrew busybodies. The new culture of Palestine will either be Jewish or nothing at all. Unfortunately, continuity is not so easily achieved when the link has, to a very large extent, been severed. For generations now, the Jewish masses have been estranged more and more from Jewish values, standards, and teachings of the past. Today, Judaism is for the great majority of us a theoretical system, stored up in old books that people understand no more, imprisoned in libraries and covered there with thick layers of dust. In actual life, it is restricted to a steadily decreasing minority. Even in these how does it survive? Owing to the circumstances of the exile, it survived in one special shape that was bound to become rigid, and that, because of its rigidity, has ceased to draw strength from its origin. And this too is another break in continuity. Before the opportunities presented in modern Palestine can lead to a new organic development, the broken chain must be mended. We must give ourselves back to the past. We must trace back the long stream of Judaism to its origin. We must make ourselves receptive, and let Judaism enter us before it can flow through us to coming generations, augmented, enriched, and reshaped by our exertions.

This is not the usual call for return to Judaism, a call that does not become more convincing because it is being ceaselessly repeated. It is not very helpful to blame those who will not listen to stirring calls for return. They do not listen because the words that reach them do not carry any convincing message for them. They do not listen because they do not understand the language in which exile-preserved Judaism is addressing them. They do not understand it, not because it is Hebraic or talmudic, but because it belongs to a life which even the specialist historian apprehends but vaguely. You cannot speak to the youth of 1940 in the words of the year 500 without it sounding like gibberish. You certainly cannot reach their hearts or stir their imagination. What we have called the "problem of the language" proves to be the main obstacle in the way of restoring the broken chain of continuity. The great task at hand in this field is the translation of the whole content of Judaism, not into one or the other of the modern languages that we speak, but into the terms and notions of our time, a translation that will provide for historic Judaism the means to speak to the present generation.

Every good translation is always a rediscovery of the original, and the translation we have here in mind will be the great rediscovery of Judaism. Such a rediscovery is the only method of mending the broken chain of continuity. As we go on rediscovering our heritage, we open our minds to the message of the past, so that it may now enter us and continue through us.

7

ON JEWISH SOVEREIGNTY

(1973)

WHEN IN THE EARLY SPRING of 1967 I decided to set down my thoughts on the problem of faith raised by the European holocaust,[1] I could not anticipate that by the time the task was completed, a threat, more fateful in its consequences than Auschwitz itself, would cloud the skies of Jewish existence. The Arab nations resolved to wipe the State of Israel off the world map. If the threat in all its seriousness could not be surmised, the possibility that the frightening drama of potential extinction would find its redemptive denouement in the return of the Jewish people to Jerusalem was not envisioned by even the wildest imagination. At the time, I wrote an extended work on the theological and religious problems arising from the darkest hour of Israel's exile. Soon after the body of the book was finished, the Jews stepped into the brightest hour that God, in his unexpected mercy, bestowed upon them since their dispersion.

But, of course, that is the question. Was it indeed "from God"? Was it in truth, to use the phrase of Isaiah, the "hiding" God of Israel who acted as the savior? How are the events and the results of Israel's Six Day War to be seen in the context of theology and Jewish history, especially in light of the Holocaust?[2] Did we really experience one of those rare occasions when

God—almost as in biblical times—made his presence manifest as the redeemer of Israel?

It was probably helpful that what I had to say on the problem of the European holocaust was developed independently of the impact of the Israeli victory. If my analysis of the Jewish affirmations in the face of Auschwitz is valid, it must be so independently of Jewish military victories. On the other hand, if the analysis has no validity, no feat of arms, however magnificent, could change that. Military victory alone does not prove divine involvement in history, just as the crematoria are no proof of divine indifference. Defeat and suffering need not mean abandonment by God, and worldly success in the affairs of man is no proof of divine support.

Nevertheless, Jews the world over, and especially in Israel, experienced the speedily developing crisis, followed by the lightning transformation of the Six Day War, as history on a metaphysical level. This was not a conscious reaction to what had happened; not an interpretation of the events, or a considered judgment. As a conscious reaction, the sensing of metaphysical meaning might be questioned. But the realization that through the events of those few days all Israel was addressed from beyond the boundaries of time was not a conscious reaction. It was a spontaneous experience, borne in upon the Jew with the power of revelation. Can this revelational character of the experience be proved? Revelation is never provable. One can only testify to its occurrence: *You are my witnesses*, says God. Once again, the words of Isaiah have found their realization in world history. Nevertheless, after the event it is incumbent upon us to understand the experience in the context of Judaic teachings and expectations. In order to do this, we would do well to recall the theological relevance of a State of Israel, to examine the place that a Jewish state holds within the system of Judaism.

A vital aspect of Jewish messianism is the faith in Israel's return to its ancestral land. All the prophets that prophesy Israel's redemption see it materialize in the land of Israel. God comforts Zion through the return of her children. Nothing could be further from the truth than to interpret these messianic hopes as a nationalistic aspiration. The prophetic mood belies such misconceptions. The messianic goal is a universal one. The Messiah ushers in universal justice and world peace. But the universal expectation is inseparable from Israel's homecoming. The very passage that directs man's hope to the time when "nation shall not lift up sword against nation, neither shall they learn war any more" also envisages that "out of Zion shall go forth Tora, and the word of the Eternal from Jerusalem."[3] There can be little doubt that Zion and Jerusalem are not merely of symbolic significance in this universalistic text, but are historic places in the land of the Jews. The prophets look forward to a time when God's plan for mankind is fulfilled, when peace and brotherhood prevail among all nations, when God's blessing embraces "Egypt my people and Assyria the work of my hands, and Israel my inheritance."[4] But the realization of all these expectations will find Israel reestablished in the land of its ancestors. The redemption of mankind includes the redemption of the Jewish people in the land of the Jews. What is the messianic significance of the land? The question is identical with the subject of our inquiry into the theological relevance of the land of Israel.

II

The rabbis in the Talmud declared that a Jew who lives outside the Holy Land is to be considered as if he were an idolater.[5] This rather startling pronouncement flows from their understanding of Judaism. It is a statement about one of its essential qualities. It links the importance of the land not so much to the Jew as to the realization of Judaism. The question is often asked: What is the meaning of the term "Jewish"? Is it a religious determination, or does it apply to a national or racial entity? Formulated in this manner, the question cannot be answered. The frame of reference within which the question is asked does not apply to the Jewish people. The concepts "religion," "nation," "race" are derived essentially from the tradition and history of the Western world. But Judaism does not derive its essential quality either from that tradition or from that history. The term "Jewish" is neither a religious nor a national concept. Yet being Jewish does mean belonging to a people. Israel is a nation. But what kind of a people and nation? What kind of a people is it that has preserved its identity under conditions that no other people was ever able to withstand? What kind of a nation, that through the longest part of its history was lacking all the vital requirements of normal nationhood, yet was discernible as a separate entity?

One of the great Jewish teachers of the tenth century, Saadia Gaon, answered the question by saying: "Our people is a people only through the

Tora." In his mind, it was the Tora that made Israel a people. Israel is a nation of Tora. A nation created in its encounter with God; a nation formed by its faith, by its submission to the will of God as made manifest in the Tora.[6] Whatever anthropological science may say about the origins of the Jewish people, it has a bearing only on the raw material, as it were, out of which Israel was formed. The historical Israel came into being, and maintained itself through all times, as the result of its self-understanding as the people of God, the people of God's Tora. The formulation of Saadia Gaon defines, in Jewish terms, the meaning of Judaism as a religion, and of Israel as a people. Judaism is a nation-creating religion, and Israel is a people created by this kind of religion.

As a rule, religions do not make nations. Nations and peoples are biological, racial, political units. They may accept a religion, but the religion they accept is accidental to the national group. Christianity, for instance, created no people; peoples, already existing as such, accepted Christianity. The same applies to the world's other religions. Israel alone is a people made to fulfill a God-given task in history; the people whom, as Isaiah expressed it, God "formed" for himself.[7] Normally, religion follows nationhood; for the Jew, his peoplehood flows from his religion. This is not only an accurate account of the emergence of Israel; in a sense, it is valid to this day. An Englishman might accept Hinduism or Buddhism in London; it will not make him Indian or Burmese. He will remain an Englishman. Similarly, a Chinese, converting to Christianity in China, does not become a European, a German, or a Frenchman. But if the same people accept Judaism—not just pro forma, but in fact, living it and practicing it—they will not merely become adherents of a religion, but will belong to the Jewish people. The founder of Judaism was not a prophet, but a patriarch; the man of faith, through the intrinsic logic of his faith, became the father of a people. On the rock of his faith he built not a church, but a people that was to enter history with a divinely invested purpose.

One may also put it this way. A key concept of Judaism is the idea of the covenant with God. In terms of the covenant, one might say that whereas in other religions, the "covenant" is between the individual and his God, in Judaism the covenant with the individual derives from the larger covenant with the people. This, however, leads us to the essential distinction between religion, as traditionally understood, and Judaism. The concern of religion is with the right belief, the credo. Especially in Christianity, it is the right belief that establishes a correct relationship between the believer and his God. Judaism's main concern is with the deed. In keeping with the words of Habakkuk, Judaism does not teach that a man is *saved* by his faith, but that the righteous *lives* by his faithfulness.[8] In Judaism, the significance of faith lies in its capacity to lead to life, to action, to the human deed. In one place in the Talmud, the question is discussed: What is more important? The teaching or the deed? And the conclusion is reached: The teaching is more important, if it leads to the deed.[9] The deed, uninformed by the teaching, is blind; teaching that does not issue into the deed as a consequence is empty. The goal is the deed, guided by the teaching.

We may now appreciate why the covenant in Judaism had to mean the creation of a people. One might say that the difference between Judaism and "religion" is due to the difference between deed and faith, between action informed by teaching and salvation effected through faith. Belief or faith belongs in the private realm. The creed is always of the individual. This is why religion does not create nations. Even if everyone in a people acknowledges the same religion, the relation thus established is not between the people as such and God, but between individuals and their God. The religion remains accidental to the national group.

A nation's historical role is carried out on a level different from that of the individual religious confession. The deed, however, always takes place in the public realm. Faith is entertained in isolation. Indeed, the deeper the faith, the more private it is. The deed is impossible in isolation. It always affects others, it impinges on their lives; it always refers beyond the boundaries of isolated individuality. Faith is the preoccupation of the soul. The deed is enacted by the entire person. Faith links the soul to God; the faith-informed deed links the whole person to his fellow by way of God. Faith fills the soul; the deed fills history. While by faith alone a soul may, perhaps, be saved, the deed's *raison d'etre* is to be effective in the world. For the sake of its effectiveness, the deed will seek for its realization a group that is moved by a common faith and united by a common cause. The extent of the group depends on the area within which the deed is to be enacted. (The trade-union idea, for instance, concerns itself with a specific socioeconomic segment of society. In order to bring about effective action, it must call into being the group that is appropriate for its realization.) So it is with every idea that aspires to enter the world in the form of the human deed. The boundaries of the group will be determined by the area that the deed aims to occupy. But what if the fruition of the idea as the deed encompasses the whole of human existence? What if the faith seeks realization in economics, morals, politics, in every manifestation of human life? In that case, the group ought to be all-encompassing. Such a group should be mankind.

But mankind is not a group; it is not a historical entity. Mankind itself is an idea, an ideal. The group to be created to suit the comprehensive deed as a historical reality is a people, in sovereign control of the major areas of its life. The faith of Judaism requires such a comprehensive deed. Realization in the largest collective, mankind, is the ideal; the instrument of its realization in history is the people. Since our concern is with the comprehensive deed of Judaism, the people is Israel. Of necessity, the covenant had to create the people with which the covenant was concluded.

If, however, the people of Israel is the instrument of realization, there must be a land of Israel as the place of realization. There must be a place on earth in which the people are in command of their own destiny, where the comprehensive public deed of Judaism may be enacted. Individuals may live in two cultures; but no distinctive culture may grow and flourish authentically in an area already preempted by another one. The individual Jew may well find a home in any democratic society; Judaism must remain in exile anywhere outside the land of Israel. Outside the land of Israel, Judaism is capable of partial realization only. The decisive areas of human endeavor are controlled by the majority culture. The "raw material," the challenge of the fullness of human life, is lacking. The Jewish deed cannot be enacted in a comprehensive way. Broad areas of Jewish teaching must remain mere book learning for lack of applicability. Values and standards degenerate into pious intentions devoid of relevance because, in the circumstances of Judaism's exile, they cannot become principles of policy for the Jewish people.

According to the Bible, Moses was not granted the privilege of entering the Promised Land. Informed of the divine decree, he prayed: "Let me go over and see the good land...."[10] One of the teachers in the Talmud, interpreting Moses' prayer in the midrashic manner, commented: "Why did our teacher Moses desire to enter the land of Israel? Was it so important for him to eat of its fruits and enjoy its good things? Rather, he thought: 'There are so many commandments that Israel was given by God which can be fulfilled only there. Let me go over, that they may be fulfilled through me.'"[11] This comment expresses the theological significance of the land.

The teachers of the Talmud assume that Moses' interest in the land could not have been of a secular nature. It could not have been due to a wish for an easy life, or to "patriotic" or nationalistic aspirations. The land was the opportunity for Judaic realization. The Tora is not fully applicable outside the land of Israel. The consequences of exile are most serious: The non-application leads to continuous frustration of the spirit. The book learning, which is never tested through the contesting claims of live issues, withers. Judaism loses its creativity and stagnates.

Those Jews who separate Judaism from Zion, Tora from the land of Israel, give up both Tora and the land. Judaism without the opportunity for its comprehensive fulfillment is a spiritual tragedy. For the longest period of its history, Jews have lived with it. But to embrace the tragedy as a desired form of Jewish existence is a falsification of the essence of Judaism. Those who sever Zion from the Tora have severed Judaism from its authentic realization. They have surrendered, as a matter of principle, Judaism's *raison d'etre*, which is fulfillment in history. They have transformed its character by reducing it to the level of religion. They have reduced it to a credo, a regimen of worship, and some customs in the home. All this may well be accompanied by fine, humanitarian resolutions; but the unique significance of the Judaism of history will have been abandoned. What historically has been an obligation of the public conscience and a standard for the public deed is narrowed to the level of private creed and individual behavior. This is not the reformation of a classical heritage, but its planned decadence. What has essentially been a religious civilization is thus stripped down to a not very exciting creed, whose main function is to be a sedative in moments of trouble and visitation. The original way of life, derived from the challenge to build this world as a kingdom of God, becomes a device for securing peace of mind for the individual, a function which it fulfills less and less effectively as this kind of religion declines.

Apart from falsifying the essence of Judaism, the severance of the land from the faith brings in its wake a reevaluation of Jewish history. Through the ages, Jews struggled, prayed, lived, and died in the conviction that their role in history would ultimately be revealed through their return to Zion. Jews were prepared to die at the stake because they knew that the final reckoning was still to come; in our own days, myriad Jews perished in the gas chambers, sustained only by their "perfect faith" in the coming of the Messiah. Basically, Jewish messianism has never been either a matter of politics or an expression of mere nationalism; it is a manifestation of the essence of Judaism. It is a faith in the inevitable triumph of the divine purpose in history, which, in the course of its unfolding, would return Israel to the Holy Land and there, in the fullness of its public life, embody Judaism.

From the beginning, Judaism included both the possibility of exile as well as the certainty of redemption. To be a Jew meant to accept the one and to wait for the other. Seen in this light, Jewish history does make sense: It is part of the cosmic drama of redemption. In it the martyrdom of Israel finds its meaning: None of the sorrow was in vain, for all along the path was being paved for the Messiah. Not a single tear was wasted, for all of it will be vindicated in his coming. Only messianic redemption can lend meaning to Israel's martyrdom. In this way must the authenticity of the redeemer be tested: Should he save only a contemporary generation, and thus compel the Jewish people to write off the tragedy of two millennia in exile as a regrettable incident about which nothing more can be done, Israel will know him to be another impostor. In a sense, every generation is the guardian of all generations, seeking and acknowledging only salvation of a kind that would redeem all Jewish history from the curse of senseless martyrdom. Jews who believe that the return to Zion is not vital for Judaism have broken the continuity of Jewish history; they have given up Jewish messianism, and thus reduced the awesome drama of redemption to meaningless misery. The prophets, the martyrs, the millions of people who perished believing and hoping, were all mistaken; the blood and tears were all in vain; the Messiah has altered course and landed at New Amsterdam. This is the logic of falsifying the nature of Judaism. If Judaism is made into a purely private creed, not requiring collective implementation in the public life of the people, then indeed, two thousand years of exile have been a tragic episode stemming from unfortunate circumstances, and the sooner it is forgotten, the better.

III

Without the return to Zion, Judaism and Jewish history become meaning-less. The return is the counterpart in history to the resolution in faith that this world is to be established as the kingdom of God. The thought has its roots in the foundations of Judaism, but might have been mere wishful thinking had it not been supported by the reality of Israel: Its existence, its survival, its return to Zion. One must appreciate the irrationality of it before one can grasp its meaning. In terms of exclusively manmade history, Israel's existence is irregular (a people like the Jews is not supposed to exist), its survival anomalous (a people as irregular as the Jews is not expected to survive), its return to Zion absurd (the irregular and the anomalous com-pounded with the realization of an impossible vision). The Jew cannot stop at this point. In terms of exclusively manmade history, which is the same as Camus' exclusively manmade meaning,[12] human existence is itself a chance event in an anomalous, absurd universe. To be judged irregular, anoma-lous, and absurd by the standards of a reality that itself is such is encourag-ing. In a human condition in which history is altogether manmade, the historical Israel is an impossibility. Yet Israel is real. It can be real only because history takes place on two levels: It is manmade, that is, the kingdom is man's responsibility; yet it is planned by God. Because the kingdom of God on earth is man's responsibility, it may be delayed by crematoria and death camps; yet come it must. The movement of the two levels toward each other is the messianic process of history. Israel is the only nation that lives on both levels. Israel's history is messianic history. For Israel, history is messianism on the way to the kingdom of God on earth. Because of that, Israel knows Auschwitz; because of that, Israel, throughout its history, has been on the way to Zion.

In our days it has arrived. It may be that a majority of Jews today do not consciously subscribe to such an interpretation of either Judaism or the kingdom of God. Yet the overwhelming majority of them experienced the recent confrontation between the State of Israel and the Arab nations as a moment of messianic history. It was an event not on the purely manmade level of history, but one that took place in conformity with the divine plan.

Especially in Israel, a wide portion of the population were convinced that "this is God's doing; it is marvelous in our eyes."[13] What justification was there to see events in such a light? Apparently, those who lived through them could not see them in any other. Generals and commanding officers were unable to render a purely military account of what happened. It was the secularist in Zion who insisted that to ignore the miraculous would be unrealistic. People who never prayed found themselves turning to God in prayer. It was not the prayer in the trenches, where, supposedly, there are no atheists. It was the prayer beyond the trenches, in the clear air of victory; not the prayer of fear, but prayer in its pristine spontaneity, as the elementary desire of the soul to reach out to God. The Jew had found himself. Hard-boiled paratroopers were embracing the cold stones of the Western Wall of the ancient Temple as lovers embrace the most beloved. There was a presence about in the land. What is there in those events of unique Jewish destiny that we are able to discern from afar?

For the first time since the destruction of the ancient Jewish commonwealth, the city of David is once again the capital of a Jewish state. Undoubtedly this is a moment in Jewish history that takes its place beside the classical occasions as recorded in the Bible. For the Jew this is a renewal of biblical times. The revelatory sense of the event is due in part to the fact that it was utterly unexpected. What happened was unplanned: The great powers could have prevented the outbreak of hostilities. Instead, they disregarded their moral responsibility and wasted the opportunity of peacemaking in recriminations and chatter. Though the leader of the Arab camp threatened a massacre that would surpass those of Genghis Khan, it is conceivable that they did not intend to go all the way. Israel wanted peace and accepted war as a bitter necessity forced upon it by the stupidity of the circumstances. What happened was unwanted, and it came upon us with dramatic suddenness. The crisis reached its crescendo almost overnight; yet its choking embrace was broken even more swiftly, and with a thoroughness that could not be foreseen. The transformation was rapid and radical. The most precious reward of Israel's long history was dropped into its lap when it was hardly looking. As the rabbis of old would say, salvation came *beheseah hada'at*, in the absence of mind. "The help of God happens in the blink of an eye." All the old sayings about messianic events took on a new and undreamed-of reality. Yet all this might have been mere chance. But then came the most unexpected event, for which Jews had been longing through the ages: The return to Jerusalem. That for which we were least prepared was what we had most longed for.

To our surprise, we discovered that if we were absent-minded, we were not absent-hearted. Our hearts were wiser than our minds. Our hearts were expecting all the while, and we did not know. It was not an expectation on the manmade level of history, waiting for political advantage and military victory. Such are the hopes of the mind, and the mind was caught unaware. The heart was expecting, with messianic wisdom. Once again, we have to say it in the words of the teaching. On the verse from Song of Songs, "I sleep, but my heart wakes," the rabbis commented: "I have fallen asleep waiting for the end of my exile, but my heart is awake to redemption."[14] We have been awakened to a messianic hour in our history and found that our hearts were awake all the time. Thus we learned that if we were absent-minded, all the generations were watching us; if we thought to operate on a purely secular level, almost forgetful of the messianic vision, Jewish history had not changed its direction. We recalled that what we did not expect consciously was the expectation of the ages. And now it was happening before our eyes, the vindication of our own hearts whose truth we so often denied.

What was not granted to any other generation was awarded to the people in Zion: An encounter with all of Jewish history, a communion with all the generations. It was as if they were conversing with the patriarchs, walking with King David, listening to the voice of the prophets, comforting the martyrs. According to a midrashic legend, at the time of the revelation at Sinai all the souls yet to be born were assembled together with the contemporary generation to receive the Tora for all generations to come. When the present generation stood at the Western Wall of the Temple in Zion again, all the generations whose eyes turned toward the event through the ages stood with them. The Wall recalled all the walls of the ghettos, of the dungeons, of the concentration camps, and testified that they were no mere oversight before God; it gave the Jew the assurance that somehow and somewhere in the order of things, there was an account from which redemption would issue to all the oppressed and persecuted generations. How? It was not important to be able to spell it out in detail. The decisive experience was that "the people that walked in darkness have seen a great light."[15] It was for the entire people, who had for so long walked in darkness, that the light was received.

As there was unity between past and present, among the generations, so was there also an unprecedented sense of unity within the present generation. In those days of destiny, we indeed were one people. Nowhere was the unifying power of the moment stronger than in the State of Israel itself. This was not merely the unity that is natural at moments of national peril, or the unity of exaltation in the celebration of victory. There were no official, national victory celebrations in Israel. Rather, there was a unity of the spirit, forged in the awe of the messianic experience. The sensing of the messianic was manifest in the unity of all Israel. All Israel stood face to face with its destiny and came out of the experience with a new self-understanding. This new understanding may not reach deep with many; it may not endure long with them. On it, however, will be built the future of all Israel, because only what will be built on it has a future.

IV

Is this the Messiah already? It is enough to look out the window to realize that nothing could be further from the truth—unless he, too, came unexpectedly, "like a thief." But it is a messianic moment, in which the unexpected fruits of human endeavor reveal themselves as the mysterious expression of a divine guidance which the heart always knew would come. Ever since the Holocaust, we have known that the great Jewries that perished will never be rebuilt. We have known that there is no way back to the past. But in what direction were we moving? Our steps were uncertain; reassurance was lacking; self-understanding was confused. But now we have seen a smile on the face of God. It is enough. It will be enough for a long time. We have been called to a new beginning.

In the past, after every destruction, we built something new and different. After every destruction, we were led to new unfoldings in the history of Judaism. After the first destruction, we created the synagogue, which represented a new phase of Judaism. After the second destruction, we created the Judaism of the Talmud. In our generation we experienced another *hurban*, the third destruction, that of the Judaism of exile. Having found our way back to Zion in a messianic moment, we know that God is doing "a new thing; now shall it spring forth," in which—as in the past—the old will find home.[16] What the nature of this "new thing" is going to be no one can tell at this early juncture; but we can discern the theological significance of the circumstances in which it will have to grow and develop. Judaism in exile was lacking the completeness of life within which the deed of practical faith could flourish. In the long history of the exile, the range of application was shrinking continuously. In Babylon, for instance, there were large areas closely settled by Jews who were allowed to live under their own laws and were internally ruled by their own princes, whose authority was recognized by the state. During the Middle Ages there were many countries in which Jews enjoyed a high measure of internal autonomy, though the application of Judaism to real issues of the human condition had been greatly narrowed. This base of application narrowed further, although it was still available to some extent, in the modern ghettos. The less Jews involved themselves in the majority culture and economy, the greater the chances for the authentically Jewish deed of daily existence. As the walls of the ghettos fell, Judaism was, more and more, reduced to the status of a mere religion.

With the destruction of the great Jewries, the basis for Jewish realization in history has practically disappeared. Neither is it to be found in the communist world, where the only history permitted the Jew is one that divests him of his Jewish identity. On the other hand, in the democratic countries, where freedom of conscience is the rule, the extent of the freedom is the source of the problem. Now involved in all areas of human endeavor, the Jew is nonetheless engaged in a world to which the comprehensive deed of Judaism cannot be applied. Judaism has never been as orphaned of living reality as in our days. Even among the pious, Judaism can only be a matter of private concern. Lacking the partnership of history, it withers. However, at this moment of its greatest impoverishment of reality, destiny has blessed it with the opportunity for its fullest application in the land of the fathers, in Jerusalem. For the first time, after nineteen centuries of a continuously shrinking base of applicability, the challenge of a human condition that requires the Judaic deed has been granted the Jew. Today, outside the land of Israel the challenges to Judaism arise mainly from the Jew's involvement in a society that is non-Jewish. Those problems are insoluble. Judaism was never meant to be realized in the midst of a Christian or Marxist civilization. If the diaspora were left to itself, the future of a meaningful form of Judaism would be dim. This "new thing" that God is preparing in Zion, we do not yet know. But the unsolved problems, the numerous challenges, are addressed to Judaism from the foundation of a new reality that asks for Judaism in its fullest sense. Therein lies the promise of the future for all Jews. Will Jews understand it?

It is difficult for a Jew to detect the presence of God in the history of the nations or religions—unless it be in the history of Israel, and, only through that history, in the history of man as well. Eliminate Israel from history and there is no need for any reference to God. Without Israel, everything is explainable and expected. Economics, power, politics, and psychology will explain everything. Without Israel, man is self-explanatory. Only the reality of Israel resists explanation on the level of manmade history. Because of Israel, the Jew knows that history is messianism—that God's guidance, however impenetrably wrapped in mystery, is never absent from the life of nations.

8

TOWARDS A RENEWED RABBINIC LEADERSHIP

(1943)

FROM TIME IMMEMORIAL, the decisive authority within the Jewish community has been the rabbi, the spiritual head of the community. Today in modern Jewries, however, there hardly exists such a thing as rabbinical authority. Unfortunately, this kind of "modernism" does not mean progress. It is but another sign of the dissolution of traditional Judaism we are witnessing in modern Jewry. Jewries that are gradually losing contact with historic Judaism cannot be presided over by an authority embodying the spirit and ways of a Judaism from which modern Jews have become estranged. This is a fact that must be recognized. Rabbis who remonstrate with their communities on the matter of their authority betray a fundamental misunderstanding of the situation. No community can bestow authority on the rabbi. Rabbinical authority is of a spiritual nature and cannot be *given* to anybody; it must be accepted by those over whom it is to prevail. This is only possible where rabbinical authority represents an ideal that is commonly acknowledged and revered by the community.

This is the fundamental point in connection with the problem of authority within the community. There is such a thing, for instance, as the authority of the beadle in certain matters, or that of the honorary officers, because this kind of authority can be bestowed on people by their respective offices. Rabbinical authority, however, is not that of the office; it is the authority of a calling, of an ideal.

Let us consider what is meant by rabbinical authority. The only title attached to the name of Moses is that of *rabenu*, our rabbi, our master. In Jewish folklore the prophet Elijah is often referred to as "Rabbi." And indeed, in the Jewish conception the prophets were the great rabbis of their times, just as the rabbis of later generations performed the task formerly undertaken by the prophets. The rabbi is the successor to the prophet. In the tractate Avot, where the succession of the teachers of the Tora is given, it is said that "the prophets handed it [the Tora] down to the men of the Great Assembly" (and in the Talmud we come across an actual ruling that the rabbis learned from the prophet Haggai).[1] It can hardly be doubted that such was the historic way of passing on the Tora, from the prophets to the rabbis. The succession was much more than purely historic; it was functional as well. In later times, the rabbis stood exactly where the prophets had stood before them, fulfilling the same function within the life of the nation, in much the same spirit as their great masters, the prophets.

Rabbinical authority was not ecclesiastical. The rabbi was no cleric. There could be no place for the cleric within a nation that never admitted any division between the religious and secular spheres of life. A system of living, like Judaism, that embraces all spheres of life in one great unifying spiritual structure, cannot allow the existence of a special caste, endowed with special power and dignity and charged with special responsibilities for the guidance of the community. It is of the very essence of the Jewish art of living that all should share in the same responsibility of practicing it. If this responsibility means priesthood, then indeed the task before us is to become a "kingdom of priests and a holy nation," but it is incumbent upon every Jew to the same extent. The rabbi was the national leader toward the realization of Judaism only as the most outstanding layman. That he should be a scholar was important, because Jewish life is impossible without knowledge; but it is equally impossible for any Jew. The study of the Tora is a nationwide obligation and has never been limited to a select group of individuals. The Tora is not theology but the knowledge of the Jewish art of living. As a Jew, one cannot move properly without it, just as no European can dispense with a certain minimum of general ethical and social knowledge.

There were no special rabbinical colleges. The rabbi had no process of education to go through that was different in any way from general Jewish education. Within the old Jewish school system one did not prepare oneself to become a rabbi, but to become a Jew; one did not choose the "rabbinical career," but grew into the rabbinical calling as one succeeded in becoming a Jew. A whole community of rabbis was very well imaginable and possible. And it was, indeed, the ultimate aim of Jewish education. The rabbi was the type of the well-educated *ba'al habayit*. He was no official of the synagogue. The rabbis never constituted a caste within the community, separate from the mass of the people. They were themselves laymen, without any power of office. They had no privileges, and had the same duties as any other Jew. They were to be found in all walks of life. They were craftsmen, laborers, traders, professional men, teachers. They worked in all occupations open to Jews. They were poor or rich as the case might be, and earned their living like any other Jew in their respective occupations. This was the case even as late as the close of the Middle Ages.

Naturally, as in all living communities, throughout Jewish history there were certain offices that had to be filled by people with special qualifications; but even when these offices demanded learning and scholarship, the candidates were drawn from the large mass of learned laymen, and never represented a distinct class of experts. Anybody was eligible for office. The knowledge demanded, for instance, for the office of *dayan*, or judge, was of the same kind and quality that could be expected from any Jew who had a proper Jewish education. Such offices did not provide careers. One did not pave the way to a splendid future by preparing oneself for such offices. There were no salaries attached to such posts. It was understood that the teaching and administering of the Tora should be done freely and without payment.[2]

The great examples set by Moses when he protested, "Not one ass have I taken from them," or by Samuel when he exclaimed, "Here I am: Witness against me before the Eternal.... Whose ox have I taken? Or whose ass have I taken? Or whom have I defrauded, whom have I oppressed? Or of whose hand have I taken a bribe, to blind my eyes herewith?..." were always before the eyes of the nation, and it was in this spirit that rabbis and judges worked.[3] They lived as best they could, and as other Jews did; and by voluntarily fulfilling certain important functions within the community, they were performing a task that could have been required from any other Jew. At all times they were the communal leaders because they were the great Jews of their generation. Their authority rested upon what they actually were, the best representatives of the nation and of all that the nation stood for. It was an authority not of office but of being, the authority of a personality in which an ideal has taken concrete shape.

Even at later periods after the Middle Ages, when the rabbi had become more attached to the community in an official way, receiving a fixed salary, his position and authority did not change. He was one of the people who had been asked to devote himself entirely to certain communal tasks, and who could therefore not earn his living as he used to. His authority was not a consequence of his office, but on the contrary, it was the authority already possessed by him as a person representing and living Judaism which he now used in the communal interest. It was he who, by identifying himself with the office, rendered it authoritative.

Rabbinical authority was the authority of living Judaism, the authority of the ideal in the process of its everyday realization. And as the ideal was the driving force in all spheres of national existence, the rabbi was the communal leader, the politician, the statesman, the national authority.

II

It is natural that in Jewries within which Judaism is in a process of dissolution, there can be no such thing as the authority of the ideal embodied in the rabbi. There is no room, nor is there any call, for rabbinical authority in communities that have reduced Judaism to synagogue ceremony and the sentimentalism of the Jewish cemetery. This clericalized relic of Judaism is in need of nothing more than officials to give it service; and so arises a new priestly caste. The community consists of the laymen on the one side, and, on the other side, of those who have been initiated into the mysteries of giving service. There is certainly no sense in expecting every Jew to be able to preach a sermon or to conduct a service. Once the unity of Jewish life has been broken up into a religious and a secular sphere, once it has been admitted that there are certain hours and places for religious concentration, then life itself becomes governed by entirely different principles from those upon which Judaism insists. Then it becomes necessary to establish a clerical order with the task of rendering unto God the things that are God's, while the great majority of laymen are busy rendering unto Caesar the things that are Caesar's. And so, in modern times, the rabbi has been replaced by the "minister of religion." The minister of religion is, however, not the modern rabbi but the modern priest, a man expected to know all about service and religious ceremony, for he has been especially trained for the "job"; a man who is of course socially active in charitable undertakings, as becomes a servant of the synagogue; a man who is expected to lead a life different from that of any other Jew, a "holy man," specially engaged by the community with the duty of being holy within the limits of the modernism of the congregation that pays him. Whereas the function of the rabbi was to lead and to guide Jewish life as a whole, and, whenever necessary, to adapt it to new circumstances, this modern priest, as with all priests, has to fit into an existing scheme, good or bad. He has to "serve," and woe unto him if he does not meet the expectations of the authority of the synagogue, the social powers actually dominating synagogue Judaism. Certainly such synagogue authority may do excellent work. Possessing the social influence which in a capitalist society is usually associated with wealth, it can organize, it can administer, it certainly can "manage" the affairs of a community; what it cannot do is lead the community, determine its development, plan its future, for it lacks the Jewish knowledge, culture, and historic consciousness which alone can give the requisite sense of responsibility and imaginative power.

It is true that in these days we have learned to look to political leadership for guidance and planning. No one will deny that political leadership is of great importance; but it is very doubtful whether by itself it can shape the future of Judaism. Political leadership will be disastrous in its results if it comes to represent ultimate authority within the nation. What we should look for from our politicians is a successful struggle for political rights; what we cannot hope for is that they will infuse the nation with the desire to use political rights in such a way that the intentions of historic Judaism should be brought nearer to realization. It is certainly very unpleasant to live without elementary human rights, but we have managed to do so for quite a long period; we have not, however, been able as yet to survive without Judaism. Even today, after the great tragedies of the European Jewries, the real crisis is not a political one, but rather of a spiritual nature. Our very survival is in jeopardy, not only because a barbarous anti-Semitism has crushed the European Jewries, but firstly because Judaism is ceasing to be the spiritual strength and moral backbone of the nation. Political leadership, in its preoccupation with political problems, is losing contact with the spiritual problems of Judaism, and may one day find itself in a position in which, after having concluded a victorious struggle for Jewish rights, there are no Jews left to enjoy the long hoped-for fruits of political endeavor. On the occasion of one of the early Zionist Congresses, Ahad Ha'am boldly asserted that the Jewish nation will be redeemed not by politicians and diplomats but by prophets. It is a grave sign for modern Jewry that his words not only remained unheeded at the time, but that there is hardly anyone among our politicians who seems to be aware that they were ever uttered.

III

It was Ahad Ha'am who pointed for all time to the kind of national authority and leadership from which alone we can expect ultimate guidance. It is clear that we cannot produce the prophets that will redeem the nation; they must happen to us like a miracle. But the ground must be prepared on which the miracle may happen, and the soil must be plowed from which alone the prophetic personality can emerge. The prophetic type must have its appropriate background, and its emergence becomes possible only where there is a group from which it can grow organically. Ultimately, all this depends on nationwide education, on the spirit prevalent within it and on the way it determines the character of the average Jew. A nation that looks for its salvation from prophets must first reestablish an authority of prophetic quality, and that means the authority of the historic ideals of Judaism embodied in living personalities—which again means the reestablishment of rabbinical authority, in the historical sense of the term.

It should be clear by now that my point is not to ask for rights and powers to be delegated to the rabbinical office, and certainly not to urge more respect and deference to be shown to its holders. Rather, the point is to urge the need for personalities to exercise rabbinical authority in the sense of national leadership, based on the decisive influence of Judaism in all spheres of Jewish life. It cannot be said that we have the personalities we need, and that because Judaism is no longer the decisive force with us, their guidance remains ineffectual. If, as is only too true, Judaism is without real influence on the modern Jew, then it is part of the task of rabbinical authority to help to change this. And rabbinical authority exists only insofar as it is effective in performing its task. True, rabbinical authority as we have known it in the pre-emancipation period has come to count for little as Western Jewries have gradually lost contact with Judaism. This means that a certain rabbinic type, which at one time served us well, now belongs to the past. It may linger for quite a long time, and even may be preserved as an impressive monument of bygone days, but it is no longer a living force, and it never will be one again. Parallel to the regeneration of Judaism runs the regeneration of rabbinical authority. Just as we have to plan to bring about the great spiritual renaissance, so we must, as part of it, consciously create a new rabbinic type as the bearer of a regenerated rabbinical authority.

At a time like ours, with a spiritual crisis arising out of the tragic break between Jewish teaching and the non-Jewish surroundings dominating the everyday life of the Jew, no guidance is to be expected from the rabbi of the past who is not clearly aware of this dualism. It is certainly true that in the ghettos, and even later in many of the Eastern European countries, there lived great rabbinical personalities who displayed the highest idealism, great nobility of character, and all the qualities of spiritual national leadership. Often, by the mere fact of their existence, they set an inspiring example of a great humanism shaped entirely by Judaism. But they were the products of their time and in later days have become increasingly scarce. For Judaism in their time was, as yet, essentially untouched by any European civilization that could compete with it. The unity still present in the existence of the Jew brought forth that great rabbinic type that was in so many respects exemplary. Since then, Jewish emancipation has basically changed Jewish existence in Western European countries and even in Eastern Europe. The conflict between the traditional world of the Jew and his modern life shaped by a new and dynamic civilization shattered the spiritual unity within the Jew, and to the extent that this happened, the old rabbinic type disintegrated.

Unfortunate though this may be, it is nevertheless a fact of history. The past cannot be called back, and moreover it should not be called back. The great rabbinical personalities of the past are not the men to solve the problems of modern Jewries. We can hardly make any greater mistake than to call in the old type of *gaon* of the Russian or the Polish Jewries to assist us in our difficulties. The new situation demands new men, men who themselves are children of this new situation. They must themselves have suffered all the agonies of the dualism in the life of the modern Jew. The conflict of the two worlds must have torn their own hearts and minds; without this they cannot realize how genuine and serious the problems are, or begin to seek a remedy. As long as the present period of transition lasts, it is vital that leadership should grow from the great spiritual travail in the clash of the two civilizations. This can only happen where men actually live in the two worlds. Living in two worlds obviates one-sidedness in two respects. It obviates the one-sidedness of a rabbinical authority rooted in the past, and the one-sidedness of exclusive attachment to Western European civilization. The rabbi who is fitted for authority and leadership today in Jewry must be deeply rooted in both historic Judaism and modern European civilization. He must be a *talmid hacham* and a scientist, philosopher, or historian in one. Europe and Sinai should meet in his soul. And only as far as he is able to maintain his Judaism in his own personal experience of the conflict will he be able to give guidance to Jewry today. Only a personality harmonized within itself, after a struggle of conflicting ideas, will be able to reveal the message of Judaism to this generation, for such alone will be in a position to translate it into the terms of our age.

Such an achievement demands knowledge and character; real knowledge of Judaism combined with critical insight into the structure and workings of Western civilization, and a character that is strong enough to bear the strain of leaving many problems unsolved, strong enough to think sincerely while deliberate in translating thought into action, cautious and yet bold.

Owing to the complexity of a situation that makes such manifold demands on the limited faculties of man, we cannot expect from the new rabbi the vast and often all-embracing knowledge of traditional Jewish literature which we so often admired in the great personalities of the past. We can no longer expect the knowledge of the whole to be always present in any one man as we have had it before. What we must insist on is the ability of the rabbi to concentrate at any time on any one part or theme of our traditional literature with a thoroughness and ingenuity that should be akin to that of our former great scholars. We may go still further and say that Jewish knowledge can even be deepened today, firstly through our ability to point out previously unseen significance in Jewish conceptions by contrasting them with related ideas in non-Jewish thought; and secondly by applying to the study of the traditional literature of Judaism modern methods of research. For his actual behavior the rabbi of today can have no better and more inspiring example than that of his predecessors in Jewish history. The personal humility and great idealism of the noted rabbis of the past, their deep sense of social justice, their unwavering stand by what they thought right, combined with gentleness of character—to mention only a few of their virtues—will for all time remain a beacon for all who follow them in carrying the burden of rabbinical responsibility.

It is possible that the type of rabbi needed today will come into being, and that when he appears he will be as successful as his forerunners. It is improbable that he can be trained according to a fixed pattern, but Jewish education, when it is worth its name, should be able to produce him.

9

THE SPIRITUAL CRISIS
IN ISRAEL

(1979)

RECENTLY THE PROBLEM of Israeli identity came to my attention again in two similar, rather paradoxical cases. A friend of mine and her husband, both products of left-leaning, anti-religious kibbutzim, were in the United States for a limited period of continued professional education. In a recent letter, referring to Passover, she wrote:

> The holiday was an exciting experience for us. We saw the television mini-series *Holocaust*. That introduced us into the atmosphere of Judaism. We celebrated Passover with a Jewish family. Then came [Israeli] Independence Day, and we marched together with other Jews. We realized for the first time that we are part of a great people, and so is the State of Israel.

The same ignorance of Judaism, the same estrangement from everything Jewish, a similar "discovery" of the Jewish people are all revealed in the words of an Israeli writer in an interview published in the weekend supplement of the daily newspaper *Ha'aretz*. Speaking of his own life and that of his generation, he said, among other things:

> We were not Jews, but Israelis. The word "Jew" was hardly ever heard. We were courageous, *sabras*, different. When one of us traveled in a foreign

country, he would come back, saying proudly: "They didn't notice at all that I was a Jew."

For this man, the meeting with other Jews was the most severe trauma of his life. Where did he meet the other Jews? Not in Israel. But meeting some of the Jewish children in Europe who survived the Holocaust caused him to realize that he was indeed a Jew. What kind of Jew? "The truth is," says he, "that I cannot say what this Jewish identity of mine is."[1]

The paradox, of course, is that Israelis have to leave Israel in order to discover that they are Jews. But what kind of Jews, and why? Mostly, they themselves do not know. There is a severe identity crisis in Israel, so severe that a majority of Israelis are not even aware of the "existential vacuum" (to use Viktor Frankl's terminology) in which they live. This identity problem in Israel is, unfortunately, the direct outcome of a basic mistake of modern Zionism: "Normalization." The cause of the traumatic experience which overcame that Israeli author when he was "meeting with Jews," remnants of European Jewry, was probably due to the fact that for the first time in his life he realized that, after all, we are not a normal people. There was a collapse of the dreamworld in which he had lived as an Israeli non-Jew.

To become a normal people meant, of course, to become like all the other nations. This involved, first of all, looking at ourselves from without—that is, judging ourselves, Judaism, and Jewish history in light of values assimilated from alien cultures. Characteristic of this kind of self-judgment through alien eyes is the rather well-known (in Israel) short story by the distinguished Israeli writer Haim Hazaz, "The Sermon," in which a young man delivers a kind of secular sermon. The gist of his speech is that the Jews have no history. They have been, most of the time, objects of history. Their history is that of the nations in the midst of which they have lived. Their history has been made for them by others; it is imposed upon them. It is all passivity. And, thus, one reaches the conclusion that the Jews are not really a nation. Only now, in the State of Israel, are they made into a nation.

All of this is true if one looks at the Jewish people from without, if one judges the Jews by a concept of history taken from others. One looks at the history of the nations and concludes: "That is not us." Indeed, it is not us. But is there, because of that, no Jewish history? Is it, indeed, all passively endowed history prescribed by others for the Jew? The truth is that throughout the exile of the Jewish people, there were always options available to the Jew. It was already noted by Judah Halevi in his *Kuzari*. In the lands of their exiles, all that Jews had to do in order to join the ruling majority was to repeat a few words, known as the Creed of the various churches, and thus become Christians or Moslems, as the case might be.[2] At the cost of commitment to the truth of their own being, and in the face of great personal sacrifice, they rejected these options and made their choice in the full freedom of spirit and will. If Ahad Ha'am commented on the assimilated Jew of the Enlightenment period that he lived in subjection in the midst of freedom, one may say of the Jewish people prior to that period that, on the whole, they lived in independence in the midst of subjection. It was a form of self-affirmation, of authenticity of being, without comparison in the history of the nations.

The argument also runs: The Jews had no country of their own, no government, no armies; therefore, they were no nation. Again, this is true if one looks at us from without. But what do we find within? Scattered all over the world, the Jews were *one*. Except for minor local variations, they all lived by the same values, pursued the same lifestyle. Wherever Jews met, they encountered each other in mutual recognition. Notwithstanding language differences, they all prayed in the same tongue, according to the same order and, essentially, the same prayers; observed the same holy days; observed the same laws. The literature of the various communities was Jewish literature for all. The talmudic as well as philosophical works written in any one community were meant for all communities. They had no government, yet they governed themselves. For centuries, Jews lived by an internal autonomy. The rabbinical courts were a generally recognized and effective judiciary. The communities were guided only by elected committees. The communal ordinances (*takanot hakahal*) were the laws that prescribed order in all matters affecting the material and spiritual well-being of the communities. Whereas in the rest of the world, general education for all social levels was introduced relatively late, the institution of general education was in existence in all the lands of Jewish exile and had an uninterrupted tradition going back to talmudic times. In all communities there were, for the poor and the sick, welfare services whose historic continuity paralleled that of the educational system. All this internal autonomy was maintained without state power; it required no police enforcement. On the whole, it functioned by the moral force of a self-imposed discipline, unique in human history.

Certainly, there was Jewish history of the Jews' own making, but a different one.

Certainly, we are a people, though unlike the other nations. Not a normal people? Looking at the history of the "normal" nations, one need not be embarrassed by the qualification.

Zionism's striving for "normalization" meant a misreading of Jewish history. Thus, it destroyed the Jew's self-understanding. Moreover, knowingly or unknowingly, "normalization" implied the rejection of Judaism and required the reshaping of the Jewish people in an alien image. But this is impossible. A nation may grow, develop, renew itself from its own resources of the mind and the spirit, in a continuous process of loyalty to its own identity. But a people that refuses to understand itself from within, that cuts itself loose from the meaning of its historic course, that has no respect for its historic identity, is bound to fail. National identities cannot be exchanged; neither can a people turn its back on its past and start from scratch. There are no such beginnings in history. The image, therefore, in which this people was to be reshaped was essentially a negative one, a shattering of the historic molds.

Israel was built with rebellion. This was, in a sense, necessary, and worked well for the founding generation. The giants of that generation were all children of the Judaism of the ages against which they rebelled. Joseph Haim Brenner testified that in his youth he had a thousand pages of Talmud in his head. The same Brenner would also write: "I live in shame as I recall God's kindness that keeps me alive every minute, and that yet I rebel against him."[3] His writings are rich with biblical and talmudic phrases and allusions. That was a generation that had its identity rooted completely in historic Judaism. Its emotions came from the shtetl, its intellectual patterns had been largely forged in the *beit midrash*, the Jewish study hall. The founding generation came because they were returning to the land of their fathers. Thus, A.D. Gordon would write of the situation in the land:

We all agree that our position is dangerous. Our fate hangs by a hair between life and death. Yet we are unwilling to confess to ourselves that our salvation will come only from a giant, almost miraculous effort of the will, so that in a certain sense we may say, together with the masses of the people, that we shall be redeemed and saved for eternal salvation only by way of a miracle.[4]

This rendering into English is somewhat awkward because Gordon uses classical Jewish messianic terminology. The power of the faith that moved him and his contemporaries was essentially a manifestation of the force of Jewish messianic belief in return, an authentic transformation of that belief in a new context, in a new historic situation.

Notwithstanding their rebellion, their values had their origin in the "old home," though they were applied in a new context and, as a result, often became enriched. Let us recall here Gordon's idea of nationhood. He writes: "The nation as a 'collective individual' is a tearing animal. There is not another one like it for cruelty and meanness among all the wild beasts of prey. Acting as a nation, it is not only permitted to tear, to kill, to rob, to steal, to lie, to forge, to defile, to commit all kinds of abominations, but such acts redound to the nation's fame and glory, for which it is worth sacrificing one's life."[5] That is what Gordon sees as history and nationhood, the absence of which among Jews is so deeply regretted by Hazaz's hero in "The Sermon." When we read Gordon, we immediately feel the passion of the Jew behind his words. His ideal is what he calls *am-adam*, a phrase one can render only awkwardly as "man-nation." Behind his Hebrew *adam* one hears its Yiddish equivalent, *mensch*, not just in the sense of a human being, but a humane human being. *Am-adam* is a humane nation. Gordon also puts it this way:

> Where there is no humane nation, there will be no humane human, no humane individual either. And who should more insist on this than we, the children of Israel! We were the first to declare that man was created in the image of God. We have to go further and say: The nation has to be made in the image of God. Not because we are better than the others; but because everything [in human experience] that demands it we have endured and suffered on our own shoulders.[6]

There is no "normalization" here, but complete identification with all of Jewish history. Gordon is also going further here, beyond the "Old Word." But what is spoken is the Old-New Word of Judaism.

All this was rebellion within the continuity of Jewish history. It was internal, Jewish rebellion, carried out with an inherited idealistic fervor. Unfortunately, however, all this is no more. The rebellion of the founding generation is long past. The *sabra* may well live in existential frustration, but he is not a rebel. He has nothing to rebel against. It is worth noting how Berl Katznelson, one of the outstanding leaders of the early Labor movement, who was also the founder of the Histadrut, expressed his misgivings about the future:

> That one generation should rebel against another is natural.... That, however, one generation should tear itself loose from another, which then becomes like one that never existed, is a special curse from our *tocheha* [the portion in the Bible describing the punishment that will befall the Jewish people for not keeping the Tora's commandments].... A generation that does not know its father does not know itself; it does not know what it has inherited and against what it rebels.[7]

Unfortunately, the present generation in Israel not only does not know "the father" of whom Katznelson spoke, who is its "grandfather"; it does not even know its own fathers, such as Katznelson, Brenner, Gordon, and others. The founders, who in spite of their rebellion were heirs, did not succeed in becoming ancestors. This was succinctly expressed by a *kibbutznik* of the older generation, whose words were quoted in an article in the literary publication of the kibbutzim, *Shedemot*. Speaking of his son, the man remarked: "He is not a Jew. I wished he were, at least, a socialist."[8]

This son is no exception, not even in the kibbutzim. Outside of them, in the cities, such souls are much more numerous. Nature does not tolerate a vacuum; much less does the life of a people. The spiritual and value vacuum caused by a Zionism without Judaism has been filled by a crude Levantinism and a vulgar imitation of American materialism. In the earlier days of Zionism, one was apprehensive of the dangers of national assimilation. We have since learned that only a minority may become meaningfully assimilated. There is a great deal that is objectionable in contemporary America. But a minority has the option to assimilate itself to what is positive and noble in the American tradition and civilization. The same is true of any minority in the midst of any other historic culture and tradition. Not so a majority that lives in its own land. It has nothing into which to assimilate. It must be itself; it must live by its own spiritual resources, lest it become the inheritor of the cultural refuse that, in these days of easy worldwide communication and disintegrating value systems, reaches its undiscerning populace in large and intense doses.

In the aftermath of the Yom Kippur War there has been, in limited circles, some awakening to the nature of the problem. Questions have been asked: "Why Israel, and for what?" If one is an Israeli outside of the historic continuity of the Jewish people and of Judaism, a people without a past, without Jewish ideals, cut off from the historic culture and tradition of Judaism, separated from the source of its creativity, then indeed what is Israel for? Why the never-ending struggle, the wars, the internal and external problems, the tension of a little country under continuous siege? Under these circumstances, nothing is more natural than the large emigration of *sabras* in search of greener and quieter pastures. What is more difficult to understand is why so many of them, assuming that they do have the opportunity to leave, remain. Is it some form of macabre blood-and-soil nationalism?

Some mean to address the problem through what they call a "return to the sources." What they actually engage in is a form of literary activity of looking for universalistic, humanitarian "gems" in the midrash and Talmud. It is doubtful whether this kind of literature can replace a people's lack of faith in its historic destiny. The news that the old-time rabbis were not always old-fashioned will provide neither a goal nor direction for the Israeli masses, and certainly not a disciplined will and commitment to pursue a new and different course of behavior. Ideas are not ideals, and for such "quotations" to be effective, one needs foundations.

The Israeli author to whose interview I referred at the beginning of this essay also declared: "Yes, I seek my Jewish identity. However, I cannot find it here." In that context, he was saying that the search for his Jewish identity among the Jews in the United States, where he had spent some time previously, was much more promising than in Israel. Here, of course, the paradox is all too clear. Unfortunately for Israel, it is not altogether unjustified.

This takes us to the other aspect of Israel's identity problem, that of the religious sector in Israel. Needless to say, the majority of religious Jews, rather like the majority of the secular ones, are hardly aware that such a problem exists for them as well. For who can be more sure of his Jewishness than an Orthodox Jew living in the Holy Land of his fathers? The question, however, is whether this is the Jewish identity that the Tora intended for the Jew living in a Jewish state. Is this the Judaism required by the Tora for the Jewish people in its homeland? Given the ignorance about what Judaism really is, the majority of Israelis see Judaism in the image presented by the rabbinate, the heads of the yeshivot, the religious establishment. One may be extremely critical of Israeli secularism, as obviously this writer is, and yet realize—with an aching heart—that this rabbinate, these teachers of the Tora, these guardians seldom command one's respect. On the whole, but for a very few exceptions, they are incapable of conveying the meaning and relevance of Judaism to the people in the context of this completely new reality of statehood.

The image that is thus presented makes it easy for the secularist intellectual to produce his straw man, call it religion or Judaism, and self-assuredly knock him down with the worn-out arguments of a nineteenth- or even eighteenth-century Enlightenment. The image presented is essentially that of the exilic Jew. It is so unimpressive because it is placed in the altogether wrong setting. Exilic Judaism, as the only possible form of Judaism in exile, has its validity. Transferred to the condition of Jewish statehood, it becomes inauthentic. In order to explain what this means, it is necessary to recall some of the essential qualities of classical Judaism.

Religions are usually founded by prophets; Judaism was founded by a father. At the beginning of Judaism stand patriarchs; the prophets employ history to teach what was intended by the fathers. Abraham did not establish a church; his concern was not with the salvation of souls. He was a father, concerned with the life of his children. God says of him: "For I have know him, that he will command his children and his household after him, that they may keep the way of the Eternal, to do justice and righteousness."⁹ A family whose ideal was to observe the way of God, to act justly and righteously, became the Jewish people. Judaism is not a salvationist religion, but the way of life of a people, lived in the under-standing that life is forever in the presence of God. God is the eternal witness. The words of the psalmist, "Let me walk in the presence of the Eternal, in the land of the living," are explained by R. Yehuda: "'The land of the living': That is the marketplace."¹⁰ It is in the midst of life that Judaism is to be realized.

To live with the awareness that life takes place in the presence of the Eternal is an all-inclusive task. It includes man's relationship to God as well as to his fellow men. It is not only a matter of creed, but essentially one of deed. It has ramifications in all fields of human life: Spiritual and material, social and political, economic and cultural. It could not be limited to a church or a religious sect, but had to become the life purpose of a people. Only a people is capable of realizing such an all-embracing life purpose. Therefore, the normal, natural habitat of Judaism is a land of the Jews, the land of Israel. Outside the land of Israel, in all the places where Jews have lived, the social, economic, and political order is determined by cultures that are alien, and often inimical, to Judaism. In those places, wide areas of Jewish teaching, especially as they were formulated in Jewish law, have no application. For instance, wide sections of *Hoshen Mishpat*, the halachot dealing with the judiciary and civil and criminal law; or important parts of *Even Ha'ezer*, concerning family law and marital relationships, remain a mere subject of study, a matter of theory, without any practical application. Judaism is then reduced, halachically, to a regimen of the permitted and the forbidden. But it was meant to bring about the realization of the larger purpose of the Jewish people. In the dispersion, not only the Jewish people, but Judaism, too, is in exile. Congregations, synagogues, and temples can realize the goal only fractionally—services, observances, the family, the Jewish child—but the overarching fullness of life is not their domain. Only the people, in control of its own national existence, is capable of realizing the comprehensive goals of Judaism.

The rabbis taught: "There is no Tora like the Tora of the land of Israel."[11] But why so? If it is Tora, it is Tora everywhere; if it is not, it is not Tora anywhere. How is one's understanding of Tora tied to geography? If the quality of one's understanding depended only on study, geography would not matter. However, understanding of Tora is inseparable from its application. In exile, the application of Tora is limited essentially to the private domain: The individual, the home, the congregation. Very little room is left to Tora in the public domain. We may better appreciate the importance of applying Tora to the full range of actual life situations by recalling that the halacha—that is, the discipline of such application—was originally an oral Tora. R. Joseph Albo, in his *Book of Fundamentals*, explains the need for an "oral teaching" in the following manner:

> The law of God cannot be perfect so as to be adequate for all times, because the ever-new details of human relations, their customs and their acts, are too numerous to be embraced in a book. Therefore Moses was given orally certain general principles, only briefly alluded to in the Tora, by means of which the wise men in every generation may work out the details as they appear.[12]

Halacha was meant to deal with the specific life situation. But that situation is forever changing. The new, the unexpected in the human condition is the material with which halacha has to contend. It examines the situation, it considers its basic principles and then renders a decision. Now, the situation of exile is essentially non-Jewish; it is brought about by developments in a non-Jewish reality. Thus, when halacha is asked to speak its word in a completely new situation, an unfair burden is placed on it. The question put to it is: How may Jewish life be ordered in the midst of a changing, non-Jewish situation? It can be done, and it has been done for many generations, with heroism and sacrifice. But it is not the natural function of halacha to address this question.

It is, for example, the natural function of halacha to teach the observance of the Sabbath in all kinds of changing human situations. But the Tora was given to the Jewish people with a view to their living in the land of Israel, with the power to determine the rhythm of the work week. It is, of course, possible—and Judaism considers it an obligation that has been accepted by the Jewish people for its entire history—to observe the Sabbath even in exile, but that is not the natural setting for the Sabbath. Problems of the Sabbath in exile, such as how to make a living in an economic order that rests on Sunday, are not genuine problems of Sabbath observance, but part of the much wider issue of how to be a Jew in the unnatural setting of Jewish dispersion. The original function of the halacha is thus adulterated, when it is forced to contend with the ever-changing "particulars" of a non-Jewish reality in which Jews happen to live.

As a result, the halacha is negatively affected in two directions. It cannot shape and guide the specific, time-conditioned situation, for it must defend itself—it must defend Jewish existence—against the pressure and inroads of the "outside world." In exile, halacha becomes a rampart, and yet, as the word itself indicates, it was intended to be a pathway. In exile, halacha is Jewish existence, managed via the Tora, in spite of a form of life and culture that is alien to the spirit of Judaism. On the defensive, halacha becomes stunted in its creative capacity. This has far-reaching consequences for its very nature. Halacha as the application of general principles to changing particulars, once again to use Albo's formulation, needs the challenge of those "particulars," the challenge emanating from the situation of the Jewish people at a given time. It needs the challenge of a situation that is Jewish, not because it is endured by Jews, but because, in its physical and mundane structure, it is the work of the Jewish people. That, alone, is the authentic challenge to halacha. Only in response to this challenge can halacha become creative, formulating the eternal word of the Tora for the new hour, the hour of new "particulars."

All this, of course, is possible only in a state of the Jewish people. This is the meaning of the uniqueness of the "Tora of the land of Israel." In the State of Israel, Albo's "new particulars" are Jewish. They are Jewish raw material for halacha to work with. The exilic, defensive posture is no longer valid. One has to go out and meet this new challenge and show how this new Jewish reality is to be structured meaningfully and effectively by the creative power of halacha. One has to leave the ramparts built around the "private domain" of the congregation, the Jewish school, or the home in exile, and restore halacha to its original function as a pathway for the "public domain," for the life of the Jewish people in a Jewish state. To mention just a few areas: Halacha in the State of Israel ought to concern itself with the social gap, with questions of economic honesty and fairness, with issues of the work ethic and problems of labor relations, with medical ethics, even with such matters as meaningful driving laws in the cities and on the highways and with adequate enforcement.

How far removed we are from a proper understanding of what Tora and halacha are about cannot be more strikingly illustrated than by the one-sided educational ideal of the yeshivot in Israel. Most of them frown on what is called *limudei hol*, "secular studies." But a state needs an army, an economic system, health and welfare services, technology, scientific research, and so forth. If the Tora desires a Jewish people living in its own land, it must also desire soldiers, physicians, scientists, architects, engineers, policemen, and social workers. In a Jewish state, halacha cannot refuse responsibility for the effective functioning of the entire polity. This requires, however, a new educational philosophy, which would lead, in turn, to new ways of learning Tora and Talmud, and new ways of teaching both.

The new reality of the State of Israel demands an understanding of what halacha is about in its original, classical essence. Perhaps one of the major issues to which such new understanding ought to pay attention is the fact that in a state of Jews, one is dealing not with congregations but with a people. It is relatively easy to manage the congregational structure. Congregations have their declared ideologies. Those who subscribe to them are in, those who do not are on the outside. One may lament the attitude of the outsiders, but one need not be concerned about them very much. A people, however, is always within. Halacha, in its authentic function, must address itself to the Jewish people and not to members with congregational ideologies. What we have in Israel today is an understanding of halacha and its application to an exilic reality that no longer exists. It is the halacha of the shtetl, not the halacha of the state; it is not the Tora of the land of Israel.

It is this that robs teachers and interpreters of convincing authority and respect. In the shtetl they were part of the community, deeply involved in its life and problems. In Israel they live in estrangement from this new reality of the Jewish people. The psychological effects of such alienation are often responsible for a behavior that is deeply regretted by many Jews to whom the dignity of Judaism is dear.

There is widespread secularism in Israel today. But there is also an awakening to the truth that, especially in Israel, secularism is leading the people toward a spiritual and moral dead end. There are many who search for a Jewish way. The people will not be the Jewish people and the state not a Jewish state without Judaism, and Judaism will not be true to itself without finding the way to the people.

Alienation from Judaism is the source of the existential vacuum among the secularists. Alienation from the new reality of Israel's statehood calls into question the authenticity of the image of Judaism that has been transferred from exile by the religious establishment.

And yet, this is the land and this the people. It is here, in the land of Israel, that the destiny of all Israel will be decided for all generations to come. Thus, the problems of this land become the problems of the Jewish people the world over. Their solution is the responsibility of us all.

III

JEWISH THEOLOGY

10

THE ENCOUNTER
WITH THE DIVINE

(1959)

I. THE PARADOX OF THE ENCOUNTER

THE AIM OF THIS ESSAY is to examine the nature of the prophetic encounter as it emerges from the biblical record.

The encounter is an actual experience in which all of man's senses are involved; yet it is certainly no material vision of the deity that is revealed.[1] There are signs, a voice, which convey with irresistible force the knowledge of the Presence, which itself is yet invisible. The knowledge is not derived, but is immediate. The Presence is "felt"; it envelops the whole human being. It communicates itself with such overpowering certainty that no doubting is possible for those whom it confronts.

One may not always understand of what this sense of certainty consists, but often it is associated with an experience of danger. God's presence seems to be threatening; it imperils the life of the very person to whom it expresses itself. When Moses realized that it was God who spoke to him from the bush, the Bible reports that he hid his face, "for he was afraid to look upon God."[2] Standing at the mountain of Sinai, the children of Israel trembled with fear at the voice of God, which yet was conferring on them their greatest distinction. That their fear was justified, that they were in real danger from the very act of revelation, is confirmed by the words in Deuteronomy, addressed to them by their leader and teacher: "Did ever a people hear the voice of God speaking out of the midst of the fire, as you have heard, and live?"[3]

Numerous are the biblical passages that tell of the fear and trembling that seize the prophet at the moment when the divine Presence actualizes itself for him. This is not, however, because of the stern rigor that is supposed to be the hallmark of the "Jewish" deity. Such generalizations are proof that centuries of religious philosophy were not sufficient to help people understand the fundamental experience without which biblical religion is inconceivable. The peril resulting from "contact" with the divine Presence has nothing to do either with the sinfulness of man or with the judgment of the Almighty. It is something quite natural, almost "physical," if one may say so. A man wilts in the heat of the midday sun, or dies of exhaustion if exposed too long to the cold. Often mere lightning and thunder or the tempest of the elements frighten him. How, then, can he hope to stand in the presence of the source of all energy and power in the cosmos; how dare he approach it and survive? "Suppose a thousand suns should rise together into the sky,"[4] the Bhagavad-Gita asks, what would happen to our earth? Yet the "thousand suns" are a crude comparison, as all comparison must be, with God. By referring to him here as the ground of all power in the cosmos, I do not mean to suggest a material likeness of him. But whatever the unimaginable essence of the Almighty be, it does imply a concentration of power and energy (and who indeed would say these days what energy is?) that surpasses any imaginable such concentration.

The Almighty is indeed "a consuming fire";[5] not because he is angry with a sinful world, but because the potency of his being cannot be sustained by anything created. The Presence imperils men, not on account of God's will directed against man, but because divine nature is so charged with the vitality of being that its nearness naturally overwhelms all individual existence.

Thus, we are faced with a paradox. The God of religion, we have observed, must be a living one.[6] And a living God is one who stands in relationship to the world—that is, a God who not only *is*, but is also *for* man, as it were, who is concerned about man. We may know of the relationship only if it is real, if the divine concern is actually revealed to man. This is what we have called the encounter, which is the fundamental religious experience. Now we find that the encounter threatens the very existence of man. Without the encounter there can be no religion, but the encounter itself man cannot endure. There can be no religion without some active relationship between man and God; in the relationship, however, man cannot survive.

The paradox is resolved by God, when he "shows" himself to man. God, who reveals his "unbearable" Presence to the helpless creature, also sustains man in the act of revelation. The prophet Ezekiel, for instance, reports on one of his encounters: "And I fell on my face. Then the spirit entered into me, and set me upon my feet, and spoke with me...."[7] The key phrase is "and set me upon my feet." The prophet fell on his face because he was thrown to the ground by the force of the encounter. But in that condition of weakness, his ability as a messenger of God to Israel was taken from him. Only after the spirit had set him on his feet could God address him. The encounter crushed Ezekiel; but it was in the encounter that he was granted the strength to stand up and, notwithstanding the terror, face the Presence. God can meet man only by sustaining him against the impact of God's own Presence.

Obviously, not just any form of life sustained in the prophet will allow the encounter to take place. It is not enough to grant him a kind of life that may make of him some new creation, in the old external garb. The spirit has to set Ezekiel on his feet, so that he may again be himself. His own self must be returned to him; otherwise no encounter with Ezekiel per se is possible. But Ezekiel may retain his personal identity in the encounter if God, in revealing his presence, protects the prophet against his "consuming" essence. All protection that shields the prophet, however, hides God from him. God can only reveal himself to man by hiding himself in the very act of revelation.[8] In the peril, which is implied (and yet restrained) in the encounter, God both reveals and hides himself. He reveals himself, that his concern for man may be known; he hides himself in the very act of revelation, so that the subject of his concern may not be consumed by the very knowledge shown to him. He reveals himself as a "hiding" God, so that man may live in his sight. As Isaiah said of him: "You are surely a God who hides himself; O God of Israel, the savior."[9]

We may now see more clearly what is implied in the encounter. It creates a relationship that is charged with ambivalence. In the encounter, man is threatened as well as sustained. The peril reflects the transcendence of God, which man cannot sustain. The danger is a reflection of the edge with which divine transcendence juts out into human experience. But man is also protected in the encounter. He is sustained by God, so that the encounter may be possible; that God may turn toward him, as it were. Notwithstanding the terror of divine transcendence, man is assured of God's nearness and accessibility.

Under the crushing burden of the Presence, man discovers his own nothingness before God, his complete dependence on him. But there can be no encounter with nothing. Man is therefore raised up again and granted strength to retain his individuality and to be himself. Unless there is man, there can be no revelation; unless man is permitted to be himself, there can be no religion. All relationship requires two participants; man as well as God must exist. In the encounter, the identity of man must remain inviolate. Experiencing his complete dependence, man is at the same time granted a measure of independence. He is free to be himself because God cares for him.

Without that freedom, the relationship would be of no value, for man would cease being a person. The encounter is significant because it happens between God and a person who is free to be himself. The hiding God is, therefore, not only a "physical necessity," as it were, in order to protect the human being against the "consuming fire"; it is a moral necessity too that he should "hide," in order to preserve the personality of man, without which no encounter is possible. Man may confront the divine Presence only because God curbs, as it were, his transcendence. God "denies" himself in order to affirm man. By an act of divine self-denial, man is made free to deny him. In order to be encountered, man must possess his own self with a measure of freedom; and if so, he is also free to refuse the encounter. But it is because of such freedom that the encounter becomes a fellowship. The act of divine self-denial is the precondition of the fundamental religious experience.

Thus, the encounter is significant also for what it implies about the God of religion. In the terror, which is a hint of the divine transcendence, God is revealed as the "Wholly Other"; yet man is able to gain a glimpse of the "Wholly Other" solely because God, hiding his transcendence, makes himself accessible to man. In the encounter, man does experience what has been called the *mysterium tremendum*,[10] but he also hears the "still, small voice" that reassures and affirms. The "Wholly Other" reveals itself as the "friend," the sustainer and preserver. This is of the essence of Judaism. God is far removed, and yet he is near. "For though the Eternal be high, yet he regards the lowly."[11] The combination of the idea of divine transcendence with that of divine concern for man has found one of its noblest formulations in the words of Isaiah, when the prophet declares:

> Thus says the Eternal:
> The heaven is my throne,
> And the earth is my footstool,
> Where is the house that you may build for me?
> And where is the place that may be my resting place?
> For all these things has my hand made.
> And so all these things came to be,
> Says the Eternal;
> But on *this* one will I look,
> Even on *him that is poor and of a contrite spirit*,
> And trembles at my word.[12]

Bolder still than the prophets were the teachers of the Talmud, who possessed sufficient spiritual courage to make the daring statement: "Where you find the mightiness of the Holy One, there you also find his humility."[13] The humility of God is a frightening term; yet God's concern for lowly man cannot be explained in any other way. In the encounter, it is God's self-denial which "sets man upon his feet." One might say that only through divine humility is man granted strength of individuality to be able to endure, even briefly, the slightest measure of divine might. In the very terror of the encounter, man is affirmed.

Just as the divine self-revelation in the encounter is dual, so too is man's self-cognizance correspondingly dual. Man is threatened and affirmed at the same time. Through the peril that confronts him, he is bound to recognize his nothingness before God; yet in the divine affirmation, the highest dignity is bestowed on him: He is allowed into "fellowship" with God. A striking example of the dual significance of the encounter is found in the case of the patriarch Abraham pleading on behalf of the people of Sodom and Gomorrah. Abraham acknowledges his own position with the words: "Behold now, I have taken upon me to speak unto the Lord, who am but dust and ashes." Yet he does speak, and in the clearest terms: "Far be it from you to act in this manner, to slay the righteous with the wicked... shall not the judge of all the earth do justly?"[14] It is from God that the patriarch derives the strength to face him; it is God who granted this heap of "dust and ashes" the dignity of a conscience, which must be asserted even when confronting God. In the encounter, not only does God reveal himself to man, but man is revealed to himself.

The dual nature of man, which emerges in the basic religious experience, found its classical formulation in the words of the psalmist:

> What is man, that you are mindful of him?
> And the son of man, that you think of him?
> Yet you have made him but little lower than the angels,
> And have crowned him with glory and honor.[15]

Man, who is "dust and ashes" and yet "crowned with glory and honor," is the corollary to God, whose throne is the heaven and whose footstool is the earth and who yet looks on him who is "poor and of a contrite spirit." It is the mightiness of God that reduces man to nothing, and it is his "humility" that elevates man to a rank "but little lower" than that of the angels.

Through the encounter Judaism first learned of God, who is Almighty and yet cares for man, Supreme Lord and yet a friend. From his presence emanates assurance as well as terror. He is King and Father. But since, as we saw, man's ability to survive the terror of his presence is due only to the assurance of God, it is through the Father that we know of the King. Therefore, the Jew invokes God in the liturgical phrase "our Father, our King." And so is man, too, son as well as subject. The subject cannot but tremble, for the sense of one's own nothingness before the King may never depart; however, the son, the human personality redeemed from the state of dust and ashes and elevated in the presence of the Father, cannot but rejoice. The worship of the Jew is, therefore, one of fear and love.[16] Or as the psalmist puts it: "Serve the Eternal with fear, and rejoice with trembling."[17]

It is important, however, to distinguish between our interpretation of the prophetic encounter as the basic religious experience and the way of the mystic.

The encounter should not be confused with the mystical communion. The mystic's goal is the surrender of personal existence. His desire is to merge himself in the One, to pour himself into God, to be drawn into the All. The mystic finds his fulfillment in the extinction of his dignity through being consumed by the Absolute. For him individuality is a burden and a shame. Only the One or the All is real, and every form of separateness from it is an unworthy shadow existence. In the encounter, on the other hand, the original separateness is affirmed; in fact, it is granted its highest dignity by being sustained by God. The encounter may occur *because* the individual personality is safeguarded. Where there is encounter, there is fellowship; and fellowship is the very opposite of the mystical surrender of man's identity in an act of communion. Judaism is not a non-mystical religion; Judaism is essentially non-mystical because it is religion. The mystical communion is the end of all relationship and, therefore, also the end of all religion.

Judaism is essentially non-mystical because, according to it, God addresses himself to man, and he awaits man's response to the address. God speaks and man listens; God commands and man obeys. Man searches, and God allows himself to be found; man entreats, and God answers. In the mystical union, however, there are no words and no law, no search and no recognition, because there is no separateness.[18] Judaism does not admit the idea that man may rise "beyond good and evil," as it were, by drowning himself in the Godhead.

There is a natural affinity between mysticism and pantheism. All mysticism tends toward pantheism. Once the mystical union is completed, there is nothing left but the Absolute, in which all is contained. The appropriate worldview of the mystic is pantheism. It is his justification for devaluing individual existence, as well as for attempting to redeem it through return into the All. On the other hand, mysticism is the only available "religion" for the pantheist. His worship of the Absolute demands the denial of his own separateness from it. Thus, we are led to the Spinozistic *amor dei*; since nothing exists apart from the infinite, man's love for God "is the very love of God with which God loves himself."[19] One is inclined to agree with those who see in this the monstrous example of absolute self-love.[20] The truth, of course, is that where there is no separateness, there is no love either. Where there is no encounter, there can be no care or concern. The mystic endeavors to overcome all separateness; the pantheist denies it from the very beginning. Judaism, on the other hand, through its concept of the encounter, affirms the reality as well as the worth of individual existence. Judaism is not only non-mystical, it is also essentially anti-pantheistic.[21]

II. FAITH, REASON, AND THE ENCOUNTER

The question may be asked: If the encounter is the fundamental religious experience, what does this imply about the nature of faith? What is its relationship to the encounter?

On its own, the proposition that God exists, even if proved, need not lead to religion. Religion maintains not only that God exists, but that he is also concerned about man and the world.[22] Faith, therefore, requires belief not only in God's existence, but also in his concern. Originally, we know of the divine care for man only by actual experience. This thought gave us the concept of the encounter. While the encounter lasts, we know of God's concern beyond any doubt. But what of the time after the encounter? Does God withdraw himself from the world? Does he become the Absolute of metaphysics, for whom all involvement in life is inconceivable, until the next encounter? Such an idea would, of course, be absurd. It would destroy all meaningful religion. During the encounter man knows with immediate certainty of God's concern; afterwards, he knows about it by an act of faith.

In the encounter man is "shown" not that God happens to care at one particular moment, but that he is a caring God. Therefore, even after the actual experience of the relationship has passed, the knowledge remains with man that God does not withdraw, that he does not abandon man, that the relationship of concern is not severed even though it is no longer experienced. The knowledge follows logically from the encounter. But what is logic in the absence of the experience? Logically speaking, a caring God ought to care always. But we generally do not recognize his care and concern; most of the time God is silent, as if absent. Transcendental divine indifference seems to replace the short and extremely rare moments of the relationship in the encounter. It is here that faith has its place. Faith turns the theoretical consequences of the encounter into living reality. Through faith we know that even though God seems to be absent, he is present all the time; even though he is far, he is close at hand; even though he transcends all life, still we confront him every moment of our existence. Through the power of faith we know, as if by actual experience, that his gaze is always upon us, that no matter where we may turn, we are forever in his presence. The psalmist expressed this in the words:

I have set the Eternal always before me;
Surely he is at my right hand, I shall not be moved.[23]

The essence of faith is a sensitivity of the entire personality to the Presence, even when the realness of the Presence is not as directly evident as in the acute form of the encounter. The act of faith holds on to the encounter beyond its actualization. Thanks to faith, the encounter never passes; the Presence remains forever on the threshold of possible experience.

This function of faith is of vital significance for Judaism. We call Judaism a historic religion because it was constituted by a number of encounters between God and the patriarchs and prophets of Israel, encounters whose meaning has remained valid for all generations of Jews. Eliminate Abraham, Isaac, and Jacob and their intercourse with God, deny the revelation at Sinai and the words of the prophets, and you have destroyed the foundations of Judaism. On the other hand, the encounter as the basic religious experience means that all religion must be personal. Unless God is accessible to me, unless I am able to confront him myself, unless he is concerned about the way I live and behave, however insignificant I may otherwise be, religion is not possible for me. But the confrontation between God and Israel, the Judaism-constituting encounters, occurred many centuries ago. How can they be personalized for me? It is true, these encounters are on record, and we have elsewhere advanced reasons for the credibility of the biblical testimony.[24] However, to accept a recorded event as credible does not constitute religion, but belongs to the discipline of history. That God revealed himself to the children of Israel in the wilderness is history. As such, though a most unusual event, with far-reaching historic consequences, it would concern us only as a matter of information. Giving credence to the record becomes religion when the event is accepted as if what happened at Sinai had happened to oneself now. The problem of personalizing the public encounter in history is solved within Judaism by viewing God's revelation at Sinai as a continuing address to all the generations of Israel.

The solution is clearly expressed in the Bible in the well-known words of Deuteronomy: "Neither with you only do I make this covenant and this oath; but with him that stands here with us this day before the Eternal our God, and also with him that is not here with us this day."[25] It is noteworthy that the ancestors are not said to have concluded the covenant on behalf of their children. It is extremely doubtful that such a procedure could have been valid. The text insists that the oath and covenant were made with those too who were not yet born. The later generations did not inherit it; the covenant was originally made with them directly, as it was made with their forefathers. The need for so strange a concept derives from the very essence of religion. The covenant is the most intense form of the encounter. But the encounter must be real for me, or else it does not exist for me; and so it is with the covenant too. The covenant with my ancestors was concluded with them. As an event in history, it could not but affect the lives of their children as well; yet it could not be a covenant with the children. For me it is history, not encounter, that my forefathers encountered God. However, where there is no encounter, there may be philosophizing about religion, but there is no religion. For the revelation at Sinai to be revelation for me, it must be addressed to me. And so the covenant had to be concluded with all generations.

This could be done because, while the generations of the wilderness did pass away, God is timeless and therefore the manifestation at Sinai is timelessly directed to Israel. The revelation at Sinai never belongs to the past, it never ceases to be. It is as if the divine Presence, never departing from the mountain, were waiting for each new generation to come to Sinai to encounter him and to receive the word. Judged from the aspect of God's relationship to Israel, as revealed at Sinai or in the exodus from Egypt, these encounters are ever-present events. The miracles and the signs, the thunder and the lightning are gone; but not God, nor the word, nor Israel. And so it is for the eye of faith to see what has been withdrawn from the senses, and for the ear of faith to hear, notwithstanding the silence.[26]

We may now say that while the encounter is the foundation of religion, faith is its edifice. Without the encounter, we could not know the God of religion, the God who is concerned about us and our world. With the encounter alone, we could not face the contradiction between what is conveyed in the encounter, which is God's concern, and what often follows after it, namely, his apparent indifference. Faith, in keeping the truth communicated in the encounter alive at all times, is the answer to the contradiction. Since the encounters are few and quickly passing, and since most of life is spent without their being granted to man, without faith the encounter itself would be like a tiny island of freakish fellowship with the Supreme Being in an ocean of loneliness.

It may now be advisable to take a closer look at the material, as it were, which goes into the making of faith. What is at hand to justify faith, according to our interpretation?

There are, of course, the memories of the experiences of the encounter. For those few people who themselves had the experience, the prophets and the saints, these are personal memories. The impression that the event itself made on them is indelible; it will easily change the entire course of a man's life. Yet even these chosen may doubt, not the existence of God, but whether the relationship has not been severed, whether God is still "mindful" of them. The quest of the pious for God is the quest for nearness to him, for fellowship with him. It originates in the anguish of the soul that feels the loss of "contact" as the result of personal unworthiness. Only one who has known such fellowship may call out, with the psalmist:

> My God, my God, why have you forsaken me,
> And are far from my help at the words of my cry?
> O my God, I call by day, but you answer not....[27]

Only he who has learned of the nearness of God as a matter of immediate experience may exclaim:

> Upon you I have been cast from my birth;
> You are my God from my mother's womb.
> Be not far from me; for trouble is near....[28]

The immediacy of contact can never be recovered outside the encounter. But the continuous recourse to the memory of it, as well as the quest of the soul for the renewal of the experience, causes one to develop an awareness of the Presence which, though withdrawn and silent, remains concerned.

This, however, is equally possible in the case of an entire people like Israel, whose memories of the encounter are mediated by its history. The memories of Israel are our own memories. The events to which they refer are our own history; they formed us and determined our destiny. And so we know of Israel's encounters with God as if they had been our own. As we delve into our memories, our hearts long for "the renewal of our days as of old" and for overcoming the estrangement. The longing is the beginning of the quest; it supplies the tension which sustains the soul in gaining awareness of the Presence through the act of faith, even when God is "hiding" from us.

The awareness of the divine Presence may not in itself be very conclusive; in itself such a sense may be completely subjective, a feeling to which nothing in reality corresponds. However, for him who starts out in his quest with the memory of the actual encounter, and the very real sense of estrangement from God which followed it, the awareness in faith of the Presence is like finding a lost treasure which is recognized by its familiar marks. In view of the original encounter, all faith is an act of recognition.

This idea may help us in discerning other sources from which faith may draw its strength. Any serious meditation on existence and the nature of being, any effort to attune the sensitive soul to the imponderable quality of reality, fills one with a sense of awe and mystery. Now, by itself, neither the awe nor the mystery is decipherable. On their own, they do not lead to God. Nature as such may justify both. Left to themselves, the experience of the mystery and the sense of awe are riddles without solution. But in the light of the encounter, we may occasionally recognize them as the traces of the Presence. The memories of the encounter are the key with which to unlock the secret of the mystery about us. They are guidance for the soul in quest of a lost fellowship. Only by the way of recognition may the mystery and the awe find their rightful place within the kingdom of faith.

The principle of recognition in the light of the encounter may also enable us to redefine the function of reason within the realm of religion. We have established the independence of religion from philosophy or metaphysics, but not for a moment did we mean to take recourse to any form of irrationalism as a source of religion.[29] The arguments demonstrating that reason by itself can never lead to the God of religion are themselves rational ones. This, we have shown, is not due to any skepticism concerning the value of the intellectual faculty, but to the nature of religion. Had God not actually revealed his concern for this world, it would be impossible for man to know about it. This revelation of the divine concern constitutes the independence of religion. That religion is based on an actual experience, and is not derived logically, does not make it irrational. For any non-dogmatic mind, once the credibility of the records of religious experience has been ascertained, the unexpected event of the encounter will expand the frontiers of the possible and modify accordingly the notion of rationality.

Once the encounter is made the starting point, we may understand the significance of a religious metaphysics and philosophy. All the known proofs for the existence of God yield no more than a "most likely hypothesis" that a First Cause, an Infinite Supreme Being, may well be assumed as existing.[30] This is about all that philosophy may accomplish for us, and it is not religion. But for the man for whom the encounter has laid the foundations of religion and who, possessed of its memories, is in search of the hiding Presence, the "most likely hypothesis" of a religious metaphysics becomes a source of continuous encouragement in the quest and a signpost for guiding him to the threshold of the Presence. The "most likely hypothesis" by itself has little convincing force, but if one comes upon it in one's search for the "lost" encounter, the hypothesis may be a potent factor in leading man to the form of recognition that he attains in an act of faith.[31]

In another place we have discussed the intrinsic fallacy of the negative attributes of God.[32] But they do make sense for one who reaches the idea after the encounter. In the encounter, man is permitted a passing glance at the transcendence of God; it is that which fills man with insupportable terror. As he then meditates on the essence of the Godhead, he may really acknowledge that it can be described in negative terms only. However, the negative attributes are revealed by the "terror," which itself is a positive mark of divine nature. The negative attributes, therefore, become an affirmation of the divine transcendence. In this way, against the background of the encounter, the negative attributes remain true to their logical implication, in that they do describe the divine essence and not nothing.[33] And we may again say that a soul steeped in the memories of the encounter may recognize in the negative attributes some positive features of divine transcendence at which man was permitted to glance in the terror of an actual experience.

In other words, in addition to the memory of the encounter and the longing of the soul for the renewal of "contact" with the divine Presence, the sense of mystery and awe as well as the philosophical quest for the ground of all being may serve as sources for the justification of faith. In themselves, as we have seen, neither the sense of awe nor the intellectual search will lead to the God of religion. But when re-evaluated in the post-encounter phase of man's experience, in the context of the effort of recognition, both may become significant forces in the constitution of religious faith.

At the same time, faith may never replace the certitude of the moment of the encounter itself. There is always an element of risk involved in faith. One may spend one's entire life believing, yet God may remain silent, and the loneliness of the soul may never be healed on this earth. To affirm, then, that God is "silent in his love"[34] is the highest creative commitment of which a man may be capable. The element of risk is the source of the tension that keeps the act of faith forever young. Because of the risk, one has to believe every day anew, one has to affirm again and again. Therein lies the essential significance of faith. Faith is commitment on behalf of God; it is a stand taken on the proposition that God is forever concerned about man and the world. It is a stand taken by man in freedom, in a situation in which the denial of God's existence need not be a logical impossibility. Only because faith is a commitment made in freedom is it a commitment at all; only because of this is it a continuation of the fellowship initiated by God in the encounter.

Commitment in freedom is the hallmark of fellowship. This may explain why the encounters themselves have to be rare and fleeting. We have maintained that in the encounter itself, God may reveal his Presence only by hiding himself. The essential disparity between the transcendental "vitality" of the Almighty and the nature of man imperils man's existence. But even though in revealing himself God hid his power, the threat to the human personality would remain if the encounter occurred frequently. Frequent encounters need not cause the actual absorption of the individual in the Absolute, but they would certainly bring to naught his freedom of commitment. Two human beings meeting each other may or may not enter into fellowship; because of a general equality between them, they may accept or reject each other. With God, however, it is not so; one who encounters God cannot refuse him. Frequent encounters between God and mankind would give us certitude, but of such a compelling kind that it would crush our freedom to acknowledge him. In the interest of religion itself, the Almighty has to be a "hiding" God.

We may now, perhaps, even make peace with the idea that reason knows of no convincing way to God. In conformity with the requirements of religion, the intellect should be able to yield no more than a "most likely hypothesis" for the existence of God. All conclusive proof is a form of intellectual coercion. It is true, as we have argued, that philosophical proofs would still not give us the "caring" God of religion; nevertheless the logical necessity of valid proofs would considerably reduce the element of freedom and risk necessary for the act of faith. Because of the infinite inequality between the Absolute Being and man, the intellectual compulsion alone would undermine the value of man's commitment to God.

Religion does not reduce man to being a puppet of God; it elevates him to his highest dignity by enabling him to acknowledge God in free commitment. The "fellowship" is initiated by God in the encounter; it is sustained after the encounter in the ever-renewed act of faith by man. To make this possible, God must hide: During the encounter, to safeguard man's own survival; in history, to protect the spiritual independence of man in making his decision for God; and, finally, God must remain elusive to the conclusive grasp of reason so that man may retain his intellectual freedom. Where there is compulsion, there can be no fellowship.

III. GOD ENCOUNTERED

One of the major problems of all philosophy of religion is that of the divine attributes. It is inconceivable that man's understanding should be able to penetrate to the essence of the Infinite. It is, therefore, unclear how the divine being may be described, except in a formula such as "the Eternal, he is God."[35] But what is really gained by this apparent tautology?

We shall here consider the "information" that is conveyed about God in the encounter, that which is revealed to man in the basic religious experience.

No doubt, the most significant thing that we learn from the experience is that God is present for man,[36] that he stands in relationship to this world. The relationship is fundamental to all religion; but it can only be known if it has been "shown" to man.

We are told in the Bible that God is One.[37] It is not the Neo-Platonic One that is thus revealed. We know nothing about the One of Neo-Platonism. In the Bible it is the Eternal our God, known from the encounter, the Eternal who led us out of the land of Egypt, who spoke to us at Sinai, who was with us in our wanderings through the wilderness, a "familiar" God, of whom it is affirmed that he is One.[38] But his oneness, too, has to be revealed, or else it could not be known. The philosophical reduction of Being to the One is not at all convincing. There is no end to the possibilities of explaining the ground of reality either by the principle of unity or by that of multiplicity. In metaphysics, the conflict between the one and the many remains forever unresolved. The intellect's aspiration to discover unity and order in the midst of multiplicity is an endless adventure. The achievements of this adventure are unceasingly challenged by the continually emerging elements of disunity. At all times, new waves of the primordial chaos seem to be welling up from the deep to mock man's neat discovery of order in the universe. Especially when judged from the angle of amoral purpose, Being seems to be much more readily explainable as the multiplicity of interests than as unity. Individual as well as historic experience appears to provide ample bias toward the Manichaean philosophy of a dualistic universe, in which two antithetical principles are locked in a perennial struggle for dominion. Furthermore, even if the principle of oneness could be conclusively established, we would know that the ground of reality was one only insofar as reality might be encompassed by our experience and our intellect. But "our" reality is of necessity limited, and, therefore, the One thus gained would be finite itself.[39] We would never know that "there is none else beside him."[40] The God of the Bible, however, is the only One.[41] We cannot know that he is alone in his oneness, except as it is "shown" to us by an act of revelation in an actual encounter.

As to the essence of God itself, the notion of its transcendence is undoubtedly communicated. However, transcendence is not conveyed as a concept or as a clearly definable metaphysical idea, but in an experience of its realness in which the entire human being participates. It is the experience of the divinity as "Wholly Other" which is the source of the *mysterium tremendum*.[42] The experience of divine transcendence is granted to man in the moment of terror, which is inseparable from the encounter.

The transcendence of the Supreme Being is thus touching man, as it were, in a moment of excruciating, overwhelming awe. Man receives no hint of the further reaches of divine transcendence. This, of course, could not be otherwise. Man could never survive the burden of an encounter with the realness of the Infinite, or even the mere vision of the full compass of the Absolute. Infinitude and Absoluteness are intellectual concepts; it is not possible to experience their corresponding reality. On the other hand, the fleeting breeze of transcendence, which shakes man in the encounter for a quickly passing and saving moment, is an experience. For this reason, all biblical descriptions of the transcendent nature of God are couched in terms of finite experience.

In order to illustrate the point, we quote one of the classical passages of prophetic elaboration of divine transcendence, in the book of Isaiah:

> Who has measured the waters in the hollow of his hand,
> And meted out heaven with the span,
> And comprehended the dust of the earth in a measure,
> And weighed the mountains in scales,
> And the hills in a balance?...
> Behold, the nations are as a drop in the bucket,
> And are counted as the small dust of the balance;
> Behold, the isles are as a mote in weight....
> All the nations are as nothing before him;
> They are accounted by him as things of naught and vanity....
> Do you not know? Do you not hear?
> Has it not been told you from the beginning?
> Have you not understood the foundations of the earth?
> It is he that sits above the circle of the earth,
> And the inhabitants thereof are as grasshoppers;
> That stretches out the heavens as a curtain,
> And spreads them out as a tent to dwell in....
> To whom then will you liken me, that I should be equal?
> Says the Holy One.[43]

Now and then one comes across philosophical writers who point to the naivete of passages such as this one. Metaphysically speaking, the Absolute is in a category of its own. It is indeed incomparable, but not because it is much bigger and much more powerful than anything else, but because it is *essentially* unlike anything else. Notwithstanding such criticism, the entire passage is aglow with religious inspiration. It is not meant to be read as a metaphysical dissertation on the subject of the Infinite, but as an interpretation of the moment in which transcendence touches man in the actual encounter. Since it is a positive experience of God as Wholly Other, the incomparability of the divine being is described in comparative terms, relative to experience. It is not an attempt to encompass the Absolute, but to convey the vision of divine transcendence as it takes shape, heavily veiled, at the transitory moment of its contact with the finite realm. Strictly speaking, the Absolute per se is not a subject of religion. The focus of all religion is the Absolute in its relationship to man and the world. It is the moment of transcendence in its relatedness to man which is described in the biblical passage in terms of "comparative" incomparability.

If, however, the notion of the Absolute itself cannot be conveyed in the encounter, how does religion acquire the idea? In the answer to this question, we should recall what has been said above regarding the function of reason in religion. In the question of attributes we are presented with yet another example of that function. The religious thinker starts out with a number of certitudes which are germane to religion. Religion has shown him that God is One, and that "there is none else." He also has definite cognizance of the "edge" of divine transcendence jutting into the sphere of human experience. If he then, impelled by intellectual curiosity, inquires into the logical or metaphysical consequences of the fundamental religious experience, he may discover the entire discipline of a philosophy of religion. He will find that the One has to be thought of as incorporeal; that if "there is none else beside him," then God must be infinite. These insights may further lead the religious thinker logically to the idea that the transcendence of an incorporeal, infinite being has to be absolute. In this way, we may be able to readmit a great deal of the philosophy of religion, which we were at first compelled to reject.[44] There is no path from the metaphysical Absolute to the God of religion, but there is one from the revealed God of religion to the Absolute of metaphysics and its incorporation into the body of religious affirmations.[45]

The combination of the religious experience with philosophical reasoning will therefore yield the incorporeal, infinite, and absolute Godhead. But with it we seem to have slid back into the rut of the "negative attributes." The essence of the one God remains unexplored. What is being asserted is the denial of multiplicity, of corporeality, of finitude or dependence in the divine essence. We have seen that once we reach the negative attributes coming from the encounter, their metaphysical meaninglessness is redeemed by meaning and significance. In the post-encounter phase of human experience, they do describe quite "positively" the inconceivable essence of the Supreme Being, which is no longer an unknown "stranger" to man. The rut of all religious metaphysics is thus avoided; nevertheless, this

solution to the problem still offers too meager a fare to justify the requirements of the logic of religion.

It was clearly appreciated in the history of religious philosophy that the
negative attributes by themselves were unable to sustain a Godhead which
would justify religion. In order to remedy the situation, the negative
attributes of essence were supplemented by the positive attributes of divine
action.[46] These attributes of action were usually seen formulated in the
passage of Exodus where God is described as "merciful and gracious, long-
suffering and abundant in goodness and truth; keeping mercy to the
thousandth generation."[47] But the blight of the negative attributes is cast
over even attributes of action. Can religion, for example, accept the interpretation of Maimonides when, explaining this passage, he says that "what
is meant here is not that God possesses moral qualities, but that he produces
actions similar to the ones emanating from ourselves by virtue of such
moral qualities, or rather states of the soul"?[48]

Whatever might be said in favor of the negative attributes when discussing such metaphysical concepts as unity, omniscience, or omnipotence, the
idea is untenable from the religious point of view when one deals with the
moral attributes of the deity. According to Maimonides, the psalmist's
claim that "as a father has compassion upon his children, so was the Eternal
merciful to those who feared him"[49] is not to be taken literally. And when in
the book of Malachi it is said: "And I shall be merciful to them as a man is
merciful unto his son,"[50] the words have, according to the same school of
thought, only some symbolical meaning. "Of course," says Maimonides,
"God is not experiencing the feeling of affection or tenderness, but such
actions as a father will do for his child through pure love, compassion, and
affection do emanate from God with regard to his favorites, though they are
not caused by affection...."[51] Now, this is an opinion that denies the most
precious and intimate aspect of God's relationship to the world and to man.
The negative attributes will never do. Religion cannot forgo the love and
the mercy of God, or even his justice and anger. Such attributes have to be
related to him in a positive sense, or else there is no basis for a living God of
religious relevance.

What Maimonides denies God, namely affection and tenderness, are of
the very essence of the encounter. As we have observed, the Supreme Being
seeks out man in order to encounter him, as a manifestation of his care and
concern for man; indeed, as a revelation of his affection. God upholds man

in the encounter, hiding himself for man's sake, protecting man against the peril of divine transcendence so that man may endure him and, in this way, know him. This is an act of divine love. And so we maintain that the "thirteen dispositions" cited in Exodus do indeed describe God himself, expressing positive aspects of his being. God does not act *as if* he were "merciful and gracious, long-suffering and abundant in goodness"; God is as he is here proclaimed. He is a caring God.

It is, however, to be noted that in the "thirteen dispositions" no attempt is made to describe God in his absoluteness. All the "dispositions" are related to man. We have seen that the Absolute as such is no concern of religion, but only the Absolute in its relatedness to man. It was, therefore, natural that Moses' quest for knowledge of "the ways" of God should have been answered by the exposition of the nature of divine relatedness to man. The attributes of the God of religion are, of necessity, relational attributes.

KNOWLEDGE OF THE WORLD AND KNOWLEDGE OF GOD

(1962)

IT IS WITH A SENSE of intellectual discomfort that one approaches the theme of this essay. It is deeply embarrassing that in our time it is still necessary to discuss the relationship between *limudei kodesh*, or religious studies, and *limudei hol*, secular studies, with a view to justifying their integration within a wholesome and complete form of Jewish education. There are still many individuals as well as substantial groups who, in the name of Judaism, question the religious propriety of teaching Jewish youth secular subjects. Grudgingly, they put up with the prevailing situation in Jewish day schools, in which secular subjects are taught side by side with religious ones, but they object to higher forms of secular studies at colleges and universities. One must count it among the frustrating anachronisms of our day that in yeshivot in this country as well as in the State of Israel, teachers and students often violently reject the idea of a higher professional secular education as being contrary to Jewish faith and piety. I know of a young man, studying at one of the great yeshivot in Israel, who wrote to his younger brother in this country advising him to throw all his secular books out and to concentrate on nothing else but his talmudic studies. The reason given for such a radical suggestion was: Let *goyim* be physicians; for a Jew there is nothing else but the study of Tora.

The young man overlooked, of course, the fact that even in the famous interdict that R. Solomon Aderet and his rabbinical court invoked for the duration of fifty years against anyone who in their congregations would read "in the books of the Greeks," one finds the following exception: "We have excluded from our interdict the science of medicine even though it is based on nature; for the Tora gave the physician permission to heal."[1]

It should not be difficult to show, even halachically, that the same exception applies to all other scientific disciplines, which are based upon the study of nature, and whose pursuit is no less essential for the maintenance of life than that of medicine itself. Needless to say that in the present state of the close interrelation of all branches of science, the science of medicine is inconceivable without the sciences of physics, chemistry, biology, zoology, and many others. One cannot pursue any scientific discipline effectively without having scientists carrying out research in numerous related areas. But it is not my intention to discuss the question from its halachic angle. The halacha in this case has been decided by life itself—not in the sense that life, as so often, ignoring halacha, has gone past it; but that there are certain fundamental requirements of life which halacha cannot ignore, and without whose satisfaction halacha itself becomes impossible.

The living example of the State of Israel offers the most compelling case in point. It is inconceivable that the Jewish people could exist in the State of Israel for a single day without effective mastery of those sciences which form the foundation of present-day civilization. Since it is the intention of the Tora that there be a people of the Tora, living in the land of Israel, it must also be the intention of the Tora that Jews be physicians, engineers, physicists, mathematicians, men of creative search and practical application in every field of human endeavor, without whose knowledge and skill no nation can survive. This is obvious in our own days, and the situation was undoubtedly the same whenever Israel lived as a people in its own land. Agriculture, commerce, industry, national administration, and defense, whether on an advanced, modern level or during the periods of the First or Second Temple, have always required education and training in those disciplines called *limudei hol*.

The very existence of the State of Israel demonstrates that the raising of the question of permissibility of secular studies, as if a question of halacha were involved, is one of the unhealthy manifestations of the exilic mentality. Only in the diaspora could the fantastic idea have arisen that scientific knowledge and education were only for the Gentiles, whereas a Jew should occupy himself only with the Tora. When one views the matter from the perspective of the life interest of the Jewish people in its historic normalcy, the idea of limiting Jewish education to the "four cubits of the law," to the exclusion of all secular and worldly knowledge, vanishes in its own meaninglessness.

In the well-known letter which he addressed to the rabbis of Marseilles, Maimonides complains that our ancestors "did not occupy themselves with learning the arts of war and conquest." Speaking of this mistake, Maimonides continues: "This is what caused the loss of our kingdom, the destruction of our sanctuary, the length of our exile, and brought us to our present condition. Our fathers have sinned, but they are no more."[2] If one tried to express the thought of Maimonides in the form of a general principle, one would have to say that the neglect of any branch of learning which is essential for the survival of the Jewish people is an anti-religious act, directed against Judaism itself. In this sense, the pursuit of scientific inquiry and the acquisition of scientific techniques, upon the application of which the survival of the Jewish nation in a Jewish land depends, is not only to be tolerated but must be considered a religious demand that emanates from the very intention and purpose of the Tora itself.

II

While there is no question of halacha involved in the issue before us, there is certainly a question of ideological consistency. The problem may be felt most intimately in the realm of Jewish education. It is a fact that in Jewish primary and secondary schools, as well as at higher institutes of learning, at Jewish colleges and universities, in this country as well as in the State of Israel, our education effort is divided into two branches, one secular, the other sacred. Most of the time, there is hardly any connection between the two. Each stands under its own independent authority. Our youth are being educated in the intellectual climate of two worlds that do not recognize each other.

But can the two worlds ignore each other in the heart and in the mind of the student as well? There can be no education without an educational philosophy, and consistency is the main requirement of such a philosophy. This, of course, means that all subjects must conform to the basic educational purpose; the educational goal must be reflected in the teaching of all the subjects. Such an educational philosophy may only be conceived on the basis of a philosophy of Judaism, which in the name of Judaism itself is able to formulate a worldview within which the sacred and the secular become harmonized in a more fundamental unity.

In classical Jewish thought there is a rich treasure of relevant material that may guide us in formulating such a comprehensive Jewish view. For the sake of illustration, it is worth looking at a number of significant ideas from the works of some of the great teachers of Israel.

There is, at least, one concept that has specific importance in relationship to knowledge in general no less than in relationship to the study of the Tora itself. It is the concept of truth. Without truth, there is no Tora; without truth, there is no knowledge of any kind. The question of truth may be asked epistemologically; it may also be asked ontologically. One may inquire about the means by which we reach the knowledge of truth; and one may investigate the essential nature of truth, its contents. Concerning the epistemological question, Saadia Gaon, in the introduction to his *Book of Beliefs and Opinions*, maintains that there are three sources for the knowledge of truth: Sense perception, immediate rational insight, and inference by means of logical necessity. There is, however, also a further source of knowledge: *Hagada ne'emenet*, or "reliable tradition." Our acceptance of the Tora is based on such tradition. It is noteworthy that, in the name of Jewish monotheism, Saadia Gaon most determinedly rejects skepticism regarding the original three sources of knowledge. Since our acceptance of the Tora depends on a reliable tradition, the question cannot be avoided: How does a tradition become reliable? Saadia Gaon's answer is that, like any other knowledge, tradition too must be validated by the three basic sources of truth. If sense perception is not to be trusted, then the revelation at Sinai itself could be no proof of the handing down of the Tora; if reason is not to be relied upon, we should of course not be able to grasp the contents and meaning of the Tora either. Thus, Saadia concludes that the validity of the "reliable tradition" is established "by reason of the fact that it is based upon the knowledge of the senses as well as that of reason...."

For Saadia Gaon, the epistemological question "How do we know?" is solved in a comprehensive manner. For him, there is no twofold epistemology, one for matters sacred and another one for matters secular. All truth must ultimately be validated by sense perception and by reason. In this respect, the concerns of Judaism and of the sciences are identical. One may, of course, disagree with Saadia and see in the act of revelation a way of reaching the truth that is essentially religious and different from other sources of knowledge. Such, indeed, was the position adopted by Judah Halevi. However, the difference would only apply to those to whom revelation is actually granted. Undoubtedly, our acceptance of the Tora is based on the revelation at Sinai. But we know of that event not by means of revelation, but by what Saadia calls "reliable tradition." Thus we are back to the question: How does tradition become "reliable"? How is it to be validated?

One need not accept Saadia's epistemology, but one cannot escape his conclusion that the question can only be answered within a general theory of knowledge within which no distinction can be made between secular and sacred. Such a comprehensive theory of knowledge is a religious necessity. Without it, the floodgates are opened for superstitions of all kinds, which are bound to distort and to degrade genuine religion. Without due respect for a sound theory of knowledge, even the famous leap of faith may be a form of tumbling into darkness and futility. This is the ultimate significance of Halevi's repeated statement: "God forbid that there should be anything in the Tora that contradicts reason." For the sake of religion itself, religion dare not ignore these requirements for the validation of truth to which all human inquiry is subject. Truth, as such, is a religious value.

III

As to the ontological character of truth, the actual nature of the object of knowledge for which it stands, differences in the importance of the various disciplines of knowledge are obvious. The statement that last winter saw more snow in Chicago than any other winter in the past twenty-five years may be true, but it is far less exciting than that in the beginning God created heaven and earth. No doubt, from the point of view of the significance of the truth taught, there is ample room for distinguishing between knowledge and knowledge. Nevertheless, there are also such among the teachers of Israel who, on the strength of the truth contents of the various disciplines of knowledge, were able to recognize a harmonious pattern among them, subserving a superior concept of unity. The outstanding one among these men was, of course, Maimonides. According to him, the purpose of man on this earth is to know God, and the goal of Judaism is to lead men to the knowledge of God. This knowledge Maimonides identifies with the knowledge of the supreme truth. But how can one reach it? How can one reach God, how can one know him? As is well known, according to Maimonides, the essence of God remains forever unknown to human nature. Man can know God only from his deeds and from his handiwork. Since it is man's purpose on earth to know God, he must search in God's works for him. Only from the knowledge of the creation can one know the Creator. Maimonides lays down, therefore, the rules: "It is thus necessary to examine all things according to their essence, to infer from every species such true and well established propositions as may assist us in the solution of metaphysical problems," without which the knowledge of God is impossible.[3] The truth in nature points to the supreme truth which is above nature.

Thus, in order to know God, one must be familiar with the natural sciences. These, however, are based on certain auxiliary disciplines like mathematics and logic. Maimonides has occasion to declare: "He who wishes to attain to human perfection must therefore first study logic, next the various branches of mathematics in their proper order, then physics [i.e., the sciences of nature], and lastly metaphysics."[4] Even the commandment "you shall love the Eternal your God with all your heart"[5] he explains in the light of this thought. Only a person who understands the nature of the universe and is able to meditate on God's wisdom revealed in it is capable of loving God with all his heart.[6] One may see in Maimonides the most extreme proponent of the concept of unity. Truth is one because all reality is one—the creation of the one God. All knowledge and all wisdom lead to the knowledge of the One. In the realm of truth, there is no distinction between the secular and the sacred. Truth is, as the Talmud teaches, "the seal of the Holy One"; all truth leads man to its source, to God.

It is worth noting that even Bahya ibn Pakuda, whose *Duties of the Heart* is highly valued in the yeshivot as a work of moral wisdom, adopts a position very similar to that of Maimonides. As he states in the work's "Examination of Creation" (*sha'ar habehina*), it is through our meditations that we come to appreciate "the manifestations of God's wisdom in all created things…. For all wisdom is one; even though its signs vary among the things created, in its foundation and essence it is all one…."[7] There is a certain intellectual boldness in this concept of the essential unity of all knowledge which derives from our knowledge of the universe and which in its various partial manifestations adds up to the one divine truth. Because of that, Bahya declares it to be man's duty to study God's creation in order to come nearer to God's wisdom. In another passage, elaborating the idea further, he practically develops a plan for the scientific study of nature, inspired by the purely religious motivation of coming closer to God.[8]

It may be difficult to accept the extreme rationalistic position of Maimonides. Yet he and Bahya ibn Pakuda have prepared the ground for us for a religious approach to a scientific investigation of all reality and to the evaluation of the truth that it may reveal. The basic principle is that this world is God's world—and all truth has its source in God. The laws of nature are God's laws; and the wisdom in the creation is of his wisdom. The truth revealed in God's creation and the truth revealed in the Tora are alike: Both have their origin in the same "highest truth" (*emet elyona*), to use the terminology of Maimonides. Trying to establish that it is man's duty to study the nature of all creation in order to understand God's wisdom, Bahya quotes the words of the Talmud: "Had the Tora not been given to Israel, we could have learned modesty from the cat, chastity from the dove, conduct from the rooster, and respect for the property of others from the ant."[9] According to him, the saying shows that in the opinion of the teachers of the Talmud one may find Tora in the wisdom revealed in creation as well.[10] In this sense, Maimonides occasionally emphasizes that nature and Tora emanate from the same source.

A different approach, no less significant, is found in the views of R. Judah Loeb ben Betzalel, the Maharal of Prague. The Maharal does not accept the opinion that "all wisdom is one." He recognizes a difference in essence between knowledge grasped by the human intellect as the result of human endeavor and the knowledge that comes from God in the form of revelation. The truth of God is inaccessible to man unless it be revealed to him. Nevertheless, he considers it a religious duty, incumbent on every Jew, to occupy himself with the study of those manmade disciplines of knowledge which try to penetrate the nature of reality in order to understand the existence of the universe. He finds a basis for his contention in the well-known saying of the Talmud: "R. Yehoshua ben Levi said in the name of Bar Kapara: He who knows how to calculate the turn of the seasons and the motions of the planets but does not do it, about him the verse says: 'But they regard not the work of the Eternal, neither have they considered the operation of his hands.'"[11] R. Shmuel bar Nahmani even adds that to make the astronomical computations of the motions of the planets is a commandment of the Tora, which he derives from the words of the Bible: "For this is your wisdom and your understanding in the sight of the peoples."[12] The originality of the Maharal's interpretation consists in seeing clearly that this statement of the Talmud should not be limited to the study of astronomy alone, but that it applies to every type of human knowledge that investigates God's creation.

This, of course, is supported by the verse from Isaiah, which serves as the justification of the original talmudic opinion: "But they regard not the work of the Eternal, neither have they considered the operation of his hands." In keeping with the wider meaning of this verse, one not only should meditate on the revolutions of the planets, but is obligated to penetrate to the understanding of all works of the Creator. Thus, the Maharal sums up his position in the following words: "From this we may learn that a man ought to study everything that will enable him to understand the essential nature of the world. One is obligated to do so, for everything is God's work. One should understand it all and through it recognize one's Creator."[13]

IV

We have before us, then, a classical tradition of Jewish thought which in our own days may serve as a guide in the development of a Jewish religious worldview that will embrace the whole of reality and relate all human knowledge to the focal point of Jewish religious affirmation and commitment. We are, of course, still far removed from such a comprehensive and consistent outlook. The foremost intellectual challenge of our generation is to create one. It is inconceivable that Jews as individuals and Israel as a nation should make practical use of successful scientific inquiry, and yet the genius of Judaism should nonetheless ignore the fact that the same scientific disciplines carry within themselves certain insights or suggestions which carry consequences for religious faith and for that ultimate truth which is God's own seal. In the continuous progress of human knowledge and search for the truth, there is ever present a spiritual challenge that influences the life of man in its entirety.

A scientific understanding of certain biological processes, interpretations of laws of nature, and interpretations of historical developments may often tend to undermine some forms of established religious faith. How is Judaism to meet such challenges? Not by closing its eyes to them. The attitude of disdain toward all secular knowledge that is propagated in certain circles is based on a profound ignorance of what it despises and rejects, and, far from being a solution, is in fact a sign of spiritual incompetence and intellectual cowardice. If religious faith is joined by intellectual honesty, it must find the idea intolerable that the truth of religion should be defended by such questionable means. What is worse, a truth so defended must itself become questionable. If any branch of human knowledge poses problems to religion, then out of religious zeal for the truth and for the truthfulness of religion itself, religion must take such problems seriously. It will meet such problems effectively, or at least live with them comfortably, not by rejecting secular knowledge but by mastering it. All so-called *limudei hol* are now within the scope of Jewish religious interest and concern. Without a knowledge of their premises, methods, and conclusions by the believing Jewish scholar, a comprehensive worldview of Judaism cannot be formulated.

There is, however, a more serious consequence of the failure to integrate the entire scope of human knowledge within the framework of religious concern. Earlier I referred to a talmudic passage which quotes the verse, "for this is your wisdom and your understanding in the sight of the peoples." Most medieval Jewish philosophers justify on the basis of this text the demand for a rationally meaningful interpretation of Judaism. Maimonides quotes the verse to prove that even *hukim*, laws possessing no obvious explanation, are to be interpreted rationally.[14] It would be wrong to assume that the intention of these thinkers was to impress the nations with the wisdom of the Tora. Their efforts in interpreting Judaism were directed inward to the Jews, not outward to the Gentiles. What they wanted to emphasize was that the truth of Judaism has universal meaning and applicability. Because of its universal import, it must be, at least potentially, recognizable as "your wisdom and your understanding in the sight of the peoples." It must retain its ability to deal meaningfully with the human situation, even though only the Jew must accept its pronouncements as binding for himself. The moment Judaism loses this ability, it ceases being a world religion and degenerates into a marginal sect. This is, however, the danger if we turn away from the challenges of the various branches of human knowledge. A negative attitude to secular knowledge will not only prevent "the peoples" from seeing in Judaism "our wisdom and our understanding," it will not even allow the Jewish people to gain a comprehensive Jewish worldview. It may lose us the historic Israel and replace it with a handful of life-estranged Jewish sectarians.

There are, of course, dangers along the path we must take; one must tread carefully. But the challenge must not be ignored, and the responsibility cannot be avoided. Our faith that Judaism's intellectual and spiritual power is equal to the task is identical with our faith in the inexhaustible vitality and eternal validity of the Tora. In the world of the spirit, one need not fear the truth; as to the untruth, one must know it in order to defeat it. Undoubtedly, the secular disciplines have often served as the basis of philosophies of life which the believing Jew cannot accept. Yet when confronted with the challenge of overcoming an untruth, one must understand the source of its strength. The powerful grip which secular and materialistic philosophies hold on the modern mind is in large measure due to the truth-contents of the sciences upon which they are based. But it must be remembered that each of the sciences may bring into relief only one facet of the truth. Philosophy often turns the partial aspect of the truth that is uncovered in some domain of knowledge into an absolute concept; this is the lie in such philosophy. The power of such a lie is at times frightening, but only because it has its root in something that is valid and true. In order to meet the spiritual challenge of our age, we must learn how to evaluate the truth-contents of all those disciplines of human knowledge that to a large extent determine the fabric of our civilization. Only thus shall we succeed in formulating that comprehensive Jewish worldview which will make manifest the truth-contents in the various disciplines of human knowledge as a part of a meaningful pattern which derives its validity and value from the truth which is of God.

Through the ages, Jews, as individuals, have greatly enriched every branch of human knowledge. However, in most of the separate branches a partial truth reigns supreme. And man's world is broken. With the rise of the State of Israel, the Jewish people has been called by historic necessity to become a people of science in the widest sense of the word. For the religious Jew who sees in Israel's return to the land of its fathers the hand of God, the historic necessity for scientific effectiveness imposed by the return becomes a divine command. We interpret it as meaning that Israel, the people of the Tora, must acquire mastery in the realm of worldly knowledge and weave the pattern of unity between fact and value, faith and reality, between life and Tora. "For this is your wisdom and your understanding in the sight of the peoples."

12

THE CONCEPT OF HOLINESS

(1969)

I. THE HOLY ONE AND THE LORD OF HOSTS

WE SHALL BEGIN OUR INVESTIGATION of the biblical concept of holiness with the revelation granted to Isaiah: "Holy, holy, holy is the Lord of Hosts."[1] Since the prophet finds it necessary to affirm that the Lord of Hosts is holy, it is fair to assume that whatever is meant by "holy" needs to be explicitly attributed to the Lord of Hosts; that is, the idea of the holy is in itself not implied in the idea of the Lord of Hosts. We shall, therefore, have to see what these terms convey when they are used independently of each other. How does Isaiah use the concept of the Lord of Hosts, and how that of the holy?

Let us look at a number of passages in which Isaiah refers to God as the Lord of Hosts:

O *Lord of Hosts*, the God of Israel, that sits upon the cherubim; you are the God, you alone, of all the kingdoms of the earth; You have made heaven and earth.[2]

Thus says the Eternal, the King of Israel and its Redeemer, *the Lord of Hosts*: I am the first and I am the last, and beside me there is no God.[3]

For I am the Eternal your God, who stirs up the sea, that the waves thereof roar; *the Lord of Hosts* is his name.[4]

Therefore says the Lord, *the Lord of Hosts*, the Mighty One of Israel: Ah, I will ease me of my enemies; and I will turn my hand upon you, and purge away your dross with lye.[5]

For *the Lord of Hosts* has a day upon all who are proud and lofty, and upon all who are lifted up, and they shall be brought low.[6]

For, behold, the Lord, *the Lord of Hosts*, does take away from Jerusalem and from Judah stay and staff, every stay of bread, and every stay of water.[7]

Hark, a tumult in the mountains, as of a great people! Hark the uproar of the kingdoms of the nations gathered together! *The Lord of Hosts* musters the host of the battle.[8]

Therefore I will make the heavens tremble, and the earth shall be shaken out of her place, for the wrath of *the Lord of Hosts* and for the day of his fierce anger.[9]

One could multiply the quotations almost at will; they would all show the same character and would well find their place in the above grouping.[10] The Lord of Hosts alone is God; he is at the beginning of time and at the end of it; he alone and no one besides him. He is the creator of heaven and earth; he is the sovereign power over all nature, as well as over all the kingdom of men. Of this sovereign Lord it is maintained that he is "the Mighty One" who deals with his enemies, Jew or Gentile, as he pleases. He acts, however, as a judge, who "purges away the dross with lye." He brings low the haughty and the proud. He executes punishment, when punishment is required; and, as he does so, like a warlord he musters his armies. For Isaiah, "the Lord of Hosts" expresses the idea of divine transcendence, of elevation above everything created. This idea of transcendence is connected with divine might and power, which is exercised by the universal sovereign in his capacity as the supreme judge and ruler. Isaiah uses the phrase "the Lord of Hosts" consistently in this sense.

No less consistent and definite is he in his handling of the word "holy." Throughout the book of Isaiah, the word occurs most frequently in the phrase "the Holy One of Israel" (*kedosh yisrael*). Again we shall look at some verses in which the term is mentioned:

> Sing unto the Eternal; for he has done gloriously; this is made known in all the earth. Cry aloud and shout, inhabitant of Zion; for great is *the Holy One of Israel* in your midst.[11]

> And you shall rejoice in the Eternal, you shall glory in *the Holy One of Israel*.[12]

> When you pass through the waters, I will be with you; and through the rivers, they shall not overflow you; when you walk through the fire, you shall not be burned, neither shall the flame kindle upon you. For I am the Eternal your God, *the Holy One of Israel*, your savior.[13]

> And it shall come to pass in that day that the remnant of Israel, and they that are escaped of the house of Jacob shall no longer rely upon their oppressors, but shall rely upon the Eternal, *the Holy One of Israel*, in truth.[14]

These passages show that "the Holy One of Israel" occurs in contexts whose message is opposed to those that speak on behalf of the Lord of Hosts. The "Holy One of Israel" is the cause of joy and happiness. He is the friend of the poor and the needy; he protects them when they are in trouble. He is the savior. He is "with you"; he is "in your midst." He is the One on whom man should rely. The idea is maintained with such conviction that it is recommended by Isaiah as a cornerstone for the foreign policy of the Jewish state of his time. Caught in the power struggle between Assyria and Egypt, the people seek their salvation in a political alliance with Egypt. Thus they reject God, on whom alone they ought to rely. It is noteworthy, however, that in the various passages that deal with this theme, God is referred to as the Holy One of Israel. Concerning those in favor of the Egyptian alliance, the prophet proclaims that they "trust in chariots, because they are many; and in horsemen, because they are exceedingly mighty; but they look not unto the Holy One of Israel." The policy suggested by Isaiah is a different one. "For thus said the Lord, the Eternal, the Holy One of Israel: In sitting still and rest shall you be saved, in quietness and in confidence shall be your strength."[15] In times of crisis, one should have trust in the holiness of God. Instead of making alliances with military might, one should ally oneself with the Holy One. Faith in him brings salvation in peace and quietude.

These attributes of the Holy One are different from those in which the Lord of Hosts makes himself manifest. The Lord of Hosts is transcendent; the Holy One is immanent. The Lord of Hosts is far removed, he is above man and all creation; the Holy One of Israel is near. The Lord of Hosts judges; the Holy One of Israel saves. Quite obviously, the Holy One is not the *mysterium tremendum*.[16] He is in the midst of Zion, the cause of joy and happiness. The *mysterium tremendum* seems to describe the Lord of Hosts more aptly. It is significant that, after having heard the threefold "Holy, holy, holy," Isaiah should exclaim: "Woe is me, for I am undone; because I am a man of unclean lips... for my eyes have seen the King, *the Lord of Hosts*."[17] Not the Holy One, but the beholding of the Lord of Hosts is the cause of his terror.

One who reads the Bible in English might, however, point to at least one passage in which the holy does appear in the form of the divine wrath. The Revised Version reads:

> And the light of Israel shall be for a fire, and his Holy One for a flame; and
> it shall burn and devour his thorns and his briers in one day.[18]

This surely is an activity that, in the light of so many other passages, we would expect to be performed by the Lord of Hosts. Reading the text in the Hebrew original, however, it becomes clear that the English version is somewhat misleading. The phrase *vehaya or yisrael le'esh ukedosho lelehava* should be translated as: And the light of Israel shall *become* a fire, and his Holy One a flame. The Hebrew *haya le* means to become; it expresses a change of status, condition, or nature.[19] Light is normally something very beneficial. So is, of course, the light of Israel, which is an appellation for the God of Israel here. The prophet, however, warns that the light of Israel will change its nature, as it were. It will cease being light and become a consuming fire. Similarly—and it should be obvious because of the parallelism in the text—the Holy One will *become* a flame. Far from associating any form of destructiveness with the concept of the Holy One, the words imply the opposite. The Holy One will suppress his natural quality. He will change and become a destructive force. He will cease manifesting himself as the holy and will act in another capacity, like a flame.

The same distinction, which is made by Isaiah between the two concepts referring to God, also appears in the book of Psalms. We shall list only a few examples:

> Who is the King of glory? The Eternal strong and mighty, the Eternal mighty in battle.... Who then is the King of glory? *The Lord of Hosts*; he is the King of glory.[20]

> Nations were in tumult, kingdoms were moved; he uttered his voice, the earth melted. *The Lord of Hosts* is with us.... Come, behold the works of the Eternal, who has made desolations in the earth. He makes wars to cease unto the end of the earth; he breaks the bow and cuts the spear asunder... I will be exalted among the nations, I will be exalted in the earth. *The Lord of Hosts* is with us.[21]

> For, behold, the kings assembled themselves, they came onward together. They saw, straightway they were amazed; they were affrighted, they hastened away. Trembling took hold of them there, pangs, as of a woman in travail. With the east wind you break the ships of Tarshish. As we have heard, so have we seen in the city of *the Lord of Hosts*.[22]

In these and other passages, the psalmists employ the phrase "the Lord of Hosts" in the same sense as does Isaiah. Note that in the last quotation, Zion is referred to as the city of the Lord of Hosts. The usual appellation for Zion is the "city of the holy" (*ir hakodesh*), or the "mount of the holy" (*har hakodesh*). Here, however, as the psalmist describes the mighty deeds of judgment, performed by God who uses the east wind as the messenger to do his bidding, all this is witnessed in the city of God, who has made himself manifest on this occasion as the Lord of Hosts.

The distinction we have established is further strengthened as we compare the psalmist's use of *kadosh*, or "holy," in contrast to "the Lord of Hosts." The following passages offer some examples of the ways in which the idea of the holy occurs in Psalms:

> Sing praise unto the Eternal, you his godly ones, and give thanks to the *name of his holiness*. For his anger is but for a moment, his favor is for a lifetime.[23]

> Our soul has waited for the Eternal; he is our help and our shield. For in him our hearts rejoice, because we have trusted in the *name of his holiness*.[24]

> A father of the fatherless and a judge of the widows is God in the *habitation of his holiness*.[25]

> I also will give thanks unto you with the psaltery.... I will sing praise unto you with the harp, you *Holy One of Israel*.[26]

As with Isaiah, the manifestation of divine holiness is the cause for rejoicing and thanksgiving. Far from signifying separateness, the idea of the holy conveys a sense of intimacy and relatedness. Here I have insisted on the more accurate translation, "the name of his holiness," rather than the way it is usually rendered, "his holy name." The name of his holiness means the manifestation of divine holiness.[27] Such manifestation is a sign that "his anger is but for a moment, his favor is for a lifetime." "His holy habitation" might be a point in space. But such a term does not occur in the Bible even once. "The habitation of his holiness," rather, is the indwelling of divine holiness; it is divine holiness, the saving force immanent in creation. By means of his association with the world, God is a "father of the fatherless and a judge of the widows."

A striking support for our analysis of the term "holy" can be found in the book of Hosea:

> My heart is turned within me, my compassions are kindled together. I will not execute the fierceness of my anger, I will not return to destroy Ephraim; for I am God, and not man, the *Holy One* in your midst, and I will not come in fury.[28]

The familiar traits of the Holy One, as we found them in Isaiah and Psalms, are stated here almost in the form of a definition. With Hosea, too, the Holy One is "in your midst." His signs are neither fury nor anger, but compassion and love.[29]

The same idea may be seen by comparing two passages in the book of Amos. In both cases God takes an oath, once "by his holiness" and once "by himself." It would, however, be mistaken to assume that both have the same meaning. When, in one place, God swears "by his holiness," it is against the "kine of Bashan... that oppress the poor, that crush the needy."[30] He swears by his holiness, because it is his concern for the poor and the needy that causes him to resolve to act in order to save them. But when, in a later passage, he swears "to deliver up the city with all that is there," no mention is made of the oppression of the poor. Those that are "at ease in Zion" and "secure in the mountain of Samaria" are punished because of their pride and depravity. What is resolved this time is not for the sake of the poor and needy, but purely as punishment for the haughty and degenerate. This time no reference need be made to God's holiness. He swears "by himself," and the oath is declared in the words "says the Eternal, the God of Hosts."[31]

Jeremiah, too, mentions God taking an oath "by himself," and links it to the Lord of Hosts: "The Lord of Hosts has sworn by himself: Surely I will fill you with men, as with the cankerworm, and they shall lift up a shout against you."[32] In these words, judgment is announced in the name of the Lord of Hosts. But when, according to the psalmist, God promises David that he will sustain him and his dynasty forever, he swears again "by his holiness":

Once I have sworn by my holiness: Surely I will not be false unto David; his seed shall endure forever, and his throne as the sun before me. It shall be established forever as the moon, and be steadfast as the witness in the sky.[33]

The sustaining and protecting attribute of divine mercy and love is God's holiness.

Most revealing are those biblical passages which make use of both terms, the Holy One and the Lord of Hosts. There is, for instance, God's answer to Hezekiah's prayer in the book of Isaiah. It appears in the form of an address to Sennacherib, king of Assyria. In its opening words we find the following:

Whom have you taunted and blasphemed? And against whom have you exalted your voice? Yes, you have lifted up your eyes on high, even against *the Holy One of Israel.*

This speech, at the start of which God is referred to as the Holy One of Israel, concludes with the words: "The zeal of the Lord of Hosts shall perform this."[34] Between the beginning and the close of the address, Sennacherib is put in his place. In his pride, he imagined that his conquests of nations were his own doing, whereas in truth God used him as his instrument. But now Sennacherib's time has come.

> Because of your raging against me, and since your uproar is come up into my ears, therefore will I put my hook in your nose, and my bridle in your lips, and I will turn you back by the way you came.

Quite obviously, the judgment to be executed over Sennacherib is a task for the Lord of Hosts. Thus, it is the zeal of the Lord of Hosts that shall perform it. On the other hand, the conqueror king of Assyria did not taunt and blaspheme the Lord of Hosts. He did not know him. Had he known him, he would have thought better of it. What was his message to Hezekiah? "Let not your God whom you trust beguile you, saying: Jerusalem shall not be given into the hand of the king of Assyria."[35] Now, of course, the God in whom Hezekiah trusts that he will protect Jerusalem is the God who is "in your midst," the Holy One of Israel. It is the Holy One, on whom Israel relies, that was blasphemed, when Sennacherib declared him not to be relied upon. It is, however, the Lord of Hosts that brought low his pride and conceit.

As the Lord of Hosts executes judgment on Sennacherib, so he grants power and dominion to another conqueror, Cyrus, to fulfill a divine mission. This mission, however, is related also to the liberation of God's people. Cyrus is chosen "for the sake of Jacob my servant, and Israel my elect." Thus, in the description of the events in which Israel and Cyrus are together involved, the Holy One and the Lord of Hosts occur alternately. We read:

> Thus says the Eternal, *the Holy One of Israel*, and its maker: Ask me of the things that are to come; concerning my sons and concerning the work of my hands, command me. I have made the earth, and created man upon it; I, even my hands, have stretched out the heavens, and all their hosts have I commanded. I have roused him up in victory, and I make level all his ways; he shall build my city, and he shall let my exiles go free, not for price nor reward, says *the Lord of Hosts*.[36]

The calling of Cyrus, granting him victory and success, putting it into his heart that he rebuild God's city and let the exiles go, is something which only the divine sovereign can perform. He has the power to do it, because he is the Lord over the universe, the creator of heaven and earth. Therefore

the prophecy concludes with "says the Lord of Hosts." In the beginning of
the prophecy, however, these weighty matters are related to the exiles
themselves. God speaks "concerning my sons and concerning the work of
my hands," meaning Israel. Here he is called the Holy One of Israel.[37]

The most striking passage of this type is found in chapter 5 of Isaiah. It
is the familiar verse:

> But the Lord of Hosts is exalted through justice (*mishpat*), and God the
> Holy One is sanctified through righteousness (*tzedaka*).[38]

The distinction between justice and righteousness is parallel to the distinction between the "Lord of Hosts" and the "Holy One," as well as to the
distinction between being exalted and being sanctified. This becomes more
obvious if we compare the Hebrew terms *mishpat* (judgment or justice) and
tzedaka (righteousness or charity). *Mishpat* is justice based on adherence to
the law; *tzedaka* is doing right with charity or compassion. *Mishpat* is
dispensed with authority; *tzedaka* with kindness. He who administers
mishpat must not consider the person; only because one does consider the
person does one practice *tzedaka* toward him. The one who enacts *mishpat*
is a judge; he is above you; he who practices *tzedaka* is a friend who is with
you. God dispenses justice, *mishpat*, as the Lord of Hosts; he practices
righteousness, *tzedaka*, as the Holy One. As the one who imposes justice, he
is exalted; doing *tzedaka*, he is sanctified. To be exalted indicates remoteness; it is a quality properly ascribed to the Lord of Hosts. To be sanctified
is befitting the Holy One. We are not yet in a position to define the
meaning of being sanctified. However, on the basis of the parallelism
between the three pairs of opposite terms in the sentence, we may venture
the guess that as the exaltation of the Lord of Hosts through justice implies
distance between the judge and the judged, so the sanctification of the Holy
One by his acts of *tzedaka* is somehow related to the fact that he is "in your
midst."

A closer look at the context in which this verse occurs will show clearly
why reference is made to a twofold manifestation of God's action. Declaring the woes that await those who enjoy a life of unbridled pleasures, and
who therefore show no regard for the work of God, the prophet exclaims:

> And down goes their glory, and their tumult, and their uproar... and man
> is bowed down, and man is humbled. And the eyes of the lofty are

humbled. But the Lord of Hosts is exalted through justice (*mishpat*), and God the Holy One is sanctified through righteousness (*tzedaka*). Then shall the lambs feed as in their pastures, and the waste places of the fat ones shall wanderers eat.[39]

The verse we have analyzed speaks of two functions of God, as the dispenser of justice and as the one who practices *tzedaka*. The context in which these two functions are mentioned speaks of two types of people: The lofty and arrogant ones, and those who are meek like lambs; the "fat ones," and the "wanderers" who are the homeless poor. God deals with both of them. As to the former, they are silenced and humbled, justice is done to them; as to the latter, they are the meek ones who inherit the land, *tzedaka* is practiced toward them. For the "fat ones," he appears as the Lord of Hosts; for the "lambs" and "wanderers," he is the Holy One. Thus, the Lord of Hosts is exalted through justice, and God the Holy One is sanctified through *tzedaka*.

Neither is this stylistic idiosyncrasy limited to Isaiah. In Psalm 89, the psalmist addresses himself to God with the words, "O Lord God of Hosts"[40] and praises him for all his transcendent majesty:

Righteousness and justice (*mishpat*) are the foundation of your throne; mercy and truth go before you.[41]

However, as we read on, we hear of a people that walks in the light of God's countenance. Of them it is said: "In your name do they rejoice all the day; and through your righteousness (*tzedaka*) are they exalted. For you are the glory of their strength, and in your favor our horn is exalted. For it is due to the Eternal, our shield, and to the Holy One of Israel, our king."[42] While the incomparable sovereign of the universe is addressed as the Lord of Hosts, the one in whom people rejoice because he treats them with *tzedaka*, with kindness and charity, who is the source of their strength, is the Holy One of Israel.

It may also be useful to compare the use of the word "exalted" by the psalmist and the place it has in the verse of Isaiah which we discussed above. Isaiah said that the Lord of Hosts was exalted through justice. The psalmist, on the other hand, said of the people that they are exalted through *tzedaka*. Both usages belong to the same world of discourse. Justice exalts God, it elevates him. But the more he is exalted, the further removed he is from man. Through divine *tzedaka*, the people are exalted and elevated. And the more they are elevated, the closer they are to God.

A most surprising affirmation of our analysis appears in the book of Samuel. In the opening chapters we encounter two prayers of Hannah; in the one she addresses the Lord of Hosts, in the other she acknowledges the Holy One. The following appears in the first prayer:

> O Lord of Hosts, if you will indeed look on the affliction of your handmaid, and remember me, and not forget your handmaid.[43]

In the second prayer, she says:

> My heart exults in the Eternal, my horn is exalted in the Eternal, my mouth is enlarged over mine enemies; because I rejoice in your salvation. There is none holy as the Eternal, for there is none beside you; neither is there any rock like our God.[44]

The two prayers betray two exactly opposite moods. The first may be called a prayer of intercession, the other is one of thanksgiving. The first one Hannah prayed "in bitterness of soul," and she "wept sore." She was a barren woman. The second prayer she recited in a spirit of elation. Her prayer was answered; God blessed her womb.

In the prayer of intercession, she addresses God as the Lord of Hosts. What is her situation? She feels that God has abandoned her. He does not look on her affliction. She is forgotten, forsaken by God. God is far removed from her; he is inaccessible to her. Thus she calls on the Lord of Hosts. It is what God is to her at the moment. But, later, she was remembered after all; God turned toward her, and looked on her affliction. And now she exults in God, rejoices in his salvation. What happened to her is what centuries later Isaiah would declare of the "humble and the neediest among men," who shall "increase their joy in the Eternal" and shall exult in "the Holy One of Israel." The surprising thing, of course, is that this woman "from the hill country of Ephraim" knows how to pray anticipating the ideas and the style of an Isaiah and of the psalmist by centuries. The God of her salvation, the cause of her joy and exultation is the Holy One; he is the rock on whom to rely. Hannah distinguishes between the concept of God as the Lord of Hosts and that of God as the Holy One in much the same way as was done generations later by Isaiah and the psalmist. Feeling

God's remoteness, his anger or judgment, she calls him the Lord of Hosts; experiencing his salvation, the "light of his countenance" turned to her, she knows him in his manifestation of the Holy One.

Occasionally we find the expression "Redeemer, the Holy One of Israel." Since the Holy One is "in your midst," since he is the rock on whom one may rely, the salvation of the poor and the needy, it is natural that God acting as the Redeemer should be linked to his manifestation as the Holy One. But the two concepts are not identical. The Redeemer has a function which is not always implicit in that of the Holy One. The Redeemer has to redeem, and thus he has to deal with those who prevent redemption, who would hold his people in subjugation. He is the Redeemer because he is the Holy One; but as the Redeemer he cannot remain "in your midst" altogether. He must also direct his attention toward the oppressors and confound their plans and aspirations. Let us consider some of the passages that mention the "Redeemer, the Holy One of Israel," which are all found in Isaiah.

> Fear not, you worm Jacob and you men of Israel; I help you, says the Eternal, and your *Redeemer, the Holy One of Israel*. Behold, I make you a new threshing-sledge having sharp teeth; you shall thresh the mountains and beat them small, and shall make the hills as chaff. You shall fan them, and the wind shall carry them, and the whirlwind shall scatter them; and you shall rejoice in the Eternal, you shall glory in the Holy One of Israel.[45]

We are now familiar with some of the ideas in these verses. After the encouragement and promise of help, we are prepared to find Holy One of Israel mentioned. We also expect that those saved should "rejoice" and "glory" in the Holy One of Israel. However, a new term is introduced and connected with the Holy One, the term "Redeemer." But an activity, too, is described which we do not normally associate with the Holy One of Israel. It is the activity of threshing the mountains and scattering them like chaff in the wind, symbolizing the reduction of the enemies or whatever obstacles that may stand in the way of redemption. Help for Israel requires action against the taskmaster. In other passages, too, where the combined phrase occurs, the twofold function is unmistakable.[46]

One may, however, readily see how the function of the Redeemer combines within itself the two manifestations of God, as the Holy One of Israel and as the Lord of Hosts. God's activity as the Redeemer moves in two directions: Against those who oppress, and toward those who are to be redeemed. For the oppressor, the Redeemer is the Lord of Hosts; for the redeemed, the Holy One. Accordingly, there are some passages which combine the Redeemer, the Lord of Hosts, and the Holy One of Israel. In the midst of the prophecy about the approaching downfall of Babylon, Isaiah exclaims: "Our Redeemer, the Lord of Hosts is his name, the Holy One of Israel!"[47] The reader of the verses immediately preceding this exclamation will find that the heavy blows predicted against Babylon are indeed such as are normally said to emanate from the Lord of Hosts: "Your nakedness shall be uncovered, yes, your shame shall be seen; I will take vengeance, and will let no man intercede." On the other hand, immediately following the exclamation and explaining why the "daughter of the Chaldeans" will no longer be called "mistress of kingdoms," it is said: "I was angry with my people, I profaned my inheritance, and gave them into your hand; you showed them no mercy; upon the aged have you laid heavily your yoke."

The implication is that because of the cruelty with which Babylon treated Israel, God turns from his anger against them. He acknowledges his inheritance and will no longer let it be profaned. He will treat mercifully those to whom no mercy was shown. We are reminded of that other verse in Isaiah about the Lord of Hosts who is exalted through justice and the Holy One who is sanctified through *tzedaka*. It is the Redeemer, the Lord of Hosts, dispensing justice for Babylon, and the Holy One of Israel treating his people with mercy.

Unfortunately, often the nuances get lost in the translation. For instance, there is a verse in Isaiah that is commonly rendered:

> For your maker is your husband, the Lord of Hosts is his name; and the Holy One of Israel is your Redeemer, the God of the whole earth shall he be called.[48]

The dual function of the Redeemer is lost in such a translation. The word "husband" suggests an intimate relationship; to call him the Lord of Hosts is jarringly incongruous. The Hebrew for husband is, of course, *ba'al*; the masoretic reading, however, gives us the verbal noun *bo'el*. The *ba'al* is; the *bo'el* does. The prophet wishes to indicate that Israel's maker makes himself her "husband" again. The promise follows immediately after the words: "and the reproach of your widowhood shall you remember no more." Israel will no longer remain without a husband, for her maker will possess her again. The passage recalls the complaint of Israel, in which the same verb, *bo'el*, occurs, and it should be understood in its light. The complaint was: "O Eternal our God, other lords beside you *have had dominion* over us."[49]

Only the Hebrew text, using the same terminology in both cases, shows that the promise was meant to counter the complaint. God, becoming once again the "husband," takes sole "dominion" over Israel; he replaces the "other lords," who mistreated this people. Now, of course, the twofold function of the Redeemer appears in our text, too. Only by shattering the yoke of the "other lords" can God make himself Israel's Lord. In order to repossess Israel, the Redeemer must act in history as the Lord of Hosts; he has compassion on the "widow" and becomes her "husband" again as the Holy One of Israel.[50]

II. HOLY AND AWESOME

The foregoing analysis, however, has to contend with a difficulty arising from those occasions in which the word "holy" (*kadosh*) is combined with *nora*, which means awful or awesome. There are two such passages in the Bible; both are found in the Psalms. In view of the numerous passages on which our interpretation is based, two exceptions to the rule would not weigh heavily. Nevertheless, since the term holy, with reference to God, is employed with such uniform and consistent meaning, exceptions that would indicate a meaning contrary to the one found everywhere else do require careful examination.

One of the passages we find in Psalm 99: "Let them praise your name as great and awful (*nora*). Holy is he."[51] "Holy" and *nora* are placed here in a rather uncomfortable proximity. It seems to associate the awful with the holy, declaring the awful to be holy.

Beginning with the second verse, we shall quote the psalm in its three main parts:

(i) The Eternal is great in Zion; and he is high above all the peoples. Let them praise your name as great and awful (*nora*). Holy is he....

(ii) You have executed justice (*mishpat*) and *tzedaka* in Jacob. Exalt the Eternal our God and prostrate yourselves at his footstool; holy is he....

(iii) O Eternal our God, you answered them; a forgiving God you were to them, though you took vengeance of their misdeeds. Exalt the Eternal our God and prostrate yourselves at the hill of his holiness; for the Eternal our God is holy.[52]

The above quotation is divided in order to indicate the three distinctive parts of the psalm. Though distinct, they are similar in conceptual structure, as well as in style. This is quite obvious of the second and third sections, but it is also true of the first one. At first, we shall direct our attention to (ii) and (iii). The sentences beginning with "Exalt the Eternal" are practically identical. "His footstool" is parallel to "the hill of his holiness"; it is Zion, the symbol of God's presence "in your midst." In both cases, the reason why he should be exalted seems to be given in the immediately preceding sentence: In (ii) it is the execution of justice and *tzedaka*; in (iii) it is the fact that God answered his people when they called to him and he forgave their sins.[53] However, rather hesitantly it is remembered, almost as an aside, that nevertheless they were punished for their misdeeds. And yet in this, too, there is a similarity between the second and third parts. In (ii) the execution of justice (*mishpat*) and *tzedaka* is mentioned. But God's answering of prayers and forgiving of sins is certainly an act of *tzedaka* on his part; and taking "vengeance of their misdeeds" is an exercise of *mishpat*. In both cases, then, the psalmist calls for exalting God for the same reason. But we have learned already that the doing of justice alone exalts God, and the practice of *tzedaka* sanctifies him. Shall we then say that the phrase "Exalt the Eternal our God and prostrate yourselves at his footstool" (or "at the hill of his holiness") calls for a twofold acknowledgment of God's twofold actions? Exalt the Eternal for his justice, and prostrate yourself before him as an act of worshipful gratitude for his *tzedaka*?

Let us now look again at the first section of the psalm. Like the other two, (i) presents a twofold manifestation of God. But whereas in the last two sections God makes himself known "in Jacob" by means of *mishpat* and *tzedaka*, in the first the duality of his manifestation comes about by the division between Zion and "all the peoples." It should be noted that, as the text puts it, God is great "*in* Zion," and he is "high above all the peoples." "In Zion" recalls once again the God "in your midst," the Holy One of Israel; whereas God "high above all the peoples" leads to the association with the Lord of Hosts. In a sense, this passage too speaks of God's twofold function as executing justice and *tzedaka*. It would seem that the following phrase, "Let them praise your name as great and awful," is now easily explained. "Great" corresponds to "the Eternal is great in Zion," and "awful" corresponds to "he is high above all the peoples." This is in keeping with what we have found earlier—that it is his remoteness as the sovereign and judge which inspires awe and fear. That "awful" is the manner in which God's name is known among the nations is explicitly stated by Malachi, who presents God as saying:

> For I am a great king, says the Lord of Hosts, and my name is awful (*nora*) among the nations.[54]

It was the same prophet who proclaimed that "from the rising of the sun even unto the going down of the same," God's name was great among the nations. Yet they knew him not as Israel did. They knew him by the awesomeness of his name, as the Lord of Hosts; with the intimacy of the Holy One he was not known to them.

Quite clearly, in our psalm the idea of the holy is not to be associated with that of *nora* (awful). *Nora* describes one specific form of divine self-revelation which is different from that of "holy." In our psalm the idea of the holy occurs at the end of each section. In the first section, it is even separated by syntax from the preceding sentence. "Let them praise your name as great and awful" is addressed to God. "Holy is he" stands clearly by itself.[55] It is certainly not spoken to God. It is the private meditation of the author. It expresses the idea that God, who is known in a twofold capacity in Zion and among the nations, is for him holy. He is holy because he is in the midst of Zion. In the second part of the psalm, we understand its place more readily. Mention is made there of God's *mishpat* and *tzedaka*. We have, however, learned from Isaiah that it is in his capacity as the Holy One that God executes *tzedaka*. Whereas in the first section, "Holy is he" stands by itself, in the second it should be read as concluding the thought "prostrate yourselves at his footstool," as an expression of gratitude for *tzedaka* received; "holy is he" as the bestower of *tzedaka*. If we now compare (ii) and (iii), we find that although both contain the ideas of *mishpat* and *tzedaka*, they do not treat them with the same emphasis. In the second part, justice and righteousness are of equal weight. In the third, the emphasis is on God's answering and forgiving, on his *tzedaka*; of his justice we are reminded only in passing. In other words, the emphasis is on God's holiness. May this be the reason why in this section "his footstool" is replaced by "the hill of his holiness," and why instead of the quiet "holy is he" we have the triumphant affirmation, "for the Eternal our God is holy"? It is the crescendo toward which the psalmist has been moving.

The second passage combining "holy" and "awful" reads:

> He has sent redemption to his people; he has commanded his covenant forever; holy and awful is his name.[56]

As I have discussed elsewhere, the term "his name" refers to God's self-manifestation, by which he becomes known.[57] "Holy and awful" would, of course, correspond to the combination we found in the concept of the Redeemer, that of the Lord of Hosts and the Holy One of Israel. However, what is the reason here for such a combination? A careful reading reveals that as two attributes are associated with God's name, so also are two actions of God mentioned. On the basis of the principle of parallelism, we may, perhaps, assume that "he has sent redemption to his people" corresponds with "holy," and "he has commanded his covenant forever" is paralleled by "awful." Now, the sending of redemption to his people may well be considered a manifestation of divine holiness. It would indeed be the function of the Holy One of Israel. This is in keeping with what we have seen thus far. As to the second phrase, independently of our immediate concern, it requires elucidation. "He has commanded his covenant forever": What exactly does this convey? Fortunately, the idea of the everlasting covenant occurs once more in the same context, preceding our text by several verses. The entire passage reads:

> He has given food to them that fear him; he will *forever be mindful of his covenant*. He has declared to his people the power of his works, in giving them the inheritance of the nations.[58]

This time, it is the second part of the passage which offers no difficulty of interpretation. God showed his power to his people when he led them into the Promised Land and gave them the "inheritance of the nations." In this connection, we cannot help thinking of the Lord of Hosts. The first part of the text, however, is unclear. Is God mindful of his covenant by giving food to those who fear him? One would be inclined to connect the thought of the fulfillment of the covenant with what follows, with "giving them the inheritance of the nations." By doing that, God was mindful of his covenant with Israel and the patriarchs.

Once again, the translation confuses rather than clarifies. The Hebrew rendered here as food is *teref*. The verb from which the noun derives, *taraf*, means to tear, to rape, to rob. The more adequate word for food is *ochel*. *Teref* would normally be food of wild animals, who feed by tearing asunder. There is one verse in the Bible in which both terms occur, in the Psalms: "The young lions roar after their prey (*teref*), and seek their food (*ochlam*) from God."[59] *Teref* has come to mean food in relationship to the wild animals that subsist on prey. In a more general sense, anything torn away by force from its owner, anything taken by force, may be called *teref*. Our text does not speak about food at all. It would be highly incongruous to call the food given to "them that fear him" *teref*. What God gave them emerges clearly from the context. He gave them "the inheritance of the nations," the land he promised them. It is this that is referred to as *teref*. And *teref* indeed it was. It had to be taken by force from the Canaanites and given to the Israelites. Failing a better word, it would be more correct to translate: "He has given prey to them that fear him." And now the succession of the ideas becomes much more coherent. By giving them *teref*, God was mindful of his covenant. In this manner, he has "declared to his people the power of his works."

We may now return to the starting point of this discussion. Our difficulty began with the phrase "he has commanded his covenant forever." The meaning is that he maintains his covenant, he orders it to stand forever; he is loyal to the covenant. From the preceding verses, we have learned that God is ever mindful of his covenant by giving his people the "prey," the "inheritance of the nations."

Again, to recall the verse under discussion: "He has sent redemption to his people; he has commanded his covenant forever; holy and awful is his name." The parallelism now becomes evident. As the one who sends redemption to his people, his name is holy; as the one who sustains his covenant by giving them *teref*, his name is awful. In conclusion, it may be worth noting that the very expression "holy *and* awful is his name" suggests that the concept of awful is not included in that of holy.

We might then say that "holy and awful" (*kadosh venora*) expresses two different and opposing attributes of God. In this sense, the idea is similar to that of the Redeemer, who, in his relationship to those to be redeemed, acts as the Holy One, but toward those from whose power he redeems, he behaves as the Lord of Hosts.

There is, however, another term which encompasses the twofold function of the Redeemer most dramatically. It is the phrase *zeroa kodsho*, which should not be translated as "his holy arm," but literally, as "the arm of his holiness." It is the tool which God uses to bring to fruition the plans prompted by his quality of holiness. The phrase occurs in one of the most stirring prophecies of Isaiah, which begins with the words: "How beautiful upon the mountains are the feet of the messenger of good tidings." As we read on, we come across the passage:

> Break forth into joy, sing together, you waste places of Jerusalem. For the Eternal has comforted his people, he has redeemed Jerusalem. The Eternal *has made bare the arm of his holiness* in the eyes of all the nations; and all the ends of the earth shall see the salvation of our God.[60]

What is described in this great prophecy of redemption is, of course, God's act in history as the Redeemer. We have found in numerous other passages that God is the cause of comfort, joy, and salvation in his capacity as the Holy One. The Redeemer, however, cannot limit himself to dealing with his people alone. All the nations are involved in Israel's redemption. It is out of their midst that God's people have to be redeemed. The act of redemption takes place in the sight of all the nations. Because God is the Holy One, he is impelled to redeem; but in order to redeem, his might must become effective in the world. This is symbolized by the baring of the arm of his holiness.

A parallel to this passage appears in the opening verses of Psalm 98:

> O sing unto the Eternal a new song... his right hand, the arm of his holiness, has wrought salvation for him. The Eternal has made known his salvation: His righteousness (*tzedaka*)[61] he has revealed in the sight of the nations... all the ends of the earth have seen the salvation of our God.[62]

Salvation is the function of the Holy One, but in history it has to be "wrought"; and that requires an arm. The working of salvation is the revelation of divine *tzedaka*, but it has to take place in the sight of the nations. It must be effective. It is performed by "the arm of his holiness."

It will be rewarding to look at another passage, appearing in Psalm 77, which associates the word "arm" (*zeroa*) with redemption, but does not mention "the arm of his holiness": "You have with your arm redeemed your people, the sons of Jacob and Joseph."[63] The reference to the other nations is not lacking here either. The immediately preceding verse declares: "You are the God that does wonders; you have made known your strength among the peoples." The reference to holiness, which is the motivating desire to redeem, is lacking here—but not altogether. After declaring that he will meditate on all of God's works and doings, the psalmist introduces his meditation with the sentence: "O God, your way is in holiness; who is a great god like unto God?" We now have all the material we have been looking for: The "arm," redemption, and the idea of holiness. How do they function in our text, how are they related to each other?

Following our method of interpretation, we note that "who is a great god like unto God?" is a way of saying, through a rhetorical question, that no one is like unto God. It expresses, to speak theologically, God's incomparability, transcendence and remoteness. In other words, it expresses what we have identified as the meaning of "Lord of Hosts." This, however, is not holiness. Shall we then assume that this too is one of the dual-function passages which we have discussed, like the passage using "holy and awful"? In order to answer the question, we have first to determine what is meant by "your way is in holiness." Fortunately, the psalmist explains himself. Toward the end of the psalm, he mentions once again God's "way." Of it he says:

> Your way was in the sea, and your path in the great waters, and your footsteps were not known. You led your people like a flock, by the hand of Moses and Aaron.[64]

This conclusion is most revealing. God's way was the path across the waters. But it was not God who went across. It was God's way because he led his people across. His "footsteps were not known," for who indeed could have imagined that there was a path for men there to be led through the waters? This, then, is God's "way in holiness." It would indeed be the exact concept on the basis of our understanding of the term "the Holy One": The savior who dwells in the midst of the poor and needy. It is God's way of holiness, because along with it God exercised his quality of holiness. Thus, we indeed have before us another such dual-function passage. The psalmist meditates on God's holiness as well as on his quality as "Wholly Other," on his immanence as well as his transcendence, his nearness as well as his remoteness. Both qualities are needed in order to accomplish what is to be accomplished.

We shall again quote the psalmist's meditation, with the verses in order. He muses on the miracle of the dividing of the waters and the salvation of the children of Israel:

> O God, your way is in holiness; who is a great god like unto God? You are the God that does wonders; you have made known your strength among the peoples. You have with your arm redeemed your people, the sons of Jacob and Joseph.[65]

With this introduction, the theme is set. God is holy, but he is also supreme. Because he is supreme and above all other powers, he does wonders; because he is holy, he redeems. Because his way is in holiness, he performs miracles in order to redeem. What follows in the psalm is the description of how all this was wrought:

> The waters saw you, O God; the waters saw you, they were in pain; the depths also trembled.... The voice of your thunder was in the whirlwind; the lightnings lighted up the world; the earth trembled and shook. Your way was in the sea, and your path in the great waters, and your footsteps were not known. You led your people like a flock, by the hand of Moses and Aaron.[66]

Performing the miracle at the Sea of Reeds, God revealed himself as the Lord of nature and as the shepherd of his people, as the awesome, inaccessible power above all powers and as the Redeemer who will lead us as if "by the hand," as the Lord of Hosts and as the Holy One of Israel.[67]

The above psalm was certainly inspired by the Song of the Sea, which Moses and the children of Israel sang after they escaped Egypt in the book of Exodus.[68] There is a great similarity in the ideas and tone pervading both texts. At least one phrase has been almost literally borrowed by the psalmist. The words "you led your people like a flock" recall the parallel phrase of the song, "in your love you have led the people that you have redeemed." The thought is the same in both places, and the verb "to lead" appears in both, in the same grammatical form; it is the Hebrew *nahita*. This similarity leads us to have a closer look at the song from the point of view of our study.

After introductory verses, the song may be divided into two parts. The first deals exclusively with the destruction of Pharaoh and his armies. There is no mention at all of Israel. The second part still refers to what has happened to Pharaoh and describes vividly the fear that befalls the Philistines, Edomites, and Moabites, and all the inhabitants of Canaan, when the tidings of these wondrous events reach them. But quite clearly, the emphasis there is on the acts which God performed in order to save his children and to lead them to his sanctuary. The first part is introduced with the words: "The Eternal is a man of war, the Eternal is his name." The second part begins with the exclamation: "Who is like unto you, O Eternal, among the mighty? Who is like unto you, mighty in holiness?"[69] This is as we would expect it to be, in light of our discussion. It is appropriate that God should be called "a man of war" in a description of the vanquishing of Pharaoh and his chariots. But when the emphasis is on redemption, and the acts of war appear as prerequisites of the redeeming purpose, we are again confronted with a dual manifestation of divine performance. It is no surprise that this section of the song should open with a reference to God that makes mention of his elevation above all powers as well as of his being "mighty in holiness." "Mighty in holiness" is the parallel to "your way is in holiness" in the psalm we have interpreted, just as "who is like unto you, O Eternal, among the mighty?" corresponds to "who is a great god like unto God?" in the same psalm.

But what exactly is meant by "mighty in holiness"? We may suggest that the concept is identical with "the arm of his holiness." It is the attribute of the Redeemer, who uses might for the sake of preserving the purpose he envisages because of his holiness. It is worth observing that the first part of the song contains a phrase which is exactly in opposition to "mighty in holiness" (*ne'dar bakodesh*), and which is therefore its stylistic parallel, and that is "mighty in power" (*ne'dari bakoah*). It is an almost perfect correspondence of opposites. The first part, describing the perspective of the warlord, speaks of God's "right hand" as "mighty in power"; the second part, elaborating on God's actions as the Redeemer, speaks of him as "mighty in holiness."

III. HIGH AND HOLY

There are, however, several passages that seem to suggest that it is the Holy One who is incomparable, that he dwells inaccessibly in a "high and holy" place. The heavens are often called his holy dwelling. We now turn to those passages, in order to see what they convey. A significant one appears in Isaiah, where we read: "To whom, then, will you liken me, that I should be equal? says the Holy One."[70] Earlier we have seen that God's incomparability was an indication of his remoteness and transcendence, proper to his quality as Lord of Hosts. Here, however, it is the Holy One who speaks of it. As always, we have to consider the context in which the phrase appears. Having declared that God is unlike anything imaginable, he continues:

> Lift up your eyes on high, and see: Who has created these? He brings out their host by number, he calls them all by name. By the greatness of his might, and because he is strong in power, not one fails.[71]

Quite clearly, the theme of divine transcendence is further sustained. That God is the creator of the heavens and their hosts is an indication of the fact that he cannot be compared to anything created; the "greatness of his might" and his "strong power" illustrate his elevation above all other powers. Nevertheless, transcendence is not the only theme of this verse. The concluding part of the verse hardly requires further interpretation. God uses his might and power in order to preserve the heavenly hosts so that "not one fails." In English, the expression should probably be extended: "Not one fails" in its course or function. The intention of the prophet comes through much clearer in the Hebrew original. The word is *ne'dar*, which is better rendered as "missing."[72] God uses his power in order to preserve each individually, so that not one will be lost. As for the phrase "he brings out their host by number, he calls them all by name," surely it could not mean that God is an excellent astronomer who knows the exact number of all the stars and planets and is even familiar with their names. To number is mostly a preserving activity. One usually counts that which one wants to keep, which is of value; normally, what one counts one does not wish to lose. One counts one's money in order to know whether any has been lost.

And to call someone by name means to know him, to pay attention to him, to turn to him in order to have some relationship to him. What Isaiah says is that God, who created "these," continues his interest and care for all these. He numbers them, he knows them individually, he preserves them. God is the Creator, but after the creation he is the Preserver. With his might he created, with his might he sustains and protects.

The verse, "To whom, then, will you liken me, that I should be equal?" now takes on a deeper meaning. This phrase should perhaps be understood differently from those of a similar nature, which we came across earlier. Its meaning is not the same as that of the exclamation in Psalm 77, "who is a great god like unto God?" or as that which appears in the song in Exodus, "Who is like unto you, O Eternal, among the mighty?" In both these cases, the impossibility of the comparison is with the mighty; in both cases the Hebrew word used is the same: In the Psalms, the singular *el*; in Exodus, the plural *elim*. In both cases, the subject is God's mightiness, which is incomparable. In our present text, no reference is made to might. What is said is that no one may be likened to God. The reason emerges from what follows. God is, indeed, above all creation; yet he uses his might to preserve his creation. By his essential nature, he is far removed from all things created; yet he knows them all "by name." He infinitely transcends them all; yet he cares for them such that "not one shall be missing." Not only is he incomparable because he is infinite in essence and power; his true incomparability to anything else is to be recognized in the fact that, notwithstanding his infinitude, he lowers himself to his creations with preserving care.

These thoughts of the prophet are aptly followed up with the application of the universal truth to the historic situation of the Jewish people:

> Why do you say, O Jacob, and speak, O Israel: My way is hid from the Eternal, and my right is passed over from my God? Have you not known? Have you not heard that the everlasting God, the Eternal, the Creator of the ends of the earth, faints not, nor is weary? His discernment is beyond investigation. He gives power to the faint; and to him that has no might, he increases strength.[73]

How can Israel believe that their way is hidden from God? It is true that God is far removed from man; nevertheless, he is not the God of the deists. As he knows every one of the heavenly hosts "by name," so does he know Israel, their "way" and their "right." He is the Creator; but having created the world, he has not abandoned it; he has not grown weary of it. On the contrary, his power and his might sustain the weak and the powerless. How this may be, why the One who infinitely transcends man should be concerned about him, we may never understand. "His discernment is beyond investigation." But just because of that, he is even more unequal to anyone to whom he might be compared. "Says the Holy One," maintains Isaiah. Indeed, only the Holy One can speak like that.

We are now better prepared to understand another passage in Isaiah which contains a similar thought. "For thus says the high and lofty One that inhabits eternity, whose name is Holy."[74] Once again, the opening phrase concerns divine transcendence. Of this transcendent God it is said that his name is Holy. But how does the prophet continue? "I dwell in the high and holy place, with him also that is of a contrite and humble spirit, to revive the spirit of the humble and to revive the heart of the contrite ones."

The reference to the "high and holy" place, as it appears in the Revised Version, seems, of course, to strengthen the impression gained by the opening line that holiness is in transcendence. Yet practically in the same breath, the prophet also informs us that the God who dwells so high also dwells rather low, with him who is of "a contrite and humble spirit." But this is exactly what we found expressed in numerous other passages about the Holy One, who is the salvation of the needy and the poor, the source of strength for the lowly, without any mention of divine transcendence. A more literal translation would be more to the point. The Hebrew original does not have "the high and holy place," which is rather misleading. A more accurate reading would be: "I dwell high and holy, with him also that is of a contrite spirit." "High and holy" does not qualify a place, but the manner in which God "dwells," the way in which he is "present." On the strength of all the passages we have examined, it is justified to say that "high and holy" is a paradoxical concept which yet is true of the God of the Bible. "High and holy" is the way God is related to his creation. As the infinite Being, as the Creator, he is inaccessible, he is far removed from everything created; as the Holy One, he is accessible, he is near, he is "in your midst." He is transcendent as well as immanent. The rabbis of the midrash used to say of him: *Rahok vekarov*, far and near.[75] "I dwell high and holy" means: Even though I am so far removed by my absolute nature, I am nonetheless near through my actions. And because of that, as I dwell on high, I also dwell with the "contrite and humble spirit" and revive him.

We know that in the biblical text the "name" of God refers to his manifestation, the acts of self-revelation by which he makes himself known. The opening line of the text under discussion, "For thus says the high and lofty One that inhabits eternity, whose name is Holy," should be understood as saying: It is true, I am the high and lofty One, and I inhabit eternity. Such am I as the Absolute and Infinite, but my manifestation in the world is holy. The Infinite Being does what is beyond all human comprehension, he dwells high and holy.

It is important to note that whenever God's "holy habitation" is mentioned in the Bible, often identical with the heavens, it is the "place" from which God turns toward man, knowing him and considering him. In Deuteronomy, we read the prayer:

> Look forth from the habitation of your holiness, from heaven, and bless your people Israel, and the land which you have given us, as you swore unto our fathers.[76]

God's "holy habitation" is not what sets God and man apart; it is the point from which his blessings are expected. God relates himself to his people by blessing them and their land. Similarly, of the prayers of the priests and the Levites at the time of restoration of the Temple service under King Hezekiah, it is said:

> And their voice was heard, and their prayer came up to the habitation of his holiness, unto heaven.[77]

God's "holy habitation" is not really very far away. It can be reached through prayer. Isaiah, too, prayed in the same spirit: "Look down from heaven, and see, even from the habitation of your holiness and of your glory; where are your zeal and your mighty acts, the yearning of your heart and your compassions, now restrained toward me?"[78] God's zeal and mighty acts are due to the yearning of his heart and his compassion. Could anyone have known of God's nearness more intimately than the one who knew of "the yearning" of God's heart for man? It is that intimacy which the prophet is missing, and it is for its renewal that he prays. But he directs his plea to heaven, to God's holy habitation. Even though it is high, it is still God's "holy place," whence prayers are answered. Needless to say, the place is not a geographic point, but the quality of holiness with which God relates himself to the world and to man.

The psalmist, too, uses the concept of God's "holy habitation" in the same way: "Now I know that the Eternal saves his anointed; he will answer him from the heaven of his holiness with the mighty acts of his saving right hand."[79] The passage is a typical dual-function one. He saves and he does so with mighty acts. It is the dual function of the Redeemer. Because he dwells on high, he has the power to save; because his habitation is also holy, he has the "yearning and compassion" to save. Thus he answers his anointed from "the heaven of his holiness." In another place, the psalmist calls on man to "extol him that rides upon the skies, whose name is the Eternal." And he adds: "A father of the fatherless and a judge of the widows is God in the habitation of his holiness."[80] Though God is exalted above the skies, it is from the habitation of his holiness that he acts like a father and protector of orphans and widows. Similarly, God turns his attention toward the inhabitants of the earth, "To hear the groaning of the prisoner; to loose those that are appointed to death";[81] but in order to do so, he looks down "from the habitation of his holiness, from heaven."

The prophet Jeremiah employs the term *me'on kodsho*, the habitation of his holiness. The passage may, however, require some elucidation in order to be seen in its full significance. It runs as follows:

> The Eternal roars from on high and utters his voice from the habitation of his holiness; he mightily roars because of his sanctuary.[82]

The Hebrew *navehu*, in the text, is God's sanctuary in Zion. It is the *neveh kodsho*, the habitation of his holiness, which occurs in the Song of the Sea, to which God was leading his people in his love. The same word, *navehu*, is used by King David when, on his flight from Zion because of Absalom's rebellion, he says to the priest Tzadok: "If I shall find favor in the eyes of the Eternal, he will bring me back and show me... his habitation."[83] Jeremiah juxtaposes *me'on kodsho*, the habitation of his holiness, with *navehu*, his "earthly habitation" in Zion. His "mighty roar because of his sanctuary" is a symbolic expression of his sorrow over the destruction of the Temple in Zion, which has become necessary.[84] God's "holy place" in Zion symbolizes God's nearness to his people; it is a witness to his divine providence; it is a manifestation that "great is in your midst the Holy One of Israel."[85] The destruction of the Temple is the elimination of that manifestation; it is the withdrawal of the Holy One from the midst of the people. The divine "yearning and compassion" have to be curbed; the quality of divine holiness has to be controlled, its function must be withheld. Thus, it is from the habitation of his holiness on high that God roars because of the destruction of the habitation of his holiness below. God's quality of holiness is tragically involved in the destiny of Zion and her people.

IV. HOLY IS THE LORD OF HOSTS

We are now in a better position to appreciate the significance of the revelation granted to Isaiah, with which we began our study. "Holy, holy, holy is the Lord of Hosts; the whole earth is full of his glory." In the light of our analysis, one might say that the exclamation declares a coincidence of opposites. It would seem that "holy" and the "Lord of Hosts" represent contradictory forces of divine self-revelation. The one stands for love, mercy, and compassion; the other, for might, anger, and judgment. The one speaks of God as near, a friend, and a protector; the other, as remote, a stern judge, and even as the Wholly Other. But however contradictory both functions may be, they are attributes of the one God. The Lord of Hosts is the same as the Holy One of Israel. The Lord of Hosts is holy. In God, both attributes are one. This brings the "Lord of Hosts" himself closer to the world and to man than he appeared by his own characteristics. If he is holy, then even the divine anger and judgment must somehow be related to God's nearness, to the "yearning and compassion." Only because God remains related to his creation does he act in it; only because he considers man does he address himself to him, even if in "anger" and "judgment."

It would seem that the idea that "the whole earth is full of his glory" is a further elaboration of the same theme. Quite obviously it is a statement about divine immanence. If God's glory is present everywhere, then God is not inaccessible. It should be noted that the manifestation of the divine "glory" (*kavod*) may be brought about by both the quality of holiness and that which distinguishes the Lord of Hosts. The "high holiness" of God, as we have defined it, is explicitly called by the psalmist the greatness of God's glory, when he says:

All the kings of the earth shall give thanks, O Eternal.... Yes, they shall sing the ways of the Eternal; for great is the glory of the Eternal. For though the Eternal be high, yet he regards the lowly, and the haughty he knows from afar. Though I walk in the midst of trouble, you quicken me....[86]

Occasionally, in his prophecies of redemption, Isaiah makes reference to the glory of God, which is being revealed through his comforting acts of salvation.[87]

While these and similar revelations of "glory" may well be ascribed to the Holy One, others are obviously the function of the Lord of Hosts. The psalmist calls the Lord of Hosts the "king of glory." The glory of God often appears through his power and judgment. According to Isaiah, the glory of God will be feared, "for distress will come in like a flood, which the breath of the Eternal drives." The relationship between glory and judgment is found in Ezekiel, who says:

And I will set my glory among the nations, and all the nations shall see my judgment that I have executed, and my hand that I have laid upon them.[88]

This is, however, an activity that we have found always emanating from the Lord of Hosts. Both the Lord of Hosts and the Holy One reveal the divine glory in the earth. Both express qualities of divine immanence and nearness. Even his judgment is, though beyond human understanding, not apart from his yearning for his creation and from his compassion for it. For holy, holy, holy is the Lord of Hosts.

V. THE MEANING OF HOLINESS

Thus far, we have investigated the manner in which the term *kadosh*, holy, is used in the Bible in relationship to God. We have tried to derive the meaning from the work that the word is doing in the numerous passages in which it appears. However, in order to grasp the application of the concept of holiness to man and to objects, we shall have to attempt to discover the most basic meaning of the term "holy" as it appears in the Bible. It seems that this appears mainly in those passages in which "holy" has no religious significance at all. There are quite a few such passages in the Bible. We shall list most of these neutral passages together, so that the meaning of the word may emerge with accumulative force. In the following quotations, words which are derivative of the root *kadosh* are set in italics.*

> And they *set apart* Kedesh in the hill country of Naphtali, and Shechem... and Kiryat Arba... these were the appointed cities for all the children of Israel... that whoever kills any person through error might flee there. (Joshua 20:7-9)

> And Jehu said: "*Designate* a solemn assembly for Baal." And they proclaimed it. (II Kings 10:20)

> I have commanded my *designated* ones, yes, I have called my mighty ones for my anger.... Hark the uproar of the kingdoms of the nations gathered together! The Lord of Hosts musters the host of the battle. They come from a far country, from the end of heaven, even the Eternal, and the weapons of his indignation. (Isaiah 13:3-5)

> *Prepare* war against her.... (Jeremiah 6:4)

> Pull them out like sheep for the slaughter and *prepare* them for the day of slaughter. (Jeremiah 12:3)

> And I will *prepare* destroyers against you, every one with his weapons. (Jeremiah 22:7)

> Set up a standard in the land, blow the horn among the nations, *prepare* the nations against her, call together against her the kingdom of Ararat, Minni, and Ashkenaz... *Prepare* against her the nations, the kings of the Medes. (Jeremiah 51:27-28)

> *Designate* a fast, call a solemn assembly, gather the elders and all the inhabitants of the land unto the house of the Eternal your God. (Joel 1:14)

> Blow the horn in Zion, *prepare* a fast, call a solemn assembly; gather the people, *prepare* a congregation, assemble the elders, gather the children. (Joel 2:15-16)

---

* [In order to facilitate the discussion which follows, citations for the biblical sources are presented in the text, rather than as endnotes.—Ed.]

Proclaim this among the nations, *prepare* war; stir up the mighty men; let all the men of war draw near, let them come up. (Joel 4:9)

Hold your peace at the presence of the Lord the Eternal, for the day of the Eternal is at hand, for the Eternal has prepared a sacrifice, he has *designated* his guests. (Zephaniah 1:7)

As usual, we have followed the translation of the Jewish Publication Society. However, we deviated from it in the quotations from Kings, Isaiah, and Zephaniah, as well as in the first two quotations from Joel. As far as possible, the rendering "prepare" has been retained.

The passage in Joshua has, of course, no implication of sanctity in the religious sense. The cities of refuge were not sanctified. They were set apart to serve a specific purpose. The Revised Version has "appointed," which may be even more exact than "set apart." It brings out more strongly the positive idea of being set apart *for* something. The cities were designated to serve as places of refuge. It is in this sense that Jeremiah uses the term. "Prepare them for the day of slaughter" means, of course, mark them out, give them over for that day. Similarly, "prepare war against her" means mark her out for war. The nations and the kings that are to be "prepared" against Babylon are the powers that have been chosen to wage war against her. In the light of these passages we have translated *mekudashai* in Isaiah as "my designated ones," and not "my consecrated ones." As in Jeremiah, where God marks out the nations that are to wage war against Babylon, so here too, he causes the warriors, whom he has designated for the task of destruction, to do their work. "My consecrated ones," while not wrong, is misleading because of its religious connotation. The Revised Version has here "my sanctified ones," which is meaningless. *Mekudashai* are the armies that gather from all the corners of the earth, as "the weapons of his indignation." God calls them *mekudashai* because they have been given a specific task; they have been designated by the divine plan to perform in a certain manner. Nor should one render the phrase *hikdish kru'av* in Zephaniah as "he has consecrated his guests." "He has invited his guests" would be much nearer to the correct sense. We prefer here the Revised Version, which has: "He hath bid his guests." To invite implies to mark out from among others and to designate with a definite purpose in view.

As to our deviations in translation in the quotations from Kings and Joel, they explain each other. *Kadshu tzom* in the two passages we have quoted from Joel should certainly not be translated as "sanctify a fast." These are the only two occasions in the Bible where the phrase is met. To sanctify a fast sounds suspiciously unbiblical. Moreover, a careful examination of the texts will show that the rendering "sanctify," in this connection, is a misunderstanding.

In the first passage from Joel, *kadshu tzom* is followed by *kir'u atzara*, call a solemn assembly. Now in the quotation from Kings, we find the phrase *kadshu atzara*. To translate this phrase, as has been done, as "sanctify a solemn assembly" is quite wrong. For the text continues: "And they proclaimed it"; or in more exact, literal conformity with the Hebrew, *vayikra'u*, "and they called it."[89] According to the context, *kadshu atzara* means "call" or "proclaim" a solemn assembly. As such, the term is in keeping with what we have found to be neutral, not specifically religiously significant. What Jehu said was: Set apart a day. That the Bible informs us with the word *vayikra'u*, that they *called* such an assembly as they were asked to, proves that *kadshu atzara* in Kings is identical in meaning with *kir'u atzara*, call a solemn assembly, which is used by Joel. One might say that *kadshu* in this context equals *kir'u*; the meaning in both cases is obviously the same: Call a solemn assembly, designate a day to be observed as such. For this reason we translate in Joel *kadshu tzom, kir'u atzara* as: Designate a fast, call a solemn assembly.[90]

Similarly, in our second quotation from Joel, *kadshu kahal* should not be rendered as "sanctify the congregation." As such the phrase would keep rather strange company. It is immediately preceded by "gather the people" and followed by "assemble the elders, gather the children." The verb "sanctify," flanked by the verbs "gather" and "assemble," would be poorly placed. It is jarring to the ear as well as to the mind. Prophets did not write like that. What is meant is preparing a congregation, bringing it together for the occasion. It is synonymous with "gather" and "assemble." It is the appointing of the people as a congregation for the observance of the fast proclaimed.

On the basis of these passages, it seems reasonable to conclude that the word *kadosh* does have a meaning without any specifically religious connotation.[91] *Kadosh* is that which is set apart, marked out, assigned, designated. We are employing these many descriptions in order to indicate that no one by itself gives us the full meaning. The *kadosh* is set apart from others, but it is also assigned to something; it is marked out, but for a definite purpose, and it is thus designated as something to something. To make something *kadosh* is to remove it from one context and to place it into another. The cities of refuge set apart by Joshua at first belonged to one group, with all other cities of the land. Later, they were singled out, removed from their group and given a function which related them to a different context. Originally, the day to be proclaimed a fast is like any other day. In order to be designated as a day of fast, it has to be selected, set apart from all other days, and associated with a new meaning or purpose.

The primary neutral meaning of the term "holy" is fully retained in its specifically religious implication. "Holy" in the religious sense—and as the word is normally understood—is that which has been removed from its original frame of reference and placed into one in which everything derives its position by reference to God. This is quite obviously so, when we consider the purely ritualistic meaning of the term. Holy objects and animals are holy because they have been severed from their "natural" place within the neutral scheme of things and given a function within a realm that is reserved for the service of God. Their character is now determined by their relatedness to the divine; the purely ritualistic meaning of the term is still close to its primary non-religious significance. Essentially, it means being set apart from and being assigned to. The assignment, however, is a specific one: Assignment to God.

Our main interest in this study is, however, not the purely ritualistic aspect of the holy. Quite obviously, there are forms and grades of holiness that designate a man in his relatedness to God.

We may distinguish between the ritual and the spiritual aspects of holiness. The holy in relationship to man belongs in the category of the spiritual, as does the holiness of God. One might, however, consider the sanctification of the priests as the bridge between the spiritual and the merely ritualistic. Much more than ritual is involved in the appointment to priesthood. We adduce this clearly from a passage in Numbers, regarding the rebellion of Korah against Moses and Aaron. He and his followers sought priesthood. In answer to their request, Moses had occasion to explain how priesthood comes about. He put it this way:

> In the morning the Eternal will show who are his, and who is holy, and
> will cause them to come near to him... and it shall be that the man whom
> the Eternal chooses, he shall be holy.[92]

These are most illuminating words. Holiness, nearness, and being chosen
are mentioned and related to each other. The holy is brought near to God.
The chosen one is brought near to God. One is brought near by being
chosen. Furthermore, the one whom God chooses is holy. This gives us the
definition: To be holy is to be chosen by God, by being brought near to
him. This is the spiritual factor in the sanctification of man for priesthood.
We may say that to sanctify means "to choose in order to bring near." What
in the neutral meaning of the term "holy" meant to be assigned to, or to be
designated for, becomes in the spiritual sense nearness, closeness; it describes a personal relation between God and the priest.

We may now better understand what is meant when the concept of the
holy is applied to God, as it appeared earlier. While the concept of choosing
does imply singling out and separating, it is not yet sanctification. Sanctification consists of bringing near, establishing the relation, the closeness of
association. To single out or separate is a prerequisite of sanctification. This
is, in fact, explicitly stated in Chronicles, where it is said of the appointment
of Aaron: "and Aaron was separated, that he should be sanctified as most
holy."[93] Separation is quite clearly not sanctification; it is a precondition for
sanctification. The holy is separated away, but it is not holy because of its
separation. It is holy because it is near, because it is close to God. It can be
close because it is separated from associations and involvements that would
render nearness to God impossible.

How does all this affect the application of the idea of the holy to God?
We have found that holiness in the priest and—anticipating what yet has to
be shown—in man in general is nearness to God, standing in personal
relationship with him. Correspondingly, holiness in God should mean
nearness to what alone there is besides God, his creation. As far as man is
concerned, it is God turning toward him with love and compassion; it is,
indeed, as we have found it, the Holy One "in your midst." As with man the
precondition for human holiness is separation from that which may prevent
nearness to God, so too with God, as it were, separation and withdrawal are
the prerequisite of his holiness. But God is already separate by his essential
nature; he is unlike anything created; he is Absolute and Infinite. However,

as the Absolute he cannot be near, he cannot dwell in the midst of his people. The Infinite is unrelated to the finite by its essence; it is indifferent toward it. Thus God, too, as it were, has to separate himself from his absoluteness in order to turn with care and consideration toward his creation; he has to "withdraw" from the "natural" indifference of his infinitude in order to be "the father of the fatherless and the judge of the widows in the habitation of his holiness." He has to "curb" his nature as Wholly Other so that he may come near for the sake of his holiness. It is the awe-inspiring greatness of his holiness that he who is infinitely removed draws near and makes himself accessible.

VI. YOU SHALL BE HOLY

The spiritual aspect of holiness arises most forcefully from the relationship which, according to the Bible, exists between God and Israel. Only on the basis of that relationship could the children of Israel be commanded: "You shall be holy, for I the Eternal your God am holy."[94] With Israel, holiness has dual significance: It is a condition and a goal. They are God's holy people, as God has sanctified them. They shall become a kingdom of priests and a holy nation unto God; they have to sanctify themselves.

God has sanctified them in much the same way that the priests were designated, by choosing them and bringing them near. In Deuteronomy it is written: "For you are a holy people unto the Eternal your God: The Eternal your God has chosen you to be his own treasure, out of all the people that are upon the face of the earth."[95] Israel was made a holy people by God by his choosing them from among the other nations and taking them to himself. This is a form of sanctification very similar to the ritualistic one. The people themselves were passive. They were singled out and brought near to God. They had as little share in it as did the Aaronites, who were chosen to serve in the sanctuary.

Strangely enough, this people that is sanctified by God is, in the book of Leviticus, commanded to sanctify itself. "Sanctify yourselves and be holy, for I am the Eternal your God; and keep my statutes and do them. I am the Eternal who sanctifies you."[96] These words almost convey the idea that Israel has to sanctify itself because it is already sanctified by God. At least in one other place it is indeed put so, though in somewhat different phrasing.

Toward the end of the same chapter in Leviticus, we read: "And you shall be holy unto me, for I the Eternal am holy, and have set you apart from the peoples, that you should be mine."[97] Thus it seems that God sanctified Israel by setting them apart and taking them to be his. It is the essence of their being sanctified by God. The children of Israel are thus commanded to be holy because God, who made them holy, is holy.

That they shall sanctify themselves and be holy because God is holy is, of course, expressed repeatedly.[98] However, in the first of the above quotations from Leviticus, the reason that holiness is demanded of them is "for I am the Eternal your God." In yet another passage, the command to be holy seems to be related to their redemption from Egypt. "For I am the Eternal that brought you out of the land of Egypt to be your God: you shall therefore be holy, for I am holy."[99] Not only Israel's obligation to become holy, but God's own holiness is here related to the exodus. This is further emphasized in another verse later in Leviticus, where we learn that God's sanctifying Israel is explicitly linked to his bringing them out of Egypt: "I am the Eternal who sanctifies you, who brought you out of the land of Egypt to be your God."[100] We have collected now a rather confusing combination of ideas. Israel shall be holy because God is holy; they shall be holy because God is their God. They shall be holy because God has made them holy. Because God has brought them out of Egypt to be their God, they shall be holy, for he is holy. God, who has brought them out of Egypt in order to be their God, made them holy. The confusion is due to a multitude of concepts, which at first sight appeared to be unrelated to one another. In truth, however, a logical consistency prevails among them and connects them.

The phrase "for I am the Eternal your God," which we have found to be used in parallel with "for I am holy," is indeed identical with it. What is meant by "I am the Eternal your God" becomes clear if we render it as "I am the Eternal your *elohim*." As we have demonstrated elsewhere,[101] this does not mean: I, God, am God, the God whom you acknowledge to be God. Similarly, the two quotations that make mention of the exodus should read: "I am the Eternal that brought you out of the land of Egypt to become your *elohim*." God became their *elohim* by bringing them out of Egypt. "Your *elohim*" is God who has redeemed them, who has guided them and protected and saved them; the God who is with them, "in your midst." But this is exactly what we have found to be the function of the Holy One of Israel.

Thus, "Sanctify yourselves and be holy, for I am the Eternal your *elohim*." But in redeeming the children of Israel from Egypt, God chose them from among the nations and took them to be his. This again we have found to be the meaning of their sanctification by God. Thus, through the exodus God revealed his own holiness, and in so doing, in acting as their redeemer because of his holiness, he also sanctified them in choosing them and taking them for his own. Thus the various passages we have quoted say one and the same thing: Sanctify yourselves and be holy, for God is holy. He revealed to them his holiness by making himself *their elohim* through his redeeming acts; in making himself their *elohim*, he sanctified them by taking them unto himself. We are then left with the one concept requiring interpretation, the command that Israel become holy because God is holy.

What is the connection between Israel's obligation to become holy and God's being holy? God sanctified the priests and Israel by choosing them and bringing them near to himself. This is passive holiness. One is actively holy by bringing about the same relationship to God by one's own effort. "Sanctify yourself," therefore, means: Seek the nearness of God, choose him, relate yourself to him, cling to him. This is necessary because God is holy; he is your *elohim*. And he cannot be yours unless you are his. God is not holy because he saves; he saves because he is holy, because he is near, because he is with you, because of his love and compassion, because of his "yearning" for you. His nearness is not a spatial determination, but one of the spirit. His holiness is the bond between himself and his creation. Therefore, it requires mutuality. In his mercy, he may help man, even though man does not acknowledge him. But he cannot be near man unless man is near him. Nearness of spirit is mutuality of relationship. God sanctified Israel by choosing them and taking them to himself. He brought them near to himself because he is holy. But his holiness must be met with holiness. He took them for his own, but they cannot be his own in spirit unless they choose him as he chose them, unless they draw near as they were brought near. They cannot be his very own unless they give themselves to him to be his very own. Therefore, "You shall be holy, for I, the Eternal your *elohim*, am holy."

How does man sanctify himself, how does he choose God and move close to him? In the numerous passages that enjoin Israel to become holy, the obligation is connected with listening to the voice of God and doing his will.[102] Nor is this limited to any specific aspect of the law, such as rituals or sacrifices. Israel sanctifies itself by striving to fulfill God's will in all matters in which it has been revealed or may be ascertained. In Exodus we find the characteristic passage, supported by all the other related passages:

> Now therefore, if you will hearken to my voice indeed, and keep my covenant, then you shall be my own treasure from among all people; for the earth is mine; and you shall be unto me a kingdom of priests and a holy nation.[103]

As the various passages show, this applies to every branch of the divine commandments, those "between man and God" as well as those "between man and man."

The idea should be understood in its twofold relevance. Holiness is not the child of faith. One can have faith in a God who is far removed, who is "hiding his face." Faith in itself is not relation to God; it is essentially one-sided. The strength of faith is believing in God, even though he is "hiding his face," even though he seems silent and indifferent to man's personal destiny. Faith is not mutuality. Holiness is living with God, near him, in his company. But how can a man do that? How can a human being move near God, establishing contact in actuality with the divine? But for the moments of revelation, when God turns to man in a convincing human experience, how can man be with God in reality? And even those rarest of moments are altogether God's doing and not initiated by man. According to biblical teaching, man comes near to God by doing God's will. God revealed to man his will, so that by doing his will man may link himself to God. God is in his voice, in the covenant. By hearkening to his voice and keeping the covenant, man holds on to God; it is his very real bond with God. Thus he comes close to God, answering God's holiness by sanctifying himself through his own nearness to God.

The idea also implies that holiness originates not in what a man does, but in the fact that he does it in fulfilling the divine intention; that what is done is done for the sake of God. Holiness is not, for example, ethics. Holiness is a specifically religious category. The highest form of ethics may be unrelated to holiness. It is a noble thing to do the good for its own sake, but it is not holiness. Holiness is being with God by doing God's will. Now, it is the will of God that man should act ethically. But if he acts ethically for the sake of the good, he is an ethical man; if he does so for the sake of God, in order to do God's will, he is striving for holiness.

The connection between sanctification and listening to the voice of God may help us to clarify another concept that is relevant to our investigation. It is the concept of "sanctifying God," or of its opposite, that of "profaning his name." At least in one place, both are related to the keeping of God's commandments. The passage is found in Leviticus:

> And you shall keep my commandments and do them: I am the Eternal. And you shall not profane the name of my holiness; but I will be sanctified among the children of Israel: I am the Eternal who sanctifies you, who brought you out of the land of Egypt, to become your God.[104]

We are introduced here to the idea that God, too, has to be hallowed or sanctified. The idea, of course, occurs in other places as well, and we shall yet turn our attention to them. Here, however, it is linked to the keeping of God's commandments. We have found earlier that Israel, which is sanctified by God, has to sanctify itself. Now we hear that God, who is holy, has still to be hallowed. This is indeed surprising. In what sense may it be said that God will be sanctified by human action? How is it to be understood that the sanctification of the divine, or its profanation, is dependent on the keeping of God's commandments or on their rejection?

By doing the will of God man chooses God, he holds on to him and lives in his company. He sanctifies himself. But man's sanctification is the response to God's holiness. He is to become holy because God is holy. It is the human end of the mutuality which is required by holiness. The revealed will of God, his voice and his law, is the instrument of man's sanctification. As man does the will of God, he moves toward God in response to God's movement toward him; he sanctifies himself in response to God's holiness. Thus by keeping the commandments as a means of human sanctification, man acknowledges God's holiness, which requires that man, too, be holy. Thus God is being hallowed. On the other hand, the violation of God's commandments is a rejection of the instrument of human sanctification and of the demand to "be holy, for I, the Eternal your God, am holy." It implies a denial of God's holiness. It is tantamount to a profanation of "the name of his holiness."

To put it in simpler language, the violation of God's will is an act of separation between man and God. It is a deed against the manifestation of divine holiness, in which God is "in your midst." It is an attempt to remove God from the midst of men. It is a rejection of his quality of holiness. But he who does the will of God establishes closeness. He does what needs doing in order to bring God into the midst of men. He acts in harmony with God's holiness, making it manifest in the world through his own way of living. In this way, God is being hallowed through the deeds of man.

VII. SANCTIFYING GOD'S NAME

The profanation and sanctification of God's name forms one of the major themes in the book of Ezekiel. Although with Ezekiel the concept is not directly connected with the keeping of the commandments, in essence the idea is the same as we have described it above.

Ezekiel does not mention either the Lord of Hosts or the Holy One of Israel. He uses the term "name of his holiness" (*shem kodsho*), which we interpret to mean the manifestation of his holiness. A recurring subject in his prophecy is the profanation of this name, and what God will do so that it may be sanctified again. A striking passage, for instance, is the following:

> And when they went among the nations, where they had gone, they profaned the name of my holiness; in that men said of them: These are the people of the Eternal, and are gone forth out of his land.[105]

The strange idea conveyed here is that the exiles profaned the divine name in being exiles, in having moved from their native land. The traditional Jewish interpretation is that since they are God's people, God should have protected them and their land. To their enemies, the fact that they are in exile proves that their God is unable to protect them. He is lacking in power. This is a diminution of the glory of God.[106] They brought about this degradation of the divine name through their sins, which were the cause of their expulsion from their land. On the basis of our analysis, we would call any suggestion that God was lacking in power a desecration of the name of the Lord of Hosts, and not of the name of his holiness. However, independently of our own investigation, it is difficult to accept the traditional interpretation because of the local textual evidence in Ezekiel. The profanation of God's name, here attributed to Israel, is in another passage the doing of God himself. Thus God promises: "Neither will I cause the name of my holiness to be profaned any more."[107] This has occasioned a great deal of embarrassment for translators. How is it conceivable that God could have actively brought about the profanation of his name? In the JPS translation, for example, it has been toned down to "Neither will I suffer my holy name to be profaned any more."[108] The fact is that the Hebrew original is *ahel*, which is the active causative. God himself profanes the name of his holiness. Indeed, when the destruction of Jerusalem is prophesied, the prophet says so in a manner which does not permit any circumlocution:

> Thus says the Lord the Eternal: Behold, I will profane my sanctuary, the pride of your power, the desire of your eyes, and the longing of your soul; and your sons and your daughters whom you have left behind shall fall by the sword.[109]

God himself does the profaning. True, no explicit mention is made here of the name of his holiness. Or so it would seem, if one reads only the English translation; the Hebrew, however, has *mikdashi*, which means "my holy place" or "my sanctified place." This comes very close to the profanation of his name. When King David spoke of the same sanctuary, he said: "to build you a house for the name of your holiness."[110] The *mikdash* is holy because it is dedicated to God's name of holiness. In our terminology, it is the visible symbol that God dwells in Israel's midst; it symbolizes the manifestation of God's holiness, the "name" of his holiness. God threatens that he himself will bring about the profanation of the manifestation of his holiness, as he later promises not to do so again. What then is meant by such profanation that can be executed by the people as well as by God?

We may elucidate the meaning of profanation by discovering what is meant by sanctifying the name. This is what is said about it, what God promises to do for the sake of the name of his holiness:

> And I will sanctify my great name… and the nations shall know that I am the Eternal, says the Lord the Eternal, when I shall be sanctified in you before their eyes. For I will take you from among the nations, and gather you out of all the countries, and bring you into your own land.[111]

Thus it is by taking back Israel unto himself, purifying them and placing his spirit within them, that God sanctifies his name, revealing himself as the Holy One. The thought is repeated several times in the book of Ezekiel, such as in the following example: "With your sweet savor will I accept you,

when I bring you out from the peoples and gather you out of the countries
where you have been scattered; and I will be sanctified in you in the sight of
the nations."[112] By redeeming them from among the nations and accepting
them again, God is being sanctified. This is stated even more clearly in the
following verses:

> Therefore, thus says the Lord the Eternal: Now will I bring back the
> captivity of Jacob, and have compassion upon the whole house of Israel;
> and I will be jealous for the name of my holiness... when I have brought
> them back from the peoples and have gathered them out of their enemies'
> lands and am sanctified in them in the sight of many nations.[113]

God is jealous for the name of his holiness, and thus he is motivated to
have compassion on Israel and to redeem them from among the nations.
But we have found that to redeem them, to have compassion, to accept, to
take Israel for his own, are the manifestations of the Holy One of Israel. In
exile, God's face is hidden; he seems to be far removed from his people, as if
he no longer considered them. God is not revealed as the Holy One of
Israel. Thus he is jealous for the name of his holiness. He takes his people
back for his own, and in this act of reconciliation, God once again becomes
known as the Holy One. He sanctifies his name; he makes manifest his
attribute of holiness. It is important to note that in all our quotations God
is said to be sanctified "in you" or "in them," and "in the sight" or "before
the eyes" of the nations. God's sanctification is his self-revelation as being
"in your midst." This is expressed most powerfully in the passage referred to
above, in which God promises not to cause again the profanation of the
name of his holiness. This is the passage in its entirety:

> And I will send a fire on Magog, and on them that dwell safely in the isles;
> and they shall know that I am the Eternal. And the name of my holiness I
> will make known in the midst of my people Israel; neither will I cause the
> name of my holiness to be profaned any more; and the nations shall know
> that I am the Eternal, the Holy One in Israel.[114]

One is reminded of the dual-function passages in Isaiah, of the Redeemer,
who is at once Lord of Hosts and Holy One of Israel. The Holy One is in
Israel, the quality of his holiness will be made known in the midst of his
people. But the nations, too, will know he is the Eternal, for the power of
Magog will be shattered and the oppressed and persecuted will go free.[115]

We may therefore say that God sanctifies the name of his holiness by acting again as the Holy One, by revealing himself as the one who is with the poor and needy, who may well rely on him. But when God withdraws, when he "hides his face," when he withholds the manifestation of his attribute of holiness, he profanes the name of his holiness. He suppresses his "yearning and compassion," he violates the quality of his relatedness to his creation. But man too can profane God's name of holiness. When man withdraws from God, when he removes himself from association with him, when he severs the relationship, he rejects God's nearness; he denies the manifestation of God's holiness, he profanes it. We may suggest that it is of such profanation that Ezekiel accuses Israel. A careful reading of one of the key passages seems to indicate this. We already had occasion to quote it in part; we shall now examine it as a whole.

> And when they *went* among the nations, *where they had gone*, they profaned the name of my holiness; in that men said of them: These are the people of the Eternal, and *are gone forth* out of his land. But I had pity for the name of my holiness, which the house of Israel had profaned among the nations, *where they had gone*. Therefore say unto the house of Israel: Thus says the Lord the Eternal: I do this not for your sake, O house of Israel, but for the name of my holiness, which you have profaned among the nations, *where you have gone*.[116]

In this passage, the recurring idea of "going among the nations" has been emphasized. The seemingly unnecessary repetition is quite obviously a stylistic method of emphasis. It contains the point the prophet wishes to make. One senses it especially since it is conceptually connected with the burden of Israel's guilt—they are the people of God, and they are gone forth out of God's land. Now, to have been driven out from one's land may be the result of guilt, but it is no guilt in itself. The continuous repetition of the idea that "they went among the nations, where they had gone," however, suggests that they came freely, voluntarily. They were, of course, exiles, but their conduct in the land of their exile was such that it led the host nations to conclude that they "are gone forth out of his land." They had settled down as if they never meant to return, as if they were glad to have left the land. The emphasis here is on "his land." They reject God's land. But the land is God's because it is the place where he makes manifest his nearness to Israel. Rejecting God's land, they reject God's nearness to his people; they separate themselves from God, who desires to dwell in their midst. Thus they profane the name of his holiness. That this is the issue at stake one may gather from the change in the minds of the nations that comes about as a result of God's jealousy for the name of his holiness. In connection with that it is said:

> And the nations shall know that the house of Israel went into captivity for their iniquity, because they broke faith with me, and I hid my face from them.[117]

It is regarding this matter that the nations are originally mistaken. The behavior, the way of life, of the exiles causes them to believe that the people of Israel have rejected God. And so indeed they have. As God, however, takes pity on his name and restores his association with Israel, even though they do not deserve it, the nations learn to understand the true meaning of the exile of God's people. God's name becomes sanctified again, not through Israel but as a result of God's intervention in the course of history.

If, however, man's separation from God and rejection of God's nearness indicate man's profanation of God's holiness, then man's clinging to God and living testimony to his nearness are a form of sanctifying the name of his holiness through human behavior. Isaiah, too, speaks of such a form of sanctification in a passage which normally causes a great deal of difficulty to commentators. The translation from which we have usually been quoting runs as follows:

> Say not "a conspiracy" concerning all whereof the people say "a conspiracy"; neither fear their fear, nor account it dreadful. The Lord of Hosts, him shall you sanctify; and let him be your fear, and let him be your dread.[118]

This, of course, is an obscure passage. What conspiracy has the prophet in mind? Even more difficult is the parallelism in the text. According to it, to sanctify the Lord of Hosts would be the counterbalance to the demand not to acknowledge as a conspiracy everything that the people are willing to judge as such. What, however, could be the possible connection between the two?

As to our first problem, we prefer the Revised Version's rendering of the Hebrew *kesher* as "confederacy." The reference in the preceding context to "Rezin and Remalia's son" shows that the prophet is discussing the policy of alliances of the time. *Kesher* stands here for association, alliance. The people enter into alliances because they are afraid of Assyria. The prophet warns against such alliances. They are not to be relied upon; nor is the power to be feared whom they fear. Instead of relying on alliances, they should rely on God; instead of trembling before Assyria, they should fear God. Now, we have heard Isaiah declare often enough that Israel should rely on the Holy One of Israel. It was the "policy" recommended by him in place of the alliance with Egypt; the same policy is recommended here in a different constellation of power politics. God's people should withdraw from participation in power politics and instead put its trust in God. However, such reliance on God alone is a sanctification of God. It is based on man's conviction that God is to be relied upon, that he is the savior, that he is near, that he looks upon man with love and compassion—in other words, it is the affirmation that God is the Holy One. It is not affirmation by mere words; it is entrusting one's life unto him in the face of an overwhelming enemy, at a moment of supreme crisis. Not to be afraid, because he who fears God need fear no man; not to rely on alliances with any earthly power, because he who is allied to God needs no other alliances. Such complete trust that God is near and helps, all appearances to the contrary, is the highest form of sanctifying the name of God's holiness.[119] This is, indeed, how Jews understood the meaning of *kidush hashem*, the "sanctification of the name," through the ages. To give one's life for the sake of God, in loyalty to his command, is the supreme act of trust and reliance on him. In the knowledge of his nearness, death itself is being conquered.

In Ezekiel, God is sanctified through divine action, which reveals that God is near his people; in the passage we have just discussed, Isaiah speaks of God's sanctification through human action, which testifies to man's faith in the nearness of God. It seems, moreover, that both these forms of sanctification are encountered in the book of Numbers in close proximity. According to the biblical narrative, Moses and Aaron failed at the waters of Meribah. The traditional Jewish interpretation is that their failure consisted in smiting the rock, which eventually yielded water, instead of talking to it, as they were told by God to do. Of their punishment for this transgression the Bible says:

> And the Eternal said unto Moses and Aaron: "Because you believed not in me, to sanctify me in the eyes of the children of Israel, therefore you shall not bring this assembly into the land which I have given them." These are the waters of Meribah, where the children of Israel strove with the Eternal, and he was sanctified in them.[120]

It is surprising to hear that Moses and Aaron were punished for not sanctifying God before the children of Israel, since the passage concludes with the words "and he was sanctified in them." We may suggest that the moment of great crisis in which the children of Israel found themselves in a waterless wilderness was an occasion for a twofold sanctification of God: One in Ezekiel's style, with God sanctifying himself and revealing, through his saving act, his compassion for the people; the other in the manner of Isaiah, sanctifying God through complete trust and reliance on him, who is near to save. The first form of sanctification did take place; water was given to them and they were saved by the grace of God. Concerning this matter it is stated: "and he was sanctified in them." The other form of sanctification was to be the responsibility of Moses and Aaron. Had they quietly spoken to the rock to yield up its water, it would have been a more convincing demonstration of their unqualified reliance on God than was the forceful smiting of the rock. They missed an opportunity to illustrate to the people the attitude of ultimate reliance on God at a time of crisis. It is of this that the Bible says: "Because you believed not in me, to sanctify me in the eyes of the children of Israel." God was sanctified through his own act of salvation; but they did not sanctify him by demonstrating a complete trust that his salvation was near because he was the Holy One.

VIII. THE HIDDEN FACE OF GOD

It is difficult to ignore the fact that a number of prophets either do not mention the "Holy One" as such at all, or refer to him only incidentally, while they use the term "Lord of Hosts" quite frequently. This in itself need not be too surprising. The material that has been preserved in the name of some of those prophets is not very extensive. That there is no reference to the Holy One in the few chapters of Micah or in the not much larger books of Haggai and Malachi may be of no specific significance. The scanty references in Jeremiah are, of course, much more unexpected. We raise the point mainly because Jeremiah and Zechariah use the term "Lord of Hosts" in two different ways. They use it, as do Isaiah, the Psalms, and other books of the Bible, to indicate the remote mightiness of God, who executes judgment and punishment; but they also speak in the name of the Lord of Hosts in order to offer hope and to promise salvation. We would expect, however, that hope and salvation should be prophesied in the name of the Holy One, a term almost completely absent from the writings of these two prophets.

In numerous places, Jeremiah speaks in the name of the Lord of Hosts as Isaiah would;[121] but the prophecy that once again "the voice of joy and the voice of gladness, the voice of the bridegroom and the voice of the bride" will be heard in Jerusalem, is associated with the Lord of Hosts, as well.[122] Zechariah is conspicuous for the frequent mentioning of the Lord of Hosts. But the great chapter of comfort begins with the words: "Thus says the Lord of Hosts." There we find, for instance, those precious words, the faith in which has sustained Israel through its exile:

> There shall yet old men and old women sit in the broad places of Jerusalem, every man with a staff in his hand for very age. And the broad places of the city shall be full of boys and girls playing, in the broad places thereof.[123]

But this prophecy too, as others of similar quality, is prefaced by the words: "Thus says the Lord of Hosts." While this deviation from the pattern found in other books of the Bible has no direct bearing on our analysis of the concept of the holy, it nonetheless requires an explanation. The way they employ the term "Lord of Hosts" seems to indicate that with them the Lord of Hosts absorbed the function of the Holy One. This is all the more surprising since both Jeremiah and Zechariah, when they do refer to the holy, do it in the manner we would expect.

Earlier we discussed Jeremiah's use of the term "habitation of his holiness," which bears out our interpretation. When Babylon's punishment is prophesied, Jeremiah says, "for she has been arrogant against the Eternal, against the Holy One of Israel."[124] The verse recalls a passage in Isaiah, which we also addressed earlier, where something similar is said of the king of Assyria: "Whom have you taunted and blasphemed? And against whom have you exalted your voice? Yes, you have lifted up your eyes on high, even against the Holy One of Israel."[125] As we saw, Sennacherib "taunted and blasphemed" by declaring that it was foolish for Israel to rely on God for help and salvation. But this is exactly what the Holy One is to Israel, the One to rely upon. Thus Sennacherib has lifted up his eyes against the Holy One of Israel. Similarly does Jeremiah declare about Babylon that she was arrogant against the Holy One of Israel, believing that Israel was helpless and completely handed over into her grip. There was nothing for them to hope for. This, too, was blaspheming against the Holy One of Israel. The Holy One of Israel occurs in one other place in Jeremiah, rather interestingly for our purpose, in closest proximity to the Lord of Hosts. The theme is still the fall of Babylon. In that connection it is said:

> For Israel is not widowed, nor Judah, of his God, of the Lord of Hosts...
> for their land is full of guilt—of the Holy One of Israel.[126]

We have departed from the generally accepted translations. The grammatical form of "of the Holy One of Israel" (*mikedosh yisrael*) is the exact parallel to "of the Lord of Hosts" (*me'adonai tzva'ot*), and to "of his God" (*me'elohav*).[127] The phrase "for their land is full of guilt" is an insertion which refers to the reason why Babylon is being punished. This is well borne out by the entire context. The purpose of the insertion is to remind Israel that even though she is not widowed, what is done to Babylon is not done altogether for Israel's sake. She herself may not deserve her deliverance. Nevertheless, an important statement is made about the relationship between God and Israel. In spite of all appearances to the contrary, Israel is not forsaken by God, who is the Lord of Hosts and the Holy One of Israel. Once again we are reminded of Isaiah, of the dual function of the Redeemer. In the case of Jeremiah, God is the Lord of Hosts who executes judgment over Babylon, "for their land is full of guilt"; and he is the Holy One of Israel, and therefore Israel's cause is not forgotten. In addition, the association between Israel's status as a possible widow, on the one hand, and the concepts of the Lord of Hosts and the Holy One of Israel, on the other, recalls that specific passage in Isaiah which we discussed earlier, in which Israel is promised that she will remember the reproach of her widowhood no more:

For your maker is your husband, the Lord of Hosts is his name; and the Holy One of Israel is your Redeemer, the God of the whole earth shall he be called.[128]

While Jeremiah applies the term "holy" as expected, Zechariah employs it most originally in the two places in which it has been preserved for us. For now we shall examine only one of the passages. In that great chapter of comfort, to which we have already alluded once, we read the following:

Thus says the Eternal: I return unto Zion, and will dwell in the midst of Jerusalem; and Jerusalem shall be called the city of truth, and the mountain of the Lord of Hosts the mountain of holiness.[129]

According to this prophecy, the name of Zion will undergo a change. When God returns to Zion, the mountain of the Lord of Hosts will be called the mountain of holiness. Why the change? The reason for it seems clear in light of our analysis. Prior to God's return to Zion, Israel experiences divine judgment, as if God had departed, withdrawn from the midst of his people. At such a stage of history, Zion is not the visible manifestation of the Holy One of Israel. In its ruin, Zion is a witness to judgment and divine anger. It is the mountain of the Lord of Hosts. But when God, through the act of Israel's deliverance, returns to Zion, he reveals himself once again as the Holy One "in your midst." At that time, what was known as the mountain of the Lord of Hosts will rightly be called again the mountain of holiness, the manifestation of God's nearness and indwelling in Israel.

However, this passage in Zechariah may contain the clue we have been seeking in order to solve our present problem, which is the use of the term "Lord of Hosts" as the remote Judge and as the near Redeemer. Jeremiah and Zechariah have something in common: Both are witnesses to the judgment executed over Zion and her people. Their prophecies of redemption are made from a situation of either expected or fulfilled doom. The Holy One has severed his association with Israel. He treats them as the Lord of Hosts; it is as such that he deals with them at this stage of their history. We recall how at a time of a similar personal experience Hannah turned in prayer to the Lord of Hosts, and only after her prayer was granted did she in her joy address God as the Holy One. There are at least two psalms which affirm the idea that at a time of estrangement and separation from God, one addresses oneself to the Lord of Hosts. One appears as an intercession on behalf of Israel as a whole:

> O Lord God of Hosts, how long will you be angry against the prayer of your people? You have fed them with the bread of tears, and given them tears to drink in large measure... O God of hosts, restore us; and cause your face to shine, and we shall be saved....
>
> O God of Hosts, return, we beseech you; look from heaven and behold and be mindful of this vine, and the stock which your right hand has planted, and the branch that you made strong for yourself. It is burned with fire, it is cut down; they perish at the rebuke of your countenance....
>
> O Lord God of Hosts, restore us; cause your face to shine, and we shall be saved.[130]

The mood is very similar to the one we find in Hannah's first prayer, but here it arises from a national experience of being forsaken by God. God has punished Israel, and they plead that the punishment be taken from them; God has left Israel, and they pray that he may return. Significantly, the appellation is to the Lord, or God, of Hosts. We know, however, that when God "returns" and saves, he is the Holy One. Thus, the deeper meaning of the prayer is that God, who deals with them at the present as the Lord of Hosts, may make himself known again as the Holy One. The idea comes through rather intensely in the refrain that God may cause his face to shine so that they may be saved. The moment is then one of the "hiding of the face"; and the shining of the face is identical with being saved. But we know from Ezekiel that the "profanation" of the name of holiness by God is his withdrawal from Israel; and the hour is that of the "hiding of the face." Correspondingly, God's return in his people, the revelation of his holiness, is the hour in which he causes his face to shine. For in the context of the passage in which we have heard God declare that he will be "jealous" for the name of his holiness, we read: "Neither will I hide my face any more from them; for I have poured out my spirit upon the house of Israel, says the Lord the Eternal."[131] When God makes manifest his holiness, his "face shines" on man; but at the time of the "hiding of the face," one can turn only to the Lord of Hosts.

The second relevant psalm begins rather surprisingly: "How lovely are your tabernacles, O Lord of Hosts."[132] The opening phrase sounds as if it were spoken by a man at ease, who enjoys the nearness of God. However, anyone who might think so is soon disabused, for the psalmist continues: "My soul yearns, even pines for the courts of the Eternal."[133] This is an indication that the psalm was composed by someone who was banished or, against his will, separated from the "courts of the Eternal." In his yearning love for the sanctuary of God, he was recalling in memory the loveliness of God's tabernacles. The reference to the sparrow that "has found a house and the swallow a nest for herself"[134] suggests that the individual experience at the root of the psalm is exile and homelessness. Thus the psalmist pleads from the heart of his experience of separation:

> O Lord of Hosts, hear my prayer; give ear, O God of Jacob. Behold, O God our shield, and look upon the face of your anointed. For a day in your courts is better than a thousand: I had rather stand at the threshold of the house of my God than to dwell in the tents of wickedness.[135]

Clearly, these are still the words of one whose "soul yearns" for the threshold of God's house and who is yet condemned to dwell in the tents of wickedness. The phrase "look upon the face of your anointed" reminds one of "cause your face to shine, and we shall be saved" of the first quotation from Psalms. The experience is similar; as if God's face were turned away, as if he did not see, did not consider. Thus, as expected, the intercessions in the psalm are addressed to the Lord of Hosts. Nevertheless, the mood of this psalm is rather different from that in the prayer of Hannah or in the plea on behalf of Israel in the previous psalm. The tone of agony, almost despair, is absent here. This psalmist, too, pleads with God in a moment of the hiding of the face; yet even though it is the Lord of Hosts whom he approaches, he does so in a spirit of confidence and reliance on God. The psalm comes to a hopeful conclusion with the words: "O Lord of Hosts, happy is the man that trusts in you."[136] This is, indeed, the authentic strength of faith. It is rather easy to trust in the Holy One of Israel. For this means to trust in God who is near, who makes himself known as the Redeemer, who does cause his face to shine. The test of faith comes in the hour of the "hiding of the face," when God is known as the Lord of Hosts, when he comes as a judge to execute justice. When, notwithstanding such experiences, a man can turn to him in quiet confidence and say, "O Lord of Hosts, happy is the man that trusts in you," he has lived by his faith. Even when God treats him as the Lord of Hosts, the man of faith trusts in him, even in the Lord of Hosts. For is not holy, holy, holy the Lord of Hosts? Even though he may hide his face, he is the same One, who is also the Holy One, no matter what his specific manifestation may be.

From these considerations we may derive two points. We have seen that in times of the "hiding of the face," one turns to the Lord of Hosts. It is the essence of the moment that the closeness to God has been shattered, the contact has been lost. Yet in spite of it all, it is the Lord of Hosts that now becomes the source of hope; for he is God.

This may explain why, beginning with Jeremiah, the term "the Holy One" hardly occurs in the prophetic writings. Most of the prophets of the post-exilic period do not mention the concept of the Holy One at all. With Jeremiah begins the gloom of the "hiding of the face." More and more, God makes himself manifest as the Lord of Hosts. Whatever hopes of future redemption are held out to this people, it is done against the background of divine judgment and active wrath. It is the hour of the Lord of Hosts; it is to him that they must turn for their redemption. It is noteworthy that all the prophecies of comfort found in either Jeremiah or Zechariah contain a very natural reference to the prevailing situation of ruin and desolation. We shall list only a few from among them. There is, for instance, the passage in Jeremiah where, although the Lord of Hosts is not mentioned, the promise of redemption is nonetheless made against the experience of the "hiding of the face":

> For thus says the Eternal, the God of Israel, concerning the houses of this city and concerning the houses of the kings of Judah, which are broken down for mounds and for ramparts; whereon they come to fight with the Chaldeans, even to fill them with the dead bodies of men, whom I have slain in my anger and in my fury, and for all whose wickedness I have hid my face from this city: Behold I will bring it healing and cure, and I will cure them; and I will reveal to them the abundance of peace and truth.[137]

Not even the promise of cure and healing and abundance of peace can be made in the name of the Holy One in the sight of the rubble of the houses turned into mounds and ramparts and covered with the bodies of the dead. Similarly, in the same chapter, when the prophecy is made that "this place" will once again become "a habitation of shepherds causing their flocks to lie down," the present condition of "this place" cannot be overlooked, "which is waste, without man and without beast." The prophecy is proclaimed in the name of the Lord of Hosts.[138]

The same reference to the present moment of the "hiding of the face" we also find in all the prophecies of salvation by Zechariah. For example:

> For thus says the Lord of Hosts, who sent me... unto the nations which despoiled you: "Surely, he that touches you touches the apple of his eye. For, behold, I will shake my hand over them, and they shall be a spoil to those that served them"; and you shall know that the Lord of Hosts has sent me.[139]

They are still among the nations and are being despoiled. Even though God will shake his hand over the nations, so that they in turn will become a spoil to their former servants, at the moment they are still serving the nations. Therefore, even the prophecy of hope is introduced with the words "thus says the Lord of Hosts," and concluded similarly. The very promise of future redemption implies the present condition of rejection.[140]

Most revealing, however, is the conclusion of the second chapter of the book of Zechariah. The passage opens with the well-known words:

> Sing and rejoice, O daughter of Zion; for behold, I come, and I will dwell in your midst, says the Eternal.[141]

The verse reminds us of the one in Isaiah: "Cry aloud and shout, inhabitant of Zion; for great is the Holy One of Israel in your midst."[142] Zechariah, however, does not mention the Holy One of Israel, whereas Isaiah does. The difference between them is probably that whereas Isaiah can declare, "for great is... in your midst," Zechariah may only announce, "for behold, I come, and I will dwell in your midst." God who is in your midst is the Holy One of Israel; but as long as he is on the way to dwelling in your midst, he is not yet in your midst; he is not yet revealed as the Holy One. The promise that God will in the future dwell in the midst of Zion is repeated in the next verse in Zechariah, upon which follows the conclusion, "and you shall know that the Lord of Hosts has sent me to you." The prophet who brings good tidings is, of course, sent before the fulfillment of the promise. He is sent by God at a moment when God has not yet returned to Zion; he is sent by the Lord of Hosts. But then follows the most illuminating part of the prophecy:

> And the Eternal shall inherit Judah as his portion in the land of holiness
> and shall choose Jerusalem again. Be silent, all flesh, before the Eternal;
> for he is aroused out of the habitation of his holiness.[143]

While the Holy One is still not mentioned, the concept of the holy occurs
twice. The land in which Judah is once again taken to be God's portion is
the land of divine holiness, as the place which makes manifest again God's
association with Israel through Israel's redemption. More significant, however, is the phrase "for he is aroused out of the habitation of his holiness."
We have seen earlier that "the habitation of his holiness" (*me'on kodsho*)
reflects God's responding to man with the quality of his holiness. During
Israel's exile, God is silent; God does not respond, he is as though removed
and apart. Yet even when he is manifest as the Lord of Hosts, he is holy. His
attribute of holiness is not active, as if it were at rest, asleep. But when the
hour of redemption approaches, one witnesses in silent awe how God is
aroused out of the habitation of his holiness to come and dwell in the midst
of Zion.

IX. THE HOLY AND THE 'MYSTERIUM TREMENDUM'

We have seen that the biblical concept of the holy, far from being one with
the *mysterium tremendum*, indicates its very opposite, the attribute by
which God relates himself to the world as the source of human salvation, as
the one who is near, notwithstanding his being Wholly Other. God is, of
course, the Wholly Other, and as such the *mysterium tremendum* is rightly
associated with him, but through his attribute of holiness he covers up, as it
were, the *mysterium*, in order to be near his creation and to make himself
accessible for man. It is through holiness that the remote moves close, that
the transcendent becomes immanent. There are, however, a number of
passages in the Bible that do seem to associate the holy with the fear and
danger associated with the *mysterium tremendum*. Before we enter into a
deeper analysis of these passages, we may observe that they all have one
thing in common: The holiness, which seems to be the source of the
trembling and the peril, is not directly associated with God, but with some
object or place which is considered holy due to its being, somehow, related
to God. In the first revelation that was granted to Moses at the beginning of

his mission, he was told not to approach, and to take off his shoes because the ground on which he stood was one of holiness.[144] Nadav and Avihu, who died when they offered strange fire before God, came near the sanctuary, a place sanctified.[145] The danger for the Kehathites emanated from the holy vessels, should they touch them or see them without their covers.[146] Uzza was slain because he touched the ark.[147] When King Uziah, even though not a priest of God, burned incense in the sanctuary, leprosy broke out on his forehead because he desecrated the sanctuary.[148] In all these cases, the danger is due not to closeness with God, but to contact with sanctified objects or places. In view of the consistently spiritual meaning of the term "holy" as a divine attribute, it is difficult to accept the theory, suggested by some scholars, that in these passages we have remnants of the primitive concept of holiness as *avanda*, the almost demonic divine mightiness which spells danger for everyone who comes near it.[149] Nor is it likely that, if such primitive ideas should indeed have been retained, they should uniformly be applied to holy objects and places, but never to God himself.

There is one important distinction between the primitive *avanda* or *mana* and the peril that threatens in the Bible from the holy. *Avanda* works automatically, blindly, with the power of a natural force. Some authors refer to it as divine electricity. The danger in the Bible, however, is due to some improper action. It is not the approach that is dangerous, but the wrong approach. Moses does stand on holy ground; he is ordered to take off his shoes. The sons of Aaron are obviously punished for offering a "strange fire" which they were not commanded to do. Uzza did not die *of* touching the ark, as if he had been in contact with a high-power wire. He was killed *because* he touched the ark, which he was not permitted to do. "God smote him for his error."[150] Neither was the leprosy of Uziah caused by some automatically effective *mana*. It was punishment for transgression.

This may explain why the Bible associates the peril only with holy things. Holy objects or places are holy either because they are dedicated to God or because God uses them for the manifestation of his holiness. In either case they are set apart for God; they symbolize God's nearness, his indwelling. Through their sanctification, they become, indeed, what they symbolize. Because of that they have to be treated with awe and respect. There are, therefore, ritualistic rules regulating the reverent approach to them. He who violates these rules acts with disrespect, or even abuse, toward the One whose nearness they symbolize. It is in this way that the passage in Numbers, too, which we have quoted, must be understood. In light of the other passages we have discussed, it should be understood that not to touch the holy vessels and not to look at them without their being covered is the law of approach for the Kehathites. As with Uzza, it is not the touching or the seeing that spells disaster, but the breaking of an explicit law, which in this case is equal to sacrilege. So it happened to the men of Beth Shemesh, who gazed upon the ark of God. They did not die of gazing at the ark; rather, *because* they gazed, which they were not permitted to do as a sign of reverence, they were punished by God.[151]

The connection between God's nearness and the peril of the improper approach to his holy places is dramatically illustrated by what is said by Moses to Aaron concerning the death of Nadav and Avihu. Explaining the significance of the event to Aaron, Moses says:

> This is as the Eternal spoke, saying: Through them that are nigh unto me I will be sanctified, and before all the people I will be glorified.[152]

God is sanctified whenever his quality of holiness is made manifest. This may be done by God himself, who, as we saw in Ezekiel, may sanctify the name of his holiness by accepting Israel again and redeeming them from among the nations. It may be done by man, as Israel was enjoined by Isaiah to "sanctify him" by relying on God unquestioningly, because he is near. And now we hear of a third form of sanctification: Punishment for improper approach to the sanctuary. This, too, is sanctification, because it reveals that God dwells in the midst of his people. The holy place is the visible and tangible symbol of the nearness of God. Because God is indeed near, the symbols are true and testify to God's indwelling, to his holiness. Only because they are such true symbols does one have to treat them with awe and can one offend against God by approaching them contrary to the prescribed form of service. When men are then punished for their improper approach, God's holiness is affirmed, and he is sanctified. Most significant, however, is the statement that "Through them that are nigh unto me I will be sanctified." It relates sanctification to nearness. The further removed God is, the less the likelihood that man may approach him without due respect. The Infinite cannot be approached at all. Only because he is near can one violate the boundaries set by awe and respect. The nearer one is to him, the greater the risk of trespassing the boundaries. Only a priest, who is engaged in the Temple service, will make the mistake of offering a "strange fire." The nearer the person, the greater the risk that he may become too "familiar" with the tangible accouterments that symbolize divine holiness. Thus it is through those who are nearest to him that God will be sanctified.[153]

We are now in a better position to appreciate those last words Joshua addressed to the people before his death:

> You cannot serve the Eternal, for he is a holy God, he is a jealous God; he will not forgive your transgressions or your sins. If you forsake the Eternal, and serve strange gods, then he will turn and do you evil, and consume you, after he has done you good.[154]

Is this an indication that God's holiness excites fear and trembling? It seems unlikely. Human transgressions are to be feared, the forsaking of God by man. There is of course a connection between God's holiness and human transgressions. Only God, who is close to man and considers man, can be forsaken by man. Were he not holy, he could not be forsaken. Only because he is holy and considers man does he consider human transgressions as well. Only because he is holy and turns toward man with his providential care does it matter to him how man lives. Only because he is a holy God is he also a jealous God. The Infinite, the transcendent Wholly Other, cannot be approached by man either rightly or wrongly; it can be neither forsaken by man nor jealous for man. Only the Holy One knows man; only because God knows man is man a responsible being, a being responsible to God. Because God is holy, man is graced by responsibility. In responsibility lies man's risk as well as his opportunity. For he is a holy God and, being a holy God, he is a jealous God.

The rules governing the ritual treatment of sanctified places and objects also have their spiritual counterpart, which we find in the book of Psalms.

> Who shall ascend the mountain of the Eternal, and who shall stand in the place of his holiness? He that has clean hands and a pure heart, who has not taken my name in vain and has not sworn deceitfully.[155]

Because God is near, man may ascend to the place of his holiness. Because he may ascend, he should ascend. Since he should ascend, let him know how to ascend. Let him accept the nearness of God by drawing nigh.

Let him sanctify God, who, by revealing his will and his law for man, sanctified man.

X. HOLY AS AN ADJECTIVE AND AS A NOUN

In this study, we have been rather insistent on translating such terms as *zeroa kodsho* or *shem kodsho* not as they normally are rendered, as "his holy arm" or "his holy name," but as "the arm of his holiness" or as "the name of his holiness." The adjective "holy" is *kadosh*; in these and similar terms, however, we have the noun *kodesh* in a construct with a possessive suffix, meaning "his holiness." It is not for the sake of pedantry that we prefer our rather cumbersome English to the simpler rendering of the word as an adjective. The adjectival form is confusing and often misleading; it frequently obscures and distorts the Hebrew concept. For example, "his holy arm" was interpreted as being holy because it is God's. This, and similar terms, gave rise to the idea that holy meant either belonging to God or being of God. And since no one gives an arm to God, and one cannot speak of ritual sanctification of the divine arm, the conclusion was drawn that to be holy meant to be of God, to be God. It was only a very short step from here to the misleading thought that holy was an "otiose epithet," identical with the nature of God.[156] The exact Hebrew rendering could never have given rise to such misinterpretations.

One must distinguish carefully between holy as adjective and holy as noun, as it occurs often in the construct. Holy is that which has been sanctified, either ritually or spiritually. For instance, a "holy place"; a "holy people"; a "holy camp"; a "holy man"; Aaron, God's "holy one"; a "holy congregation"; and so forth.[157] These things or persons are holy, because they have been made holy in one way or another. However, the *makom kadosh*, the holy place where the "ram of consecration" was prepared, is not to be confused with the *admat kodesh* on which Moses stood when God appeared to him in Midian. The first one is a holy place, dedicated as such to the divine service of the tabernacle. The ground on which Moses stood was not dedicated or consecrated in this sense at all. Nor does the text refer to it as *adama kedosha*, holy ground. It was ground like any other ground. It possessed only the momentary distinction that God made his presence known to Moses there. God revealed to him his nearness, his concern for

Israel. At that spot, he revealed himself as the Holy One. This is what the Bible calls not holy ground, but "ground of holiness," or ground associated with God's revelation of his holiness. Its distinction lasts as long as the revelation lasts. Similarly, "his holy arm" should be *zero'o hakedosha*, which is meaningless. The Hebrew has *zeroa kodsho*, which must be rendered as "the arm of his holiness," referring to the power that God employs in order to take actions reflecting his attribute of holiness. "His holy name" would be a name reserved for God alone. But the name of God, as we have shown, stands in the Bible for the actions by which God makes himself known in the world. "His holy name" would mean "his holy manifestation," and we are back again to the spurious interpretation according to which everything that appertains to God is holy, because holiness is identical with divine nature. But the Bible does not speak of "his holy name," but of "the name of his holiness," which is a specific type of divine manifestation, namely, that of his holiness. Neither is *shemei kodsho* "his holy heavens," but "the heaven of his holiness," whence, as we saw earlier, he reveals his holiness by answering the prayers of those who call him.[158] *Kiseh kodsho* is not his holy throne, but "the throne of his holiness," implying that God rules and judges like a king, yet acts with compassion because of his quality of holiness.[159] Zion is called *har hakodesh*, "the mountain of holiness," the mountain on which God, through his sanctuary, reveals that he is the Holy One who dwells in the midst of Zion.[160] In the same sense does Isaiah speak of "cities of your holiness," emphasizing the aspect of their distinction due to God's making his holiness manifest in them or through them. In Deuteronomy, where the emphasis is that God has chosen Israel to be a nation unto him, they are called *am kadosh*, "a holy nation"; holy because God sanctified them.[161] But when Isaiah proclaims the approach of God's salvation, the time when Zion will be "sought out" and "not forsaken," he says of the people in Zion that they will be called *am hakodesh*; which does not mean "a holy nation" but "a nation of holiness." What Isaiah declares is not the sanctification of Israel through God, but the redeeming acts of God on behalf of Israel. God reveals his holiness by what he does as the Redeemer of Israel. That road, on which God's redeemed ones will return singing to Zion, is not a *derech kedosha*, a holy road, but *derech hakodesh*, the road of holiness. It is the road of return, of salvation and help, along which God makes effective his quality of holiness.

Nor do we find anywhere in the Bible the expression *ruah kedosha*, "holy spirit"; but either *ruah kodsho*, spirit of his holiness, or *ruah kodshecha*, spirit of your holiness. It will be interesting to take a good look at the three passages in the Bible where the term occurs. Two of them are found in the same context in a passage in Isaiah. We read there:

> In his love and in his pity he redeemed them; and he bore them and carried them all the days of old. But they rebelled and grieved *the spirit of his holiness*; therefore he was turned to be their enemy, and he fought against them.[162]

It is said most appropriately that it was the spirit of God's holiness that was grieved by their rebellion, for it is the continuation of the thought that God redeemed them in his love and pity and cared for them "all the days of old." We have found in numerous places that God's redeeming love and caring pity are the activity of his holiness. When Israel rebelled, they offended the spirit of divine holiness that redeemed them and protected them. And Isaiah continues:

> Then his people remembered the days of old, the days of Moses: Where is he that brought them up out of the sea with the shepherd of his flock? Where is he that put *the spirit of his holiness* in their midst? That caused the arm of his glory to go at the right hand of Moses? That divided the water before them... that led them through the deep... *the spirit of the Eternal* caused them to rest; so did you lead your people....[163]

The entire context shows that the "spirit of his holiness" is the power with which God led them across the waters of the Sea of Reeds, guiding them and saving them. This is, as we know, the work of the Holy One. "He put the spirit of his holiness in their midst" means that God as the Holy One was helping them. The passage is reminiscent of the verse in Psalm 77, which we discussed earlier. There, too, the psalmist describes the miracle of the crossing of the sea, as God "led his people like a flock, by the hand of Moses and Aaron." The striking similarity of construction we see in what follows. The psalmist begins his meditation by mentioning God's "way" in holiness. What is meant by it becomes clarified in the development of the theme, but especially at the point where the term "your way" is taken up again in the sentence: "Your way was in the sea, and your path in the great waters, and your footsteps were not known. You led your people like a flock."

We have seen that in reintroducing the idea of God's way, the concept of God's way in holiness is defined. Isaiah, too, describing the same event in Israel's history in very similar terms, mentions first the "spirit of his holiness in their midst" and then, after elaborating the idea further, reintroduces the spirit of God in the words: "The spirit of the Eternal caused them to rest; so did you lead your people." This, then, is "the spirit of his holiness in their midst": The spirit of God that leads them and brings them to rest and lets them find peace. It is the power of love and compassion through whose activity God reveals his holiness.

This, too, is the meaning of "spirit of holiness" in the third passage in which it occurs in the Bible, in Psalm 51. We find there:

> Cast me not away from your Presence; and take not the spirit of your holiness from me. Restore unto me the joy of your salvation; and let a willing spirit uphold me.[164]

To be cast away from the presence of God is to be separated from him. It is the dissolution of the bonds with the Holy One. The restoration of the joy of God's salvation is a plea that God may act as the Holy One. It is most fitting in this context to pray that the spirit of God's holiness be not taken from man, that the power of divine holiness may sustain man, that he may stay in the Presence and be upheld by God's salvation.

XI. CONCLUDING NOTES

A Bible scholar of my acquaintance has insisted that *shem kodsho* is "his holy name" (and similarly in the other cases in which I limit the suffix to the second noun in the construct). His reference to E. Kautzsch's edition of Gesenius' *Hebrew Grammar* is certainly very much to the point.[165] However, I do not mean to suggest that "his holy name" is incorrect, but that it is inexact and therefore confusing. While normally it is sufficient to translate the pronominal suffix of the second noun of the construct as referring to the entire phrase, Gesenius-Kautzsch fails to prove that that is indeed the exact meaning of the Hebrew usage. For example, *elilei kaspo* may well mean "the gods of his silver," meaning gods made out of his silver.[166] As such it would contain the sarcastic allusion, not unfamiliar in the Bible, to the fact that man makes himself gods from what he owns and controls. For all practical purposes, *kelei milhamto* may well be rendered "his weapons of war."[167] May it nevertheless not be the case that the Bible preferred to speak of the weapons of his war, since the ownership of the weapons as such is irrelevant? Similar is the phrase appearing in Ezekiel, *kelei mashhito*, normally rendered "his instruments of destruction," the ownership of the instruments of destruction is irrelevant; the men were charged with the task of destruction, each to his destroying task.[168] Again, no harm is done if one translates *beit tefilati* as "my house of prayer"; the emphasis in Hebrew, however, is on "my prayer." *Beit tefilati* is the house where prayers are offered to God; it is God's house because of "my prayer." The literal rendering as the "house of my prayer" may reflect the spirit of the Hebrew concept more exactly.[169] The distinction in meaning between the translation and the exact Hebrew construction is well illustrated by *tza'adei ono*, "the strides of his strength." Gesenius misses the point here by translating "his strong strides."[170] Even an average person may walk with strong strides. The "strides of his strength" conveys a different picture from the colorless "his strong strides." Again, the rendering of *alizei ga'avati*, following Gesenius, as "my proudly exulting ones" is a considerable weakening of the forcefulness of the Hebrew original.[171] The term *ga'avati* is paralleled by *mekudashai* (my designated ones) and *giborai* (my valiant ones). Those called by God are not the proudly exulting ones. But the exulting ones who are called are God's pride, representing his might as do his *giborim*. In the case of all the other examples to which Gesenius-Kautzsch makes reference, it is possible to show that by limiting the pronominal suffix to the second noun of the construct, the meaning of the concept becomes enriched, whereas its application to the entire phrase impoverishes both style and meaning.

Be that as it may, it is certainly permissible to refer the pronominal suffix only to the second noun, especially where to do so makes good sense. In fact, there are sufficient examples in the Bible to show that in certain cases no other reference is possible.[172]

Christian Bible scholars seem to agree among themselves that the original meaning of the term "holy" is hardly recoverable now. On the whole, they are inclined to follow Wolf W. Baudissin's interpretation that the word *kadosh* probably signifies separation and withdrawal.[173] However, notwithstanding the etymological difficulty of establishing the original meaning of the word, certain concepts are associated with the idea of the holy. It would appear that A.B. Davidson, in his Ezekiel commentary, has succeeded in interpreting the idea in a manner that was accepted by many scholars after him. According to him, "holy" does not express any definite attribute of the deity. It is a rather general notion of what is meant by the godhead. The holy God is the same as God. He is holy because he is God. Holy is a mere "otiose epithet" for God. For this reason, the word may be used elastically, depending on what we mean by God. Whatever our idea of the godhead may be, it is the contents of God's holiness. If one's idea of the deity is that of some mysterious power before whom one must tremble, then the holy God means the fearsome, superhuman being. If, on the other hand, one's concept of God comprises his righteousness and love, then the idea of the holy will be identical with divine righteousness and love.[174]

This interpretation has been adopted by W. Robertson Smith in his *Prophets of Israel*:

> Its force [of the word "holy"] lay in its very vagueness, for it included every distinctive character of godhead, and every advance in the true knowledge of God made its significance more profound; thus the doctrine of the Eternal's holiness is simply the doctrine of his true godhead.[175]

According to Robertson Smith's insight, in the Hebrew Bible God alone is holy, because he alone is the true God. H. Wheeler Robinson follows in the same tradition, as he concludes that the essential fact to be remembered about man's approach to God is the gradual transformation of man's ideas about God. In his opinion, only with the eighth-century B.C.E. prophets of Israel does holiness become associated with morality, because only then were the moral ideas of God's righteousness and love fully comprehended. At this stage, holiness stands for the transcendent majesty of God. The original, primitive concept of holiness as separation and inaccessibility of the godhead because of the mysterious dangers connected with the approach becomes now the transcendent holiness of God which may be manifest in divine righteousness and grace.[176]

The idea of transcendence as the meaning of holiness is, of course, closely connected with the concept of the Wholly Other that is the subject of Rudolf Otto's famous investigation, *The Idea of the Holy*.[177] For him the holy is the numinous, the mysterious, the unknown power to which man responds with fear and trembling. There are of course levels of development in the religious experience of the human race. Abraham's reaction is the classical biblical example of the numinous experience. Standing before God, Abraham sees himself as the creature in his "absolute profanity," as "dust and ashes." Sensing God as the Wholly Other, one becomes aware of the unbridgeable gulf between creature and Creator. In one's creaturely worthlessness one experiences God as "absolutely inaccessible," the *mysterium tremendum*. However, the holy has an ambivalent quality. While as the *mysterium tremendum* it is inaccessible, it is also the *fascinans* that fascinates and attracts. One desires the inaccessible and unapproachable.[178] Otto maintains that in the Hebrew Bible, the divine "anger," "wrath," "zeal," and "consuming fire" are terms related to that of holiness.[179] It is quite understandable that on the basis of his interpretation, he should declare that the holy in itself is indifferent toward the ethical and that it may be considered independently of it. In the history of religious development the holy has to be "moralized." In its essential nature, it represents the irrational element in religion. Through its moralization, the holy incorporates the rationality of ethical principles and ideals.[180] Eventually, the holy does become accessible. This, however, is not to be taken for granted. On the contrary, it is altogether due to the incomprehensible grace of God.[181]

These various aspects of the holy are neatly united into one pattern by a more recent author. N.H. Snaith, in *The Distinctive Ideas of the Old Testament*, follows in the footsteps of all his predecessors. He accepts Otto's interpretation that the holy is identical with the concept of the Wholly Other, the *mysterium tremendum*. He also agrees with Davidson that the holy is a mere "otiose epithet" of the deity. "Whatever that Other was realized to be, that was holiness. *Kodesh* never meant anything else among the Hebrews. It meant precisely that which at any period was recognized to be the inner nature of the Deity." He accepts the idea of the "moralizing" of the concept. As with Robinson, Snaith sees it as having been brought about by the eighth-century prophets. Since their conception of the Deity "was without parallel," the idea of the holy became associated with righteousness. For Snaith, too, this association with righteousness gives us the concept of "transcendent holiness." Since holiness for him is identical with divine nature, we assume that by transcendent holiness he means the transcendent quality of divine righteousness. It is still holiness as the "otiose epithet," the meaning being: God is God and not man; and God, who is God, is righteous.[182]

Theologians normally understand by the holiness of God his absolute transcendence in the metaphysical sense of the word. Thus Paul Tillich, for instance, declares: "The unapproachable character of God, or the impossibility of having a relation with him in the proper sense of the word, is expressed in the word 'holiness.' God is essentially holy, and every relation with him involves the consciousness that it is paradoxical to be related to that which is holy."[183] According to Tillich, the idea of the holy expresses the ontological discrepancy between the finite and the infinite, between the absolute and the contingent. The holy is a quality that belongs only to God, the ground of all being.

In the light of the preceding interpretations of the term, we might say that to theological and historical research, "holy" means the nature of the godhead as that nature is understood at each phase in the history of religion. For the psychological investigator, "holy" expresses the impact made on the human mind by the Wholly Other in its mysterious inaccessibility and otherness. For the philosophical understanding, the concept of the holy is identical with that of absolute divine transcendence.

In Jewish tradition, the word *kadosh* is taken to mean separateness. The idea is adopted by the classical commentators of the Bible. The interpretation seems to have its source in a midrashic explanation of the biblical injunction "You shall be holy, for I the Eternal your God am holy."[184] The observation is made: "As I am holy, so shall you be holy; as I am separate, so shall you be separate."[185] In the sense of separateness, *kadosh* applies both to God and to man. With God it is transcendence beyond everything created. This is how the term is understood, for example, by Nahmanides.[186] Applied to man, it is the demand for self-control, separating oneself from certain forms of conduct which are contrary to—or not in keeping with—the will of God. Judah Halevi, explaining the significance of the word "holy" in relationship to God, writes:

> Holy expresses the notion that he is high above any attribute of created beings…. For this reason Isaiah heard an endless "Holy, holy, holy," which meant that God is too high, too exalted, too holy, and too pure for any impurity of the people in whose midst his light dwells to touch him.

> For the same reason, Isaiah saw him sitting upon a throne, high and lifted
> up. Holy is, further, a description of the spiritual which never assumes a
> corporeal form, and which nothing concrete can possibly resemble.[187]

Holy, according to Halevi, apparently means "unlike anything created,
transcendent, divine." It is the essence of the separateness of God.

These various interpretations are on the whole unconvincing. The idea
that "holy" is identical with the nature of the godhead, in whichever way
that may be understood, is the least convincing. Quite obviously the word
kadosh in the Bible is not an "otiose epithet." "Holy, holy, holy is the Lord
of Hosts" does not mean, "Godly, godly, godly is God." The only proof
Davidson offers for his contention—a proof which is repeated by Snaith—
are two verses in Amos.[188] In the one, God swears by his holiness; in the
other, by himself. Davidson remarks that God does so in both cases
"without difference of meaning."[189] This is no proof. He is begging the
question. If "holy" means what he says it does, then there is no difference of
meaning between the two passages. On the other hand, if "holy" should
have a specific meaning of its own, there may well be a difference in
meaning between the two passages in Amos. That God swears in each case
need not mean that that by which he swears is the same in each case.

As to the theory of Otto that the holy is the *mysterium tremendum*, one
should note that, as far as the Hebrew Bible is concerned, he does not quote
a single passage to sustain his interpretation. He quotes the expression "the
terror of the Eternal" (*eimat adonai*) from Exodus and Job.[190] However,
neither of these passages makes mention of God's holiness. Needless to say,
we know of the concepts of God's terror, wrath, and anger from the
Hebrew Bible; and Otto is justified in saying that they are the character of
the numinous. However, in none of the passages he quotes are those terms
associated with the attribute of holiness. When Jacob awakes from his sleep
at Bethel, he is afraid and exclaims, "How full of awe is this place! This is
none other than the house of God, and this is the gate of heaven."[191] The
passage might justify the association of fear and awe with the numinous,
but Otto should not use it—as he does—to connect the holy with fear and
awe. The term "holy" does not occur in that context. There is one more
passage which he quotes to prove his point. It is God's address to Moses
from the burning bush: "Draw not nigh; put off your shoes from your feet,
for the place where you stand is holy ground."[192] The word "holy" is

mentioned here. However, as we have seen earlier, it is not said here that God is holy, but that the ground on which Moses stands is holy. There are many biblical verses in which holiness is attributed to God himself. The most significant aspect of Otto's study of the idea of the holy is his complete neglect of all the numerous passages which mention the holiness of God. In view of the rich biblical material on divine holiness, one cannot hope to define the idea either by relying on a few passages that speak of the *mysterium tremendum* but not of holiness, or by the one passage quoted which does mention holiness but not in relationship to God.

A remarkable failing in Otto's study is that it does not at all define divine holiness, but presents us with the description of human reaction to the Wholly Other. The numinous and the *mysterium tremendum* do not exist objectively. They result from a certain form of human reaction to a certain type of human experience. The holy emerges from Otto's study as a subjective quality of a state of mind which is characteristic of man when he is confronted with the unhuman or superhuman. Otto's distinction between the *fascinans* and the *augustum* cannot overcome this criticism.[193] The *augustum* too is the outcome of a purely subjective evaluation of the Unknown. Tillich, in his *Systematic Theology*, insists that Otto's analysis is phenomenological and not psychological.[194] If so, it is the phenomenological analysis of a certain state of mind, but not that of the holiness of God.

The theological view of the holy as the absolutely transcendent is not very convincing either. The classical passage in Isaiah runs: "Holy, holy, holy is the Lord of Hosts; the whole earth is full of his glory." Surely, rather than speaking of divine transcendence, the words seem to suggest God's immanence in the world by means of his "glory." The phrase "the Holy One of Israel," so often found in Isaiah as well as in other books of the Bible, does not indicate inaccessibility either. On the contrary, it would seem to suggest a close relationship between the Holy One and Israel. The greatest difficulty that renders the transcendence theory difficult to accept is the fact that the term "holy" does not apply to God alone. It is useless to maintain in this connection, as some scholars have done, that it applies also to people and objects in a secondary sense, as that which belongs to the holy, which is the godhead alone.[195] We are not thinking here of the merely ritualistic usage of the word. Holiness is an obligation upon all Israel to be a holy people. Surely, the injunction "You shall be holy, for I the Eternal your God am holy" does not speak of ritualistic belonging to the sphere of the holy, but of holiness as a form of human existence. If holiness is a concept which can be ascribed to the deity alone, if it stands for divine transcendence and inaccessibility, to enjoin man to be holy "for I the Eternal your God am holy" does not seem to make sense.

The difficulty is not quite as pronounced if we follow the traditional Jewish interpretation that "holy" means separate. One can perhaps ask man to separate himself from certain practices, for he should imitate God, who too is separate. But this, too, is difficult to accept. God's separateness is his transcendence. To say to man, "transcend yourself, for I the Eternal your God am transcendent," carries very little convincing logic within itself. It would almost make more sense to say to a mere human being: Do not even attempt to be holy, for holiness applies to God alone.

In the analysis suggested above, interest was concentrated on the meaning of the term as it is applied to God and man, but we have not lost sight of its purely ritualistic significance either. We have found that the word "holy" does not stand for divine nature, in whatever way that nature is understood. It is not a mere "otiose epithet" of God; rather, it is a specific attribute of the deity, and it is consistently used all through the Bible in that specific sense. Rather than indicating transcendence, it seems to be inseparable from the idea of immanence. Far from meaning inaccessibility, it reveals closeness and association. It is not the *mysterium tremendum*. If anything, it is its very opposite.

13

FAITH AFTER
THE HOLOCAUST

(1973)

FOR NUMEROUS JEWS, the Jewish fate in the ghettos and death camps led to a crisis of religious faith. "Where was God all the time? How could he countenance the infliction of such suffering and degradation on helpless millions?" The faith of many a Jew in the God of his fathers was choked in the smoke of the crematoria. And today, in the third decade after the last of the German death factories was destroyed, the questioning has not subsided. On the contrary, it seems to be on the increase. The Jews are gradually recovering from the quasi-paralysis of the imagination that at first protected the surviving remnant of their people. As they do so, the extent of the tragedy may now slowly sink in without rendering them incapable of confidence in a meaningful Jewish destiny. Thus, the quest for the place of God in that tragedy is gaining momentum.

Our concern here is with the authentic form of the quest. For there is also an inauthentic quest. It is the quest of those who, independently of any confrontation with the Jewish fate of our generation, have renounced faith in a personal, providential God. They reject any faith in God or conceive God as an impersonal cosmic process that is, by definition, indifferent toward individual human existence. When they raise the question of God's silence at Auschwitz, it is done with the impure intention of proving how right they were all the time. I call it impure, because the quest is a pretense. One must approach the problem of faith presented by the crematoria in the agony of one's soul. He who approaches the problem cleverly, using it as proof, vulgarizes. Only one who believes in the living God of Israel is involved in the crisis of faith of the death camps; only he can lose his faith on account of it. Undoubtedly, for our generation Auschwitz represents the supreme crisis of faith. It would be a spiritual tragedy if it were otherwise. After the Holocaust, Israel's first religious responsibility is to "reason" with God and, if need be, to wrestle with him.

The "reasoning" with God is a need of faith; it issues from the very heart of faith. When, in Elie Wiesel's *Night*, at the hanging of the little boy, someone asks: "Where is God now?" it is the right question to be asked.[1] Not to ask it would have been blasphemy. Faith cannot pass by such horror in silence. Faith, because it is trust in God, demands justice of God. It cannot countenance God's involvement in injustice and cruelty. And yet, for faith, God is involved in everything under the sun. What faith is searching for is, if not to understand fully, at least to gain a hint of the nature of God's involvement. This questioning of God with the very power of faith stands out as a guidepost at the earliest beginnings of the Jewish way in history. Abraham wrestled with God over the fate of Sodom and Gomorrah. We note how the man who, in his piety, sees himself as mere "dust and ashes," nonetheless has the audacity to challenge God with the words: "Shall the Judge of all the earth not do justice?" There is no contradiction here. The man of faith questions God because of his faith. It is the faith of Abraham in God that cannot tolerate injustice on the part of God.

This is also the essence of Job's dilemma. The sustained fire of his plaint is derived not from his personal plight, but from the passion of his faith. There is no weakening of faith with Job. On the contrary: It is the very power of the faith that lends force to the accusation. What has happened to Job is wrong; it is terribly wrong because it is judged by the ideal of justice that Job formed for himself on the strength of his faith in God. That Job will not accept the arguments of his friends in defense of divine providence is not a matter of stubborn self-righteousness, nor is it due to a sense of exaggerated self-importance. What the friends attempt to do is to defend a wrong as justice. By doing so, without being aware of it, they degrade Job's idea of God. Because of his faith, Job cannot accept a defense of God that implies an insult to the dignity of the God in whom he believes.

The questioning of God's providence in the death camps was taking place within the classical tradition of Judaism. Unfortunately, unlike the case of Job, God remained silent to the very end of the tragedy, and the millions in the concentration camps were left alone to shift for themselves in the midst of infinite despair. To this day, theologians are arguing about the meaning of God's answer to Job. Be that as it may, one thing is certain: In the denouement, God appears to Job. He makes himself known to him. Thus Job is able to find peace with God in the words:

> I had heard of you by the hearing of the ear;
> But now my eye sees you
> Wherefore I abhor my words, and repent,
> Seeing I am dust and ashes.[2]

No such denouement to the drama of faith took place in the camps. To the very end, God remained silent and in hiding. Millions were looking for him, in vain. They had heard of him by the hearing of the ear, but what was granted to their eyes to behold was "dust and ashes," into which they and everything dear to them were turned. There were really two Jobs at Auschwitz: The one who belatedly accepted the advice of Job's wife and turned his back on God, and the other who kept his faith to the end, who affirmed it at the very doors of the gas chambers, who was able to walk to his death defiantly singing his *ani ma'amin*—"I believe." If there were those whose faith was broken in the death camp, there were others who never wavered. If God was not present for many, he was not lost to many more. Those who rejected did so in authentic rebellion; those who affirmed and testified to the very end did so in authentic faith.

Neither the authenticity of rebellion nor the authenticity of faith is available to those who are only Job's brother. The outsider, the brother of the martyrs, enters on a confusing heritage. He inherits both the rebellion and the witness of the martyrs: A rebellion not silenced by the witness; a witness not made void by the rebellion. In our generation, Job's brother, if he wishes to be true to his God-given heritage, "reasons" with God in believing rebellion and rebellious belief. What may he hope for? He is not searching for an understanding, in terms of his faith, of what has befallen his people. He is not attempting to steal a glance at the "hand" of the Almighty in order to appreciate what meaning the destruction of European Jewry might have in the divine scheme. To understand is to justify, to accept. That he will not do. He looks to his religious bearings. He desires to affirm, but not by behaving as if the Holocaust never happened. He knows that this generation must live and believe in the shadow of the Holocaust. He must learn how this is to be done. If his faith is to remain meaningful, he must make room for the impenetrable darkness of the death camps within his faith. The darkness will remain, but in its "light" will he make his affirmations of faith, and it will accent his affirmations. The inexplicable will not be explained, yet it will become a positive influence in the formulation of that which is to be acknowledged. The sorrow will stay, but it will become blessed with the promise of another day for Israel to continue on its eternal course with a new dignity and a new self-assurance. Thus, perhaps in the awful misery of man will be revealed to us the awesome mystery of God. But when this happens, who can say that it will not be we who, seeking his consolation, in consoling him shall find our comfort?

II

There is a simple way to resolve the crisis of faith presented by the Jewish death-camp experience. One may meet the problem with a resolutely negative approach and say that what happened was possible only because God has abandoned the Jew, because he is not concerned with what happens to man. One might cut the Gordian knot, invoking the classical formula: "There is no justice, and there is no judge." This would be the Jewish version of what today has become known as radical theology. In its ultimate consequence, such a conclusion is a comprehensive statement about an essential quality of existence in general. What it says is that the universe is indifferent toward human destiny. Considerations of value are alien to the universal order, which is impervious to questions of meaning. Anything that can happen may happen, for there is no one providentially concerned with the course of nature or history. Indeed, such or similar is the position of some existentialists. Camus, for instance, gave expression to such an attitude in his *Letters to a German Friend*, writing: "I know that heaven, which was indifferent to your horrible victories, will be equally indifferent to your just defeat. Even now I expect nothing from heaven."[3] This is what is meant by the absurdity of existence. Life is absurd, it is without meaning. The only meanings, the only values, are those created by man. There is nothing beyond this existence, beyond this ethical indifference of the cosmos. There is no possibility of reference to the transcendent for values and standards. Life is altogether man's responsibility, his choice, and his decision; it is his fight against a meaningless fate. The meaning that man alone can create is the only justification for a meaningless universe.

It is the most uncomfortable aspect of such a position that, if carried to its logical conclusion, it leads to a justification of Nazism itself. If there is no possibility for a transcendent value reference, if existence as such is fundamentally meaningless and man alone is the creator of values, who is to determine what the values are going to be or what the manmade meaning is to be? Man, of course. But which man? Man as such, in the abstract, as a norm, does not exist. There is no Man; there are only men. There are only people; and they are of all kinds, with different temperaments, varied desires, and manifold self-created goals which set them at cross-purposes with each other. Camus spoke nobly when, after having declared his disbelief in an ultimate meaning of the world, he continued: "But I know that something in it has a meaning and that is man, because he is the only creature to insist on having one. The world has at least the truth of man, and our task is to provide its justification against fate itself. And it has no justification but man...."[4] These are beautiful words, but only because "the truth of man" here means the truth of the man Camus and that of other men like him; they are beautiful if one sympathizes with Camus' manmade meaning. There is no such thing as "the truth of man"; there are only the truths of men.

Himmler, too, was giving expression to his "truth of man" when at the close of the Final Solution he said to the assembled SS leadership: "To have gone through that, and to have remained an honest man just the same, save for the exceptions due to human nature, that is what has made you tough and strong. This is a glorious page in our history, never before, never again to be written."[5] There is no hypocrisy here. The "honest man" and the "glory" are genuine; they are the truth of the man Himmler. Camus opted for the persecuted; Sartre, for an existentialism as a form of humanism. But why should one not also be able to opt, in the full honesty of one's self-made truth, for the idea of a master race as the supreme man-created value?

It is true that far greater human suffering is likely to be found in a world in which the master-race idea constitutes the meaning of life, but this is the complaint of those who suffer. The infliction of suffering as such may well be reconciled—as indeed it has often been—with the manmade values and meanings of the persecutors. Some like to side with the persecuted; others find meaning in an otherwise absurd universe by feeding the crematoria. In a universe in which all values are based on human choice and decision, anything may become such a value.

What emerges as a Jewish version of a death-of-God theology, on account of the Jewish experience at Auschwitz, has both an ironic and a tragic aspect. Its starting point is the problem of faith raised by the German barbarism of the Nazi era. In search of a solution to the problem, it arrives at a position from which one may not only reject Nazism, but, indeed, find a "moral" validation for it as one of the man-created truths. This is the bitterest irony. What is tragic about such a position is that it presents us with one of the truly great triumphs of the Nazi proposition. It is of the very essence of that proposition that there is no personal God who is concerned with justice, morality, or human suffering. Law and meaning are manmade, and the man is the Fuhrer of a Teutonic master race. A negative response of the Jewish people to the Auschwitz experience, the response of religious denial, affirms the first part of the Nazi proposition, which is the premise to its Teutonic conclusion: There is no personal God; no divine justice or divine providence, as proved by what happened to the Jews. It is the true Hitlerian victory, the victory over Judaism in the hearts and minds of Jews, by whose treatment Nazi Germany too was going to prove God's indifference toward the plight of Israel.

If existence as such is absurd, it is vain to speak of man as the sole source of meaning. In an absurd universe, man too is absurd, and so are his self-made values and meanings. Camus himself felt this occasionally. One of the most lovable characters in his novel The Plague is Tarrou. In that important self-searching and self-revealing conversation that he has with the doctor, we are given the key to his personality. He is a modest man, he does not wish to be a maker of history. There is something lacking in his mental makeup, as he puts it; he cannot be a national murderer. All he understands is that there are pestilences on this earth and there are victims. And it is up to us, so far as is possible, not to join forces with the pestilences. Of this he says, "I know it's true." But how does he know? Perhaps he is on the side of the victims because of that flaw in his mental makeup? It would seem, however, that Tarrou himself would like to know how he knows, how he could know with such certainty. For Tarrou, too, has a problem. What really interests him is how to be a saint. But since he does not believe in God, his problem is: Can one be a saint without God? "In fact [that is] the only problem I am up against today," he confesses. But is there a solution to the problem? One might say that nothing could be easier than its solution. Indeed one might fail to see a problem here at all. For without God anyone may be a saint within the terms of his truth. In Valhalla, Himmler's minions are "honest men."

Of course, Camus' problem arises from the fact that for him to be a saint is defined in an exclusive manner, as being on the side of the victims and against the pestilence. But can one, without God, define sainthood thus exclusively? This indeed is a problem, an insoluble one. And Camus seems to have had some notion that there was no solution to his problem along the road he was walking. After Tarrou has unburdened himself of his self-revelation to Dr. Rieux, the two friends feel that they ought to do something. At this point, one cannot help being reminded of the haunting question in the aimlessness of *Waiting for Godot*: "And what shall we do now?" The two friends decide to go for a swim. For "really it's too damn silly living in and for the plague. Of course a man should fight for the victims, but if he ceases caring for anything outside that, what's the use of the fighting?"[6]

And so, to prove to themselves that they do care for something outside that, they go for a swim. At first this may seem rather opaque, until we understand the symbolic meaning of the swim. For in order to be able to swim, one has to leave the town, one has to pass through the closely guarded gates of the city of the plague; one must have special passes. Finally, far out in the fresh water of the bay, one is "at last free of the town and the plague." The town with its pestilence is the symbol of the absurdity of existence, and the fight for the victims is the meaning introduced into this absurdity by man. It is the attempt to be a saint without God. But it is not enough; it does not work. One has to go for a swim in the bay, outside the gates of this absurdity. The swim symbolizes the need for the Beyond, for a transcendent value reference. Without a sphere of reality where one is "free of the town and the plague," existence is indeed too damn silly; without it, why indeed should one fight for the victims?

Of course, one might say: It is indeed so; without that "swim," reality is damned silly. Yet there is no Beyond to which to go for the "swim"; there is no possibility of a transcendent reference. This has, to some extent, been the position of logical positivism, which denies the validity of all transcendent value judgments and reduces all ethics to questions of subjective likes and dislikes. Of course, the logical positivist is not an existentialist, nor is he a radical theologian. He will not say that existence is damned silly, because he is a much better logician than the existentialist. For if existence were indeed meaningless, no one within its scope could be bright enough to notice it. If life were indeed absurd, its absurdity could only be judged from a standpoint that would enable one to understand the distinction between the absurd and the meaningful. But this point cannot be found within the absurd itself; one would have to move beyond the realm of the absurd and take that "swim," the possibility of which is denied by the premise.

While the existentialist is not as logical as the logical positivist, he certainly speaks more truly. For it is indeed the case that, as we have heard Camus say, man has meaning because he insists on having one. Now this may not be very logical, but it is a fact, and facts enjoy the privilege of not having to conform to logic. Man's insistence on meaning is meaning. Even a nihilistic rejection of all meaning, including man's, is insistence on meaning and its affirmation. It presupposes certain standards of values by which existence is being judged. These values are acknowledged to be meaningful, but in their light existence is found wanting. As a result, the original value concepts are rejected as mere illusions, and the meaninglessness of everything is proclaimed. Finally, a certain form of behavior is adopted as the only meaningful thing to do in view of all that absurdity. All the time man is in search of meaning. In the very denial of meaning, he affirms it. Man is meaning.

But he is meaning in the universe. In a meaningless universe the denial of meaning would be not only illogical but impossible. Only because there is meaning in the universe can the question of its absurdity arise, not only logically but also existentially. If, then, man's insistence on meaning declares the world to have no ultimate meaning, what this means is that existence from a standpoint of realized meaning makes demands upon itself for more meaning. Whether such demands are realizable is another matter. The nihilist declares that they are not. This, of course, he cannot prove, because such a statement is not provable. Nihilism is not a logical conclusion but a choice, an act of faith in the purposelessness of existence, a decision whose purpose it is to adjust ourselves to the fact that the meaning originally demanded of existence was found unrealized. But the adjustment is meaning, and the original demand for meaning, whether realized or not, too, is meaning in the universe.

The idea of the absurdity of the universe may be entertained as a dogma to which a person may emotionally commit himself; it cannot be argued as a truth that takes sufficient cognizance of all of man's experience. At least, one would have to concede that there is enough reason in the universe to judge a great deal that is happening in it as absurd. Not only is there enough meaning to judge, but there is enough vital force to act for the realization of meaning. Camus never solved this problem of how one could be a saint without God, yet he—and many others like him—were such saints, struggling "against this universe in which children suffer and die."[7] But of course, the "saint without God" is part of the same universe in which he finds the suffering children; and what is wrong with that universe because of the suffering of the innocent is right with it because of those who struggle against such a universe. In the very power of his rebellion, Camus affirms this world, which he loathes. The extent of his rebellion against the evil which is life, is also the affirmation of the good, which is life, too. The problem of the good is no less serious a problem than the problem of evil. Anyone who, because of the problem of evil, concludes that existence is absurd has aggravated the problem of the good. He has closed a gap and torn open an abyss.

III

The universe cannot be dismissed that simply, and certainly not after the Holocaust. It is true that nowhere on earth and never before in history could one experience the absurdity of existence as in the German death camps; but it is also true that nowhere else in this world and never before could one experience the nobility of existence as there and then. And the one is not unrelated to the other. At Auschwitz and Treblinka, in the camps and the ghettos, man sank to his lowest level yet, but there too he was exalted to his highest dignity. The story of man's degradation is well known. Perhaps, in our sorrow over it, we have paid little attention to the greatness of man. Let a few examples stand here for what we mean by the experience of the nobility of existence even next door to the crematoria.

One of the survivors of the Warsaw Ghetto tells the story of how he and a woman were sought by the Gestapo. They were chased for weeks, living continually under the shadow of imminent death, changing their hiding place from day to day, until finally they were trapped behind the accumulated garbage of a ghetto attic. The man was determined to sell his life dearly. As the policeman approached his corner, he jumped forward and got him by the throat. The policeman went limp in his hand, completely at his mercy. At this moment, "Sonya ran from her hiding place and shouted hysterically: Don't kill him! Don't kill him!"[8] What manifestation of human dignity in this Jewish woman, who after having been stalked by death for weeks, became hysterical at the thought that her companion in hiding should kill their pursuer. And the greater the inhumanity that surrounded her on all sides, the more striking is the nobility of existence that she exemplified. At that moment, there was no place on earth holier than that dark corner in that attic in the Warsaw Ghetto. It was the Holy of Holies on earth, sharing in the majesty of Sinai, when God, descending upon it, proclaimed: "You shall not kill." Who knows whether that wretched attic was not wrapped in even greater majesty than Sinai? At Sinai God proclaimed; in the ghetto a hunted human being, at the risk of her own life, enacted God's commandment.

The same witness tells us about his final escape from the clutches of the SS, helped by fellow men, among whom an underworld character in prewar Warsaw was most instrumental. Recalling his feelings at the time when he finally was able to climb out from his secret hiding place, he writes: "I was a little dizzy and walked unsteadily. But I felt a lifting of the spirit. In this dismal, terror-ridden life, three men out of the gray, frightened, brutalized mass had shown humanity, tenderness, and friendly consideration. Under no greater compulsion than a decent feeling of compassion, they had risked their lives for a fellow man."[9] Instances of this kind could be multiplied without number. They occurred not only in the less dehumanized conditions of the ghettos, but also in the death camps. Another one of the survivors reports: "I saw death many times in the ghetto and in the concentration camps; I looked into its eyes often. Yet always the way out would come suddenly, as if by a miracle. Always a fellow sufferer would appear to help out in a dangerous situation, by giving a hand.... Once—I shall never forget that—a friend, risking his own life, brought me a dose of anti-tetanus serum."[10]

The cases of self-sacrificing humanity that have been testified to from the ghettos and the death camps fill volumes. There is, for example, the farewell letter by a member of the Jewish Council for the Warsaw Ghetto to a young woman who was his assistant in his work for the starving children of the ghetto and who, being a foreigner, was able to leave Poland. The man had been rich before the war and, thanks to his international connections, could have easily escaped the ghetto and left Poland. He wrote to her: "I wish you a safe journey. I am not sorry that I remain here. Of all the decisions of a life which has not been a short one—I have just turned seventy—I consider the one to stay here among my brothers and sisters the wisest. And if my eyes shed but a single tear… it was reward enough. Peace to you, my daughter."[11] When, one day, the last written messages from the ghettos and the death camps will be assembled in an edition worthy of the depth of their truth and inspiration, mankind will possess in them a new collection of holy scriptures.

We have heard a great deal about the disgraceful behavior of some members of the Jewish police in the Warsaw Ghetto and the inhumanity of the *kapos* and of some of the ordinary inmates of the concentration camps. It is maintained that, occasionally, they were more cruel than even the Germans. However, before one makes such comparisons, one ought to look with greater objectivity at the conditions of those who are so judged. Anyone who is willing to take upon himself the trying responsibility of studying the records and documents of the conditions in the ghettos and the camps will soon realize that even in ghettos like Warsaw, life was so degrading and dehumanizing that it defies the imagination of anyone who did not actually share in the experience.[12] And the ghettos were sheer luxury compared to the concentration camps, of which a German official reported home that Dante's hell was a mere comedy compared to them.[13] The cruelty of the Germans surpasses everything known in human history. Yet their greatest crime was not their cruelty, but their sophisticated system of planned destruction of the human status of their victims. Their terrible, barbarous power over their helpless victims was used not just to destroy them physically, but to degrade them to the extent of losing the last vestige of their self-respect. The world has never known anything like that before. The cruelty of the Germans was different not only in degree from other forms of cruelty practiced by man against his fellow. Unique was their system of the planned dehumanization of their victims. It is the uniquely German crime against humanity, against the status of man. It is the crime most difficult to forgive or to forget.

It has rightly been said that what the people had to face in the liquidation of the ghettos and on entering a concentration camp was immeasurable with all human experience, and it defies all moral criteria.[14] Reading the reports and studying the documents, I personally cannot visualize how one could survive a single day in a German death camp. All the values of human existence were deliberately destroyed. Family ties were torn apart, not only physically, but morally, too. Parenthood was trampled underfoot. Compassion was derided. Whatever a human being ever cherished was degraded. And all this in conditions of ultimate physical misery and wretchedness. How could human beings endure it without losing their senses? How was it possible for them not to break down and lose the last vestiges of their humanity? A well-known type in the concentration camps was the "Moslem," the person who, though completely destroyed as a human being, went on living. Leon Poliakov describes the "Moslems" in the following words:

> When they could still walk they moved like automatons; once stopped, they were capable of no further movement. They fell prostrate on the ground; nothing mattered any more to them. Their bodies blocked the passageway. You could step right on them and they would not draw back their arms or legs an inch. No protest, no cry of pain came from their half-open mouths. And yet they were still alive... they had become insensible to everything.[15]

Human beings can be crushed in spirit as well as in body. As there were physical "Moslems," so were there also moral "Moslems"—both the victims of German barbarism. The truth is that any act of cruelty committed by the victims of this inhumanly degrading system against their fellow sufferers was itself a German crime, the greatest of all their crimes, the crime of dehumanization. To compare members of the ghetto police or some of the *kapos* to their German taskmaster is a sign of insensitivity to the monstrosity of the German crime against the metaphysical status of man. There is a universe of difference between the inhumanity of people who strut about as the lords of creation, battening on the fat of a raped and looted continent, who, in free choice, embrace a religion of cruelty and murder and use their terrible might for the systematic physical and moral destruction of helpless people; and the inhumanity of some of their wretched victims, whose innate humanity was crushed under the weight of Nazi barbarism. The first form of inhumanity is unnatural; the other, natural—the natural and direct result of the unnatural. Inexplicable is the fact that the overwhelming majority of the inmates did not surrender their humanity to the very end; that, on the contrary, there were not a few among them who attained heights of self-sacrificial heroism and dignity of human compassion and charity. This was the true mystery of the ghettos and the death camps.

In former generations, at times of severe persecution, Jews would affirm their faith through the supreme act of *kidush hashem*, sanctification of the name of God. Placed before the choice of baptism or death, they would choose death and thus sanctify God's name. One of the tragic misunder-standings of our generation is that people often imagine that during the German-Nazi era in Europe, Jews were robbed even of this opportunity of preserving their dignity through the sanctification of the divine name. That there was no choice: One could not opt out of being a Jew. Nothing could be further from the truth. Choosing death, when betrayal by baptism may secure life, is only one form of *kidush hashem*, but not its only form.

The classical example of Jewish martyrology is the manner of the death of R. Akiva. As they were tearing the flesh from his body with iron-pronged combs, "he took upon himself the yoke of the kingdom of heaven." His disciples asked him: "Thus far?" His answer was: "All my life I was worried by the verse, 'You shall love the Eternal your God… with all your soul,' that is, even when he takes your soul. I said to myself: When will I have the opportunity to fulfill it?" As he surrendered his soul, with the completion of the verse of the *shema*, "Hear O Israel, the Eternal our God, the Eternal is One," he prolonged the pronunciation of the word "One."[16] When R. Akiva was captured by the soldiers of Hadrian, he had as little choice to die or not to die as the average Jew in the death camps in Europe. He already had forfeited his life. When his disciples asked him, "Thus far?" they did not mean to suggest that their master save his life by renouncing Judaism. It would not have helped him. He rebelled against Rome and was under sentence of death. As the sentence was carried out, R. Akiva was fulfilling a religious commandment: He recited the *shema*, whose meaning is the acceptance of the yoke of the kingdom of heaven, the affirmation of one's love of God. The "Thus far?" of the disciples meant: Is one obligated to fulfill this commandment even at a moment of one's being forsaken by God? The question becomes even more poignant just because there was no choice before R. Akiva.

One might say that in the Middle Ages, when Jews were confronting the Church, their abandonment by God was not complete. The decision was still theirs; there was a way open to them, which they could choose and save their skins. As long as the decision still lies within man, a human being draws strength from his sense of self-respect. When it comes to matters of man's ultimate concern, strong personalities will rather die than save their lives by acknowledging a lie as the truth. This is not an exclusively religious act. Religious and secular people both have been capable of such martyrdom. The confrontation in such situations of choice is between man and man, man and society, man and some other earthly power. The defiant "no" with which a man meets a tyrant or a persecuting church or a humiliating falsehood is itself a supreme act of living self-affirmation. If it is done for the sake of God, in whose truth alone one finds fulfillment, it is a heroic act of *kidush hashem.* One dares speak only with great hesitation and trembling on the subject.

It would, however, seem that with this act alone, the highest form of *kidush hashem* is not yet reached. There is still a great deal in it for man. At this stage, man is still acting within the frame of reference of this world. He preserves his dignity in the face of a this-worldly challenge. The ultimate phase of *kidush hashem* begins after the choice has been made, when the martyr approaches the stake at which he is to be burned. The world has died to him, he is no longer of it. He no longer confronts man and his works. He is alone—with his God. And God is silent, and God is hiding his face. God has abandoned him. Now man is truly alone. If at this moment he is able to accept his radical abandonment by God as a gift from God that enables him to love his God with all his soul, "even when he takes your soul," he has achieved the highest form of *kidush hashem.* "Thus far?" asked the disciples; "thus far," answered the master. R. Akiva does not complain to his God, asking why he has forsaken him. His radical abandonment is the great moment for which he has been waiting all his life. For no one can so completely surrender to him as the one who is completely forsaken by him.

The Jews in the camps never had the choice. They were placed directly into the situation at which their ancestors in the Middle Ages had arrived after they had made their decision. For them the challenge of *kidush hashem* commenced at the stake as the faggots were about to be set afire. From the very beginning they were beyond the gates of this world; from the very beginning they were facing God and not man. And God was absent; he had abandoned them. From the very beginning it was "when he takes your soul." It was the classical situation of R. Akiva. They did not choose it for themselves as was the case of thousands of instances during the Middle Ages. They were catapulted into it. But once in it, they were confronted with the ultimate phase of *kidush hashem*, to love him with all one's soul, at the very moment when he takes one's soul. For many the test was beyond them in strength; many doubted. Many exclaimed in their agony: My God, my God; why have you forsaken us? But there were others, in the thousands and tens of thousands, who affirmed and acknowledged in the classical style of their master, R. Akiva, whose act of sanctifying God's name reached the ultimate in the love of God, because it occurred in the dark hour of ultimate abandonment by God.

There is also another aspect of *kidush hashem* that should not be overlooked as we consider the human behavior in the ghettos and the death camps. The Talmud introduces the story of R. Akiva's martyrdom with the words: "The hour when they took R. Akiva to his death was the time for the recitation of the *shema*." These laconic words hide the greatness of R. Akiva's deed. We usually imagine an act of *kidush hashem* as the drama of the soul as it reacts to an extraordinary situation. This is how Jewish martyrs through the ages gave their lives and breathed their last with the words of the *shema* on their lips. It was an affirmation, an "acceptance of the yoke of the kingdom of heaven," brought about by the extraordinary nature of the challenge; specific acceptance, meeting a specific hour. Not so in the case of R. Akiva: It was the hour of the daily recitation of the *shema*. Accepting "the yoke of the kingdom," R. Akiva was doing what he had been doing every day of his life. It was, one might say, routine. The extraordinary situation invested the routine with extraordinary meaning and dignity. But R. Akiva was not responding to a situation; he ignored it. The Roman soldiers came to fetch him; they abused his body. It happened to be the time of the day when a Jew recites the *shema*. Let the Romans do to him whatever they please: R. Akiva could not be concerned with it. He had more important things to which to turn his attention—it was time for the recitation of the *shema*. What did it matter what Rome did to him? He went about his business of living the daily life of a Jew. Continuing with the "routine" of Jewish existence and ignoring the world that is bent on crushing the Jew is one of the marks of *kidush hashem*. Often it is practiced long before the hour of radical abandonment arrives. Sanctification of God's name in this sense is not one final heroic act of affirmation. It may be a form of behavior and daily conduct.

Numberless are the instances which show how widely this form of *kidush hashem* was present in the ghettos and in the death camps. Emanuel Ringelblum, the historian of the Warsaw Ghetto, writes as follows in his journal. "I marvel at the pious Jews who sacrifice themselves by wearing beards and the traditional frock coats. They are subjected to physical abuse.... An elderly Jew passed the guard on Twarda Street and did not— for reasons of piety—take off his hat in salute, although the Jewish guards warned him. So they tortured him a long time. An hour later, he acted the same way. 'They can go to hell!' were his words."[17] Now these Jews did not act this way in fulfillment of any religious duties. From the point of view of religious law, it was quite permissible for them to shave their beards, to change their traditional garb. Nor was there for them the least religious obligation not to remove their hats as they were passing the German guards. Yet they refused. And perhaps one should not use that word. They continued in their Jewish "routine," living their own life and ignoring the world around them. "They can go to hell" is a magnificent expression of this indifference to what others are to do. One goes on being a Jew in one's everyday way. This, too, was *kidush hashem*.

A similar story appears in the diary of Hillel Seidman. A group of young Hasidim, their names are on record, are assembled at the point whence they were to be taken to Treblinka. The cattle trucks are not ready yet. There is time. It is Saturday at dusk, the hour for the traditional third Sabbath meal. One of them finds some bread, some water. With the water they wash their hands; they sit down to the Sabbath meal. They intone the traditional song: "Let us prepare the repast of faith, perfect and joyous, of the Holy King," and, as customary, "The Eternal is my shepherd."[18] All this was done in the tradition of R. Akiva—contempt for a form of reality that does not even deserve a reaction. The hour happened to be the time for the third meal, just as R. Akiva's hour chanced to be the time for the saying of the *shema*. One is unimpressed by Nazi Germany as one was unimpressed with Hadrian's Rome: One continues the "routine" of being a Jew. This, too, is sanctification of God's name, and it was practiced by many not only in the ghettos and at the assembly points to the extermination camps, but also in the camps in the very shadow of the gas chambers.

Confronting Auschwitz one faces ultimate evil, but also the ultimate of goodness. The more vast the degradation and the misery, the more miraculous the manifestation of man's faith in the values and meaning he cherishes. If the evil was unnatural, so too was the good. Or shall we say supernatural? If the humiliation was inhuman, so was the preservation of man's dignity at all cost inhuman as well. Shall we rather say superhuman? In our generation, nowhere on this earth have man's conscience and his faith in a transcendent meaning of existence been defended and vindicated as nobly and as heroically as in the ghettos and the concentration camps, in the very dominion of their worst denial and degradation. Where we find man's deepest fall, there also do we find his most sublime ascent. If man's ability to perpetrate incomprehensible crimes against his fellow bespeaks the absence of God, the nonexistence of divine providence, what shall we say of his equally incomprehensible ability for kindness, for self-sacrificial heroism, for unquestioning faith and faithfulness? Is this all man's doing? Is it possible to separate human nature from the nature of the universe and from its meaning? Is it possible to reject the universe and accept man? Is it possible to accept man in view of his limitless ability for evil? Is it possible to reject him, witnessing his equally limitless ability for good?

These are, of course, questions and not answers. But it is important to understand their relevance as we attempt to cope with the problem of existence as it emerges anew from our confrontation with the Holocaust. One must recognize the ambivalence which is inseparable from human destiny in the death camps. The ambivalence is the source of the tragedy as well as the promise of existence. Meaninglessness recognized and fought is unrealized meaningfulness. It is doubtful that any philosophy will ever penetrate the secret of this ambivalence. It is, however, important that the faith by which a man lives—and we all live by some faith—should take adequate cognizance of its presence, woven as it is into the structure of existence as it concerns and affects man. The question of faith for the Jew is, therefore, not to explain why God was silent while the crematoria were consuming a third of the Jewish people. The question is whether within the frame of reference of Judaism it is possible to take cognizance of the tragedy and promise of existence and whether one may hold onto the promise in spite of the tragedy. One of the survivors of Auschwitz-Birkenau concluded her recollections with the words: "I believe that the still, small voice of Israel will remain and continue to proclaim the law of truth and justice. I have survived… now I know that fire cannot extinguish the heart of man, and gas cannot stop the breath of God."[19] It is not our intention to justify God's ways with Israel. Our concern is with the question of whether the affirmations of faith may be made meaningfully, notwithstanding God's terrible silence during the Holocaust.

Appendix:

Writings of Eliezer Berkovits

BOOKS

1. *Hume and Deism* (University of Berlin, 1933). [German]

2. *What Is the Talmud?* (Berlin: Judischer Buch-Verlag, 1938). [German]

3. *Towards Historic Judaism* (Oxford: East and West Library, 1943).

4. *Between Yesterday and Tomorrow* (Oxford: East and West Library, 1945).

5. *Judaism: Fossil or Ferment?* (New York: Philosophical Library, 1956).

6. *God, Man, and History: A Jewish Interpretation* (New York: Jonathan David, 1959).

7. *Prayer* (New York: Yeshiva University, 1962).

8. *Conditionality in Marriage and Divorce* (Jerusalem: Mosad Harav Kook, 1966). [Hebrew]

9. *Man and God: Studies in Biblical Theology* (Detroit: Wayne State, 1969).

10. *Faith After the Holocaust* (New York: Ktav, 1973).

11. *Major Themes in Modern Philosophies of Judaism* (New York: Ktav, 1974).

12. *Crisis and Faith* (New York: Sanhedrin, 1976).

13. *With God in Hell: Judaism in the Ghettos and Death Camps* (New York: Sanhedrin, 1979).

14. *Halacha: Its Authority and Function* (Jerusalem: Mosad Harav Kook, 1981). [Hebrew]

15. *Not in Heaven: The Nature and Function of Halacha* (New York: Ktav, 1983).

16. *Logic in Halacha* (Jerusalem: Mosad Harav Kook, 1986). [Hebrew]

17. *Unity in Judaism* (New York: American Jewish Committee, 1986).

18. *The Crisis of Judaism in the Jewish State* (Jerusalem: Rubin Mass, 1987). [Hebrew]

19. *Jewish Women in Time and Tora* (Hoboken, N.J.: Ktav, 1990).

SELECTED ARTICLES AND ESSAYS

1. "In Search of Fundamentals: Five Addresses" (Sydney: Central Synagogue, 1947).

2. "Jewish Living in America," *Judaism* 2:1, January 1953, pp. 68-74.

3. "The *Galut* of Judaism," *Judaism* 4:3, Summer 1955, pp. 225-234.

4. "From the Temple to the Synagogue and Back," *Judaism* 8:4, Fall 1959, pp. 303-311. Also appeared in Jakob Josef Petuchowski, ed., *Understanding Jewish Prayer* (New York: Ktav, 1972), pp. 138-151.

5. "Reconstructionist Theology," *Tradition* 2:1, Fall 1959, pp. 20-66.

6. "What Is Jewish Philosophy?" *Tradition* 3:2, Spring 1961,

pp. 117-130.

7. "An Integrated Jewish World View," *Tradition* 5:1, Fall 1962, pp. 5-17.

8. *A Jewish Critique of the Philosophy of Martin Buber* (New York: Yeshiva University, 1962).

9. "The Laws of *Koah Koho* and *Tzerorot*," in *The Oral Law: Lectures from the Fourth Congress on the Oral Law*, ed. Y.L. Hacohen Maimon (Jerusalem: Mosad Harav Kook, 1962), pp. 73-79. [Hebrew]

10. "The Twofold Tetragrammaton of the Thirteen Attributes," in *The Leo Jung Jubilee Volume* (New York: Jewish Center, 1962), pp. 45-52.

11. "Dr. A.J. Heschel's Theology of Pathos," *Tradition* 6:2, Spring-Summer 1964, pp. 67-104.

12. "Faith and Law," *Judaism* 13:4, Fall 1964, pp. 422-430.

13. "Orthodox Judaism in a World of Revolutionary Transformations," *Tradition* 7:2, Summer 1965, pp. 68-88.

14. "Judaism in the Post-Christian Era," *Judaism* 15:1, Winter 1966, pp. 74-84.

15. "Rabbi Yechiel Ya'akov Weinberg, My Teacher and Master," *Tradition* 8:2, Summer 1966, pp. 5-14.

16. "The Biblical Meaning of Justice," in H. Gvaryahu, Y. Hocher-man, M. Lahav, and B.Z. Luria, eds., *Zer-Kavod: In Honor of Dr. Mordechai Zer-Kavod* (Jerusalem: Kiryat Sefer, 1968), pp. 115-134. [Hebrew]

17. "God's Silence in the Dialogue according to Martin Buber," *Tradition* 11:2, Summer 1970, pp. 17-24.

18. "Jewish Education in a World Adrift," *Tradition* 11:3, Fall 1970, pp. 5-12.

19. "The Role of Halacha: Authentic Judaism and Halacha," *Judaism* 19:1, Winter 1970, pp. 66-76. Reprinted as "The Centrality of Halacha," in Jacob Neusner, ed., *Understanding Rabbinic Judaism from Talmudic to Modern Times* (New York: Ktav, 1974), pp. 63-70.

20. "Babylonian Talmud," *Encyclopaedia Judaica* (Jerusalem: Keter, 1971), vol. 15, pp. 755-768.

21. "A Contemporary Rabbinical School for Orthodox Jewry," *Tradition* 12:2, Fall 1971, pp. 5-20.

22. "Death of a God," *Judaism* 20:1, Winter 1971, pp. 75-86. Also appeared in *Faith and Reason: Essays in Judaism* (New York: Ktav, 1973), pp. 345-356.

23. "The Halacha Concerning Autopsies," *Sinai* 69:1-6, 1971, pp. 45-66. [Hebrew]

24. "Jewish Universalism," in W. Wagar, ed., *History and the Idea of Mankind* (Albuquerque: University of New Mexico, 1971), pp. 47-71.

25. "The Laws of *Grama* and *Garmi*," in *Proceedings of the Fifth World Congress of Jewish Studies* (Jerusalem: World Association for Jewish Studies, 1972), vol. 3, pp. 51-65. [Hebrew]

26. "Tora and Nature in the Philosophy of Maimonides," in *World of Jewish Philosophy* (1974), vol. xi, pp. 64-74. Appeared in Hebrew as "Tora and Nature in the Philosophy of Maimonides," in Menahem Zahari, Aryeh Tartakover, and Haim Ormian, eds., *Jewish Thought in America* (Tel Aviv: Brit Ivrit Olamit, 1972).

27. "Instant Mysticism and Chemical Religion," in Leo Landman, ed., *Judaism and Drugs* (New York: Commussion on Synagogue Relations, 1973), pp. 97-133.

28. "The Authority of the Rabbis to Contradict Biblical Commandments," *Sinai: A Journal of Torah and Jewish Studies* 75:1-6, 1974, pp. 227-238. [Hebrew]

29. "Conversion 'According to Halacha': What Is It?" *Judaism* 23:4, Fall 1974, pp. 467-478.

30. "Crisis and Faith," *Tradition* 14:4, Fall 1974, pp. 5-19.

31. "On the Laws of Conversion," *Sinai* 77:1-2, 1975, pp. 28-36. [Hebrew]

32. "The Scientific and the Religious Worldview," *Gesher* 1976:5, pp. 75-87.

33. "A Jewish Sexual Ethics," *Jewish Life*, Fall 1976, pp. 19-28.

34. "The Methods of R. Judah Halevi and Maimonides in Light of the Interpretations of the Scriptures in Their Writings," in *The Intellectual Legacy of R. Judah Halevi* (Jerusalem: Ministry of Education and Culture, 1978), pp. 13-20. [Hebrew]

35. "Exile and Redemption," in *Redemption and the State: The Redemption of Israel, Visions and Reality* (Jerusalem: Ministry of Education and Culture, 1979), pp. 141-148. [Hebrew]

36. "The Miracle: Problem and Rationale," *Gesher* 1979:7, pp. 7-14.

37. "Identity Problems in the State of Israel," *Judaism* 28:3, Summer 1979, pp. 334-344.

38. "The Authority of the Rabbis," *Sinai* 87:1-2, 1980, pp. 1-25. [Hebrew]

39. "Judaism: A Civilization," *Judaism* 30:1, Winter 1981, pp. 53-58.

40. "Speech, Voice, and Deed in Halacha," in Meir Benayahu, ed., *Studies in Memory of the Rishon Letzion R. Yitzhak Nissim* (Jerusalem: Yad Harav Nissim, 1985), vol. 2, pp. 81-93. [Hebrew]

41. "When Man Fails God," in Abraham Ezra Millgram, ed., *Concepts That Distinguish Judaism* (Washington: Bnei Brith, 1985), pp. 183-196.

42. "Judaism: After the Holocaust, in the Age of Statehood," in Joseph A. Edelheit, ed., *The Life of the Covenant: The Challenge of Contemporary Judaism, Essays in Honor of Herman E. Schaalman* (Chicago: Spertus College, 1986), pp. 9-16.

43. "Maimonides as a Source for Draft Deferral for Yeshiva Students," in Ze'ev Falk, ed., *Glory of the Lance* (Jerusalem: Mesharim, 1987), pp. 333-336. [Hebrew]

44. "The Self-Obligation of Women Regarding Positive Time-Bound Commandments," *Sinai* 100, 1987, pp. 187-194. [Hebrew]

45. "Understanding the Present to Save the Future," in Yehuda Bauer, ed., *Remembering for the Future* (New York: Pergamon, 1989), pp. 2342-2348.

46. "Authenticity of Being," in Roger Gottlieb, ed., *Thinking the Unthinkable: Meanings of the Holocaust* (New York: Paulist Press, 1990), pp. 209-223.

47. "Final Solution: Universal?" in Daniel Landes, ed., *Confronting Omnicide: Jewish Reflections on Weapons of Mass Destruction*, (Northvale, N.J.: Jason Aronson, 1991), pp. 259-267.

SOURCES

NOTE ON BIBLICAL QUOTATIONS

Throughout this collection, translations from biblical sources are either those of the author or his modification of previously published translations. With regard to the four-letter name of God, the tetragrammaton, the translation "the Eternal" has been preferred for the sake of consistency.

SOURCES FOR ESSAYS

CHAPTER 1: "Law and Morality in Jewish Tradition." Appeared as "How to Encounter the 'Other,'" "Divine Law and Ethical Deed," and "The Holy Deed," chapters 10-12 of *God, Man, and History: A Jewish Interpretation* (New York: Jonathan David, 1959), pp. 85-132.

CHAPTER 2: "The Nature and Function of Jewish Law." Appeared as "The Nature and Function of Halacha," chapter 1 of *Not in Heaven: The Nature and Function of Halacha* (New York: Ktav, 1983), pp. 3-45.

CHAPTER 3: "Conversion and the Decline of the Oral Law." Appeared as "Conversion 'According to Halacha': What Is It?" in *Judaism* 23:4, Fall 1974, pp. 467-478.

CHAPTER 4: "A Jewish Sexual Ethics." Appeared in *Crisis and Faith* (New York: Sanhedrin, 1976), pp. 48-82. Reprinted by permission of the publishers, Hebrew Publishing Company.

CHAPTER 5: "The Biblical Idea of Justice." Appeared as "The Biblical Meaning of Justice," chapter 5 of *Man and God: Studies in Biblical Theology* (Detroit: Wayne State, 1969), pp. 224-252.

CHAPTER 6: "On the Return to Jewish National Life." Appeared as "Galut, or the Breach Between Tora and Life" and "Healing the Breach," chapters 3-4 of *Towards Historic Judaism* (Oxford: East and West Library, 1943), pp. 25-51.

CHAPTER 7: "On Jewish Sovereignty." Appeared as "In Zion Again," chapter 6 of *Faith After the Holocaust* (New York: Ktav, 1973), pp. 144-158.

CHAPTER 8: "Towards a Renewed Rabbinic Leadership." Appeared in "Organizing the *Gola*," chapter 8 of *Towards Historic Judaism*, pp. 101-111.

CHAPTER 9: "The Spiritual Crisis in Israel." Appeared as "Identity Problems in the State of Israel" in *Judaism* 28:3, Summer 1979, pp. 334-344.

CHAPTER 10: "The Encounter with the Divine." Appeared as "The Paradox of the Encounter," "Faith, Reason, and the Encounter," and "The God of the Encounter," chapters 4-6 of *God, Man, and History*, pp. 31-56.

CHAPTER 11: "Knowledge of the World and Knowledge of God." Appeared as "An Integrated Jewish Worldview" in *Tradition* 5:1, Fall 1962, pp. 5-17.

CHAPTER 12: "The Concept of Holiness." Appeared as chapter 4 of *Studies in Biblical Theology*, pp. 141-223.

CHAPTER 13: "Faith After the Holocaust." Appeared as "God and the Holocaust," chapter 3 of *Faith After the Holocaust*, pp. 67-85.

NOTES

INTRODUCTION

1. Martin Buber, *On Judaism*, ed. Nahum Glatzer (New York: Schocken, 1995), p. 92.

2. Cf. M. Herbert Danzger, *Returning to Tradition: The Contemporary Revival of Orthodox Judaism* (New Haven: Yale, 1989), pp. 24-26. See also Howard W. Polsky, "A Study of Orthodoxy in Milwaukee: Social Characteristics, Beliefs, and Observances," in Marshall Sklare, ed., *The Jews: Social Patterns of an American Group* (New York: Free Press, 1958), pp. 325-335; and Sidney Goldstein and Calvin Goldschneider, "Jewish Religiosity: Ideological and Ritualistic Dimensions," in Marshall Sklare, ed., *The Jew in American Society* (New York: Behrman House, 1974), pp. 203-221.

3. "A Statement of Principles for Reform Judaism," adopted at the 1999 Pittsburgh Convention of the Central Conference of American Rabbis, available on the CCAR's Internet site, www.ccarnet.org. According to the platform, Reform Jews "are committed to the ongoing study of the whole array of *mitzvot* and to the fulfillment of those that address us as individuals and as a community. Some of these *mitzvot*, sacred obligations, have long been observed by Reform Jews; others, both ancient and modern, demand renewed attention as the result of the unique context of our own times." According to R. Richard Levy, one of the statement's principal proponents, the use of the term *mitzva* is a deliberate break with the Reform movement's past, reflecting a new consensus among Reform rabbis in favor of a more traditional approach to Jewish practice: "The Centenary

Perspective [the Reform platform adopted in 1976] would not use the Hebrew word *mitzva* but only the English word 'obligation,' whereas most Reform rabbis and laypeople are trying nowadays to build more and more *mitzvot* into their lives." According to Levy, "Reform Jews are much more willing today to rethink Jewish practices that have been taboo for a hundred years." An earlier draft of the statement also called for a rediscovery of specific practices of *kashrut* and ritual immersion in a *mikveh*. Richard Levy, "Is It Time to Chart a New Course for Reform Judaism?" *Reform Judaism*, Winter 1998, pp. 10-22, 54.

4. On the Holocaust, see his *Faith After the Holocaust* (1973) and *With God in Hell* (1979). Berkovits' essays on Jewish philosophers are collected in *Major Themes in Modern Philosophies of Judaism* (1974).

5. Menachem Friedman, "Life Tradition and Book Tradition in the Development of Ultra-Orthodox Judaism," in Harvey E. Goldberg, ed., *Judaism Viewed from Within and from Without* (Albany: SUNY, 1987), pp. 235-255.

6. Lawrence Kaplan, "The Hazon Ish: Haredi Critic of Traditional Orthodoxy," in Jack Wertheimer, ed., *The Uses of Tradition* (New York: Jewish Theological Seminary, 1992), pp. 145-173.

7. Cf. Michael K. Silber, "The Emergence of Ultra-Orthodoxy: The Invention of a Tradition," in Wertheimer, *Uses of Tradition*, pp. 49f. This leveling effect may be seen as a response to the perceived threat of the non-Orthodox movements, whose allure may have been seen as particularly strong at a time when large, uprooted Jewish populations were coming ashore to a New World in which these movements had established a successful base; since the threat came from those who rejected the binding nature of halacha, many Orthodox leaders responded by making adherence to halacha per se, rather than a complex of traditional value judgments, the overriding value.

8. The most important account of the change is that of the historian Haym Soloveitchik, whose essay "Rupture and Reconstruction: The Transformation of Contemporary Orthodoxy" created a minor tempest in Orthodox circles when it first appeared. The essay was published in *Tradition* 28:4, Summer 1994, pp. 64-130. In addition to this as well as the sources cited above by Friedman, Kaplan, and Silber, see Menachem Friedman, "The Lost Kiddush Cup: Changes in Ashkenazic Haredi Culture—A Tradition in Crisis," in Wertheimer, *Uses of Tradition*, pp. 175-186; Jack Wertheimer, *A People Divided: Judaism in Contemporary America* (New York: Basic Books, 1993), pp. 114-233.

9. *Not in Heaven* appeared in an expanded form in Hebrew under the title *Halacha: Its Authority and Function* (1981).

10. Brachot 19b-20a; Jerusalem Brachot 3:1; Jerusalem Kilaim 9:1; cited in *Not in Heaven* (1983), pp. 22-24, 120 n. 51.

11. The question of whether the cancellation of loans was still considered to have biblical status at the time of Hillel is debated in the Talmud. According to the opinion of Abaye, which was later accepted as halacha, Hillel acted under the assumption of the position of R. Yehuda Hanasi (who lived about two hundred years after Hillel), according to which the cancellation of loans no longer was considered a biblical commandment. This was somewhat difficult, since R. Yehuda Hanasi's position was itself a minority opinion when he held it, and thus for Abaye's claim to be historically accurate would require that the *prozbul* have been a matter of contention for at least two centuries, a dispute of which we would expect to have some record. For this reason, perhaps, Abaye's position is disputed by Rava, who holds that Hillel was empowered to act even in contravention of a biblical institution. Gitin 36a-36b; see Rashi ad loc.

Two latter-day parallels to this are controversial, yet widely accepted: The *heter iska*, which enables Jewish-owned banks to lend and borrow money at interest despite a strict biblical prohibition on charging or paying interest; and the *heter mechira*, which allows Jewish farmers in Israel to circumvent the prohibition on farming during the sabbatical year by allowing them to temporarily transfer ownership of the land to non-Jews.

12. Deuteronomy 6:18.

13. By "codes" I am referring to lists of rules such as those composed beginning in the medieval period. This is as opposed to works of the oral law which are not codes: The Talmud and its commentaries comprise a collection of discussions and disputes; in general, the study of Talmud in the yeshiva is frequently understood to be a separate subject of study from "halacha," which focuses mostly on the legal rulings beginning with the *Arba'a Turim* and continuing through the centuries to our own day. While both subjects are considered crucial for the aspiring *talmid hacham*, it is the study of halacha which constitutes the immediate basis on which rabbis are to make their decisions.

14. In his proposal for the creation of a new type of rabbinical education, Berkovits includes the study of codes of Jewish law, which he understood as binding in nature. See "A Contemporary Rabbinical School for Orthodox Jewry" (1971).

15. Louis Jacobs, for example, a leading thinker of the Conservative stream in Judaism, dedicates a chapter of his *A Tree of Life* to cataloguing instances in which the talmudic rabbis altered the import of the biblical law, in a discussion reminiscent of Berkovits' opening chapters in *Not in Heaven*. Jacobs also writes that "Change is never engaged for its own sake, and there is a proper appreciation of the great caution that is required if continuity is to be preserved. But where halacha as it is at present practiced results in the kind of injustice that reasonable persons would see as detrimental to Judaism itself, frank avowal that there must be changes in the law is called for." Louis Jacobs, *A Tree of Life: Diversity, Flexibility, and*

Creativity in Jewish Law (London: Littman Library, 2000), pp. 34-41, 220-221. Other examples are: Moshe Zemer, *Evolving Halacha: A Progressive Approach to Traditional Jewish Law* (Woodstock, Vt.: Jewish Lights, 1999); Robert Gordis, *The Dynamics of Judaism: A Study of Jewish Law* (Bloomington: University of Indiana, 1990).

16. Jacobs, *Tree of Life*, p. 230. Jacobs' *A Tree of Life* is a well-researched study on the flexibility of halacha in the face of many different types of considerations: Ethical, historical, philosophical. What is missing, however, is any effort to develop a theory which unites these extra-halachic factors—in other words, which can serve as the basis for a coherent theory governing the development of halacha. As such, *A Tree of Life* is typical of the historical school which he represents, and which Berkovits rejects.

17. Robert Gordis, "A Dynamic Halacha: Principles and Procedures of Jewish Law," *Judaism* 28:3, Summer 1979, p. 265.

18. See, for example, Zemer, *Evolving Halacha*, pp. 44-57.

19. Megila 14a.

20. Cf. Zemer, *Evolving Halacha*, p. 49; Zemer cites only the first part of Berkovits' statement, that halacha may not contradict "ethics," but leaves out the continuation in which he describes the ethical principles as based within the Tora itself. For a more faithful representation of Berkovits' position, see Jonathan Sacks, *Crisis and Covenant: Jewish Thought After the Holocaust* (Manchester: Manchester, 1992), pp. 162-167.

21. On the status of women in halacha, see his *Conditionality in Marriage and Divorce* (1966); *Jewish Women in Time and Tora* (1990); as well as the essay "The Status of Woman Within Judaism" in his book *Crisis and Faith* (1976), pp. 97-122; and his essay "The Nature and Function of Jewish Law," pp. 72-86 in this anthology. On conversion, see *Unity in Judaism* (1986), as well as the essay "Conversion and the Decline of the Oral Law," pp. 89-102 in this anthology.

22. *Crisis and Faith* (1976), p. 121.

23. See, for example, Sacks, *Crisis and Covenant*, p. 167. Sacks does not present a justification for his opinion.

24. Cf. *What Is the Talmud?* (1938), pp. 40-47. An excellent example of an effort to explain the Sabbath prohibition on work with reference to the agadot of the tractate Shabbat is Yosef Yitzhak Lifshitz, "Secret of the Sabbath," *Azure* 10, Winter 2001, pp. 85-117. A similar effort to describe prayer in light of both the halacha and agada is undertaken by Berkovits himself, in *Prayer* (1962).

Berkovits is not the only modern Jewish thinker to declare the essential nature of the agadic passages of the Talmud. However, usually this claim is made by those who do not accept the binding nature of the halacha, and therefore do not view the central purpose of the agada as contributing to the integrity of the system of halachic values, but to an overall understanding of Jewish morality independent of halacha. See, for example, Abraham Joshua Heschel, *God in Search of Man* (New York: Noonday, 1996), pp. 336-337; there Heschel describes the agada as necessary for giving man his ultimate direction, whereas halacha provides a specific, non-legal norm.

25. "We do not learn out words of Tora [i.e., halacha] from words of the received [i.e., prophetic] tradition." Baba Kama 2b; cf. Rashi ad loc., s.v. *divrei kabala*; Hagiga 10b; Nida 23a.

26. The rabbis decreed that biblical texts, but not apocryphal or post-biblical ones, had the status of "defiling the hands," i.e., causing ritual impurity. The purpose of this seemingly counterintuitive law was more practical than symbolic: To prevent the storage of these texts together with the food of the priests, which had to be eaten in purity, and thereby to protect the scrolls from the rodents which tended to roam in areas where food was stored. Nonetheless, a debate ensued over which of the biblical books defile the hands and which do not, a discussion clearly meant to establish the relative sanctity of the different books. Shabbat 13b; cf. Mishna Yadaim 3:4; Tosefta Yadaim 2:14; Megila 7a.

27. On Ezekiel, cf., inter alia, the extended discussion beginning in Hagiga 11b. On Esther, cf. Shabbat 88a.

28. Mishna Rosh Hashana 2:5; Beitza 11b.

29. "Because of the roads, because of the bridges, because of the ovens for roasting a paschal lamb, and because of the Jews who left their homes in exile but have not arrived yet." Sanhedrin 11a.

30. As Berkovits points out, there are even cases in which the word *mishpat* leans so heavily to the side of consequences that it cannot even be reasonably translated as "justice" at all, but rather as "deliverance"—as in the verse "The Eternal therefore judge, and give sentence between me and you, and see and plead my cause, and *deliver* me (*veyishpeteni*) out of your hand." I Samuel 24:16, quoted on p. 136 below.

31. Martin Buber, one of the outstanding examples of this approach, undertook an extensive study of Hasidic thought to demonstrate the religious truths inherent in the movement's spiritual approach. Abraham Joshua Heschel and Joseph B. Soloveitchik used similar means to spell out the experience of the prophetic type (Heschel), or of the "halachic man" (Soloveitchik), a type whose perception of the world is seen through the prism of the law. Cf. Martin Buber's many Hasidic works, notably Martin Buber, *Hasidism and Modern Man*, trans. Maurice Friedman (New York: Harper Torchbooks, 1958), and Martin Buber, *The Origin and Meaning of Hasidism*, trans. Maurice Friedman (Atlantic Highlands, N.J.: Humanities, 1988); Abraham Joshua Heschel, *The Prophets* (New

York: Harper Torchbooks, 1962); Joseph B. Soloveitchik, *Halachic Man*, trans. Lawrence Kaplan (Philadelphia: Jewish Publication Society, 1983).

32. Buber, *On Judaism*, p. 87.

33. Buber, *On Judaism*, p. 114. Buber is aware of how difficult a goal this is. In his essay "The Holy Way," Buber bemoans the difficulty of preserving the purity of the deed, and of creating a community based on unconditional deeds:

> It is its [the deed's] nature to point beyond itself. No matter how free its intention, how pure its manifestation, it is at the mercy of its own conse-quences; and even the most sublime deed, which does not waste so much as a glance at the lowlands of causality, is dragged into the mud as soon as it enters the world and becomes visible. And the deed concerned with the growth of the true community especially has everything lined up against it: The rigorism of the habitual traditionalists and the indolence of the slaves of the moment, yet equally a rash doctrinairism and irresponsible disputa-tiousness; miserly egotism and untractable vanity, yet also hysterical self-effacement and disoriented flurry; the cult of the so-called pure idea, hand in hand with the cult of so-called *realpolitik*. In addition, it is opposed by all the established forces that do not wish to be disturbed in the exercise of their power. All these forces rage in a clouded and beclouding whirlwind around the lonely and dedicated individual who boldly assumes the task of building a true community—and with what materials! There is no undefilable perfection here; everywhere the impure challenges the pure, dragging it down and distorting it; all about him gloating derision apprises the heroic victim of his futility, and the abyss pronounces its inexorable sentence on the dying to whom victory is denied. (Buber, *On Judaism*, p. 114)

34. "It is Judaism's basic tenet," Buber writes, "that the deed as an act of decision is an absolute value. On the surface it may seem that the deed is inescapably set into the unyielding structure of causality, whose rules determine its impact; in fact, however,… when it remembers its divine goal, when it extricates itself from all conditionality and walks by its own light—that is, the light of God—it is free and powerful…." Buber, *On Judaism*, p. 67.

35. Martin Buber, "Religion and Ethics," in Martin Buber, *The Eclipse of God: Studies in the Relation Between Religion and Philosophy* (Amherst, N.Y.: Humanity, 1999), p. 95. An example of the slight but noticeable moderation of his position is found in an essay entitled "The Silent Question" (1952), where Buber allows that "inward truth must become real life, otherwise it does not remain truth. A drop of Messianic consummation must be mingled with every hour; otherwise the hour is godless, despite all piety and devoutness." Yet even here, it is still not clear whether by "real life" he actually means actions taken in purity, or a consideration for their consequences. Buber, *On Judaism*, p. 209. Cf. Buber,

Hasidism and Modern Man, p. 99, where he asserts, in the context of the Hasidic concept of intentionality (*kavana*), that "there are no *goals*, only *the goal*. There is only one goal that does not lie, that becomes entangled in no new way, only one into which all ways flow, before which no byway can forever flee: Redemption." [emphasis in original]

36. Abraham Joshua Heschel, *Man Is Not Alone* (New York: Farrar, Straus, and Giroux, 1979), pp. 277-278.

37. Brachot 17a; cited in Heschel, *God in Search of Man*, p. 309.

38. Heschel, *God in Search of Man*, p. 308.

39. Cf. Heschel, *God in Search of Man*, p. 311: "Deeds are outpourings, not the essence of the self. They may reflect or refine the self, but they remain the functions, not the substance of inner life. It is the inner life, however, which is our most urgent problem." Cf. also Heschel, *God in Search of Man*, p. 310: "A moral deed unwittingly done may be relevant to the world because of the aid it renders unto others. Yet a deed without devotion, for all its effects on the lives of others, will leave the life of the doer unaffected. The true goal for man is *to be* what he *does*. The worth of a religion is the worth of the individuals living in it. A *mitzva*, therefore, is not mere doing but an act that embraces both the doer and the deed. The means may be external, but the end is personal. Your deeds be pure, so that ye shall be holy."

40. Heschel, *God in Search of Man*, pp. 337-338.

41. Heschel, *God in Search of Man*, p. 283. A similar downplaying of the importance of consequences is evident in the thought of other Jewish writers of this tradition, such as the Orthodox thinker Joseph B. Soloveitchik. The entirety of *Halachic Man* is dedicated to the implications of the halachic norm from the individual's own subjective perspective, rather than within the historical world. In some respects, Soloveitchik's perspective is more extreme than even Buber's, as when he declares that the "halachic man" is concerned more with the decision to undertake an action than with the carrying out of the action itself. Soloveitchik, *Halachic Man*, pp. 63-64. It is telling that of all the religious types articulated in Soloveitchik's writings, the only one that is fully dedicated to a concern for the consequences of action is "Adam the first" from *The Lonely Man of Faith*—a figure who is not considered by Soloveitchik to care for good or evil: "Adam the first is always an esthete, whether engaged in an intellectual or in an ethical performance. His conscience is energized not by the idea of the good, but by that of the beautiful. His mind is questing not for the true, but for the pleasant and functional, which are rooted in the esthetical, not the noetic-ethical, sphere." Joseph B. Soloveitchik, *The Lonely Man of Faith* (New York: Doubleday, 1992), p. 19.

42. *God, Man, and History* (1959), p. 134.

43. *Major Themes* (1974), pp. 140-141.

44. Max Weber, "Politics as a Vocation," in H.H. Gerth and C. Wright Mills, eds., *From Max Weber: Essays in Sociology* (New York: Oxford, 1946), pp. 117f.

45. See Immanuel Kant, *Grounding for the Metaphysics of Morals*, trans. James W. Ellington (Indianapolis: Hackett, 1981), p. 3; there Kant determines that "in the case of what is to be morally good, that it conforms to the moral law is not enough; it must also be done for the sake of the moral law."

46. Put another way, the moral reasoning inherent in an ethic of responsibility calls into question another of the basic assumptions of ethical philosophy in the Kantian tradition: That all morality can or should be reduced to formulated rules of action. According to Kant, the aim of ethical thought is to make order out of our vague and conflicting values and intuitions by translating them into clear principles based in reason—in his words, to move "from popular [moral] philosophy, which goes no further than it can get by groping about with the help of examples, to metaphysics... which, inasmuch as it must survey the whole extent of rational knowledge of this kind, goes right up to ideas...." Kant, *Grounding*, p. 23; cf. Kant, *Grounding*, pp. 21f. In an ethic of responsibility, however, the flexibility and "impurity" of common-sense morality reflect not an insufficient degree of understanding, but the non-delineated nature of moral values that are geared toward advancing a state of affairs.

This is a crucial point in distinguishing between Berkovits' moral approach and that of the "consequentialist" movement in ethical thought. Like Berkovits, consequentialists view consequences as crucial; however, they accept the Kantian approach which reduces morality to the effort to articulate a single, absolute formula for predetermining morality—as in the phrasing of Samuel Scheffler, who defines consequentialism as the belief that "the right act in any given situation is the one that will produce the best overall outcome, as judged from an impersonal standpoint which gives equal weight to the interests of everyone." Samuel Scheffler, ed., *Consequentialism and Its Critics* (Oxford: Oxford, 1988), p. 1. While there are different schools of consequentialist thought, each offering its own formulations, what they all have in common is the Kantian reductionism of searching for a categorical imperative as the test of moral behavior. Such an effort is notably absent in Berkovits, as it is in Weber as well.

47. Berkovits singles out the writings of Jean-Paul Sartre and Martin Buber as susceptible to this problem. See "The New Morality," in *Crisis and Faith* (1976), pp. 23-33; "Martin Buber's Religion of the Dialogue," in *Major Themes* (1974), pp. 68-137.

48. Obviously this does not exhaust the shades of Western ethical thought, and Berkovits himself cites three thinkers (Spinoza, Marx, and Bergson) who understood on some level the problem with ignoring the body. See pp. 20-21, 12-13 below.

49. One example appears in Genesis Rabba 8:11: "R. Tafdai said in the name of R. Aha: The higher things (*ha'elyonim*) were created in the likeness and image of God, but cannot be fruitful and multiply; the lower things (*hatahtonim*) can be fruitful and multiply, but were not created in the likeness and image of God. Said the Holy One, 'I will make him [i.e., man] in the likeness and image, with the higher things, and able to be fruitful and multiply, with the lower things.' R. Tafdai further said in the name of R. Aha: Said the Holy One, 'If I make him of the higher things, he will live and not die; if I make him of the lower things, he will die and not live. Therefore, I will make him from both the higher and the lower things. If he sin, he will die; if he does not sin, he will live.'" See also Genesis Rabba 14:4. For additional sources, cf. Ephraim E. Urbach, *The Sages: The World and Wisdom of the Rabbis of the Talmud* (Cambridge: Harvard, 1979), pp. 221f.

50. In particular, Berkovits points to Aristotle, whose understanding of practical wisdom demands an appreciation of the ethical significance of emotions and appetites. See p. 20 below.

51. See note 49 above.

52. Cf., most notably, R. Jonah Gerondi's thirteenth-century work *The Gates of Repentance*, as well as the writings of the musar movement of the late nineteenth century, which had a decisive influence on much of the Lithuanian yeshiva world.

53. Soloveitchik, *Lonely Man of Faith*, p. 57; cf. Soloveitchik, *Lonely Man of Faith*, p. 74 n. 1.

54. Abraham Joshua Heschel, *Man's Quest for God: Studies in Prayer and Symbolism* (New York: Charles Scribner's Sons, 1954), p. 53; cited in Arnold Eisen, "Rereading Heschel on the Commandments," *Modern Judaism* 9:1, February 1989, p. 20.

55. Buber, *Hasidism and Modern Man*, p. 151. Cf. Heschel: "The body without the spirit is a corpse; the spirit without the body is a ghost." Heschel, *God in Search of Man*, p. 341.

56. It is central to Buber's neo-Hasidic approach that redemption is the result of man's inner repair, reflected in the purification of his own intentions and its reflection in his relations with others, and that only through such repair will the world, somehow, be redeemed. Buber, *Hasidism and Modern Man*, pp. 98-108; Buber, *On Judaism*, pp. 83-87.

1. LAW AND MORALITY IN JEWISH TRADITION

1. Eliezer Berkovits, *God, Man, and History: A Jewish Interpretation* (New York: Jonathan David, 1959), pp. 75-81.

2. See Plato, "Theaetetus" and "Laws," in Edith Hamilton and Cairns Huntington, eds., *The Dialogues of Plato, Including Letters* (Princeton: Princeton, 1961), pp. 880-881, 1307.

3. Deuteronomy 13:5.

4. Deuteronomy 4:24.

5. Sota 14a.

6. Jeremiah 9:22-23.

7. Leo Baeck points out that in prophetic teaching the knowledge of God means the knowledge and the practice of the good. See Leo Baeck, *The Essence of Judaism* (New York: Schocken, 1948), p. 37. We may explain it by saying: Since God may only be known from the encounter, knowing him implies the knowledge of how to encounter the "other," the world outside ourselves.

8. Several times Kant makes the observation that since the law of practical reason commands us to be better human beings, it follows that we are also able to become better human beings. Cf., for example, Immanuel Kant, *Religion Within the Limits of Reason Alone* (New York: Harper, 1960), pp. 15-49; also pp. 55-60. Now this is, of course, unconvincing. It has meaning only on the basis of a dogmatic ontology. That something is required by reason is no proof at all that it is also feasible in practice. On the other hand, it does follow that, if God commands man to become a better human being, the command itself is the assurance that man is, indeed, capable of improvement.

9. Especially since the rise of Christianity, the concept of the law has been exposed to misrepresentation. The difference between Judaism and Christianity is not that the emphasis of Christianity is on the love of God, whereas in Judaism his stern justice is in the foreground. Whether love or justice, it is always relationship. But a relationship of the Absolute to the finite requires primarily caring involvement—that is, love. The justice of God itself is such a form of caring involvement; its essence is, therefore, love. Divine love may be made manifest in various ways. Thus the Bible says: "And you shall consider in your heart that, as a man chastens his son, so the Eternal your God chastens you." Deuteronomy 8:5. Even the judgment of God, as an expression of his concern, is the proof of his fatherhood. As one of the rabbis in the Talmud expressed it: "Even in the moment of his anger the Holy One remembers his mercy." Pesahim 87b. His very "anger," made possible only by his self-denying act of involvement in the destiny of what is beside him mere "dust and ashes," is a manifestation of his love.

In what specific form divine love ought to be shown depends on our evaluation of man. In the Christian view, as the result of "original sin," man is like a helpless baby. He can exert himself for good as much as he is able to lift himself from the ground by pulling at his bootlaces. For such a creature, a law of God would, indeed, be meaningless. Judaism disagrees with the Christian interpretation of human nature. Man is, of course, not good, but he is capable of goodness. He is a responsible creature. God made his love known to him by entrusting him with a responsibility worthy of his abilities. One does not show one's love to an adult son in the same way as one does in the case of a child. From the Jewish point of view, Christianity has not discovered an idea of God which is superior to the one taught by Judaism; rather, it has adopted a radically pessimistic evaluation of human nature as compared with the critical optimism of Judaism concerning all creation. The Christian God idea is adjusted to the psychological needs of the human being as he is evaluated by Christianity. Cf. Eliezer Berkovits, *Judaism: Fossil or Ferment?* (New York: Philosophical Library, 1956), pp. 53-62.

10. Menahot 43b.

11. A somewhat free translation of the Hebrew *hamuda genuza.* See Shabbat 89a.

12. Psalms 19:8-11.

13. See Rashi's commentary on Genesis 6:9.

14. Cf. R. Joseph Karo, *Shulhan Aruch, Orah Hayim* 2:1-6.

15. Cf. the discussion between the Mutzailites and the Asharites in Islamic theology.

16. See Wilhalm Windelband, *A History of Philosophy* (New York: Macmillan, 1935), pp. 332-333.

17. Cf. Saadia ben Joseph, *The Book of Doctrines and Beliefs* (Oxford: East and West Library, 1946), pp. 96-97. See also the relevant notes of the editor, Alexander Altman; cf. also p. 103 and editor's note there.

18. Cf. Kant, *Religion Within the Limits of Reason*, p. 156.

19. In the discussion of this point I owe a great deal to the writings of John Macmurray, especially his *Reason and Emotion* (New York: Barnes and Noble, 1962); as well as to William G. De Burgh's *From Morality to Religion* (London: Macdonald and Evans, 1938). Cf. also Henri Bergson, *The Two Sources of Morality and Religion* (Garden City, N.Y.: Doubleday, 1954).

20. See Plato, "Meno," "Pratagoras," "The Republic," and "Laws," in *Dialogues of Plato.* Cf. also Alfred E. Taylor, *Plato: The Man and His Work* (London: Metheon, 1949).

21. Plato, "Laws," in *Dialogues of Plato*, p. 1317.

22. In Hinduism, for instance, the entire problem would be meaningless. All problems of ethics are problems of individual responsibility. In Hinduism, however, individuality itself is evil. The task, therefore, is not ethical conduct, but

conduct in conformity with one's karma, which alone may lead to individual extinction in the All. Cf., for instance, the problem of individual ethical responsibility in the opening verses of the *Bhagavad-Gita* and its solution in the course of the development of the theme of the song.

23. Cf. Taylor, *Plato*, p. 230; and Plato, "Phaedo," in *Dialogues of Plato*, pp. 48, 81.

24. Our discussion is based, in the main, on the ideas of Julian Huxley as propounded by him in his essays in Thomas H. Huxley and Julian Huxley, *Evolution and Ethics 1893-1943* (London: Pilot, 1947), pp. 106-111. The basic fallacy of all evolutionary ethics is that it is unable to provide the concept of obligation. Evolution describes facts. But what *is* contains nothing that, in itself, may validly propose what *ought* to be. Evolution runs its course in a certain direction, but this implies no obligation for man to imitate it. Where there is no obligation, there can be no ethics.

25. Cf. Henri Bergson, *The Two Sources of Morality and Religion* (Garden City, N.Y.: Doubleday, 1954), p. 96.

26. Bergson, *Two Sources of Morality*, p. 101.

27. Bergson, *Two Sources of Morality*, p. 29.

28. We may readily agree with Hobbes that the "will… is the last appetite in deliberating." Thomas Hobbes, *Leviathan* (London: Penguin, 1981), p. 128. We may also readily accept Bertrand Russell's statement that "all systems of ethics embody the desires of those who advocate them." Bertrand Russell, *Religion and Science* (New York: Henry Holt, 1935), p. 242.

29. See note 23 above.

30. Cf. Berkovits, *God, Man, and History*, pp. 11-17.

31. Maimonides in his *Mishneh Tora*, Laws of Kings 8:11, records the rabbinical teaching that those Gentiles who observe the seven commandments given to "the sons of Noah" are to be considered "the pious of the nations" and have a share in the world to come. However, he adds—and apparently without any support from talmudic sources—that this is true only in cases where the "seven commandments" are observed as the law of God, as revealed in the Bible. It does not, however, apply to those Gentiles who practice them as the result of their grasping of the logical validity of these commandments. It would seem to us that Maimonides' position in this context contradicts the rationalism of his *Guide for the Perplexed*. There, the highest service of God is that of the intellect; here, it seems to be the obeying of a divine command because it is commanded and not because reason "dictates" it.

His position in *Mishneh Tora* seems to imply the point of view presented here. The "seven commandments" have logical validity; but they are laws of God because they were actually commanded by God. Now, a Gentile who practices them because they were revealed by God fulfills the will of God; he is a "pious" man. But he who practices them because he recognizes their logical validity acts in conformity with reason and his own human desire and will. He is, of course, an ethical person; but he cannot be called "pious."

32. Cf. Max Scheler, *Man's Place in Nature* (New York: Noonday, 1961), pp. 63-67.

33. Cf. Berkovits, *Judaism: Fossil or Ferment?* pp. 124-131.

34. In the context of this discussion, we are using the term "matter" in the sense which it has received in modern physics, i.e., as being identical with "energy."

35. See Berkovits, *God, Man, and History*, pp. 31-39, 57-65.

36. Cf. Charles W. Stork, trans., *Alcibiades: A Play of Athens in the Great Age* (Syracuse: Syracuse University, 1967); see also Taylor, *Plato*, pp. 27-28.

37. See, for example, Aristotle, *On the Soul* 3:9 and 3:10.

38. Aristotle, *On the Soul* 3:9.

39. Cf. Benedict Spinoza, *The Ethics and Selected Letters* (Indianapolis: Hackett, 1982), pp. 162-163.

40. In the approach to this problem, what I have elsewhere called Judaism's critical optimism manifests itself in another form. See Berkovits, *God, Man, and History*, pp. 75-81.

41. See note 71 below.

42. Since we know nothing of God's essence, it is highly doubtful that the "image" of God, in which man was created, could refer to the faculty of reason. The only "image" of God of which we know is reflected in the relational attributes, expressing God's desire for "mercy, justice, and righteousness on earth." To do justice and righteousness and to judge the cause of the poor and the needy is, according to Jeremiah, the meaning of the knowledge of God. Jeremiah 22:15-16; see also note 7 above. We would rather say that the "good inclination" in man is the "image" of God, in which man was created.

43. In the Talmud, man's natural inclination for the good is compared to a "poor man" who saves the city in his wisdom. See Nedarim 32b.

44. I am not unaware of the importance that the concept of "disinhibiting" has received in modern psychology. No doubt, it is necessary to "disinhibit" the behavior of a person at times, but only in pathological situations. Normally, however, inhibition is the precondition of all civilization and culture.

45. Where no ritually permissible food is available, a man must not endanger his health and is *commanded* to sustain his life with the food he may obtain. See note 59 below.

46. On dealing with the "evil inclination" cunningly, see Brachot 5a.

47. We are treating here the significance of the law as a discipline of conduct and its effects on the body. As I suggest further down, this does not exhaust the full meaning of the law. The law does have this habit-forming effect, even though on the level of conscious religious life the rabbis have taught that "a person should not say, 'I do not eat pork because I dislike it.' But rather, 'I do like it; however, what can I do, since the Tora forbade its enjoyment?'" See Sifra Leviticus 20:26.

48. See Jerusalem Brachot 2:10.

49. We have discussed the disciplinary significance of the ritual laws in general. The specific form which these laws were given is, of course, not explained by this discussion. Often it is due to the specific religious purposes which these laws also have, and with which I have dealt in *God, Man, and History*, pp. 75-81. Often, of course, they may depend on historic considerations, like the commandment of eating *matza* on Passover in commemoration of the exodus. One may even agree that some laws were dictated entirely by certain conditions which prevailed at one time in Jewish history. As is well known, Maimonides explained some ritual laws as having been time-conditioned reactions to certain idolatrous ways of worship and practice. See, for example, his *Guide for the Perplexed* 3:32.

It is not at all illogical to say that some historic necessity determined the specific form of a ritual law. Nevertheless, the law does not pass with the passing of the historic situation. Its specific form might have been time-conditioned; its general significance within the disciplinary system of the law derives from the condition of man. As long as that condition lasts, the law will remain. This applies even more exactly to the general religious significance of the law, about which see further on.

50. Cf. Berkovits, *God, Man, and History*, pp. 11-17.

51. See pp. 217-219 below.

52. See pp. 217-219 below.

53. There is no need for entering into a discussion of the specific talmudic concept that "*mitzvot* do not require intention" (*mitzvot ein tzrichot kavana*), which may be translated as saying that conscious intention is not a *sine qua non* for adjudging a *mitzva* to have been obeyed.

54. Psalms 35:10.

55. Cf. Maimonides, *Mishneh Tora*, Laws of Prayer 5:9; see also R. Jacob ben Asher, *Arba'a Turim, Orah Hayim* 101:2; as well as Karo, *Shulhan Aruch* ad loc.

56. Adapted from Philip Birnbaum's translation in his *Daily Prayer Book* (New York: Hebrew Publishing Company, 1977), p. 334.

57. Kant, *Religion Within the Limits of Reason*, p. 180.

58. Bahya ibn Pakuda differentiated between "duties of the heart" and "duties of the body," but only in order to be able to concentrate all the more on the "duties of the heart." In reality, however, the *mitzva* represents the coalescing of the two categories of duties in the one unifying deed, which should be known as the duty of man.

59. The biblical verse, "You shall therefore keep my statutes, and my ordinances, which if a man do, he shall live by them" (Leviticus 18:5) is interpreted by the Talmud to mean that "he shall *live* by them but not that he shall *die* by them." Yoma 85b. On that basis, for instance, whenever the preservation of life conflicts with the observance of the Sabbath, the preservation of life takes precedence. According to the teachings of Judaism, a person must not expose himself to danger needlessly. Cf. Mishna Truma 8:4; Pesahim 112a; Hulin 10a.

60. Cf., for instance, Plato, "Phaedo."

61. Cf. the blessings that are to be said about the beholding of beauty in creation. There are specific blessings which are to be recited when one sees beautiful trees and handsome people. Cf. Brachot 58b.

62. The dining table is compared to the altar in the Temple of Jerusalem. Cf. Karo, *Shulhan Aruch, Orah Hayim* 167:5.

63. The thought comes to clear expression in the Tosefta Brachot 4:5, where we find the following: "R. Meir said:... If a person, on seeing bread, exclaims: Blessed be he who created this bread! How beautiful it is! Then such is its blessing...."

64. See Tosefta Brachot 6:7.

65. See Shabbat 119a, where R. Yehoshua ben Hanania calls the Sabbath the spice that makes the Sabbath dishes savory.

66. Genesis 1:28.

67. Isaiah 45:18.

68. See, for instance, Gitin 41b.

69. Sota 17a.

70. The words of the Bible, "You shall love the Eternal your God with all your heart..." (Deuteronomy 6:5), were interpreted by the rabbis in the Talmud as meaning that a man should love God with everything there is in his heart, that is, with both his inclinations, the good and the evil one. Brachot 54a; cf. also Berkovits, *God, Man, and History*, p. 180n.

71. See Leviticus Rabba 34:3, where Hillel explains to his disciples that the taking of a bath is a *mitzva*, as a deed of respect performed on the body of man.

72. In the history of Western philosophy it was Schiller who, in his *Naive and Sentimental Poetry*, struggled with the problem of man's sensuous nature. We agree with him that the "ethical man" is not the whole man. The "moral state" of man may only be established at the cost of the suppression of his bio-physical condition. Had Schiller been familiar with some of the insights of psychology which are available for us now, he might have added that just because of the required suppression, the "moral state" has thus far not been achieved in history. However, it is difficult to accept his solution that by an "esthetic education," which allows the satisfaction of man's sensuous nature "nobly," the two sides of human nature may be reconciled. The ideal is not the "beautiful soul" (*die schone Seele*)—man is not a soul—but body and soul sanctified through the holy deed.

73. The Hebrew *ruah hakodesh* ought not to be translated as "the holy spirit," but rather as the "spirit of holiness." See also Hermann Cohen, *Religion of Reason out of the Sources of Judaism*, trans. Simon Kaplan (Atlanta: Scholars Press, 1995), ch. vii, pp. 100-112.

74. The Kantian definition of the "true religion" as "the invisible religion of the heart" leads logically to the concept of the "holy will." See Immanuel Kant, *Critique of Practical Reason* (Indianapolis: Library of Liberal Arts, 1956), book 1, 1:7; and also 1:3.

75. See pp. 14-17 above.

76. Laws regulating human relationship are stricter than those affecting man's relationship to God. Cf. Sanhedrin 27a.

77. Cf. Mishna Avot 6:2.

78. We use the term which is familiar in the history of religious thought. It should, however, be clear that from our point of view the idea of *mitzvot ma'asiyot* is a tautology. The essence of every *mitzva* is a deed.

79. See the dictum of Rav in Genesis Rabba 44:1.

2. THE NATURE AND FUNCTION OF JEWISH LAW

1. For example, Baba Kama 46b.

2. Baba Metzia 47b; and the commentary of Nimukei Yosef on the relevant passage, which appears at 28b in the commentary of R. Isaac Alfasi.

3. Ketubot 22a.

4. Sanhedrin 74a.

5. By formal betrothal I am referring to *erusin,* the halachic form of marriage, which, however, does not allow husband and wife to actually live together until *nisuin,* the ceremony, usually under a *hupa,* a marriage canopy.

6. Deuteronomy 24:4.

7. Yevamot 11b; Tosafot ad loc., s.v. *l'rabot sota.*

8. The *aguna,* or "anchored" woman, is one whose husband is missing or estranged without having divorced her. Because she is not divorced, and there is no proof of his death, she continues to be legally married to him and therefore unable to remarry.

9. Ketubot 2b-3a.

10. Cf. Brachot 37a; Yevamot 108a; Gitin 15a; Ketubot 48b; Kidushin 59b.

11. Gitin 67a.

12. Shabbat 60b.

13. Brachot 23b.

14. Mishna Eduyot 1:5; Ra'avad's commentary ad loc; cf. Maimonides' comments there as well; cf. Eliezer Berkovits, *Halacha: Its Authority and Function* (Jerusalem: Mosad Harav Kook, 1981), pp. 28-29. [Hebrew]

15. Deuteronomy 21:10-14.

16. Kidushin 21b.

17. Bechorot 13a.

18. "*Heicha de'efshar efshar; heicha delo efshar lo efshar.*" Hulin 11b.

19. Gitin 28a.

20. Yevamot 36b-37a.

21. Rosh Hashana 23b.

22. Avoda Zara 36a.

23. Beitza 36b; Baba Batra 60b; Tosafot ad loc.

24. Sanhedrin 11a.

25. Succah 26a.

26. Yoma 73b.

27. Deuteronomy 15:9.

28. Mishna Shvi'it 10:3; Gitin 36a-b.

29. Yevamot 16a.

30. Sanhedrin 12a.

31. Sanhedrin 26a.

32. Shevu'ot 45a.

33. Mishna Gitin 5:3.

34. Mishna Baba Kama 10:3.

35. Rashi's commentary on Baba Kama 115a.

36. Baba Batra 175b.

37. Hulin 49b, 76b, 77a.

38. Bechorot 40a.

39. Pesahim 20b, 55b; Shabbat 154b; Baba Kama 117a; Baba Metzia 38a-b.

40. Sifrei, Re'eh 16:13.

41. Leviticus 12:6, 8.

42. Kritot 8a.

43. The reference is to Psalms 119:126, "It is time for the Eternal to work; they have violated your law," to which the rabbis gave the following midrashic interpretation: "At times one has to work for God by voiding his law." For the discussion of this principle, see Eliezer Berkovits, *Not in Heaven: The Nature and Function of Halacha* (New York: Ktav, 1983), pp. 64-70.

44. Maimonides, *Mishneh Tora*, Laws of Those Requiring Atoning Sacrifices 1:10. See also his commentary on the Mishna, Kritot 8a. [In Berkovits' *Halacha: Its Authority and Function*, pp. 157-158, one may find a full analysis of Maimonides' view in this matter.—Ed.]

45. Deuteronomy 6:18.

46. Proverbs 3:17.

47. Proverbs 2:20.

48. Gitin 59b.

49. Succah 32b.

50. Shabbat 63a.

51. The *kal vahomer*, a conclusion from a minor to a major.

52. Yevamot 87b.

53. Baba Kama 82b-83a.

54. Exodus 21:29.

55. Sanhedrin 15b.

56. Deuteronomy 25:3.

57. Makot 22a-23a; Sanhedrin 10a.

58. Brachot 20a.

59. For the sources, see Brachot 19b-20a; Jerusalem Kilaim 9:1; Jerusalem Brachot 3:1.

60. Hagiga 3:7.

61. Hagiga 26a.

62. Moed Katan 27b.

63. Ta'anit 26b, 31f.

64. Baba Metzia 10a.

65. Kidushin 63a.

66. Gitin 59a-b; Tosefta ad loc., 3:18.

67. This is not the only limitation on the law for this reason. Baba Metzia 30b, 24b; Baba Kama 99b; Ketubot 97a.

68. Baba Metzia 108a, 35a.

69. Deuteronomy 6:17-18.

70. Baba Metzia 83a; for the biblical quotation, see Proverbs 2:20.

71. Jerusalem Gitin 6:6. Usually, the stories in both the Babylonian and the Jerusalem Talmuds are confused with regard to what is known as *lifnim mishurat hadin*.

72. Deuteronomy 23:3.

73. Ecclesiastes 4:1.

74. Zechariah 4:2; Leviticus Rabba 32:8.

75. Kidushin 72b.

76. Kidushin 71a.

77. Deuteronomy 21:18-20; see Rashi's commentary there. For a more thorough discussion of the subject, see Berkovits, *Halacha: Its Authority and Function*.

78. Sanhedrin 71a.

79. Deuteronomy 13:17.

80. Sanhedrin 71a.

81. Makot 7a.

82. Leviticus 19:18.

83. Kidushin 41a.

84. Kidushin 41a.

85. Maimonides, *Mishneh Tora*, Laws of Personal Status 12.

86. Ketubot 111a, 56b.

87. Yevamot 112b.

88. Mishna Ketubot 7:10.

89. Maimonides, *Mishneh Tora*, Laws of Divorce 2:20.

90. Maimonides, *Mishneh Tora*, Laws of Divorce 2:20.

91. R. Joseph Karo, *Shulhan Aruch, Even Ha'ezer* 77:1.

92. Maimonides, *Mishneh Tora*, Laws of Personal Status 14:8.

93. For instance, the views of Tosafot on Ketubot 83b; commentary of R. Solomon Aderet (Rashba) on Ketubot ad loc.; the opinion of R. Asher (Rosh) quoted in R. Jacob ben Asher, *Arba'a Turim, Even Ha'ezer* 154; also his Responsa 53:6.

94. Proverbs 14:10; "the Rabbi," as quoted by R. Isaiah of Trani (Rid), *Tosefot Rid*, Ketubot 64a.

95. For the entire discussion, see Alfasi on Ketubot 63a-b; commentary of Rashba ad loc., and his Responsa 1:192; Responsa of the Rosh 43:8; *Hama'or Hagadol* and Nahmanides' *Milhamot Hashem* on Alfasi ad loc.

96. Karo, *Shulhan Aruch, Even Ha'ezer* 154:2.

97. Responsa of R. Samson ben Tzadok (Tashbatz) 2:8.

98. Ketubot 77a.

99. Yevamot 106a, 44a.

100. Rosh, Responsa 52:6.

101. Tashbatz, Responsa 2:180.

102. Gitin 3a.

103. Gitin 19b.

104. Yevamot 87b-88a. The legal basis for the non-application of the biblical law on testimony is discussed in Berkovits, *Not in Heaven*, pp. 47-70.

105. Gitin 33a.

106. Ketubot 2b-3a.

107. Yevamot 110a; Rashi ad loc.

108. Rosh, Responsa 42:1.

3. CONVERSION AND THE DECLINE OF THE ORAL LAW

1. Gitin 36b-37a.

2. Yevamot 88a; Tosafot ad loc., s.v., *mitoch*; Ritba ad loc., Rashi on Shabbat 145b, s.v. *le'edut isha*.

3. Yevamot 88a.

4. Baba Metzia 83a.

5. Kidushin 71a.

6. Deuteronomy 30:12.

7. Exodus 23:2.

8. Baba Metzia 59b.

9. Gitin 60b.

10. Gitin 60b.

11. Psalms 119:126; Gitin 60a.

4. A JEWISH SEXUAL ETHICS

1. Corinthians 7:1, 9.

2. Norman O. Brown, *Life Against Death: The Psychoanalytical Meaning of History* (New York: Random House, 1959), p. 31.

3. Cf. Silvano Arieti's excellent book, *The Will to Be Human* (New York: Quadrangle, 1972).

4. Ignace Lepp, *The Authentic Morality* (New York: Macmillan, 1965), p. 177. The idea that human instincts are not identical with animal instincts is a thought that was well understood by the great medieval Jewish talmudist and philosopher Maimonides. Cf. his *Introduction to Mishna Avot*, ch. 1.

5. Saadia Gaon, *The Book of Beliefs and Opinions*, trans. Samuel Rosenblatt (New Haven: Yale, 1948), p. 249.

6. Ketubot 51b. Cf. also Hagiga 16a, the advice given to a person who is incapable of controlling his sex drive. Cf. the discussion of the passage in Tosafot ad loc.

7. Kidushin 81a.

8. Kidushin 81a.

9. Cf. the case of R. Hiya bar Ashi, Kidushin 81b.

10. Ecclesiastes Raba 3:16.

11. Succah 52a.

12. Yoma 69b.

13. Cf., for instance, Eruvin 100b.

14. Joseph Fletcher, *Moral Responsibility: Situation Ethics at Work* (Philadelphia: Westminster, 1967), p. 85.

15. Isaiah 45:18.

16. Mishna Eduyot 1:13; also Gitin 41a. An interesting legal consequence in mishnaic times was the law in the case of a slave who was originally owned by two people and was set free by one of the owners. Now he was in the anomalous situation of being half-free, half-slave. As a slave he could have married a slave girl; as a free man he could have married a free woman. As half-and-half he could not marry either. Therefore, the remaining half-owner was obligated to set him free fully, for "he created it not a waste; he formed it to be inhabited." Needless to say, in contemporary society the governing phrase of the interpretation may have further application to man's responsibility in the face of the destruction of the ecological order and balance in the universe.

17. Leviticus 19:18.

18. Deuteronomy 6:5.

19. Brachot 54a.

20. Pesahim 72b.

21. Shevu'ot 18b.

22. Ketubot 62b.

23. See p. 34 above.

24. Deuteronomy 12:19.

25. Menahot 44a.

26. Numbers 15:39.

27. Cf. Sigmund Freud, *Civilization and Its Discontents* (London: Hogarth, 1949), pp. 120-122; see also the discussion of this point by Herbert Marcuse in his *Eros and Civilization* (New York: Vintage, 1962), pp. 78-105.

28. Joseph Albo, *The Book of Principles*, ed. Isaac Husik (Philadelphia: Jewish Publication Society, 1946), pp. 19-20.

29. Marcuse, *Eros and Civilization*, p. 71.

30. We are referring to the concept of the *pilegesh*, a union in which a man and a woman live as husband and wife, but without any formal enactment of a marriage ceremony and contract. For the two authorities quoted see the gloss to Maimonides, *Mishneh Tora*, Laws of Personal Status 1:4; and R. Joseph Karo's *Kesef Mishneh* ad loc.

31. Genesis 18:19.

32. Kidushin 41a.

33. Kidushin 41a. Cf. also Tosafot ad loc., s.v. *asur l'adam,* trying to justify, by pointing to the precarious situation of the Jewish communities in the Middle Ages, why the rule of Rav was not adhered to.

34. Kidushin 70a.

35. Nedarim 20b.

36. See Eruvin 100b and Brachot 62a. Cf. also the relevant passages in Maimonides' *Mishneh Tora*, Laws of Personal Status 15:17; R. Jacob ben Asher, *Arba'a Turim*, *Even Ha'ezer* 25; R. Josheph Karo, *Shulhan Aruch* ad loc.

37. Ezekiel 20:38.

38. Nedarim 20b.

39. Numbers Raba 9.

40. The subject has been treated excellently by R. David Feldman in his *Birth Control in Jewish Law* (New York: New York University, 1968).

41. R. Moses Isserlis' comment on Karo, *Shulhan Aruch, Even Ha'ezer* 1:3.

42. Yevamot 12b, for example.

43. Sota 17a.

5. THE BIBLICAL IDEA OF JUSTICE

1. Deuteronomy 1:17.

2. Numbers 27:5.

3. Cf. I Kings 3:11; the Revised Version (RV) and Jewish Publication Society (JPS) translations. [The reference here is to the older Jewish Publication Society edition, published in Philadelphia in 1917.—Ed.]

4. I Kings 3:28.

5. Psalms 1:5.

6. Leviticus 24:22.

7. Genesis 18:25.

8. Psalms 119:120.

9. Psalms 119:137.

10. Psalms 119:75.

11. Isaiah 34:5.

12. Ezekiel 39:21; 5:8-10.

13. Jeremiah 48:21-47.

14. Jeremiah 51:9.

15. I Samuel 3:13-14.

16. Zephaniah 3:15.

17. Deuteronomy 10:17.

18. Deuteronomy 10:18.

19. Psalms 68:6.

20. Exodus 23:6-7.

21. Deuteronomy 24:17-18.

22. Jeremiah 5:28-29.

23. Isaiah 1:16-17.

24. Psalms 94:1.

25. Psalms 94:2.

26. Psalms 94:3-7.

27. Psalms 146:6.

28. Psalms 146:7-9.

29. Psalms 76:9-10. Here, as in all biblical quotations, the italics are added.

30. Ezekiel 34:21-22.

31. Isaiah 51:5.

32. Numbers 35:24-25.

33. Jeremiah 21:12; see also 22:3.

34. Isaiah 59:11.

35. I Samuel 24:16.

36. II Samuel 18:19.

37. II Samuel 18:31.

38. The RV and JPS editions here are identical.

39. Judges 2:16, 18.

40. Isaiah 33:22.

41. For this interpretation of *tzedaka* see Eliezer Berkovits, *Man and God: Studies in Biblical Theology* (Detroit: Wayne State University, 1969), pp. 292-348. This quotation takes, of course, our subject much further than we are at this point prepared to go. Its significance will emerge more clearly when we reach the definition of the biblical concept of justice.

42. Jeremiah 9:23.

43. Hosea 12:7.

44. Zechariah 7:9.

45. Isaiah 56:1.

46. Isaiah 30:18.

47. Psalms 119:149, 156.

48. Genesis 40:13.

49. Joshua 6:15.

50. Judges 18:7.

51. II Kings 1:7-8.

52. II Kings 17:33.

53. I Samuel 8:9.

54. II Kings 17:26.

55. Jeremiah 5:4-6.

56. The RV translates: "For they know not the way of the Lord, nor the judgment of their God." The JPS edition has: "For they know not the way of the Lord, nor the ordinance of their God." Since according to them *mishpat* is different from *derech* (way) in meaning, they have to introduce into the text the conjunction "nor" which is not found in the Hebrew original and which, in fact, is not in keeping with the Hebrew sentence structure. Both renderings are misrepresentations.

57. Psalms 119:149, 156.

58. The JPS translation renders it correctly as: "Hear my voice according unto thy loving-kindness; quicken me, O Lord, as thou art wont." And so also in v. 156 of the same psalm. Whereas the RV has: "Quicken me according to thy judgment," which is meaningless.

59. Isaiah 40:12-14.

60. Isaiah 28:23-29.

61. Jeremiah 8:7.

62. Jeremiah 10:24.

63. Jeremiah 30:11.

64. Isaiah 42:3.

65. Deuteronomy 32:4.

66. Regarding the precise meaning of the Hebrew *emet*, here rendered "faithfulness," cf. Berkovits, *Studies in Biblical Theology*, pp. 253-291; its translation as "truth," especially in this context, is utterly misleading.

67. Psalms 25:10.

68. Job 40:6-14.

69. Job 41:2-3.

70. Job 42:1-6.

71. Job 42:7.

6. ON THE RETURN TO JEWISH NATIONAL LIFE

1. Cf. Eliezer Berkovits, *Towards Historic Judaism* (Oxford: East and West Library, 1943), pp. 15-24.

2. Brachot 19a.

3. Menahot 29b.

4. [The term *meshek* refers both to the fields of a farm and to the agricultural economy as a whole.—Ed.]

5. [The reference is to the 1902 novel by Theodor Herzl by that name, in which the author presented a utopian vision of a future Jewish society in Palestine. The title means "old-new land."—Ed.]

7. ON JEWISH SOVEREIGNTY

1. Eliezer Berkovits, *Faith After the Holocaust* (New York: Ktav, 1973).

2. [The reference is to the author's description of the Holocaust as the "hiding" of God's face, presented in Berkovits, *Faith*, ch. iv, pp. 86-113.—Ed.]

3. Isaiah 2:3-4.

4. Isaiah 19:25.

5. Ketubot 110b.

6. Saadia Gaon, *The Book of Beliefs and Opinions*, trans. Samuel Rosenblatt (New Haven: Yale, 1948). Cf. Maimonides, *Guide for the Perplexed* 2:29.

7. Isaiah 43:21; 44:2, 21.

8. Habakkuk 2:4.

9. Kidushin 40b.

10. Deuteronomy 3:25.

11. Sota 14a.

12. Berkovits, *Faith*, pp. 53-54.

13. Psalms 118:23.

14. Song of Songs 5:2; Song of Songs Rabba ad loc.

15. Isaiah 9:1.

16. Isaiah 43:19.

8. TOWARDS A RENEWED RABBINIC LEADERSHIP

1. Mishna Avot 1:1.

1. Cf. Ketubot 105a.

2. Numbers 16:15; I Samuel 12:3.

9. THE SPIRITUAL CRISIS IN ISRAEL

1. *Ha'aretz* supplement, May 12, 1978.

2. R. Judah Halevi, *Kuzari* 1:115.

3. Joseph Haim Brenner, *In Winter*, in *Writings of J.H. Brenner* (Jaffa: Beit Mishar Hasfarim Krugliakov, 1910), vol. i, p. 26. [Hebrew]

4. A.D. Gordon, *Nation and Labor* (Jerusalem: Hasifriya Hatzionit, 1952), p. 105.

5. Gordon, *Nation and Labor*, p. 260.

6. Gordon, *Nation and Labor*, p. 160.

7. Berl Katznelson, *Complete Writings of Berl Katznelson* (Tel Aviv: Mifleget Po'alei Eretz Yisrael, 1945), vol. vii, p. 163. [Hebrew]

8. *Shedemot*, Winter 1975.

9. Genesis 18:19.

10. Psalms 116:9; Yoma 71a.

11. Genesis Rabba 16:4.

12. R. Joseph Albo, *Book of Fundamentals* 3:23.

10. THE ENCOUNTER WITH THE DIVINE

1. Cf. Eliezer Berkovits, *God, Man, and History: A Jewish Interpretation* (New York: Jonathan David, 1959), pp. 11-17.

2. Exodus 3:6.

3. Deuteronomy 4:33.

4. Cf. *The Song of God: Bhagavad-Gita* (New York: Mentor Books, 1954), p. 92.

5. Deuteronomy 4:24.

6. See Berkovits, *God, Man, and History*, pp. 11-17.

7. Ezekiel 3:23-24.

8. Cf. Megila 19b, where R. Hiya bar Aba says in the name of R. Yohanan: "Had there been in the cave in which Moses and Elijah stood even as small an opening as the point of a needle, it would not have been possible [for either of them] to stand there on account of the brilliance of the light; for it is written... 'man shall not see me and live' (Exodus 33:20)."

9. Isaiah 45:15. We ought to distinguish between God's "hiding himself" and the notion of God "hiding his face." In the encounter, God does "face" man; it is the divine essence which is veiled or hidden, so that man may "face" God. The "hiding of the face," on the other hand, is the opposite of the encounter. The "hiding God" is essential for the relationship; the "hiding of the face" indicates a breakdown in the relationship and the withdrawal of the divine concern.

10. Cf. Rudolf Otto, *The Idea of the Holy: An Inquiry into the Non-Rational Factor in the Idea of the Divine and Its Relation to the Rational*, trans. John W. Harvey (New York: Oxford, 1958), ch. iv, pp. 12-24.

11. Psalms 138:6.

12. Isaiah 66:1-2; quotation based on the 1917 edition of the Jewish Publication Society.

13. Megila 31a.

14. Genesis 18:25, 27. Rudolf Otto, in his work *The Idea of the Holy*, speaks of man's realization that he is but "dust and ashes" as the Abrahamic experience (cf. Otto, *Idea of the Holy*, pp. 9, 21). What Otto does not seem to recognize is the truly surprising aspect of the experience: That "dust and ashes" has the moral independence to face God and to plead with him. Nor does Otto see with sufficient clarity the Jewish concept that whatever intimation man may have of God as the "Wholly Other" must somehow be communicated to him. But where there is communication, the "Wholly Other" is made accessible to man. For the same reason, a Jew will not be able to accept Otto's idea that the *kreaturgefuhl* (the "dust-and-ashes" experience) leads to the predication of all reality to the Godhead and its denial for the creature. This might indeed happen if God were only the "Wholly Other." But in the biblical experience of the encounter, the "Wholly Other" is concerned about man. God's concern for him makes man very real

indeed. Religion is not the reduction of man to nothingness, but the elevation of the "nothing" to the reality and responsibility of being, by the attention it receives from the Creator.

15. Psalms 8:5-6.

16. Cf., for instance, Midrash Tehilim 100:3.

17. Psalms 2:11.

18. It is indeed doubtful in what exact sense one may speak of Jewish mysticism. It may be of interest to recall what Gershom Scholem, the contemporary authority on Jewish mysticism, has to say on the sense of separateness among Jewish mystics in his *Major Trends in Jewish Mysticism* (New York: Schocken, 1954): "The fact is that the true and spontaneous feeling of the *merkava* mystic knows nothing of divine immanence; the infinite gulf between the soul and God the King on his throne is not even bridged at the climax of mystical ecstasy…. Throughout there remained an almost exaggerated consciousness of God's *otherness*, nor does the identity and individuality of the mystic become blurred even at the height of ecstatic passion." Scholem, *Major Trends*, pp. 55-56. Similarly, Scholem writes that "it is only in extremely rare cases that ecstasy signifies actual union with God, in which the human individuality abandons itself to the rapture of complete submersion in the divine stream. Even in his ecstatic frame of mind, the Jewish mystic almost invariably retains a sense of distance between the Creator and his creature. The latter is joined to the former, and the point where the two meet is of the greatest interest to the mystic, but he does not regard it as constituting anything as extravagant as identity of Creator and creature." Scholem, *Major Trends*, pp. 122-123.

19. Benedict de Spinoza, *The Ethics* (London: Oxford, 1927), 5:36, pp. 276-277.

20. Cf. Max Scheler, *On the Eternal in Man* (New York: Harper, 1960), p. 196. There is a surprising similarity between Spinoza's *amor dei* and some of the ideas of Thomas Aquinas on the same subject. In Aquinas' *Summa Contra Gentiles* we find such passages as this: "But God wills and loves his essence for its own sake. Now, the divine essence cannot be increased or multiplied in itself… it can be multiplied solely according to its likeness, which is participated by many. God, therefore, wills the multiplicity of things in willing and loving his own essence and perfection." Saint Thomas Aquinas, *Summa Contra Gentiles* (London: University of Notre Dame, 1955), book 1, 75:3, p. 246.

According to Spinoza, God loves "the multiplicity of things" because they are modes of himself ("God, insofar as he loves himself, loves men…"; Spinoza, *Ethics*, 5:36, pp. 276-277); according to Aquinas, God, insofar as he loves himself, loves the multiplicity of things, for they participate in his likeness. In both cases, God's love is a form of self-love. Aquinas actually maintains that God wills things other than himself because, loving and willing his own being, he desires it to be diffused as much as possible "through the communication of likeness." Cf. Aquinas, *Summa Contra Gentiles*, book 1, 96:3, p. 292.

About the love of man for God and the love of God for himself, Aquinas writes: "Furthermore, every perfection and goodness found in creatures is proper to God in an essential way.... But to love God is the highest perfection of the rational creature... therefore, the love is found in God in an essential way. Therefore, of necessity God loves himself." Aquinas, *Summa Contra Gentiles*, book 1, 80:6, p. 256. But not only is man's love for God a reflection of God's love for himself; since all perfection and goodness in the "multiplicity of things" are the likeness of the original perfection and goodness which is in God, man's love for God is the effect of God's love for himself. So that we get the Spinozistic conclusion that in man's love for God it is God who loves himself.

Aquinas' position seems to result from his application of the Aristotelian concept of the deity to the biblical framework of creator and creation. With Aristotle, God can only think himself (cf. Berkovits, *God, Man, and History*, pp. 11-17); the Creator, however, must think the world of creation too, think it and will it. How can he do it, if Aristotle is to remain unchallenged? The Thomistic solution is that even in thinking and willing the world, God really thinks and wills only himself. This is what happens when one crosses the Unmoved Mover of the heathens with the biblical idea of the Creator.

Be that as it may, Aquinas' God idea has little in common with that of Isaiah or the Psalms. The God whose throne is the heaven and footstool the earth when he looks "on him that is poor and of a contrite spirit" does not behold his likeness, but that which is the "wholly other" for him, his unlikeness. The Eternal, who is high, "regards the lowly," which is lowly because it is unlike God; he regards man *because* he is lowly. An encounter with oneself is no genuine encounter. God's concern for man is significant because it is directed toward one who is so utterly unlike himself.

21. Our position may be further illustrated by recalling some of the ideas of Friedrich Schleiermacher. According to Schleiermacher, man can in no way respond or react to God. Could man do that, it would be a sign of independence on his part; but an attitude of complete dependence is the religious one. This, of course, means that an encounter between God and man is not really possible. God cannot address man; religion is the obliteration of the human personality. This leads logically to a form of mystical pantheism. And so Schleiermacher sums up his philosophy in the words: "therefore... strive even to annihilate your personality and to live in the One and the All...." Quoted in Hugh R. Mackintosh, *Types of Modern Theology: Schleiermacher to Barth* (London: Nisbet, 1937), p. 55. In our view, however, the sense of complete dependence is a reflection of the objective human situation of "dust and ashes." Religion is the saving of man from this "nothingness." In the encounter with God, man's dependence becomes the source of a measure of independence. Man is granted individuality. He is free to respond to God because God himself protects and respects his gift to man.

22. Cf. Berkovits, *God, Man, and History*, pp. 14-15.

23. Psalms 16:8.

24. Cf. Berkovits, *God, Man, and History*, pp. 18-25.

25. Deuteronomy 29:13-14.

26. The idea has been expressed in many variations in talmudic and midrashic literature. According to Avot 6:2, "Every day a heavenly voice goes forth from Mount Sinai." Various verses in the Bible are interpreted by the rabbis as enjoining Jews that the Tora should be for them as if it were given from Sinai "today." Cf., for example, Brachot 63b; see also Yalkut Shimoni on Deuteronomy 26.

27. Psalms 22:2, 3.

28. Psalms 22:11-12.

29. Cf. Berkovits, *God, Man, and History*, pp. 14-15.

30. Cf. Berkovits, *God, Man, and History*, pp. 14-15.

31. About Abraham's "discovery" of God, the mishnaic sage R. Yitzhak says as follows: "The case is like that of the journeyman who saw a palace brilliantly illuminated. Said he: Could it be possible that such a palace should have no master? At that moment, the lord of the palace looked at him and said: I am the master of the palace. Similarly, Abraham asked himself: Could it indeed be that the universe should have no sovereign? And so the Holy One looked at him and said: I am the sovereign of the universe." Genesis Raba 39:1. It is significant that, according to this midrash, the patriarch started out with the familiar metaphysical questions concerning a Supreme Being as explanation for the existence of the universe. However, it was not his philosophy that led him to God. It was God who showed himself to Abraham in answer to his search. That was the beginning of Judaism. Our point is that those who already know the answer that was granted to Abraham—the descendants of the patriarch who have preserved the family tradition from generation to generation that God "looked at him" and revealed to their ancestor his "leadership" of the world (as the literal text of the midrash has it)— may now, in the possession of such knowledge, turn to the metaphysical quest and rediscover a reflection of the Supreme Being, of which they have learned through the religious experience.

32. Cf. Berkovits, *God, Man, and History*, pp. 6-9.

33. Cf. Berkovits, *God, Man, and History*, pp. 3-11. Otto, in *Idea of the Holy*, makes the point that in religious hymns we find entire chains of negative attributes, which actually say nothing and yet may thrill and intoxicate us. Reading or singing them, we do not notice that the attributes are all negative. Otto, *Idea of the Holy*, p. 34. He is right, of course; but only for the religious person who knows about God *positively* from the encounter, his own or that of the founders of his

faith. To those, however, who would wish to learn about God from negative attributes, only the logical fallacy of the concept will be communicated.

34. Zephaniah 3:17.

35. Cf. Moses Maimonides, *The Guide for the Perplexed*, trans. M. Friedlander (New York: Dover, 1956), p. 83.

36. It seems that the translation "I am that I am" (*ehyeh asher ehyeh*; Exodus 3:14) does not do justice to the Hebrew original. The imperfect "*ehyeh*," used here, means continuous being. Cf. E. Kautzsch, ed., *Gesenius' Hebrew Grammar*, trans. Arthur E. Cowley (Oxford: Clarendon, 1910), pp. 334-335. The Hebrew phrase says: "I am continually what I am continually." It expresses the "jutting out" of the divine being into time or—to use some German terminology—the phrase does not speak of *sein* (Being) but of *dasein* (Presence). The correct meaning of the text, therefore, is: I am forever present (for man). The rabbis in the Talmud give it the right interpretation when they remark: "What is the meaning of *ehyeh asher ehyeh*? The Holy One said to Moses: Go and tell Israel that as I have been with them in this subjugation so shall I be with them in their future subjugations by other kingdoms...." Brachot 9b. "I am that I am" is metaphysics, and so was it understood, for instance, by Thomas Aquinas. Cf. his *Summa Contra Gentiles*, book 1, 22:10, p. 121. The "I am continually present" or "I am forever with them" of the rabbis is religion.

37. Deuteronomy 6:4.

38. Cf. Berkovits, *God, Man, and History*, pp. 11-17.

39. Cf. Berkovits, *God, Man, and History*, pp. 11-13.

40. Deuteronomy 4:35.

41. The "Alone" of Plotinus fully applies to it.

42. But compare with what has been said above about the "Wholly Other" in relationship to other elements also contained in the encounter.

43. Isaiah 40:12f.

44. Cf. Berkovits, *God, Man, and History*, pp. 6-9.

45. It is, therefore, quite possible to hold the most inadequate metaphysical notions concerning God and yet have valid ideas about God's relationship to the world and know about his presence and concern. It is equally possible to penetrate the metaphysical depth of concepts like the Infinite and the Absolute or the All and still have no inkling of the relationship between God and the world. Good religion is not incompatible with poor metaphysics, just as excellent metaphysics by itself in no way provides the basis for a sound religion.

46. The theory was elaborated by Saadia Gaon, Judah Halevi, and Maimonides.

47. Exodus 34:6-7.

48. See Maimonides, *Guide for the Perplexed*, p. 76.

49. Psalms 103:13.

50. Malachi 3:17.

51. Maimonides, *Guide for the Perplexed*, p. 76.

11. KNOWLEDGE OF THE WORLD
AND KNOWLEDGE OF GOD

1. R. Solomon Aderet (Rashba), Responsa 60:415.

2. Maimonides, Letters to the Rabbis of the Community of Marseilles.

3. Moses Maimonides, *Guide for the Perplexed* 1:34.

4. Maimonides, *Guide for the Perplexed* 1:34.

5. Deuteronomy 6:5.

6. Maimonides, *Guide for the Perplexed* 3:28.

7. Bahya ibn Pakuda, *Duties of the Heart* (New York: Feldheim, 1970), p. 133.

8. Ibn Pakuda, *Duties of the Heart*, p. 133.

9. Eruvin 100b.

10. Ibn Pakuda, *Duties of the Heart*, p. 136.

11. Shabbat 75a. The verse cited is Isaiah 5:12.

12. Deuteronomy 4:6.

13. R. Judah Loeb ben Betzalel, *Writings of the Maharal of Prague* (Jerusalem: Mosad Harav Kook, 1960), vol. 2, p. 120. [Hebrew]

14. Maimonides, *Guide for the Perplexed* 3:31.

12. THE CONCEPT OF HOLINESS

1. Isaiah 6:3. [Biblical passages in this essay are slightly modified from the 1917 Jewish Publication Society (JPS) translation. When comparing the

original Hebrew with "the translation," it is to this edition that the author is referring.—Ed.]

2. Isaiah 37:16. Here, as in all biblical quotations, the italics are added.

3. Isaiah 44:6.

4. Isaiah 51:15.

5. Isaiah 1:24-25.

6. Isaiah 2:12.

7. Isaiah 3:1.

8. Isaiah 13:4.

9. Isaiah 13:13.

10. Cf., for instance, Isaiah 28:5; 10:16, 33; 19:4; 3:15; 5:9; 14:22-23; 17:3; 22:25; 14:24, 27; 18:7; 19:12; 29:6; 39:5; 48:2.

11. Isaiah 12:5-6.

12. Isaiah 41:16.

13. Isaiah 43:2-3.

14. Isaiah 10:20.

15. Isaiah 31:1; 30:11, 15.

16. [The reference is to Rudolf Otto's *The Idea of the Holy* (1917), the main thesis of which is identifying the essence of holiness with the feeling of complete transcendence or distance from the individual, as expressed in the term *mysterium tremendum*. See Berkovits' discussion of Otto's approach in the concluding section of this essay.—Ed.]

17. Isaiah 6:5.

18. Isaiah 10:17.

19. For *haya le*, meaning to become, see Genesis 2:24; 18:18; 34:22; Exodus 4:9; II Samuel 12:10; Psalms 31:3; 71:3. Cf. Eliezer Berkovits, *Man and God: Studies in Biblical Theology* (Detroit: Wayne State, 1969), pp. 49-54.

20. Psalms 24:8, 10.

21. Psalms 46:7-12.

22. Psalms 48:5-9.

23. Psalms 30:5-6. The usual translation, "his holy name," is inexact. "His holy name" should be rendered in Hebrew *shemo hakadosh. Shem kodsho*, on the other hand, which is how it occurs in the Bible, means "the name of his holiness."

Unfortunately, the inexact translation obscures the meaning. See the concluding section of this essay.

24. Psalms 33:20-21.

25. Psalms 68:6.

26. Psalms 71:22.

27. As shown above, the term "the name of the Eternal" stands for the manifestations by which God makes himself known.

28. Hosea 11:8-9.

29. Cf. also Habakkuk 1:12.

30. Amos 4:2.

31. Amos 6:8.

32. Jeremiah 51:14.

33. Psalms 89:36-38.

34. Isaiah 37:23-32.

35. Isaiah 37:10.

36. Isaiah 45:11-13.

37. See also Isaiah 10:20-25.

38. Isaiah 5:16. Cf. the discussion of righteousness (*tzedaka*) in Berkovits, *Studies in Biblical Theology*, pp. 292, 312-315.

39. Isaiah 5:14-17.

40. Psalms 89:9.

41. Psalms 89:15.

42. The syntax here offers some difficulty to the translator. I have departed from the usual translations. However, the argument does not depend on it.

43. I Samuel 1:11.

44. I Samuel 2:1-2.

45. Isaiah 41:14-16.

46. Cf. Isaiah 43:14; 49:7; 48:17-22.

47. Isaiah 47:4.

48. Isaiah 54:5.

49. Isaiah 26:13.

50. Only one passage is known to me where the Redeemer is mentioned together with the Lord of Hosts. While "King of Israel" does not convey the intimacy of "the Holy One of Israel," it is not difficult to see that "King of Israel and Lord of Hosts" may well be indicative of the twofold function of the Redeemer, which we discussed earlier.

51. Psalms 99:3.

52. Psalms 99:3-9.

53. See the commentary of Abraham ibn Ezra on Psalms 99:4.

54. Malachi 1:14.

55. The Revised Version (RV) has here as a clause, "for it is holy," referring holy to the name. This is impossible. *Kadosh hu* cannot mean anything different at this place from what it means at the conclusion of the second section, where it unquestionably refers to God, as the RV itself renders it.

56. Psalms 111:9.

57. Cf. Berkovits, *Studies in Biblical Theology*, pp. 85-140.

58. Psalms 111:5-6.

59. Psalms 104:21.

60. Isaiah 52:9-10.

61. The term *tzedaka* requires a more exact definition. See note 38 above. The argument in the text, however, is not affected by its traditional rendering as "righteousness."

62. Psalms 98:1-3.

63. Psalms 77:16.

64. Psalms 77:20-21.

65. Psalms 77:14-16.

66. Psalms 77:17-21.

67. That the way of holiness is the way of the Redeemer is supported by Isaiah 35:8: "And a highway shall be there, and a way, and it shall be called the way of holiness." Though it is said of it that "the unclean shall not pass over it," the entire context proves that the unclean there is not a ritualistic but a moral concept. "But the redeemed shall walk there," says the prophet of the way.

68. Exodus 15.

69. We follow the translation of Onkelos, for reasons which will arise from the following discussion.

70. Isaiah 40:25.

71. Isaiah 40:26.

72. Isaiah 40:26.

73. Isaiah 40:27-29.

74. Isaiah 57:15.

75. Deuteronomy Rabba 2:10.

76. Deuteronomy 26:15.

77. II Chronicles 30:27.

78. Isaiah 63:15.

79. Psalms 20:7.

80. Psalms 68:6.

81. Psalms 102:21.

82. Jeremiah 25:30.

83. II Samuel 15:25.

84. The verb *sha'ag* often expresses the moaning call of sorrow. See Psalms 22:2; 32:3; 38:9.

85. Isaiah 12:6.

86. Psalms 138:4-7.

87. For the passages referred to here and preceding presentation, see Isaiah 35:2f.; 40:2f.; 58:8.

88. Ezekiel 39:21.

89. The Revised Version has here correctly: "Proclaim a solemn assembly for Baal. And they proclaimed it."

90. It is regrettable that the Revised Version, which renders the passage in II Kings correctly as "proclaim a solemn assembly," should have in Joel, "sanctify a fast."

91. The philological question of whether the original meaning of the word is the religious and ritual or the neutral one is not very important for this study. Its neutral usage as "marked out," "designated," "assigned to" is the common denominator between the two, and thus they confirm each other.

92. Numbers 16:5-7.

93. I Chronicles 23:13; cf. also II Chronicles 7:16.

94. Leviticus 19:2.

95. See Deuteronomy 7:6 and 14:2.

96. Leviticus 20:7.

97. Leviticus 20:26.

98. Cf. Leviticus 11:44-45; 19:2.

99. Leviticus 11:45.

100. Leviticus 22:32-33.

101. Berkovits, *Studies in Biblical Theology*, pp. 11-66.

102. Exodus 19:6; Leviticus 11:44; 19:2; 20:7-8, 25-26; 22:31; Numbers 15:40; Deuteronomy 26:17-19; 28:9; and the contexts in which they occur.

103. Exodus 19:5-6.

104. Leviticus 22:31-33.

105. Ezekiel 36:20.

106. Cf. Rashi's commentary on Ezekiel 36:20.

107. Ezekiel 39:7.

108. The RV has: "and I will not *let them* pollute my holy name any more," which of course is a new text and not the Bible.

109. Ezekiel 24:21.

110. II Chronicles 29:16.

111. Ezekiel 36:23.

112. Ezekiel 20:41.

113. Ezekiel 39:25-27.

114. Ezekiel 39:6-7.

115. There are two passages in Ezekiel where this distinction between holy "in Israel" and in the sight of the nations is not as obvious as in the texts quoted. The one is 38:16, where the relevant phrase may well be translated: "When I shall be sanctified in you, O Gog, before their eyes." However, since God brings Gog into "my land," as the prophet puts it, and it is in God's land that Gog is utterly confounded, the divine act is at the same time one of redemption that reveals that God is holy in Israel. We accept, therefore, the grammatically correct rendering "when I shall be sanctified through you." Cf. the JPS translation. The other passage is found in Ezekiel 28:22: "And they shall know that I am the Eternal, when I shall have executed judgments in her, and shall be sanctified in her." This

time our translator has "in her" and not "through her," as in the first quotation. However, the judgment meted out to Sidon is also an act of redemption for Israel. In the same context it is said that the result of Sidon's punishment will be that "there shall be no more a pricking brier unto the house of Israel, nor a piercing thorn of any that are around them, that did have them in disdain…." In keeping with the other unambiguous passages, we would render it here: "and shall be sanctified through her."

116. Ezekiel 36:20-22.

117. Ezekiel 39:23.

118. Isaiah 8:12-13.

119. This is indeed R. David Kimhi's interpretation of the phrase "him shall you sanctify." On the other hand, cf., for instance, Dohin's hopeless struggle with the difficulty to elucidate the meaning of the parallelism.

120. Numbers 20:12-13.

121. Cf. Jeremiah 2:19; 5:14; 6:9; 7:3, 21; 8:3; 9:14, 16; 19:3; 27:4; the prophecies "about the nations" beginning with ch. 46.

122. Cf. Jeremiah 33:11; see also 31:22; 32:15; 51:14.

123. Zechariah 8:4-5.

124. Jeremiah 50:29.

125. Isaiah 37:23.

126. Jeremiah 51:5. See pp. 247-260 above.

127. The JPS translation has: "For their land is full of guilt against the Holy One of Israel"; whereas the RV renders it: "Though their land was filled with sin against the Holy One of Israel." The one is as little convincing as the other. *Mikedosh yisrael* does not mean "*against* the Holy One of Israel." What is more, if in the same verse the same grammatical form occurs three times, it is not possible to render it differently the third time than on the first two occasions.

128. Isaiah 54:5.

129. Zechariah 8:3.

130. Psalms 80:5, 8, 15-17, 20.

131. Ezekiel 39:29.

132. Psalms 84:2.

133. Psalms 84:3.

134. Psalms 84:4.

135. Psalms 84:9-11.

136. Psalms 84:13.

137. Jeremiah 33:4-6.

138. Cf. also all the other prophecies of redemption in Jeremiah 31:22; 32:15; 51:13-14. The reference to the present moment of destruction is never lacking.

139. Zechariah 2:12.

140. Cf. also the other passages in Zechariah 6:12 and Zechariah 8, and their context.

141. Zechariah 2:14.

142. Isaiah 12:6.

143. Zechariah 2:16-17.

144. Exodus 3:5.

145. Leviticus 10:2.

146. Numbers 4:15, 20.

147. II Samuel 6:7.

148. II Chronicles 26:19.

149. The suggestion is made by N.H. Snaith in *The Distinctive Ideas of the Old Testament* (London: Epworth, 1955), p. 40.

150. II Samuel 6:7; I Chronicles 13:10.

151. I Samuel 6:19.

152. Leviticus 10:3.

153. We depart here from the usually accepted interpretation as found in Rashi's commentary on Leviticus 10:3. Cf. the discussion above regarding the sanctification of God's name.

154. Joshua 24:19.

155. Psalms 24:3-4.

156. A.B. Davidson, *The Cambridge Bible for Schools and Colleges: The Book of the Prophet Ezekiel* (Cambridge: Cambridge, 1893).

157. Exodus 29:31; Deuteronomy 7:6; 23:15; II Kings 4:9; Psalms 106:16; Numbers 16:3.

158. Psalms 20:7.

159. Psalms 47:9.

160. Joel 4:17; Zechariah 8:3.

161. Deuteronomy 7:6.

162. Isaiah 63:9-10.

163. Isaiah 63:11-14.

164. Psalms 51:13-14.

165. E. Kautzsch, ed., *Gesenius' Hebrew Grammar*, trans. Arthur E. Cowley (Oxford: Clarendon, 1910), p. 440.

166. Isaiah 2:20; 31:7.

167. Deuteronomy 1:41; I Samuel 8:12.

168. Ezekiel 9:1.

169. Isaiah 56:7.

170. Job 18:7.

171. Isaiah 13:3.

172. Cf., for example, Isaiah 41:11; Psalms 41:10ff.

173. Wolf W. Baudissin, *Studies in the History of Semitic Religion* (Leipzig: Grunow, 1878), vol. ii, p. 20. [German]

174. Davidson, *Cambridge Bible*, pp. xxxix-xl, 279.

175. W. Robertson Smith, *The Prophets of Israel and Their Place in History* (London: Adam and Charles Black, 1902), pp. 225-226.

176. H. Wheeler Robinson, *The Religious Ideas of the Old Testament* (New York: Charles Scribner's Sons, 1913), pp. 69-70, 153-154.

177. Rudolf Otto, *The Idea of the Holy: An Inquiry into the Non-Rational Factor in the Idea of the Divine and Its Relation to the Rational*, trans. John W. Harvey (New York: Oxford, 1958).

178. Otto, *Idea of the Holy*, pp. 17-18, 45-47.

179. Otto, *Idea of the Holy*, p. 76.

180. Otto, *Idea of the Holy*, pp. 1-5, 117-122.

181. Otto, *Idea of the Holy*, pp. 50-52.

182. Snaith, *Distinctive Ideas*, pp. 51-53.

183. Paul Tillich, *Systematic Theology* (Chicago: University of Chicago, 1951), pp. 271-272.

184. Leviticus 19:2.

185. Sifra Leviticus 11:2, 44; 20:26. Arabic commentators on the Koran also seem to understand the term "holy" as being separate.

186. Nahmanides' commentary on Leviticus 19:2.

187. R. Judah Halevi, *Kuzari* 4:3.

188. Amos 4:2; 6:8.

189. Davidson, *Cambridge Bible*, p. xxxix.

190. Exodus 23:27; Job 9:34; 13:11.

191. Genesis 28:17.

192. Exodus 3:5.

193. Otto, *Idea of the Holy*, p. 52.

194. Tillich, *Systematic Theology*, p. 216.

195. Cf. Davidson, *Cambridge Bible*, Introduction; repeated also in Snaith, *Distinctive Ideas*, pp. 43-44.

13. FAITH AFTER THE HOLOCAUST

1. Elie Wiesel, *Night*, in *Night Trilogy: Night, Dawn, The Accident* (New York: Hill and Wong, 1987), p. 10.

2. Job 42:5-6.

3. Albert Camus, *Resistance, Rebellion, and Death* (New York: Knopf, 1961), p. 32.

4. Camus, *Resistance*, p. 28.

5. Leon Poliakov, *The Harvest of Hate* (Syracuse: Syracuse University, 1954), p. 214.

6. Albert Camus, *The Plague* (New York: Knopf, 1957), p. 231.

7. Camus, *Resistance, Rebellion, and Death*, p. 71.

8. Leo Schwarz, *The Root and the Bough: The Epic of an Enduring People* (New York: Rinehart, 1949), p. 28.

9. Schwarz, *The Root and the Bough*, p. 40.

10. Schwarz, *The Root and the Bough*, p. 234.

11. Hillel Seidman, *The Warsaw Ghetto Diaries* (Southfield, Mich.: Targum, 1997), p. 330.

12. See, for example, Emanuel Ringelblum, *Notes from the Warsaw Ghetto: The Journal of Emanuel Ringelblum* (New York: McGraw-Hill, 1958), p. 330.

13. Poliakov, *Harvest of Hate*, p. 28.

14. Poliakov, *Harvest of Hate*, p. 157.

15. Poliakov, *Harvest of Hate*, p. 222.

16. Brachot 61b.

17. Ringelblum, *Notes from the Warsaw Ghetto*, pp. 83, 88.

18. Seidman, *Warsaw Ghetto Diaries*, p. 229.

19. Schwarz, *The Root and the Bough*, p. 200.

INDEX

Aaron 266-267, 279-280, 291-292, 301-302, 304, 306

Abaye 59, 109, 343

Abraham 125, 130, 208, 219, 223, 310, 314, 316, 372

Abraham of Posquieres, R. 123

Absalom 136, 273

Achnai, oven of 95-96

Adam 347

Adar 52

Aderet, R. Solomon (Rashba) 79-80, 87, 360

agada xviii-xix, 344-345

aguna 45, 50, 83-85, 93, 357

Ahab 168

Ahad Ha'am 196, 203

Ahaziah 141

Ahima'atz 136-137

Akiva, R. 57, 73, 108, 128, 159, 327-331

Albo, R. Joseph 121, 209, 211, 363, 368

Alfasi, R. Isaac 79-80, 356, 360

Altneuland (Herzl) 173, 367

am ha'aretz 63-64

Amos 156, 252, 312

Amram the Hasid, R. 108

anti-Semitism 122, 195

Aquinas, Thomas 8, 370-371, 373

Arab 177, 185-186, 383

Ararat 276

Arba'a Turim (R. Jacob ben Asher) xv, 87, 343, 354, 360, 363

Aristotle 15, 20, 349, 353, 371

Asharites 351

Asher ben Yehiel, R. (Rosh) 82, 87, 360

Ashkenaz 276, 342

Asi, R. 42, 126

Assyria 142-143, 179, 249, 253-254, 291, 293

Auschwitz 177-178, 185, 315, 316-317, 320, 323, 331-332

Av, fifteenth of 65

Avihu 301-302

Avot   192

Baal   378

Babylon   52, 54, 68, 70, 73, 79, 83-84, 131, 141, 157, 161, 189, 259, 277, 293-294, 359

Bahad (the Movement of Religious Pioneers for Palestine)   173

Bar Kapara   241

Bashan   252

bastard (*mamzer*)   69, 72, 94-95

Baudissin, Wolf W.   308

beit midrash   204

Beit Yosef (Karo)   xv

ben sorer umoreh   xiii, 71-72

Bergson, Henri   13

Berkovits, Eliezer   x-xxii, xxiv-xxxvi, 342-345, 348-349, 375

Berlin, University of   xi

Beth Shemesh   302

Bethel   312

Bhagavad-Gita   216, 352

Bialik, Haim Nahman   173

Bible   x, xiii-xv, xvii-xix, xxvi-xxvii, 4, 24, 35, 42-45, 47-48, 52-53, 58, 63, 70-74, 84, 92-93, 95, 107-108, 117, 121, 126-127, 129-130, 135-141, 143, 148, 156, 160, 162, 167, 171, 182, 186, 206, 215, 223, 229-230, 242, 250, 252, 260, 264, 271-272, 275, 278, 281, 291-293, 300-301, 305-314, 350, 352, 355, 372, 375, 379

Birkenau   332

Book of Beliefs and Opinions (Saadia Gaon)   238

Book of Fundamentals (Albo)   209

Boston   xi

Brachot   xix

Brenner, Joseph Haim   204, 206

Brown, Norman O.   104

Buber, Martin   ix, xxii-xxiii, xxxiii, 118, 345-349

Buddhism   180

Burma   180

Caesar   160, 168, 169, 195

Camus, Albert   185, 318-323

Canaanites   264

categorical imperative   10, 12, 15-16, 348

Chaldeans   259, 298

Chicago   xi, 239

China   180

Christendom   14

Christianity   xviii-xxix, 11-14, 21, 103, 156, 162-163, 180, 189, 203, 308, 350-351

Church, the   328

Chronicles   280

commandments (*mitzvot*)   x, 7, 31-34, 36, 48, 63, 105, 113-120, 341-342, 347, 354-356

    between man and God   37, 51, 284

    between man and his fellow   37, 284

    negative   22

    positive   23

    practical (*ma'asiyot*)   37, 356

communism   189

Conservative Judaism   xvi, 91, 99, 343

covenant   xix, 97, 102, 148, 180-182, 223-224, 263-264, 284

Crisis and Faith (Berkovits)   344, 348

Critique of Practical Reason (Kant)   16

Cushite   136-137

Cyrus   254

Dan   141

Daniel the Tailor   69

Dante Alighieri   325

David   135-137, 187, 253, 273, 287

Davidson, A.B.   309-310, 312

dayan   193

Decalogue   24

deism   8

Deuteronomy   132, 215, 223, 272, 281, 305

diaspora 189, 236

dietary laws xxxi, 22, 24-25, 29, 34

The Distinctive Ideas of the Old Testament (Snaith) 310, 381

divine Presence 28-30, 33, 35, 128, 216, 218, 224, 226-227

divorce xvii, 43-45, 49-50, 73-80, 82-87, 124

Duns Scotus, John 8

Duties of the Heart (ibn Pakuda) 240

Ecclesiastes 69

Edom 131

Egypt 30, 132, 179, 224, 229, 249, 267, 282-283, 285, 291

Ekron 141

elan vital 12-13

Elazar, R. 46, 74, 84

Eli 131

Eliezer, R. 60, 95, 158

Eliezer ben Horkenos, R. 95

Elijah 96, 141, 168, 192, 369

Eliphaz 150

emancipation 155, 158, 167, 197

England 27, 136-137, 167, 180, 205, 250, 269, 287, 304, 342

Enlightenment xvii, 8, 203, 208

Ephraim 252, 257

Esther xix, 345

ethics xvii, xx, xxii-xxiii, xxvi, 6-7, 9, 10-14, 17, 19, 28, 38, 59, 103, 105, 107, 111, 114, 120-122, 125-128, 211, 284, 322, 344, 351-352

Europe xii, xxix, 8, 139, 156, 158, 167-168, 171, 177-178, 180, 192, 195-198, 202, 318, 327

Even Ha'ezer (Karo) 209

evil inclination (*yetzer hara*) xxx, 21, 25, 48, 76, 109-110, 113, 354

Exodus 30, 132, 233-234, 270, 284, 312

exodus 224, 282-283, 354

Ezekiel xix, 127, 131, 135, 217, 275, 286-287, 289, 291-292, 296, 302, 308-309, 379

Ezra 156

Final Solution 319

Fletcher, Joseph 111

forty lashes xiii

Four Species 59

Frankl, Viktor 202

Freud, Sigmund xi, 104, 108-109, 113, 120-122, 342

Friedman, Menachem xi, 342

Galilee 276

Gamliel the Elder, R. 51, 85

The Gates of Repentance (Gerondi) 349

Genghis Khan 186

Gentiles xiii, 76, 236, 243, 352

Geonim 79-80, 197

Germany xi-xxii, 82, 180, 315, 320, 323, 325-327, 330-331, 373

Gerondi, R. Jonah 349

Gershon, Rabbenu 79, 87

Gesenius, W. 307-308

Gesinnung 32

Gestapo 324

God in Search of Man (Heschel) xxiv

Godhead 221, 227, 232-233, 309, 311-313, 369

Gog 38

good and evil 8, 10, 15, 20, 221

good inclination (*yetzer hatov*) xxx, 21, 109, 113, 353

Gordis, Robert xvi

Gordon, A.D. 204-206

Greece xxix, 15, 71, 236

Guide for the Perplexed (Maimonides) 352

Ha'aretz 201

Habakkuk 181

Hadrian 327, 331

haftara xix

Haggai 192, 292

Hai Gaon, R. 79

halacha   ix-xxi, xxxi, xxxiii, xxxv-xxxvi,
    21, 41, 45-47, 57, 59, 60, 62-63,
    66-67, 69-71, 73, 75-76, 86, 89-
    90, 92, 94-102, 115, 128, 158, 174,
    209-212, 236-237, 342-345
Halachot Gedolot (Kiyara)   83
Halevi, R. Judah   xvii, 59, 239, 311-312,
    373
Halevi, R. Zerahiah (Ba'al Hama'or)
    80
halitza   48-51, 60, 81-83
Hannah   257, 295-297
Hasidism   345
hazaka   49
Hazaz, Haim   202, 205
Hebrew Grammar (Gesenius-Kautzsch)
    307
Hebrew literature   167
Hebrew Theological College   xi
Herzl, Theodor   367
Heschel, Abraham Joshua   xxii-xxiv,
    xxxiii, 345, 349
heter iska   343
heter mechira   343
Hezekiah   253-254, 272
Hildesheimer Rabbinical Seminary   xi
Hillel   53, 92-93, 105, 343, 356
Himmler, Heinrich   319, 321
Hinduism   180, 351
Hisda, R.   93
Histadrut   206
Hitler, Adolf   320
Hiya, R.   116, 119, 362, 369
Hobbes, Thomas   352
holiness   xviii, xxi, 36, 38, 247, 250-
    253, 261, 263, 265-268, 271-275,
    279-291, 293, 295-296, 300-307,
    309-314, 356, 375, 377
Holocaust   x, xii, 177-178, 188, 202,
    316, 318, 323, 331-332, 342, 367
Holy of Holies   xxiii, 324
Hosea   139, 156, 252

Hoshen Mishpat (Karo)   209
human dignity (*kevod habriot*)   xiii,
    xvii, xxxv, 62-63, 118, 170, 324
Huxley, Julian   352
ibn Pakuda, Bahya   240-241, 355
The Idea of the Holy (Otto)   309
idolatry   xiii, 43
imitatio dei   3-4, 35, 143, 152
Independence Day (Israel)   201
India   180
Isaac   223
Isaiah   ix, 35, 60, 112, 130, 133, 135-136,
    138-140, 143, 145, 147-148, 151, 156,
    177-178, 180, 217, 219, 231, 242,
    247-253, 255-259, 262, 265, 269-
    272, 274-275, 277, 288, 290-294,
    299, 302, 305-307, 311-313, 371
Islam   7, 8, 203, 326, 351
Israel   5, 14, 30, 51, 54, 57-58, 64-65,
    71, 84, 86, 91, 94, 97-98, 102, 125,
    131, 137, 139, 140-141, 146-148, 157,
    162, 168, 173, 177-180, 182, 184-
    186, 188-190, 201-202, 204, 206,
    209, 211-212, 217, 223-225, 235-236,
    238-239, 241-242, 244-245, 247-
    250, 252-260, 262-265, 267-268,
    270-272, 274, 281-291, 293-300,
    302, 305-307, 309, 313, 316, 318,
    320, 327, 332, 343, 373, 376-377,
    379-380
    children of   5, 49-50, 129, 140, 167,
        205, 215, 223, 264, 267, 276, 281-
        283, 285, 292
    land of   71, 83, 109, 164-166, 171-
        172, 174, 182-183, 209-211, 236
    love of   91-92, 98-99
    State of   89, 101, 177, 185, 188, 201-
        202, 211-212, 235-237, 244
    unity of (*ahdut yisrael*)   91-92, 98-
        99
    community of (*kneset yisrael, klal
        yisrael*)   91
Israelis   201-202, 208
Italy   71

Jacob 134, 223, 249, 254, 258, 260-261, 266-267, 270, 288, 297, 312

Jacob ben Asher, R. xv

Jacobs, Louis xvi, 343

Jeremiah ix, 4, 6, 131, 133, 135, 138-139, 142-143, 146-147, 156, 253, 273, 277, 293-295, 298, 353

Jericho 141

Jerusalem xi, 52, 63, 68, 169, 177, 179, 187, 189, 248, 254, 265, 287, 293, 295, 300

Jewish calendar xxi

Jewish people ix, xvi-xvii, xxxvi, 41, 47, 54, 69, 72-73, 90-92, 95, 101, 120, 128, 137, 157-158, 161, 177, 179-180, 182, 184, 201-204, 206-212, 236-237, 244, 270, 320, 332

Jewish philosophy x, xxii

Jewish Publication Society 137, 277, 287, 346, 364-366, 369, 374, 379-380

Jewish state 161, 163, 168-169, 173, 178, 186, 208, 211-212, 249

Joab 136

Job 148-151, 312, 316-317

Joel 277-278, 378

Joseph 140

Joshua 137, 277, 279, 303

Judah 168, 248, 294, 298, 300

Judges 137

justice xviii, xxi-xxii, 4, 12-13, 16-17, 28, 39, 61, 65, 95, 105, 125, 129-130, 132-134, 136, 138-140, 143, 146-152, 170-171, 173, 178, 199, 208, 233, 255-256, 259-262, 297, 316, 318, 320, 332, 345, 350, 353, 365, 373

Kagan, R. Yisrael Meir xv

Kant, Immanuel xx, xxiii, xxvi-xxviii, xxxiii, 8, 10, 15, 32, 47, 348, 350, 356

Kaplan, Lawrence xii, 342, 346

kapos 325-326

Karaites 101

karma 352

Karo, R. Joseph xv, 87, 363

Katznelson, Berl 206

Kautzsch, E. 307-308

kavana xxxiii, 26, 347, 354

Kedesh 276

Kehathites 301-302

ketuba 74-75, 77-79

kibbutz 201, 206

kidush hashem 291, 327-330

Kierkegaard, Soren xxii

Kings 277-278, 378

Kiryat Arba 276

Korah 279

Koran 383

Kuzari (R. Judah Halevi) 59, 203

Labor movement 206

Laish 141

Leeds xi

Lepp, Ignace 106

Letters to a German Friend (Camus) 318

Levantinism 206

Levi, R. 126-127, 241

Leviathan (Hobbes) 352

Levites 272

Leviticus 281-282, 285

Levy, R. Richard 341-342

Liberal Judaism 156, 158

lifnim mishurat hadin 67, 359

London 180

Magog 288

Maharal of Prague (R. Judah Loeb ben Betzalel) 241

Maimonides, Moses (Rambam) xviii, 43, 59, 76, 78-79, 82, 100-101, 233, 237, 240-241, 243, 352, 354, 358, 373

Major Trends in Jewish Mysticism (Scholem) 370

Malachi 233, 262, 292

Marcuse, Herbert   122, 363

marriage   xvii-xviii, 34, 43-44, 48-
50, 53, 60, 65-66, 73-75, 77-78,
81-87, 94, 110, 122, 124-126, 128,
357, 363

Marseilles   237

Marx, Karl   20, 348

Marxism   11, 20-21, 189

masoretic   259

Medes   276

Meir, R.   74-75, 81, 108, 355

Meribah   291-292

Messiah   70, 125, 178-179, 183-188, 190,
346

met mitzva   63

mezuza   72

Micah   292

Middle Ages   xiv-xv, xvii, 78-79, 127,
189, 193-194, 243, 328-329, 343, 361,
363

Midian   304

midrash   xix, xxx, 47, 62, 69, 109, 159,
207, 271, 311, 358, 372

Minni   276

Mishna   xiv, 49, 58, 60, 65, 73, 75, 79,
81, 100, 126, 156, 158

Mishna Brura (Kagan)   xv

Mishneh Tora (Maimonides)   100-101,
352, 363

Moab   131, 268

modesty   xiii, 65, 241

morality   ix-xiv, xvi-xxxvi, 10, 12-13, 18-
19, 22, 28, 32, 37, 41, 44, 52, 57-59,
68-70, 73, 90, 99, 103, 111, 116,
120, 124, 127, 133, 147, 171, 173,
182, 186, 196, 204, 212, 218, 233,
240, 309, 320, 326-327, 345, 347-
348, 356, 369, 378

Moses   86, 125, 129, 148, 159, 182-183,
192-193, 210, 215, 234, 266-267,
279, 291-292, 300-302, 304-306,
312-313, 369, 373

musar   349

Mutzailites   351

Nadav   301-302

Nahmanides, Moses (Ramban)   80,
123, 311

Naive and Sentimental Poetry (Schiller)   356

Naphtali   276

nasi   157

Natan, R.   96

nationalism   167-169, 171-172, 184, 207

Nazism   319-320, 327, 331

Nehardea   108

Nehemia, R.   68

Nehemiah   156

Neo-Orthodoxy   158

New Amsterdam   184

Night (Wiesel)   316

Noah   352

*Not in Heaven: The Nature and Func-
tion of Halacha* (Berkovits)   xii

Numbers   279, 291, 302

Nuremburg Laws   164

On Judaism (Buber)   xxiii

Onkelos   377

ones rahmana patrei   44, 86

Orthodox   xi-xii, xvi-xviii, xxxiii, 89-
91, 99, 101, 156, 158, 165, 208, 342,
347

Otto, Rudolf   309-310, 312-313, 369,
372, 375

Palestine   161, 164, 166-167, 172-175

pantheism   221, 371

Passover   xxi, 30, 52, 57, 201, 354

patriarchs   180, 187, 208, 219-220, 223,
264, 372

Paul   103

Pharaoh   140, 268

Pharisaism   111, 156, 168

pilegesh   363

The Plague (Camus)   320

Plato   xxviii, 4, 10-11, 15, 20, 33, 229

Plotinus   373

Poliakov, Leon 326

polygamy 65, 87, 126

polytheism 72

prayer xviii, xxxii-xxxiii, 7, 25,-27, 31-32, 34, 102, 109, 115, 140, 147, 162, 182, 186, 203, 253, 257, 261, 272, 295-297, 305, 307-308, 344

priests (*kohanim*) 49-51, 63, 192, 195, 272, 279-281, 283-284, 301, 303

Prophets xix, 278

prophets ix-x, xvi, xix-xxii, xxvii, xxxiv-xxxv, 3-4, 13, 29, 96, 109, 127, 131-133, 141-142, 144-147, 156, 158, 168-169, 178-180, 184, 187, 192, 196, 208, 215-217, 219-220, 223, 225, 231, 247, 249-250, 255, 259, 262, 265, 269-273, 286-287, 289-293, 295, 298-299, 309-310, 345, 350, 377, 379

prozbul xiii, 53, 92-93, 343

Psalms 100, 251-252, 260, 264, 293, 297, 303, 371

Rabba 43-44, 57

Rabba bar Bar Hana 67-68, 94

Rashi (R. Shlomo Yitzhaki) 53-54, 56, 58-60, 62, 64, 68, 70, 83, 86-87, 115, 343

Rav 68, 73-74, 94, 126, 356, 363

Rava 57, 60, 86, 343

Reform Judaism x, 341

"Religion and Ethics" (Buber) xxiii

Remalia 291

Resh Lakish (R. Shimon ben Lakish) 42, 100

Revised Version 137, 250, 271, 277, 290, 366, 377-380

Rezin 291

Ringelblum, Emanuel 330

Robertson Smith, W. 309

Romania xi

Rome 116, 119, 161, 169, 327, 329-331

Rosenzweig, Franz xxii

Russell, Bertrand 352

Saadia Gaon, R. 8, 107, 179-180, 238, 373

Sabbath xix, xxi, 22, 32, 34, 51, 60, 115, 162, 166, 210, 330, 344, 355

Sabbath goy 166

sabbatical year xiii, 53-55, 92-93, 343

Samaria 141-142, 253

Samson ben Tzadok, R. 80, 82

Samuel 46, 131, 136, 141, 143, 168, 193, 257

Sanhedrin 51-58, 64, 69-70, 73, 85, 163, 192

Sartre, Jean-Paul 319, 348

Saul 136-137, 168

Schiller, Friedrich 356

Schleieracher, Friedrich 371

Sholem, Gershom

Seder 30

Sennacherib 253-254, 294

"The Sermon" (Hazaz) 202, 205

sevara xiii, 41-46

sexuality 34, 43, 48, 103-115, 117-118, 120-124, 126-128, 362

Shavuot 57

Shechem 276

shema 327, 329-331

Shimon, R. 46, 57-59, 71

Shimon ben Gamliel, R. 50, 58, 85

Shmuel 46, 92

Shmuel bar Nahman, R. 108, 242

Shulhan Aruch (Karo) xv, 7, 77, 80, 87, 89, 91, 99-100, 128

Sidon 379

Sinai 5, 97, 159, 161, 187, 198, 215, 223-224, 229, 238-239, 324, 372

Six Day War 177-178

slavery 84, 169, 346, 362

Snaith, N.H. 310, 312, 381

Sholem, Gershom 370

Socrates 10-14, 18, 20, 21

Sodom and Gomorrah 219, 316

Solomon 129, 130

Soloveitchik, R. Joseph B.   xxxiii, 345, 347

Soloveitchik, Haym   342

Song of Songs   187

Song of the Sea   267, 273

Spain   82

Spinoza, Benedict de   ix, 20, 221, 348, 370-371

Stoa   15

Studies in Biblical Theology (Berko-vits)   xviii, xxi

succah   32, 52-53

Succot   52-53, 57, 59

Sydney   xi

synagogue   161-162, 188, 193-195, 209

Syria   99

Systematic Theology (Tillich)   313

Tablets of the Law   104

takana   56, 65, 203

talmid hacham   115, 198, 343

Talmud   x, xiii, xv-xix, 4-5, 26, 35, 41-46, 48, 50-52, 54, 56, 59, 70, 73, 78-89, 93-95, 97, 100, 108, 111-113, 115, 117, 126, 128, 156-161, 167, 179, 181-183, 188, 192, 204, 207, 212, 219, 240-242, 329, 343-344, 350, 353, 355, 373

   Babylonian   63, 68

   Jerusalem   63, 68, 70

Tarshish   251

Temple   58, 63, 186-187, 236, 272-274, 303, 355

Thirteen Rules   47

tikun olam   85

Tillich, Paul   311, 313

Tora   xii-xiv, xvii-xix, 8, 39, 41-45, 47-48, 53, 56-57, 59-60, 62-63, 66-67, 69, 74, 76-77, 83, 89-100, 102, 107-108, 116-119, 128, 158-166, 172-174, 179-180, 183, 187, 192-193, 208-212, 235-239, 241-245, 344-345, 354, 372

oral   xiv-xv, xviii-xix, 92, 96-97, 100-102, 209, 343

written   92-93, 96-98, 100-101

tora va'avoda   173-174

Tosafot   44, 55, 360, 362-363

Treblinka   323, 330

Tzadok   273

Ula   56

Urbach, Ephraim E.   349

Uziah   301

Uzza   301-302

Valhalla   321

Waiting for Godot (Beckett)   321

war   xxxi, 23, 47, 60, 78, 179, 186, 237, 268, 276-277, 308, 325

Warsaw Ghetto   324-325, 330

ways of peace (*darkei shalom*)   xiii, 59, 66

Weber, Max   xxv-xxvi, 348

Western culture   xxix-xxx, 15, 22, 69, 138 139, 163, 167-168, 171, 179, 198

Western thought   xxix-xxx, xxxiv, 3, 11, 15, 22, 69, 138-140 163

Wheeler Robinson, H.   309

Wiesel, Elie   316

World War II   xi

Writings   xix

Yanai, R.   54-55

Yavneh   169

Yehoshua, R.   95-96, 158, 241

Yehoshua ben Hanania, R.   355

Yehuda, R.   71-72, 208

Yehuda Hanasi, R.   xiv, 46, 65-66, 85, 126, 343

Yermia, R.   95

yeshiva   xii, xv, xviii-xix, 79, 174, 208, 211, 235, 240, 343, 349

yibum   48

Yiddish   205

Yishmael, R.   73

Yitzhak, R.   70, 95, 372
Yohanan, R.   42, 70, 94-95, 100, 369
Yohanan ben Zakai, R.   169
Yom Kippur   53, 65
Yom Kippur War   207
Yose, R.   46, 68, 70
Yose bar Hanina, R.   68
Zechariah   70, 139, 293, 295, 298-299

Zelophehad   129
Zephaniah   131, 277
Zidonians   141
Zion   131-132, 173, 178-179, 183-189,
        249-251, 253, 260-262, 273-274,
        276, 295, 299-300, 305
Zionism   166-167, 173-174, 202, 206
Zionist Congresses   196